THE CONSERVATIVE PARTY IN WALES, 1945–1997

by

SAM BLAXLAND

UNIVERSITY OF WALES PRESS
2024

© Sam Blaxland, 2024

Reprinted 2024

All rights reserved. No part of this book may be reproduced in any material form (including photocopying or storing it in any medium by electronic means and whether or not transiently or incidentally to some other use of this publication) without the written permission of the copyright owner. Applications for the copyright owner's written permission to reproduce any part of this publication should be addressed to the University of Wales Press, University Registry, King Edward VII Avenue, Cardiff CF10 3NS.

www.uwp.co.uk

British Library CIP Data

A catalogue record for this book is available from the British Library

ISBN   978-1-83772-081-1
eISBN   978-1-83772-082-8

The right of Sam Blaxland to be identified as author of this work has been asserted in accordance with sections 77 and 79 of the Copyright, Designs and Patents Act 1988.

Typeset by Richard Huw Pritchard
Printed by CPI Antony Rowe, Melksham, United Kingdom

STUDIES IN WELSH HISTORY

Editors

RALPH A. GRIFFITHS   CHRIS WILLIAMS
ERYN M. WHITE

40

THE CONSERVATIVE PARTY IN WALES,
1945–1997

SERIES EDITORS' FOREWORD

Since the foundation of the series in 1977, the study of Wales's history has attracted growing attention among historians internationally and continues to enjoy a vigorous popularity. Not only are approaches, both traditional and new, to the study of history in general being successfully applied in a Welsh context, but Wales's historical experience is increasingly appreciated by writers on British, European and world history. These advances have been especially marked in the university institutions in Wales itself.

In order to make more widely available the conclusions of original research, much of it of limited accessibility in postgraduate dissertations and theses, in 1977 the History and Law Committee of the Board of Celtic Studies inaugurated this series of monographs, *Studies in Welsh History*. It was anticipated that many of the volumes would originate in research conducted in the University of Wales or under the auspices of the Board of Celtic Studies, and so it proved. Although the Board of Celtic Studies no longer exists, the University of Wales Press continues to sponsor the series. It seeks to publish significant contributions made by researchers in Wales and elsewhere. Its primary aim is to serve historical scholarship and to encourage the study of Welsh history.

For my parents, Sue and Stuart

CONTENTS

SERIES EDITORS' FOREWORD	v
PREFACE AND ACKNOWLEDGEMENTS	ix
LIST OF FIGURES	xv
LIST OF TABLES	xvii
ABBREVIATIONS	xix
NOTE ON TERMS AND PLACE NAMES	xxi
NOTE ON INTERVIEWS AND ORAL CONTRIBUTIONS	xxiii
Introduction	1
1. Defeat and the response to Labour, 1945–1951	37
2. Affluence and a changing Wales, 1951–1964	101
3. Modernity and localism, 1964–1975	161
4. Thatcherism and its legacy, 1975–1997	213
CONCLUSION	259
BIBLIOGRAPHY	275
INDEX	295

PREFACE AND ACKNOWLEDGEMENTS

In order to give a sense of what has shaped or influenced them, authors who write books about modern political history sometimes begin by describing their own politics.[1] Those writing about Labour, Plaid Cymru or the Liberals in Wales have done so, too, to flag up that they are either openly sympathetic to those parties, are or were members of them, or even tried to get elected to office for the party they were writing about.[2] There is, of course, nothing wrong with that. Many people take a wider interest in their own politics and some subsequently benefit by having unusually close access to source material and people. Some of the pioneering historians of the Conservative Party were themselves Tories, and such connections did not dilute the quality of their work. Nonetheless, it is probably important to know about such things from the outset. I have fewer links to the party that I am writing about. I have never campaigned for it, supported it, or been paid to work for it, although I did do a short stint of unpaid work experience for my local member of what was then the National Assembly for Wales when I was a student in my early twenties. He – Paul Davies – was a Conservative but, much more importantly for me, he was the member for the constituency that I was born and brought up in: Preseli Pembrokeshire. *This* connection, more than anything else, lies at the heart of my academic interest in

---

[1] See Martin Johnes, *Wales: England's Colony? The Conquest, Assimilation and Re-creation of Wales* (Cardigan: Parthian, 2019), pp. vii–viii; the Introduction to Jon Lawrence's *Speaking For the People: Party, Language and Popular Politics in England, 1867–1914* (Cambridge: Cambridge University Press, 1998); John Ramsden, *The Age of Balfour and Baldwin, 1902–1940* (London: Longman, 1978), pp. xi–xii.

[2] See, for example, Laura McAllister, *Plaid Cymru: The Emergence of a Political Party* (Bridgend: Seren, 2001), p. 6; Martin Wright, *Wales and Socialism: Political Culture and National Identity Before the Great War* (Cardiff: University of Wales Press, 2016), acknowledgements.

Welsh Conservatism. I grew up in the Blair era, when elected Tories from Wales were not really a thing. But soaking up politics in an area that had once had Conservative MPs, and had one again by the time I was old enough to start thinking semi-seriously about current affairs, meant that I understood the places and the people that were receptive to these kinds of ideas. As a family, we holidayed every year in a part of Wales that was more naturally Tory than anything else. As an adult, I moved to, and grew to love, Cardiff, which had been surprisingly Conservative only a generation earlier. So, even though I regularly fight off accusations that I am a Conservative, I am not. But I know, like and understand people who are and I recognise the places where they often live. As for my own politics, they are a muddle, which I think is quite normal.

* * *

It was a study of 1970s and 80s Pembrokeshire politics when I was a Master's student at Cardiff University that marked the beginning of a very long journey that ends with this book. After an MA, I did a PhD on the broader topic of the Conservatives in Wales. Then came a long, enjoyable break when I turned my attention to writing my first monograph as part of a four-year post-doctoral fellowship at Swansea University. Only after that, with ideas having gestated in the meantime, did I return to my original academic interest. Carrying this project around with me for ten years means that I have accumulated an unusually long list of people who I wish to thank.

At the very beginning, Stephanie Ward and Bill Jones guided me through my earliest ideas, and my fellow 'history boys', Andy, James and Henning, listened patiently to my thoughts and didn't laugh too much when I said I wanted to be an actual historian. Patricia Skinner thought I could be and was instrumental in encouraging me to bid for Arts and Humanities Research Council funding to study for a doctorate at Swansea University, for which

PREFACE AND ACKNOWLEDGEMENTS

I will always be grateful. I thank both the AHRC and what was then the College of Arts and Humanities at Swansea for the resources to do that original research, some of which has survived into this volume. Within the College, the Department of History and Classics (as it then was) offered the warmest of scholarly environments in which to work. Rory Castle and Teresa Phipps were, at different times, friends and allies who offered endless support. Many members of staff, who then became colleagues, were at various times between 2013 and 2022 encouraging and kind. I owe particular thanks to Matthew Frank Stevens for his generosity and our long conversations, to Adam Mosely for his support, and to Louise Miskell and Tomás Irish for mentoring me through my first book project, which undoubtedly made this one better. Matthew Cragoe's thorough scrutiny of the original thesis in his role as my external examiner encouraged me to do a lot of thinking and wider reading. I am hugely grateful for that.

Since 2013, my research has taken me to a dozen archives and record offices. I want to thank everyone who patiently fetched me document after document and then didn't seem too exasperated when I turned up yet again to do more digging. I owe a huge amount to Jeremy McIlwaine and Anabel Farrell, the former and current Conservative Party Archivists and Rob Phillips at the National Library of Wales. Rob in particular took lots of time out of a hectic schedule to chat about my project, often overlooking Cardigan Bay, offering invaluable ideas about further material I could see.

Many conference papers where some of the ideas in this book were tested resulted in feedback that made my arguments sharper, and whilst there are too many people to acknowledge in this regard, I would like to say particular thanks to Laura Beers, Russell Deacon, Andrew Edwards, Martin Farr, Richard Wyn Jones, Jill Lewis, Laura McAllister, David Torrance, Richard Toye and Daniel Williams. For additional advice and support, I thank Jonathan Bradbury, Matthew Day, Aled Eirug, Deian Hopkin, Christoph Laucht, Daryl Leeworthy, Lord Parkinson of Whitley

Bay, Dafydd Trystan, Paul Ward and Martin Wright. Particular thanks are due to my fellow historian from Pembrokeshire, Geraint Thomas. For making me think about conveying my ideas to a wider public audience, I owe much to Rhodri Lewis, Arwyn Jones, Margaret Keenan and many others at the BBC in London and Cardiff for giving me more airtime than I probably deserved over the past several years.

For agreeing to talk to me, on and off the record, I wish to sincerely thank all those people listed in the 'oral interviews' section in the bibliography. Every conversation helped broaden my understanding of the wider world of Welsh Conservatism. I owe special thanks to Sir Julian Lewis MP, who gave me a huge amount of his time and arranged for photocopies of his personal archive to be delivered to me. I also want to thank the late Keith Flynn, as well as Charlotte Bennett, for their time and kindness and the late Hywel Francis for acting as an informal mentor for many years. It has been a particular pleasure talking on many occasions to David Melding and listen to his ideas.

When they weren't making me laugh, my friends David Jeffery and Antony Mullen read an entire first draft of this work, offering a range of comments that made it much better. David even helped make the map that is figure 1. I am grateful to him for that, and for our conference parkruns. Georgina Brewis generously gave me vital time to finish writing this work before I went to work at UCL. The team at University of Wales Press have, again, been patient and enthusiastic about this project, especially Llion Wigley.

Academically, the most important person in this whole process has undoubtedly been Martin Johnes. I could not have asked for a better PhD supervisor, who also became a colleague and friend. As soon as I arrived in Swansea, Martin was a cheerleader and a constant source of advice. If I have any praiseworthy skills as a historian, it is largely down to him. Thanks for all the post-work pints as well!

On a more personal note, my late grandparents, Ron and Nesta, had a profound impact on my upbringing and I am convinced that it was Ron's love of things from the past, be it the poetry of Thomas Gray, the American Civil War, or Laurel and Hardy films, that had some influence on my own interest in history. As an autodidactic manual labourer who hated Tories, I hope that he would at least have liked this volume. In the present, I am lucky to be part of various loving friendship and family groups, and without these people, I simply would not have had the right frame of mind to write another book. Many of the following also put me up when I was travelling around the country on research trips. Thank you for everything Ffion and James; Widders, Heather, Euan and Elin; Stacey, Jon, Ellis and Fraser; Laurence and James P.; Andy and Morgan; Tom, Stefan, Suzanne and especially Mary, who I effectively lived with for months and who is very special. My parents-in-law, Mara and Warwick, facilitate frequent trips to Australia, and I have written and edited numerous sections of this book at their home, listening to the birds, looking out towards the Sydney Harbour Bridge. Thank you.

Since I began working on Welsh Conservatives, my partner (in every sense of that word) Maxim has been there with me, sharing everything and making life happy. For too many years, I have been inviting groups of invisible deceased Tories into our home to dine with us and distract me. It is a mark of his love and kindness that he has never once asked them to leave.

Finally: Sue and Stuart made all this possible. It is as thanks for being such good parents, as well as a token of gratitude for our friendship in adulthood, that I dedicate this book to them.

LIST OF FIGURES

Figure 1: The constituency results of the 1983 general election in Wales.

Figure 2: Harry West's election address to the voters of Montgomery, 1950 (CPA, PUB 229/9/17).

Figure 3: A scene from a Conservative Party rally and fete at the country mansion, Brogyntyn Hall, owned by the Ormsby-Gore family, 1949 (Geoff Charles collection courtesy of the National Library of Wales).

Figure 4: Five women prepare refreshments in the rain at a Conservative fete at the Faenol Estate, 1960 (Geoff Charles collection courtesy of the National Library of Wales).

Figure 5: Geoffrey Howe's election address stresses to the voters of Aberavon in 1955 that he is a local man (CPA, PUB 229/11/13).

Figure 6: Peter Thomas emphasises the importance of place to the voters of Conway in his 1964 election address (CPA, PUB 229/13/16).

Figure 7: Revel Guest's election address to the voters of Swansea East, 1955 (CPA, PUB 229/11/13).

Figure 8: David Maxwell Fyfe arrives to speak to a large Conservative Party rally in Dolgellau, 1953 (Geoff Charles collection courtesy of the National Library of Wales).

Figure 9: Families sit together at a Conservative Party rally at Brogyntyn Hall, 1949 (Geoff Charles collection courtesy of the National Library of Wales).

Figure 10: A large number of children take part in a Conservative carnival in Chirk, 1953 (Geoff Charles collection courtesy of the National Library of Wales).

Figure 11: John Rendle's election address to the voters of Abertillery in 1970 implies that the Labour-voting electorate are sheep (CPA, PUB 229/15/17).

Figure 12: John Eilian Jones's election address to the voters of Anglesey in 1966 contained almost no English on the front cover (Welsh Political Archive, National Library of Wales).

LIST OF TABLES

Table 1: Seats, share of the vote and number of votes won by the Conservatives, Labour, the Liberals and Plaid Cymru, 1945–1997.

Table 2: Welsh constituencies won by the Conservative Party, years held and MPs representing each seat.

Table 3: Liberal and National Liberal candidates supported by the Conservative Party in Wales, 1945–1959.

Table 4: Number of Welsh-speaking candidates fielded by the Conservative Party at each general election, 1945–1997.

Table 5: Conservative association presidents in constituencies for which information was available, *c.*1948.

Table 6: Number of Young Conservatives in each Welsh constituency, *c.*1949.

Table 7: Residency and education of Conservative Party parliamentary candidates at each general election in Wales, 1945–1997.

Table 8: Number of women standing as Conservative candidates at each general election in Wales, 1945–1997.

Table 9: Number of Conservative candidates in Wales educated privately or by the state, 1945–1997.

LIST OF ABBREVIATIONS

AM	Assembly Member
CCO	Conservative Central Office
CPA	Conservative Party Archive
CRD	Conservative Research Department
DRO	Denbighshire Record Office
FRO	Flintshire Record Office
GA	Glamorgan Archives
JIL	Junior Imperial League
JP	Justice of the Peace
MEP	Member of the European Parliament
MP	Member of Parliament
S4C	Sianel Pedwar Cymru
SDP	Social Democratic Party
WGA	West Glamorgan Archives
WPA	Welsh Political Archive
YC	Young Conservative

NOTE ON TERMS AND PLACE NAMES

The official name of the Conservative Party in this period was 'The Conservative and Unionist Party', although this was always shortened to 'the Conservative Party' or 'the Conservatives'. Whilst 'Tory' has not been its official title since the mid-nineteenth century, the term was still commonly used in this period as an alternative name for the party, including by Conservatives themselves (despite the term sometimes being meant as an insult). Political historians and others distinguish a 'Tory' as a type of Conservative with a particular set of values, but the words Conservative and Tory are used in this work interchangeably, largely for stylistic reasons. 'Tory' is not a loaded term.

On the other hand, in writings about Wales – partly for stylistic purposes as well – the term 'the Principality' is sometimes used as a synonym for Wales. This is avoided in this work, unless in a direct quotation, because the term has fallen completely out of use.

When Welsh place names appear in the text, the more common English version is used – Cardiff, not Caerdydd, for example. Where place names have changed in the course of this period – from, for example, Caernarvon to Caernarfon – the more recent and less anglicised spelling is used, unless in a direct quotation or when discussing a seat like Caernarvon Boroughs, which was abolished before the more recent spelling was widely used. However, historic names of constituencies have been retained. For example 'Conway' is used in reference to that seat for the period before 1983, whereas it is 'Conwy' for the years after 1983 when the constituency's name changed. The same principle is applied to Merioneth and Meirionnydd, Cardigan and Ceredigion etc.

NOTE ON INTERVIEWS AND ORAL CONTRIBUTIONS

Over the course of ten years' worth of research for what eventually turned into this book, many people were interviewed on and off the record. Most were happy for their words to appear in the text. Some wished to be anonymised and therefore have been. The list of contributors in the bibliography includes many people whose words do not feature directly here but whose contributions were useful for the building up of a wider argument. Of those who wished to remain anonymous in the text and footnotes, some were happy to appear in the bibliography, whilst others were not.

INTRODUCTION

In July 1980, two bombs were planted in Wales by opponents of the Conservative Party. One was placed five feet from the sleeping son of the Secretary of State for Wales. The other was left outside a Conservative club in Cardiff. Whilst neither was detonated, this deliberately coincided with a visit by Margaret Thatcher to address the party's annual Welsh conference, whereupon her car was blocked and stones and eggs were thrown at it by angry protestors.[1] All of this happened four years before the bruising coalminers' strike of 1984 to 1985, which accorded Thatcher even greater villain status in parts of Wales. Visiting Wales at the same time as the double-bomb incident, the former Labour cabinet minister Barbara Castle said: 'Welsh Conservatives! The two are contradictory!'[2] This image of a naturally anti-Conservative Wales and an 'un-Welsh' Tory Party was a commonly painted one. As well as being embedded in the rhetoric of the party's opponents, it was also mirrored in popular culture. At one point in Kingsley Amis's 1955 satirical novel *That Uncertain Feeling*, the protagonist John Lewis – a resident of the fictional south Wales town of Aberdarcy, which was based on Swansea – pulls up in a car opposite a neighbour who 'was notorious in the district for displaying Conservative election posters in his windows. For a couple of months the previous autumn there'd hardly been a single evening when a

---

[1] 'Two bombs planted as Tories meet in Wales', *The Times*, 19 July 1980. For an account of the planting of the bombs, which was part of a series of attacks, see John Osmond, *Police Conspiracy?* (Tal-y-bont: Y Lolfa, 1984). It was never established who had put the bombs in these places.

[2] Lord Roberts of Conwy, *Right From the Start: The Memoirs of Sir Wyn Roberts* (Cardiff: University of Wales Press, 2006), p. 133.

whizz-bang, or perhaps a jumping cracker hadn't been dropped through his letterbox'.[3]

All of this reflected a real, and not just an imagined or exaggerated, hostility felt towards the Conservative Party in parts of Wales. Historians, academics and commentators have played a role in reinforcing this, noting how Wales is 'overwhelmingly anti-Conservative', or 'the most anti-Conservative area in all of Britain'.[4] Indeed, in the era of universal suffrage, the party has constantly failed to win anything close to a majority of parliamentary seats, or the most votes, in Wales. It was even wiped out, in terms of Westminster seats, twice, at either end of the twentieth century. In books on the history of the party across Britain, Wales is often used as a byword for Conservative failure.[5] The fact that the most well-known Welsh Conservatives – Geoffrey Howe, Michael Heseltine and Michael Howard – all had to leave their homeland to get elected to parliament reinforced much of this.

Yet, this image of a historically weak party in Wales should be more nuanced. If we return to the example of Thatcher, the Conservative Party won a modern-era record of fourteen seats (out of thirty-eight) in Wales at the 1983 general election (see figure 1), a tally only equalled by Boris Johnson in 2019, although Wales had forty constituencies by then. Whilst fourteen seats represented just under a third of the Welsh total, this was more than would be expected from a party long considered a 'dumb dog that cannot bark',[6] led by a supposed hate figure, that

---

[3] Kingsley Amis, *That Uncertain Feeling* ([1955] St Albans: Panther Books, 1975), pp. 59–60.

[4] David Butler and Donald Stokes, *Political Change in Britain: The Evolution of Electoral Choice* ([1969] Suffolk: Macmillan Press, 1974), quoted in Richard Wyn Jones, Roger Scully and Dafydd Trystan, 'Why do the Conservatives Always do (Even) Worse in Wales?', in Lynn Bennie, Colin Rawlings, Jonathan Tonge and Paul Webb (eds), *British Elections and Parties Review*, 12/1 (2002), 232.

[5] See John Ramsden, *The Age of Churchill and Eden, 1940–1957* (London: Longman, 1995), p. 119; Stuart Ball, *Portrait of a Party: The Conservative Party in Britain, 1918–1945* (Oxford: Oxford University Press, 2013), p. 121.

[6] The phrase was coined by the *South Wales Evening News* in 1874. Quoted in Felix Aubel, 'The Conservatives in Wales, 1880–1935', in Martin Francis and Ina Zweiniger-Bargielowska (eds), *The Conservatives and British Society, 1880–1990* (Cardiff: University of Wales Press, 1996), p. 96.

was totally incompatible with Welsh voting habits. In many parts of Wales, the Tories performed terribly, but this was not the case everywhere. A similar story is evident throughout the twentieth century. A glance at the political map after general elections in this period will occasionally show a nation carpeted in red constituencies, such as after the vote held in 1966. However, many others show a much more diverse picture. Beyond the anti-Conservative and hugely important Labour fortresses of the south Wales coalfield – often termed 'the Valleys' – were places like Pembrokeshire, Monmouthshire, Cardiff and its surrounds, the Vale of Glamorgan, Denbighshire, Flintshire and Conwy, where the Conservative Party was often the most successful at elections times (although the relatively large nature of these rural seats does exaggerate the 'blueness' of maps like figure 1). Some of these places may be less radical and 'more Anglicised and Anglican' than most other parts of Wales, but they remain parts of the nation, nonetheless, and fundamental to its history.[7] More important than the number of seats won, which under the first-past-the-post electoral system is a blunt tool for measuring party success, especially when the boundaries of these seats are redrawn relatively often, is the share of the vote parties receive. It is worth noting that 32.6 per cent of the vote yielded seven seats for the party in Wales in 1959, for example, whilst a 31 per cent share gave it double that number in 1983. For the vast majority of this period the Tories hovered around the 30 per cent mark when it came to the share of the vote, as demonstrated in table 1.[8] Again, this is not spectacular, especially for a party used to being in office in the UK for a large part of the twentieth century, but neither is it so small as to be worthy of dismissal.

---

[7] Duncan Tanner, 'The Pattern of Labour Politics, 1918–1939', in Duncan Tanner, Chris Williams and Deian Hopkin (eds), *The Labour Party in Wales, 1900–2000* (Cardiff: University of Wales Press, 2000), p. 113; Wyn Jones, Scully and Trystan, 'Why do the Conservatives', 232–3.

[8] Lukas Audickas, Oliver Hawkins and Richard Cracknell, 'House of Commons Briefing Paper: UK Election statistics, 1918–2016', 7 July 2016, pp. 18–19.

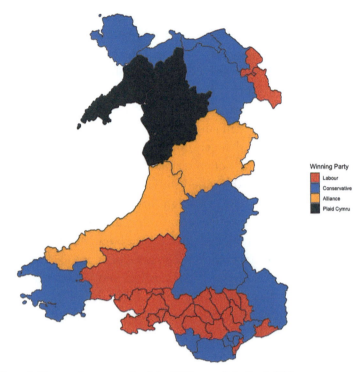

Figure 1: The constituency results of the 1983 general election in Wales.

Alongside some electoral successes, the Conservatives managed to maintain extraordinarily high membership figures in its 'heartlands' for much of the period under study here. It did so by encouraging normal grassroots supporters to join the party and, in some cases, to work voluntarily and campaign for it. In short, for by far the greater part of the twentieth century, the Conservative Party has been the second party in Wales, with thousands of people in some constituencies paying a fee to join it as a member. The party has constantly been way behind Labour, which has dominated, and which had a majority of all Welsh MPs in the period under consideration here.[9] In an era of two-party politics, there is little that is commendable about that. But in a period of multi-party politics that characterised much of the period after

---

[9] For excellent essays on Labour in Wales see Tanner, Williams and Hopkin, *The Labour Party*.

the Second World War, in terms of seats won at elections, or the share of the vote received, the Tories maintained this second-place position, ahead of both Plaid Cymru and the various incarnations of the Liberal Party. It is not accurate, therefore, to refer to 'the two main parties, Labour and Plaid', as one recent work of twentieth-century history did.[10] This book's first (but not sole) aim is to show that there is, despite popular misconceptions, a history of relative success to be told of the Tories in Wales. The party was often more popular there than historical or political stereotypes allow for.

	Con. seats[11]	Con. % of vote	Con. votes (1,000)	Lab. seats	Lab. % of vote	Lab. votes (1,000)	Lib. seats	Lib. % of vote	Lib. votes (1,000)	PC seats	PC % of vote	PC votes (1,000)
1945[12]	4	23.8	317	25	58.5	779	6	14.9	199	0	1.1	14
1950	4	27.4	419	27	58.1	888	5	12.6	193	0	1.2	18
1951	6	30.9	471	27	60.5	926	3	7.6	117	0	0.7	11
1955	6	29.9	429	27	57.6	826	3	7.3	104	0	3.1	45
1959	7	32.6	486	27	56.6	842	2	5.3	79	0	5.2	78
1964	6	29.4	425	28	57.9	837	2	7.3	106	0	4.8	70
1966	3	27.9	397	32	60.6	864	1	6.3	89	0	4.3	61
1970	7	27.7	420	27	51.6	782	1	6.8	104	0	11.5	175
1974 Feb.	8	25.9	413	24	46.8	746	2	16.0	259	2	10.7	171
1974 Oct.	8	23.9	367	23	49.5	761	2	15.5	238	3	10.8	166
1979	11	32.2	526	22	48.6	768	1	10.6	174	2	8.1	132
1983	14	31.0	499	20	37.5	604	2	23.2	373	2	7.8	125
1987	8	29.6	501	24	45.1	765	3	17.9	304	3	7.3	124
1992	6	28.6	500	27	49.5	866	1	12.4	217	4	9	157
1997	0	19.6	317	34	55	886	2	12	200	4	10	161

Table 1: Seats, share of the vote and number of votes won by the Conservatives, Labour, the Liberals and Plaid Cymru, 1945–97.

[10] Douglas Jones, *The Communist Party of Great Britain and the National Question in Wales, 1920–1991* (Cardiff: University of Wales Press, 2017), pp. 1–2.
[11] Conservative results include National Liberal votes. The party was allied with the Tories after 1945.
[12] The party fielded only twenty-one out of thirty-six candidates in this election.

Whilst the other major parties have their own academic book-length histories, this work is the first to offer that treatment to the Conservatives in Wales.[13] It concentrates on the party as an institution since the Second World War, devoting its attention to how the Conservative hierarchy mediated British-wide policies to the electorate, especially by articulating the 'dangers' of socialism; supposed women's concerns, like inflation and the cost of living; and the importance of everyday issues that impacted upon the lives of ordinary people. It also discusses how the party designed specific policy for Wales, and the attitude many of its senior members took towards the 'national question' and devolution. Despite the party often feeling uncomfortable with the topic, struggling to shake off its image as incompatible with Wales, it designed a series of specific policies for Wales after 1945, setting in train a process of administrative devolution in 1951, when Churchill's government created a Minister for Welsh Affairs. The party also undertook a series of changes to the Tory 'brand' by trying to make the institution and those who represented it more 'Welsh', whilst still attempting to retain a strong sense of a Welsh and British 'dual identity'. The book explores who many of the party's parliamentary candidates in Wales were and how they presented themselves – often badly – to the electorate.

The work also focuses on the party's mass membership and its grassroots. In doing so, it offers more than the traditional approach to political history. It explores 'ordinary' Conservatives in Wales and asks not just what they did for the Tory Party, but who such individuals were, what they thought about the world

---

[13] For Labour see Tanner, Williams and Hopkin, *The Labour Party*; Daryl Leeworthy, *Labour Country: Political Radicalism and Social Democracy in South Wales, 1831–1985* (Cardigan: Parthian, 2018); also see Martin Wright, *Wales and Socialism: Political Culture and National Identity Before the Great War* (Cardiff: University of Wales Press, 2016). For Plaid Cymru, see Laura McAllister, *Plaid Cymru: The Emergence of a Political Party* (Bridgend: Seren, 2001). For the Liberals/Liberal Democrats, see Russell Deacon, *The Welsh Liberals: The Welsh Liberals: The History of the Liberal and Liberal Democrat Parties in Wales* (Cardiff: Welsh Academic Press, 2014). For the Communist Party, even, see Jones, *The Communist Party*. See n.58 for those who have written articles and chapters on the Conservative Party in Wales.

and what kinds of backgrounds they were drawn from. It shows how the party maintained links with the landed elite well into the post-Second World War years, although these people were supplanted by a new kind of firmly middle-class elite, rooted in business and connected to a wider network of civic and local organisations. Local leadership teams in Wales were aided in the running of associations by agents, although Wales – reflecting the shaky position of the Tories there – regularly struggled to employ and then retain people of quality in this role. Active grassroots members were also drawn overwhelmingly from the middle classes, and Conservative politics throughout this period gave them an opportunity to meet like-minded people and socialise. For Tory women, in particular, the party in Wales offered an opportunity for them to incorporate their families into this world of politics and socialising, whilst some actively took a role in leading an association, or campaigning for the party, demonstrating agency and a distinct right-leaning political identity in the process. Local associations were also the place where other people, including Young Conservatives, could discuss politics and articulate the kind of conservative views that are not immediately associated with Welsh society. This book is therefore also an exploration of these societal groups.

BACKGROUND

History does not start or end in neat periods, and there are several key reasons why this work begins immediately after the Second World War. The period 1945 to 1997 encompasses some of the party's highs and lows in Wales, including some of its worst-ever performances, like the contests in 1966 and 1997. This allows us to trace how all levels of the party reacted to moments of strength and weakness, as well as how it responded to Labour during that party's zenith in Wales. The period also encompasses dramatically evolving social and cultural contexts. The 1945 general election took place in an era of old-fashioned campaigning, of door-knocking and stump speeches, alongside broadcasts on the radio.[14] By the late 1950s, the television had come into its own as a campaign tool, and by the 1960s, all political parties were having to adapt to an unfolding social and cultural revolution. When concentrating on the party's grassroots, the late 1940s and early 1950s witnessed the highest-ever number of people in Britain – including in Wales – becoming members of the party. Figures in some seats, as we shall see, were enormous. However, membership totals dropped quickly in the 1960s and then went off a cliff shortly afterwards. Again, this presents the best possible opportunity to examine how such rapid changes altered the nature of politics in Wales.

Whilst there are many threads of continuity between the pre-Second World War and the post-1945 period,[15] there are also aspects that mark the post-war years out as different, in terms of both policy and organisational initiatives, which, as the historian Tim Bale has argued, were in many cases 'genuinely innovative'.[16] The party from the mid-1940s onwards was a different and more professional outfit, which had an impact on all its levels. The years after the Second World War marked a major shift in the way the party concentrated on Wales and the issue of Welsh nationhood. The following chapters suggest that we should not overstate this latter topic. Both the party, its supporters and most of the electorate, still saw politics through a firmly British lens and cared more about class than nation in this period. But the party nonetheless thought more than ever before about its own compatibility with Wales, in a period where such things began to be discussed more frequently by ordinary people and politicians (mentions of Wales in Hansard increase steadily after 1945). It

---

[14] Kenneth O. Morgan, 'Power and Glory: War and Reconstruction, 1939–1951', in Tanner, Williams and Hopkin, *The Labour Party*, p. 173.

[15] John Ramsden, '"A Party for Owners or a Party For Earners?" How Far Did the British Conservative Party Really Change After 1945?', *Transactions of the Royal Historical Society*, 37 (1987); also see Ramsden, *The Age of Churchill*, pp. 94–5.

[16] Tim Bale, *The Conservatives Since 1945: The Drivers of Party Change* (Oxford: Oxford University Press, 2016), p. 14.

was in the immediate post-war years that the Conservatives also formally incorporated women into its local party structures, as well as establishing the Young Conservatives. Both groups are the focus of attention in following chapters. This book also draws on oral testimonies with people who were active in Welsh Conservative circles from the 1940s onwards. For both substantive and methodological reasons, therefore, the years after the Second World War are a logical place to begin.

However, a sense of the party's earlier history is vital in our understanding of it as an institution after 1945. In the nineteenth century, the Conservative Party was headed in Wales by an Anglican (or anglicised), land-owning aristocracy, which sat in contrast to a Nonconformist, more Welsh-speaking group of workers, industrial labourers and tenant farmers. Welsh society was consequently divided along the lines of class, culture, language and religion, all of which were interwoven.[17] Politics mapped on to this. The Liberal Party was best placed to represent the Nonconformist middle and working classes, stressing the key issues of disestablishment of the Church of England, temperance, Home Rule and better education.[18] On the other hand, Conservatism was both in reality, and perceived as, the political arm of an elite that was opposed to Church disestablishment. Hence, Gwyn Alf Williams commented that it was an 'unholy trinity of Toryism', comprising 'the baron, the bishop and the brewer', that oppressed the ordinary people of nineteenth-century Wales.[19] Some historians and writers have tried to temper the image of the cruel Anglican landowner or Tory capitalist 'pinning the people to the ground'.[20] For the enigmatic nationalist writer H. W. J. Edwards, it was possible to be 'a good

---

[17] Martin Johnes, *Wales: England's Colony? The Conquest, Assimilation and Re-creation of Wales* (Cardigan: Parthian, 2019), pp. 60–1.
[18] Geraint Thomas, 'The Conservative Party and Welsh Politics in the Inter-war Years', *English Historical Review*, 128/533 (2013), 878; Wyn Jones, Scully and Trystan, 'Why do the Conservatives', 233.
[19] Gwyn A. Williams, *When Was Wales?* (London: Black Raven, 1985), pp. 198, 217.
[20] See, for example, Johnes, *Wales: England's Colony*, p. 139.

Tory employer' who demonstrated a sense of patriarchal care.[21] This is reflected in the work of the historian Matthew Cragoe, who argued in his study of the Carmarthenshire aristocracy that the relationship between landlord and tenant was often much more conciliatory and mutually beneficial.[22] Others have suggested that contemporary Liberal propaganda exaggerated the negative aspects of Conservatism,[23] although the key writer Felix Aubel concluded that Anglicanism, landlordism and Englishness were the 'perceived and actual' trademarks of the party in Wales before the First World War.[24] Meanwhile, however, in the rapidly developing industrial areas of Wales, like the southern coalfield, chapels, not the established Church, were built very quickly, and Nonconformity put down strong roots in these new communities. This underpins the fact that in the eight general elections between 1885 and 1910, Conservative candidates won 34 contests out of a possible 264 in Wales. At the 1906 election, the party failed to win a single parliamentary seat.[25] Politicians like David Lloyd George tied this into a narrative of a particular kind of radical Wales.[26]

The First World War marked a major moment of change in British politics and society. The power of Nonconformism weakened, and many parts of Wales became increasingly anglicised as further waves of English people continued to migrate into industrial areas for work. The landed classes were also impacted, with a large number of estates being broken up in the immediate post-war years. After 1918, a series of industrial disputes and an economic depression, following a post-war slump

---

[21] H. W. J. Edwards, *The Good Patch* (London, 1938), p. 50.

[22] Matthew Cragoe, *An Anglican Aristocracy: The Moral Economy of the Landed Estate in Carmarthenshire, 1832–1895* (Oxford: Clarendon Press, 1996), pp. 94–5.

[23] Thomas, 'The Conservative Party', 878; Cragoe, *An Anglican Aristocracy*, pp. 94–5; Matthew Cragoe, *Politics, Culture and National Identity in Wales, 1832–1886* (Oxford: Oxford University Press, 2004), p. 3.

[24] Felix Aubel, 'Welsh Conservatism 1885–1935: Five Studies in Adaptation' (unpublished PhD thesis, Lampeter University, 1994), p. 30.

[25] Aubel, 'The Conservatives', p. 98.

[26] Geraint Thomas, *Popular Conservatism and the Culture of National Government in Inter-war Britain* (Cambridge: Cambridge University Press, 2020), pp. 205–6.

in the coal, iron, steel and tinplate industries, created widespread unemployment and poverty.[27] This, and the Great Depression which dominated much of the 1930s, was the Conservative-dominated National Government's chief legacy in much of south Wales, where unemployment rates were the worst in the entire UK.[28] Such conditions provided political opportunities for the Labour Party. Through activist groups and via winning power in local government, it integrated itself into the fabric of communities in places like the Valleys, as well as by adopting more middle-class or Welsh-speaking images in other parts of Wales.[29] As Daryl Leeworthy has argued, Labour talked effectively about building a 'humane and civilised' society in this period. It put words into action through the building of civic and community facilities, like playing fields, public halls and libraries.[30] This sat alongside holistic attitudes to welfare, education and health. But Labour could also pose as the defenders of industrial society, especially when some of the pits being closed were owned by the family of the Conservative Prime Minister, Stanley Baldwin.[31] The Conservatives managed to win only thirty-seven electoral victories in Wales between 1918 and 1935, out of a possible 252, averaging 21.4 per cent of the vote, although this is partly explained by the complexities of inter-war politics and the forging of 'anti-Socialist' pacts with parties standing under the 'National' banner.[32] But the Welsh language, some anti-Conservative rural trends and the sheer size of the working class all impeded Tory progress.[33] The

---

[27] David Williams, *A History of Modern Wales* (London: J. Murray, 1977), p. 286.
[28] Thomas, *Popular Conservatism*, p. 215.
[29] Chris Williams, 'Introduction', in Tanner, Williams and Hopkin, *The Labour Party*, pp. 7, 9; Tanner, 'The Pattern of Labour Politics', p. 118.
[30] Leeworthy, *Labour Country*, pp. 268–9. Also see Duncan Tanner, 'Gender, Civic Culture and Politics in South Wales: Explaining Labour Municipal Policy, 1918–1939', in Matthew Worley (ed.), *Labour's Grass Roots: Essays on the Activities of Local Labour Parties and Members, 1918–1945* (Aldershot: Ashgate, 2005).
[31] Leeworthy, *Labour Country*, p. 313.
[32] Aubel, 'The Conservatives', pp. 99–100; Wyn Jones, Scully and Trystan, 'Why do the Conservatives', 234.
[33] Ross McKibbin, 'Class and Conventional Wisdom: the Conservative Party and the "Public" in Inter-war Britain', in R. McKibbin, *The Ideologies of Class* (Oxford: Clarendon, 1990), p. 285.

Liberals, meanwhile, once the party of government in Britain and a dominant force in Wales, had splintered badly. One group, the National Liberals, formally allied with the Conservatives before the Second World War, and this joining together would have repercussions for post-1945 politics in Wales, as we see in chapter one.[34]

An era of Liberal hegemony in Wales, therefore, rapidly shifted to support for the new Labour Party in industrial areas, not least because those places hit hardest in the 1930s were by far the most populous.[35] The connection between Labour and the electorate there was remarkably durable, with voting for the party becoming 'a pledge of loyalty to your community, its memories, its values and its way of life' in many areas.[36] Some, including the former Labour Party leader and MP for a Valleys seat, Neil Kinnock, have argued that there was something instinctively left-leaning in the character of many Welsh people.[37] As we shall see, this was an idea that Conservatives regularly found themselves having to compete against in the post-1945 period, often to their intense frustration. Party members and senior backroom figures alike often muttered in private about the 'sentimental' temperament of Welsh people that meant they were susceptible to misleading 'Socialist rhetoric'.[38] The party also thought a culture of nepotism within Labour at local government level existed. It dreaded the prospect of by-elections in somewhere like the south Wales Valleys, where it resented losing money by having to field a candidate.[39]

---

[34] E. H. H. Green, 'The Conservative Party, the State and the Electorate, 1945–64', in Jon Lawrence and Miles Taylor (eds), *Party, State and Society: Electoral Behaviour in Britain since 1820* (Aldershot: Scolar Press, 1997).

[35] Wyn Jones, Scully and Trystan, 'Why do the Conservatives', 233.

[36] Wyn Jones, Scully and Trystan, 'Why do the Conservatives', 234; Kenneth O. Morgan and Peter Stead, 'Rhondda West', in D. E. Butler and Anthony King (eds), *The British General Election of 1966* (London: Macmillan, 1966), p. 249.

[37] Neil Kinnock, 'Preface' to Tanner, Williams and Hopkin, *The Labour Party*; Kenneth O. Morgan, 'Hughes, Cledwyn, Baron Cledwyn of Penrhos', *Oxford Dictionary of National Biography*, 8 January 2009.

[38] Conservative Party Archive, Bodleian Library, Oxford [CPA], Conservative Central Office [CCO], 500/24/56, 'Review of the Welsh political situation', 1 March 1950.

[39] For example: CPA, CCO 1/14/541, Howard Davies to the COO, 9 December 1963.

The Second World War, and the post-war settlement, changed British politics significantly. Table 2 gives a more detailed indication of the Conservative Party's performance in Wales in the decades after the war, by showing those who sat as MPs for Welsh seats between 1945 and 1997.[40] When this information is compared with figure 1, it should give some sense of the party's areas of strength in Wales. Most of these people and places will feature in the following chapters, but for now some summary comments might be useful. The party's representatives were exclusively male and drawn largely from a particular societal group. Some were schoolteachers, some had worked in broadcasting and television, but businessmen and former merchant bankers were also well represented, demonstrating their solidly middle- and sometimes upper-middle-class profiles. Some seats were held by stalwart figures like Sir Raymond Gower, the MP for Barry (and later the Vale of Glamorgan) for very long periods of time. Other people were a more fleeting presence, such as those men who briefly held seats like Bridgend or Clwyd South West. Majorities were often very small, although some seats, like Cardiff North West or Clwyd North West, had – after good elections – comfortable majorities. Perhaps the most significant moments for the party included the tenure of Hugh Rees as MP for Swansea West from 1959 to 1964, or the capturing of Anglesey, a typically Welsh-speaking rural constituency, in 1979, by Keith Best.

Both figure 1 and table 2 demonstrate how the party's success tended to map on to the 'British Wales' part of the famous Three Wales Model. This was popularised by Denis Balsom in the 1980s, building on an idea first put forward in the early 1920s by Alfred E. Zimmern. This model identified '*y fro Gymraeg*' (a Welsh-speaking region), located mainly in the north and west; 'Welsh Wales', which was Welsh-identifying but non-Welsh speaking,

[40] For extra details, see: Arnold J. James and John E. Thomas, *Wales at Westminster: A History of the Parliamentary Representation of Wales 1800–1979* (Llandysul: Gomer Press, 1981); Ivor Thomas Rees, *Welsh Hustings: 1885–2004* (Llandybie: Dinefwr Press, 2005).

and found mostly in south Wales, encompassing the Valleys; and 'British Wales', mostly along the English borders, which was British-identifying and non-Welsh speaking.[41] Although not a mirror image, the colours of the constituencies in figure 1 broadly reflect the Three Wales Model. The model itself is certainly flawed and leads to oversimplifications.[42] However, it remains a useful method of categorising a range of constituencies in a manner that makes a study of an entire nation's political history more digestible. Throughout this book, constituencies will be loosely grouped according to the categories the Three Wales Model sets out, with the areas and parliamentary constituencies encompassed by so-called 'British Wales' being those seats that Conservatives had a fighting chance of winning and where Tory politics had clear appeal to some people. The area of Welsh-speaking Wales was less fruitful territory for the party, despite the fact that such seats would have been naturally Conservative had they been located in England. 'Welsh Wales' will be used as shorthand for the places where Conservatives tended to perform terribly, with most references being specifically made to the industrialised (or de-industrialising) valleys of south Wales. It was in these areas that seats were commonly used to 'blood in' unsuitable candidates who would later win safe Home Counties constituencies, as we shall see.[43]

---

[41] Denis Balsom, 'The Three-Wales Model', in John Osmond (ed.), *The National Question Again: Welsh Political Identity in the 1980s* (Llandysul: Gomer Press, 1985), p. 6. For further comments see Thomas, 'The Conservative Party', 883–4.

[42] For a useful critique of the model, see Roger Scully and Richard Wyn Jones, 'Still Three Wales? Social Location and Electoral Behaviour in Contemporary Wales', *Electoral Studies*, 31 (2012), pp. 656–67.

[43] Kenneth O. Morgan, *Rebirth of a Nation: Wales, 1880–1980* (Oxford: Oxford University Press, 1982), p. 379.

Seat	MP and years held	Notes
Anglesey (called Ynys Môn from 1983)	Keith Best (1979–87)	
Barry; Vale of Glamorgan from 1983[44]	Raymond Gower (1951–89 (his death)) Walter Sweeney (1992–7)	
Brecon and Radnor	Tom Hooson (1979–85 (his death)) Jonathan Evans (1992–7)	
Bridgend	Peter Hubbard-Miles (1983–7)	
Cardiff Central	Ian Grist (1983–92)	Seat created in 1983.
Cardiff North	David Llewellyn (1950–9) Donald Box (1959–66) Michael Roberts (1970–4) Ian Grist (1974–83) Gwilym Jones (1983–97)	Seat created in 1950. Boundaries redrawn in 1974 and 1983, with Roberts and Grist moving to different seats in Cardiff as part of that process.
Cardiff North West	Michael Roberts (1974–83)	Short-lived seat that existed for nine years. Roberts died at the dispatch box in the House of Commons in 1983, close enough to the general election of that year for there to be no by-election.
Cardiff West	Stefan Terlezki (1983–7)	
Clwyd South West	Robert Harvey (1983–7)	
Conway (called Conwy after 1983)	Peter Thomas (1951–66) Wyn Roberts (1970–97)	Thomas became the first Conservative Secretary of State for Wales in 1970, but was then sitting as the MP for Hendon South.

[44] The seat's boundaries were redrawn, but much of the former Barry seat remained in the new Vale of Glamorgan one.

Delyn	Keith Raffan (1983–92)	New seat created out of parts of the previous Flint West and Flint East seats.
Denbigh	Henry Morris-Jones (1945–50: sat as a National Liberal) Emlyn Garner Evans (1950–9: also a National Liberal) Geraint Morgan (1959–83)	Seat abolished in 1983.
Flintshire; Flint West from 1950; Clwyd North West from 1983; Clwyd West in 1997	Nigel Birch (1945–70) Anthony Meyer (1970–92) Rod Richards (1992–7)	Meyer was the 'stalking horse' candidate who challenged Margaret Thatcher for the party leadership in 1989. Richards became the first leader of the Conservative group in the new National Assembly for Wales from 1999, although he was in the role for only a year.
Monmouth	Leslie Pym (1945 (his death)) Peter Thorneycroft (1945 b/e–1966) John Stradling Thomas (1970–91 (his death)) Roger Evans (1992–7)	Pym became the MP at the 1939 by-election. He died between the 1945 election and the announcement of the results three weeks later. His opponents found themselves congratulating a dead man.[45] Thorneycroft, Chancellor of the Exchequer from 1957–8, won the ensuing by-election.
Newport West	Mark Robinson (1983–7)	
Montgomery	Delwyn Williams (1979–83)	

[45] Gerard Charmley, 'Parliamentary Representation', in Chris Williams and Andy Croll (eds), *The Gwent County History, Volume 5: The Twentieth Century* (Cardiff: University of Wales Press, 2013), p. 306.

Pembrokeshire	Gwilym Lloyd George (1945–50: sat as a National Liberal with Tory support. Had been the MP since 1929.[46]) Nicholas Edwards (1970–87) Nicholas Bennett (1987–92)	Edwards won the seat in a highly unusual contest in 1970, where the vote was split three ways between him, an official Labour candidate and the seat's former Labour MP from 1950–70, the maverick Desmond Donnelly.
Swansea West	Hugh Rees (1959–64)	

Table 2: Welsh constituencies won by the Conservative Party, years held and MPs representing the seat.

Tables 1 and 2 demonstrate how the Conservatives were, for the vast majority of this period, Wales's second party. The 1997 general election may have been a catastrophe for the Tories, but this book does not set out to tell a story of 'dominance to decline' for the party, in the way that histories of the party in Scotland, or in places like Merseyside, do.[47] There is a frustrating tendency amongst some historians to lump together the Scottish and Welsh stories as the 'Celtic vote', as if the party's fortunes in both nations are similar.[48] For example, whilst Scottish Tories did indeed suffer 'increasingly shattering defeats' in and after the 1980s, this was not the case in Wales, as some writers have

---

[46] J. Graham Jones, 'Major Gwilym Lloyd-George and the Pembrokeshire Election of 1950', *Journal of the Pembrokeshire Historical Society*, 11 (2002), 115.

[47] Stephen Kendrick and David McCrone, 'Politics in a Cold Climate: The Conservative Decline in Scotland', *Political Studies*, 37/4 (1989); James Kellas, 'The Party in Scotland', in Anthony Seldon and Stuart Ball (eds), *Conservative Century: The Conservative Party Since 1900* (Oxford: Oxford University Press, 1994); James Mitchell, *Conservatives and the Union: A Study of Conservative Party Attitudes to Scotland* (Edinburgh: Edinburgh University Press, 1990), p. xiii; David Torrance, *'We in Scotland': Thatcherism in a Cold Climate* (Edinburgh: Birlinn, 2009), p. 27; Taym Saleh, 'The Decline of the Scottish Conservatives in North-East Scotland, 1965–79: A Regional Perspective', *Parliamentary History*, 36/2 (2017), 218–42; David Jeffery, 'The Strange Death of Tory Liverpool: Conservative Electoral Decline in Liverpool, 1945–1996', *British Politics*, 12/3 (2017), 386–407.

[48] Charles Pattie and Ron Johnston, 'The Conservative Party and the Electorate', in Steve Ludlam and Martin J. Smith (eds), *Contemporary British Conservatism* (London: Macmillan, 1996), pp. 49–50.

implied.[49] Whereas the Unionists (as the Conservative Party was called in Scotland) went from a position of near-hegemony in the mid-1950s to wipeout at the end of the century, support for the Tories in Wales in that period was reasonably consistent.[50] After 1997, the party slowly rebuilt and gained a prominent place in what is now called the Senedd, or the Welsh Parliament. If anything, support for the Conservatives in Wales has long followed the pattern of support for the party in England as a whole, except that it is always about ten to twelve percentage points below the English average.[51] Much more interesting parallels can be drawn between parts of Wales and the north of England.[52] What follows, therefore, is a history of underexplored Conservative successes in parts of Wales, but also one of systemic failure in other areas. It helps demonstrate the historian Dai Smith's famous phrase that Wales was a singular noun but a plural experience. One way of demonstrating that is this study of modern party politics.[53] Calling Wales 'the most anti-Conservative area in all of Britain' does not recognise this political diversity.[54]

---

[49] Andrew Thorpe, '"One of the Most Backwards Areas of the Country": The Labour Party's Grass Roots in South West England, 1918–45', in Worley, *Labour's Grass Roots*, p. 235; John Ramsden, *An Appetite for Power: A History of the Conservative Party since 1830* (London: HarperCollins, 1998), p. 403. Important collections like Seldon and Ball's *Conservative Century* included a chapter on Scotland, but nothing on Wales. For a chapter in another volume that sets out to compare Wales and Scotland, but devotes more time to Scotland, see Richard Finlay, 'Thatcherism, Unionism and Nationalism: a Comparative Study of Scotland and Wales', in Ben Jackson and Robert Saunders (eds), *Making Thatcher's Britain* (Cambridge: Cambridge University Press, 2012), pp. 165–79. See fn.3, where the author rechristens the primary historian who had worked on Welsh Conservatism, Felix Aubel, as 'F. Abdul'!

[50] David Torrance, 'Centenary Blues: 100 Years of Scottish Conservatism', in David Torrance (ed.), *Whatever Happened to Tory Scotland?* (Edinburgh: Edinburgh University Press, 2012), pp. 1–2.

[51] Wyn Jones, Scully and Trystan, 'Why do the Conservatives', 230. Pattie and Johnston, 'The Conservative Party', p. 39.

[52] Nick Randall, 'No Friends in the North? The Conservative Party in Northern England', *The Political Quarterly*, 80/2 (2009), 184–5.

[53] Dai Smith, *Wales! Wales?* (London: Allen & Unwin, 1984), p. 1.

[54] Butler and Stokes, *Political Change*, quoted in Wyn Jones, Scully and Trystan, 'Why do the Conservatives', 232.

HISTORIOGRAPHY

This book is, therefore, a fresh contribution to the history of the party in Britain, interest in which has been rejuvenated in the past thirty years or so, especially after the downfall of Margaret Thatcher.[55] In recent decades, key works have been produced by historians like Tim Bale, Stuart Ball, Clarisse Berthezène, Lawrence Black, Catherine Ellis, Julie Gottlieb, E. H. H. Green, G. E. Maguire, Martin Pugh, Emily Robinson, Geraint Thomas and Ina Zweiniger-Bargielowska.[56] In most discussions of the party, however, Wales is often dealt with fleetingly. That is redressed here, contributing something important to the historiography of the Conservative Party. The other side of the same coin is that this work makes a fresh intervention in the field of Welsh political history. It is not the first foray into the history of the Conservatives

---

[55] Kit Kowol, 'Renaissance on the Right? New Directions in the History of the Post-War Conservative Party', *Twentieth Century British History*, 27/2 (2016), 291; Paul Addison, 'Sixtysomethings', *London Review of Books*, 17/9 (1995), 17–18.

[56] See Bale, *The Conservatives*; Stuart Ball, *The Conservative Party Since 1945* (Manchester: Manchester University Press, 1998); Stuart Ball and Ian Holliday (eds), *Mass Conservatism: The Conservatives and the Public Since the 1880s* (London: Frank Cass, 2002); Clarisse Berthezène and Jean-Christian Vinel (eds), *Postwar Conservatism, A Transnational Investigation: Britain, France, and the United States, 1930–1990* (London: Palgrave Macmillan, 2017); Clarisse Berthezène and Julie V. Gottlieb (eds), *Rethinking Right-wing Women: Gender and the Conservative Party, 1880s to the Present* (Manchester: Manchester University Press, 2018); Lawrence Black, 'Tories and Hunters: Swinton College and the Landscape of Modern Conservatism', *History Workshop Journal*, 77/1 (2014); Lawrence Black, 'The Lost World of Young Conservatism', *The Historical Journal*, 51/4 (2008); John Charmley, *A History of Conservative Politics 1990–1996* (London: Macmillan, 1996); Catherine Ellis, 'No Hammock for the Idle: The Conservative Party, 'Youth' and the Welfare State in the 1960s', *Twentieth Century British History*, 16/4 (2015); Seldon and Ball, *Conservative Century*; Francis and Zweiniger-Bargielowska, *The Conservatives and British Society*; E. H. H. Green, *Ideologies of Conservatism: Conservative Political Ideas in the Twentieth Century* (Oxford: Oxford University Press, 2002); Green, 'The Conservative Party'; Jackson and Saunders, *Making Thatcher's Britain*; G. E. Maguire, *Conservative Women: A History of Women and the Conservative Party, 1874–1997* (Basingstoke: Macmillan, 1998); Martin Pugh, *The Tories and the People, 1880–1935* (Oxford: Blackwell, 1985); Ramsden, *The Age of Churchill*; Ramsden, *The Winds of Change: Macmillan to Heath, 1957–1975* (Essex: Longman, 1996); Emily Robinson, 'The Authority of Feeling in Mid-Twentieth-Century English Conservatism', *The Historical Journal*, 63/5 (2020); Thomas, *Popular Conservatism*; Ina Zweiniger-Bargielowska, 'Rationing, Austerity and the Conservative Party Recovery after 1945', *The Historical Journal*, 37/1 (1994).

in Wales, although the post-1945 period in particular is close to 'virgin territory'.[57] Those works that have focused on aspects of Welsh Conservatism tend to concentrate on short time periods, and the focus is almost always on aspects of the party's policy for 'the nation', or how it grappled with a growing sense of Welsh identity (which is also dealt with in detail in each chapter of this work).[58]

A sharper focus on Welsh Conservatism is part of rebalancing the canon of Wales's political history, which has traditionally lent towards a study of Labour and radical movements, often written by people themselves on the left, like the famously charismatic Gwyn Alf Williams.[59] Whilst much of this work is now relatively old, it is still considered seminal and remains well read. Kenneth O. Morgan (a Labour member of the House of Lords), who has authored some of the most epoch-defining work on Welsh history,

---

[57] Andrew Edwards, *Labour's Crisis: Plaid Cymru, the Conservatives, and the Decline of the Labour Party in North-West Wales, 1960–74* (Cardiff: University of Wales Press, 2011), p. 6.

[58] See Aubel, 'The Conservatives'; Aubel, 'Welsh Conservatism'; Matthew Cragoe, 'Defending the Constitution: the Conservative Party and the Idea of Devolution, 1945–74', in Chris Williams and Andrew Edwards (eds), *The Art of the Possible: Politics and Governance in Modern British History, 1885–1997: Essays in Memory of Duncan Tanner* (Manchester: Manchester University Press, 2015); Matthew Cragoe, '"We Like Local Patriotism": The Conservative Party and the Discourse of Decentralisation, 1947–51', *English Historical Review*, 122/498 (2007); Tomos Dafydd Davies, 'A Tale of Two Tories?: The British and Canadian Conservative Parties and the National Question' (unpublished PhD thesis, Aberystwyth University, 2011); Andrew Edwards, Duncan Tanner and Patrick Carlin, 'The Conservative Governments and the Development of Welsh Language Policy in the 1980s and 1990s', *The Historical Journal*, 54/2 (2011); Edwards, *Labour's Crisis*, chapter four; Dylan Griffiths, *Thatcherism and Territorial Politics: A Welsh Case Study* (Aldershot: Avebury, 1996); Thomas 'The Conservative Party'. Also see, by the author, 'Women in the Organisation of the Conservative Party in Wales, 1945–1979', *Women's History Review*, 28/2 (2019), 236–56. See n. 69, below, for further work on the post-devolution era by political scientists.

[59] Robert Crowcroft, 'Maurice Cowling and the Writing of British Political History', *Contemporary British History*, 22/2 (2008), 282; Andy Croll, '"People's Remembrancers" in a Post-Modern Age: Contemplating the Non-crisis of Welsh Labour History', *Llafur*, 8/1 (2000), 6. The iconic expression of this is Hywel Francis and David Smith, *The Fed: A History of the South Wales Miners in the Twentieth Century* (London: Lawrence and Wishart, 1980). Although now some years old, important works include David Smith (ed.), *A People and a Proletariat: Essays in the History of Wales, 1780–1980* (London: Pluto Press, 1980), Gwyn A. Williams, *The Merthyr Rising* (London: Croom Helm, 1978), Williams, *When was Wales?*, p. 217.

frequently presented the Tories as a marginal political force in both the nineteenth and twentieth centuries. Tories play walk-on roles and are often dismissed as 'as un-Welsh as ever'. He and others present a Wales that is 'overwhelmingly anti-Conservative', with the Tory leadership there behaving with 'insensitive arrogance'.[60] The founding, in 1970, of a society for the study of Welsh Labour history, *Llafur*, was testament to the 'communal, comradely' spirit of this left-leaning focus, as was the establishment in 1973 of the South Wales Miners' Library in Swansea, which was a physical as well as an intellectual embodiment of this trend.[61] In more recent times, new scholarship has helped provide a broader understanding of Welsh political history, although the field in general remains underdeveloped. Its focus is still on the left and on nationalism.[62] The history of coalminers, steelworkers, unrest, protest, trade unionism, and a growing Welsh national consciousness is a completely different (and sometimes more exciting) story from that which the Conservative Party tended to represent, namely relative stability, small-c conservative values, family life and Anglican influences.[63] Scholarly survey books of Wales do discuss such themes, but their very nature means they do so only in passing.[64]

---

[60] Gareth Elwyn Jones, *Modern Wales: A Concise History* ([1984] Cambridge: Cambridge University Press, 1994), p. 251; Kenneth O. Morgan, *Wales in British Politics, 1868–1922* (Cardiff: University of Wales Press, 1963), p. 9; Geraint H. Jenkins, *A Concise History of Wales* (Cambridge: Cambridge University Press, 2007), p. 286. Also see for similar comments, Kenneth O. Morgan, *Modern Wales: Politics, Places and People* (Cardiff: University of Wales Press, 1995), p. 11; and Kenneth O. Morgan, *Revolution to Devolution: Reflections on Welsh Democracy* (Cardiff: University of Wales Press, 2014), p. x. See Sam Blaxland, book review of the latter, in *Journal of British Studies*, 55/4 (2016), 855–6.

[61] Chris Williams, 'Introduction', p. 5. For an account of the formation and development of *Llafur* see Deian Hopkin, 'Llafur: Labour History Society and People's Remembrancer, 1970–2009', *Labour History Review*, 75, Supplement 1 (2010); Hywel Francis, 'Intellectual Property, First Time Round: The Re-Invention of the South Wales Miners' Library', *Llafur*, 9/1 (2004); Hywel Francis and Sian Williams, *Do Miners Read Dickens?: Origins and Progress of the South Wales Miners' Library*, 1973–2013 (Cardigan: Parthian, 2013).

[62] See n.67.

[63] Addison, 'Sixtysomethings'.

[64] See Martin Johnes, *Wales Since 1939* (Manchester: Manchester University Press, 2012), chapter 11.

This is not to suggest, of course, that the history of radical, left-wing and nationalist politics in Wales is not a crucial part of the nation's history. Labour, after all, has been so dominant and Wales has been the home of such towering socialist figures as Keir Hardie, Ramsey MacDonald, Aneurin Bevan, James Griffiths, James Callaghan, Michael Foot and Neil Kinnock.[65] The South Wales coalfield, recently christened 'Labour Country' by one historian, played a fundamental role in the history of industrial and imperial Britain and is rightly described as the 'maker of modern Wales'.[66] Plaid Cymru is understandably the focus of more attention because of its status as a Wales-only party with a fascinating history.[67] There remains, however, in the words of one writer, a 'simple but neglected fact' in the histories of Wales: 'the politics of the Rhondda valley were not those of, say, the Conwy valley'.[68] Political scientists have focused on the broad topic of the Conservatives in Wales in more depth than historians have. However, they often do so in a post-devolution context, with some exploration of the party's long-term history as part of their analysis.[69] It is a telling sign that much of the engagement with Tory history in Wales has come from a small handful of Conservative politicians, seeking either to learn more about their

---

[65] Chris Williams, 'Introduction', p. 1.
[66] Leeworthy, *Labour Country*, p. 8.
[67] See for examples John Davies, 'Plaid Cymru in Transition', in Osmond, *The National Question Again*; Rhys Evans, *Gwynfor Evans: A Portrait of a Patriot* (Tal-y-bont: Y Lolfa, 2008); McAllister, *Plaid Cymru*; Leeworthy, *Labour Country*. For a discussion of these themes see Martin Johnes, 'For Class and Nation: Dominant Trends in the Historiography of Twentieth-Century Wales', *History Compass*, 8/11(2010), 1257–74.
[68] Geraint Thomas, review of Andrew Edwards, *Labour's Crisis*, in *English Historical Review*, 128/534 (2013), 1313.
[69] Wyn Jones, Scully and Trystan, 'Why do the Conservatives'; Alan Convery, *The Territorial Conservative Party: Devolution and Party Change in Scotland and Wales* (Manchester: Manchester University Press, 2015); Martin H. M. Steven, Owain Llyr ap Gareth and Lewis Baston, 'The Conservative Party and Devolved National Identities: Scotland and Wales Compared', *National Identities*, 14/1 (2012), pp. 71–81.

party, or to justify its place in Welsh politics.[70] The most historically astute of these writers was the former member of the Senedd, David Melding.[71] Lord Crickhowell – formerly Nicholas Edwards – delivered a well-researched, if one-sided, lecture for the Welsh Political Archive on what the party had done for Wales, in 2006.[72]

No authors, however, have taken the more holistic approach that factors in the grassroots of the party, which this book does. Each chapter devotes time to Conservative members, without whom there would be no party. In doing so, it answers the call of a growing group of historians and political scientists for studies of the Conservative Party to factor in those 'ordinary' people who made it the organisation it was, as has been done with some studies of the Labour Party.[73] This is an area of interest that has grown in recent years. John Ramsden's multivolume history of the party made a deliberate – and what he at the time termed 'unfashionable' – move in this direction, devoting chapters

---

[70] Chris Butler, 'The Conservative Party in Wales: Remoulding a Radical Tradition', and Donald Walters, 'The Reality of Conservatism', in Osmond, *The National Question Again*, pp. 155–66 and pp. 210–21; Jonathan Evans, *The Future of Welsh Conservatism* (Cardiff, 2002).

[71] David Melding, 'Refashioning Welsh Conservatism – a Lesson for Scotland', in Torrance, *Whatever Happened*, pp. 127–37; David Melding, *Have We Been Anti-Welsh? An Essay on the Conservative Party and the Welsh Nation* (Barry: Cymdeithas y Kymberiaid, 2005), pp. 5, 8; David Melding, 'Unionism and Nationalism in Welsh Political Life: An Essay by David Melding AM to Mark the 20th Anniversary of Devolution in Wales' (Cardiff, 2019).

[72] Lord Crickhowell, 'The Conservative Party and Wales', *The National Library of Wales Journal*, 34/1 (2006), 49.

[73] Kowol, 'Renaissance', 302. For Labour, see Duncan Tanner, 'Labour and its membership', in Duncan Tanner, Pat Thane and Nick Tiratsoo (eds), *Labour's First Century* (Cambridge: Cambridge University Press, 2000), pp. 248–80; Worley, *Labour's Grass Roots*; Patrick Seyd and Paul Whiteley, *Labour's Grass Roots: The Politics of Party Membership* (Oxford: Clarendon, 1992); Steven Fielding, 'Activists Against "Affluence": Labour Party Culture During the "Golden Age" circa 1950–1970', *Journal of British Studies*, 40/2 (2001); Hugh Pemberton and Mark Wickham-Jones, 'Labour's Lost Grassroots: the Rise and Fall of Party Membership', *British Politics*, 8/2 (2013); Stuart Ball and Ian Holliday, 'Introduction', in Ball and Holliday, *Mass Conservatism*, p. 3. Wright, *Wales and Socialism*, p. 9.

to the local party structure and grassroots Conservatism.[74] Others, especially Stuart Ball, have followed in his footsteps, revolutionising what we know about how local Conservative associations functioned.[75] This has marked a move away from the more traditional histories of the Conservatives, authored by people like Maurice Cowling and Lord Blake, which focused largely – and understandably – on senior politicians and the party as an elite institution, although these authors were not totally blind to the importance of ideas, voters, public opinion and local politics.[76]

Those historians who have studied ordinary party members have tended to see them as part of the wider political machine, discussing what they did to raise money and campaign for the party.[77] There is an implication in much of the literature that healthy numbers of party members at the grassroots could help

[74] John Ramsden, *The Age of Balfour and Baldwin, 1902–1940* (London: Longman, 1978), p. ix and chapter 11 in particular; Ramsden, *The Age of Churchill*, chapter three; Ramsden, *The Winds*, chapter two.

[75] Stuart Ball, 'Local Conservatism and the Evolution of the Party Organisation' and 'The National and Regional Party Structure', in Seldon and Ball, *Conservative Century*; Ball, *Portrait*, chapter three in particular; Stuart Ball, Andrew Thorpe and Matthew Worley, 'Elections, Leaflets and Whist Drives: Constituency Party Membership in Britain Between the Wars', in Worley, *Labour's Grass Roots*, p. 27; Paul Whiteley, Patrick Seyd and Jeremy Richardson, *True Blues: The Politics of Conservative Party Membership* (Oxford: Clarendon Press, 1994); David Thackeray, *Conservatism for the Democratic Age: Conservative Cultures and the Challenge of Mass Politics in Early Twentieth-Century England* (Manchester: Manchester University Press, 2013).

[76] Robert Blake, *The Conservative Party From Peel to Major* (London: Heinemann, 1997); Lord Butler (ed.), *The Conservatives: A History From Their Origins to 1965* (London: George Allen & Unwin, 1977); Maurice Cowling (ed.), *Conservative Essays* (London: Cassell, 1978). For interesting comments on the historiography, see John Turner, 'The British Conservative Party in the Twentieth Century: From Beginning to End?', *Contemporary European History*, 8/2 (1999), 275–6; David M. Craig, '"High Politics" and the "New Political History"', *The Historical Journal*, 53/2 (2010), 456–7; Crowcroft, 'Maurice Cowling'.

[77] For the Conservative grassroots as a campaigning force, see Janet Johnson, 'Did Organisation Really Matter? Party Organisation and Conservative Electoral Recovery, 1945–1959', *Twentieth Century British History*, 14/4 (2003), 391–412. For a study of twenty-first-century Tory grassroots activists: Tim Bale, Paul Webb and Monica Poletti, *Footsoldiers: Political Party Membership in the 21st Century* (London: Routledge, 2019). Also see Pattie and Johnston, 'The Conservatives' Grassroots'. For comments on Labour historiography, where a similar trait is identifiable, see Matthew Worley, 'Introduction', in Worley, *Labour's Grass Roots*, p. 2.

a party win in a certain constituency, despite only a minority of members ever engaging in actual electioneering work.[78] In fact, some estimates suggest that of the 2.75 million members the party had throughout Britain in 1950, perhaps ten per cent were active campaigners.[79] Historians and political scientists have varied widely in their assessment of how important that ten per cent were to 'getting out the vote'.[80] In summary, it is probably the case that as a campaigning body, the grassroots mattered less than some might assume, and certainly less than in bygone eras, like the mid-nineteenth century, when registering

---

[78] The same was true for Labour: Steven Fielding, 'The "Penny Farthing" Machine Revisited: Labour Party Members and Participation in the 1950s and 1960s', in Chris Pierson and Simon Tormey (eds), *Politics at the Edge: The PSA Yearbook 1999* (Basingstoke: Macmillan, 2000), pp. 173–4; Fielding, 'Activists', 249; Patrick Seyd and Paul Whiteley, 'Conservative Grassroots: An Overview' in Ludlam and Smith, *Contemporary British Conservatism*, pp. 76–77; Ball, Thorpe and Worley, 'Elections', p. 22; Seyd and Whiteley, 'Conservative Grassroots', p. 64.

[79] Bale, *The Conservatives*, p. 18.

[80] Gidon Cohen and Lewis Mates, 'Grassroots Conservatism in Post-War Britain: A View From the Bottom Up', *History*, 98/330 (2013), 207. For those who see a correlation between strong membership figures in a constituency and electoral success for the party, see Ramsden, *The Age of Churchill*, p. 78, 90, 112, 114, 137. Also see Ramsden, *The Age of Balfour*, p. 53; Ramsden, *An Appetite*, p. 488; Jon Lawrence, *Electing Our Masters: The Hustings in British Politics from Hogarth to Blair* (Oxford: Oxford University Press, 2009), p. 175; Pattie and Johnston, 'The Conservatives' Grassroots',193; Robert Saunders, *Yes to Europe!: the 1975 Referendum and Seventies Britain* (Cambridge: Cambridge University Press, 2018), p. 209; Robert Waller, 'Conservative Electoral Support and Social Class', in Seldon and Ball, *Conservative Century*, p. 597; Andrew Walling, 'The Structure of Power in Labour Wales, 1951–1964', in Tanner, Williams and Hopkin, *The Labour Party*, pp. 208–9; Daniel Weinbren, 'Sociable Capital: London's Labour Parties, 1918–45' in Worley, *Labour's Grass Roots*, pp. 194–95. For inter-war Wales, see Thomas Wyn Williams, 'The Conservative Party in North-East Wales, 1906–1924' (unpublished PhD thesis, University of Liverpool, 2008), pp. 116–117, 129, 293. For those who argue that the source material draws us too readily to these conclusions, see Jeremy McIlwaine, 'The Party Archivist', *Conservative History Journal*, 2/2 (2013), 48–49; Fielding, 'Activists', 245; Peter Catterall's 'Preface' to Stuart Ball and Ian Holliday (eds), *Mass Conservatism: The Conservatives and the Public Since the 1880s* (London: Frank Cass, 2002), p. xii; Donald Stringer, 'In the Political Jungle: the Area Organisation', in Jean M. Lucas (ed.), *Between the Thin Blues Lines: The Agent's View of Politics* (Canada: Trafford, 2008), p. 116; Kowol, 'Renaissance', 295. For others generally sceptical of the argument, see Jon Lawrence and Miles Taylor, 'Introduction', in Lawrence and Taylor, *Party, State and Society*, p. 5; Bale, *The Conservatives*, pp. 20–1, 47–8; Johnson, 'Did Organisation', 409; Ball, 'Local Conservatism', pp. 308–9; Ball, *Portrait*, p. 193; Catriona Macdonald, 'Following the Procession: Scottish Labour, 1918–45', in Worley, *Labour's Grass Roots*, p. 49.

voters was one of the main factors between winning or losing a contest in a constituency.[81] However, simply by existing, often in large numbers, the impact the rank and file had on normalising Conservatism, advertising it, and encouraging discussions of it, might well have helped push the party over the finishing line in marginal seats, where a contest was very tight.[82] Ultimately, such activists could get close to voters and there remained no more immediate, direct way of contacting them than knocking on their doors.[83]

There are other reasons why they are historically significant. Particularly, as Cohen and Mates have identified, historians should be 'attentive to what those joining parties and attending meetings were actually doing and why'.[84] Such activists, throughout this period, were also the types who were plugged into the community via church or chapel congregations, or in voluntary organisations, as members of a local choir, or in roles like school governors.[85] Such people are 'an indication of the party's roots in different communities, a source of legitimacy and ideas'.[86] Senior Conservative figures in Wales realised this, commenting in 1961, for example, that good leadership at the local level 'could and should' result in the party playing a role 'in the affairs of the community'.[87] Crucially, it allowed the party to promote its values within local communities; in other words, to 'humanise' it.[88] Each chapter, therefore, goes well beyond politics by exploring the wider social and ideological worlds of Conservative supporters, especially parts of the middle classes

---

[81] Cragoe, *Politics*, pp. 84, 100.
[82] Ball, *Portrait*, p. 193; Bale, Webb and Poletti, *Footsoldiers*, pp. 1–2, 18.
[83] Bale, *The Conservatives*, pp. 17–18; Ball, *Portrait*, p. 98.
[84] Cohen and Mates, 'Grassroots', 221.
[85] Bale, Webb and Poletti, *Footsoldiers*, p. 166.
[86] Tanner, 'Labour', p. 249.
[87] Welsh Political Archive, National Library of Wales, Aberystwyth [WPA], GB0210 CARCON, file 34, The Glamorgan Group Council of the Wales and Monmouthshire Provincial Area minute book, 23 March 1961.
[88] Johnson, 'Did Organisation', 412; Ramsden, *The Age of Balfour*, p. 251.

and many women activists.[89] It approaches the world of the grassroots in a similar way to Duncan Tanner's exploration of Labour Party membership, or Catherine Ellis's treatment of the Young Conservatives, where she examined how their short involvement in the policy-making process in the early 1960s gives us an insight into 'ordinary' Conservative ideology and peoples' views on a wide range of matters.[90]

It is the blending of these areas and approaches, however, and the drawing together of various different threads in the existing literature, that offers something novel here. Wales is used as a case study to examine how Britain's most established political party had a rocky experience in a part of the UK that was not its natural territory. By the party's own admission, no Welsh seat in this period was ever really 'safe' (if we count this as having more than a 10,000-vote majority).[91] But that meant that both the central party and the regional Wales Area Office paid significant attention to some of the more marginal seats, in the hope that they could win them.[92] In having to contend with specific Welsh concerns – most notably language policy and calls for more devolution of powers – we get a window on to the party's thinking in respect to a relatively unfamiliar part of the UK in which it nonetheless wanted to be successful. By communicating with and hoping to utilise ordinary people, however, it helped create a vehicle for right-leaning individuals to express their political and social identities. This book is therefore about providing both a fresh picture and a new kind of perspective on both Conservative and Welsh history.

---

[89] Clarisse Berthezène and Julie V. Gottlieb, 'Introduction', in Clarisse Berthezène and Julie V. Gottlieb, *Rethinking Right-wing Women*, p. 4.

[90] Tanner, 'Labour', pp. 249–50; Ellis, 'No Hammock', 446.

[91] British Library Sound and Moving Image archive, C1688/19, Simon Parnell interview. For similar comments on Labour's strong seats witnessing organisational decline, see Duncan Tanner, 'Facing the New Challenge: Labour and Politics, 1970–2000', and Walling, 'The Structure', in Tanner, Williams and Hopkin, *The Labour Party*, pp. 203–4, 277.

[92] Janet Johnson, 'Conservative Party Mutual Aid: Myth or Reality?', *Contemporary British History*, 22/1 (2008), 28.

SOURCES

Any kind of study that contributes to such distinct fields can draw from a very deep well of source material. When it comes to evidence, historians of modern Britain are faced with an embarrassment of riches, and there is no exception for scholars of the Conservative Party.[93] The party's own archive, housed at the Bodleian's Weston Library in Oxford, is a rich seam of material which includes thousands of documents relating to campaign strategy, policy development, conferences and election addresses from Wales. There are also a huge number of reports from, and correspondences with, every constituency party in Wales for much of the period under scrutiny here, often in the form of Basic Reports, which were communications between the party's Wales team and Conservative Central Office (CCO) headquarters in London. These total many hundreds, and all have been read for this study. A huge amount of excellent local material is housed in the National Library of Wales's Welsh Political Archive (WPA), which contains the records of numerous associations like Monmouth, all the Cardiff seats, Pembrokeshire, Conwy, Denbigh and Caernarfon, as well as important files on small but lively Tory associations in places like Rhondda (a byword for a Labour safe seat), although it is much more common for records to exist from 'stronger' seats. The WPA also houses the political papers of various senior Welsh politicians, as well as revealing documents like the diaries of long-serving Welsh Office minister, Wyn Roberts.[94] Further material and fascinating ephemera from local record offices have been utilised. Surviving records from every part of Wales have been consulted, and this study draws upon research conducted in smaller archives across the country –

---

[93] Stuart Ball, 'National Politics and Local History: The Regional and Local Archives of the Conservative Party, 1867–1945', *Archives*, 22/94 (1996), 27; Carolyn Steedman, *Dust* (Manchester: Manchester University Press, 2001), p. 29.

[94] Rob Phillips, 'Conservatives in the Welsh Political Archive at the National Library of Wales', *Conservative History Journal*, 2/6 (2018), 56–7.

many of which contain documents from multiple constituencies – so that a truly Wales-wide picture can be developed.

Common sources like minute books, however, can be 'bland and conventional',[95] recording the outcome of a decision without detailing the fascinating conversations that would have taken place in the lead up to it. They also give no sense of those vital things like informal discussions held in corridors that, in reality, determined a lot of what was decided at all levels of politics.[96] Other documents, like reports from CCO employees, are often much franker, and sometimes amusingly rude, about people in local associations.[97] These help us understand both the decision-making process of the party and the motives or personal opinions of party members 'on the ground'. They highlight the disagreements, the 'fault lines' and the 'balance of forces' within the rank and file.[98] Although there is material in these archives that could fill a volume ten times the size of this book, it is important to stress that these archives still contain only a fraction of the material that ever existed. Occasionally, what has survived gives us an indication of why other material has not. In a minute book of the Conway Association from the late 1970s, an approach by the local record office to hand over their entire archive is noted, with the 'unanimous' decision that they will not do so, presumably because they feared prying eyes looking into their business.[99] Many people simply think the records of local political groups are of little worth so throw them away, especially when they see things like newspaper clippings, record books and personal papers as being too recent to be of pure historical interest, but too old to be worth cluttering up an attic or garage.[100] On the other hand, material that does make its way to an archive has often been sifted through, with potentially

[95] Ball, 'National Politics', 57.
[96] Ball, *Portrait*, p. 5.
[97] Jeremy McIlwaine, 'The Party Archivist', 48–9.
[98] Ball, 'National Politics', 57.
[99] WPA, GB0210 CONLES, file 8, Conway Conservative and Unionist Association minute book, 26 January 1979.
[100] Ball, 'National Politics', 39.

incriminating material taken out. This does not de-legitimise such material, but it gives pause for thought.

Whether in scrapbook-clipping form, or as original copies, a wide variety of newspapers, both national and local, have been consulted for this work. For much of this period, various Welsh, regional and local newspapers covered politics assiduously, including the machinations of grassroots parties. They recorded things like meetings and speeches in detail and became an invaluable source in the process. Particularly important for our purposes is the widely read *Western Mail*, published in Cardiff but covering all of Wales (although with a greater focus on the south).[101] At each general election, it profiled every constituency, scrutinised what candidates were saying and 'test[ed] the pulse of the local electorate'.[102] Despite the fact that, like many of Britain's important provincial newspapers, the *Western Mail* historically lent towards the Tories – and did so for a significant portion of the period studied here – writers like its long-serving political correspondent David Rosser were some of the most astute contemporary commentators on the political scene.[103] Such people's thoughts are therefore worth reading in depth not just to get a sense of how the party was received and how it presented itself, but for the detail that such reporting involved. Naturally, newspapers come with a range of issues as a historical source, including the way in which they are often compiled in a hurry for immediate consumption by a certain target audience. But they remain vital for our understanding of everything from the great events to everyday detail.[104]

Alongside this, one of the most valuable sources of information available to historians of contemporary politics is the people themselves. This work draws on the oral testimonies of a number of individuals who were in various ways connected to Conservative

---

[101] Aled Jones, *Press, Politics and Society: A History of Journalism in Wales* (Cardiff: University of Wales Press, 1993), p. 220.
[102] 'There could be a few surprises in Wales', *Western Mail*, 17 March 1966.
[103] Ball, *Portrait*, p. 95; David Rosser, *A Dragon in the House* (Llandysul: Gomer, 1987).
[104] Leeworthy, *Labour Country*, p. 12.

politics in Wales. They range from former Deputy Prime Ministers and Secretaries of State for Wales, to prospective parliamentary candidates, local activists and campaigners. Their memories were collected informally and formally over a long period of research. Such testimonies are alternatives to 'conventional' documents, and, whilst memory is notoriously unreliable and impacted by nostalgia, such reminiscences give a useful sense of what people felt about certain events or ideas.[105] Similarly, many people important for this study produced memoirs which, whilst often self-aggrandising, are useful for the information they provide and for showing us what perspective they thought was important to emphasise.[106] Finally, the biographical details of everyone who stood for election in this period were collated by Ivor Thomas Rees for his excellent book *Welsh Hustings*. The author took the information Rees collected and created various data sets from it, including information on the age, background, schooling, sex, and Welsh-language proficiency of Conservative and Labour parliamentary candidates. That data will be utilised throughout this book.[107]

THEMES AND CHAPTERS

Complications inevitably arise when writing about 'the Conservatives in Wales'. As the Three Wales Model indicates, Wales should not be used as a blanket term when discussing politics. Swathes of the country are rural and have typical non-urban concerns, including those relating to agriculture. Large parts were,

---

[105] Charles Moore, 'The Authorized Biographer', *Conservative History Journal*, 2/2 (2013), 42–3; On oral history as a method, see Stephen Caunce, *Oral History and the Local Historian* (London: Longman, 1994), p. 7; Lynn Abrams, *Oral History Theory* (Abingdon: Routledge, 2010), p. 79; Anthony Seldon and Joanna Pappworth, *By Word of Mouth: 'Élite' Oral History* (London: Methuen, 1983).

[106] See Roberts, *Right*; Nicholas Crickhowell, *Wales, Westminster and Water* (Cardiff: University of Wales Press, 1999); Peter Walker, *Staying Power: An Autobiography* (London: Bloomsbury, 1991).

[107] Rees, *Welsh Hustings*.

in the period from the end of the Second World War to the end of the twentieth century, industrial, semi-industrial or de-industrialising. The most iconic Welsh industry was coalmining, although that is only part of the Welsh economic and industrial historical story.[108] Wales has typical metropolitan hubs like Cardiff, Swansea or Wrexham. Parts tend to be Welsh speaking, most notably its rural heartlands, but even that is inconsistent: in the twentieth century and particularly the post-1945 period, most people in Wales did not speak Welsh. The significance of the language therefore varied hugely, dependent on place and, sometimes, on generation. In most areas, urban, industrial, rural and linguistic concerns overlapped. The differences between north and south Wales are often striking. Wales's border with England is permeable, and in- and out-migration between Wales and England is extremely common.[109] For the simple reasons of geography and infrastructure, many in north Wales are better connected to Liverpool and Manchester than they are to the capital city, Cardiff. Throughout this book, talk of 'Wales' is inevitable, especially because the Conservative Party dealt with it as such a bloc for the purposes of its internal administration – it divided England and Wales up into twelve 'regions', with 'Wales and Monmouthshire' being one of these.[110] Similarly, just as Wales is 'a plural experience', so too was the Conservative Party in a state of flux for the period after the war.[111] The Conservatisms of Winston Churchill, Harold Macmillan and Margaret Thatcher, for example, were considerably different from one another.[112] All three were shaped by, or helped shape, very different time periods and a changing type of Tory Party.[113]

[108] Louise Miskell (ed.), *New Perspectives on Welsh Industrial History* (Cardiff: University of Wales Press, 2019).

[109] Graham Day, Angela Drakakis-Smith and Howard H. Davis, 'Migrating to North Wales: the "English" Experience', *Contemporary Wales*, 21/1 (2008).

[110] Cragoe, 'We Like', 969.

[111] Turner, 'The British Conservative Party', 287.

[112] Arthur Aughey, *The Conservative Party and the Nation: Union, England and Europe* (Manchester: Manchester University Press, 2018), p vii; Berthezène and Vinel, 'Introduction', p. 2.

[113] Martin Pugh, 'Popular Conservatism in Britain: Continuity and Change, 1880–1987', *Journal of British Studies*, 27/3 (1988), 255.

Invariably, covering such wide-ranging subject matters over a long time period will result in omissions or in aspects having to be skimmed over in the forthcoming chapters. There is less in this work about how particular Welsh MPs operated within the House of Commons or about their parliamentary careers. Local government is only briefly touched upon; this is not a history of what Conservatives did at local authority or county council level, and future work could be done to untangle this, especially the dynamics surrounding 'Independent' and Ratepayer candidates in Wales. Similarly, while they are mentioned, many organisations that had informal links with Conservative people – the farming unions, Neighbourhood Watch [114] or the Church, for example – are only covered in passing. Research on these groups would add greater texture to the nature of middle-class life in this period. Whilst the grassroots appear regularly in this study, their role in trying to influence policy-making within the party will have to be expanded upon at another time. Neither is this a study of Wales and the Tory Party in the post-devolution era. Such a topic is deserving of a book in its own right. So much changed in the period after the 1997 referendum and the first elections to the new National Assembly in 1999, that the focus of this book would become unwieldy if that very contemporary era was tackled, although some reflections upon it are made in the epilogue.

The approach to all of this is chronological, dividing the era between 1945 and 1997 up into four sections, based on a blend of significant Welsh and British events or changes of government. The next chapter covers the period of Labour government after the Second World War, and the Conservative response to the scale of their defeat in 1945. The second chapter encompasses a period of Tory government after Churchill re-entered office in 1951 and was then succeeded as prime minister by Eden, Macmillan and Home. The late 1950s saw the coming of 'affluence' and a further change in approach to Welsh issues. The following chapter discusses what appears as an enigma: the

[114] Kowol, 'Renaissance', 301–2.

period from the mid-1960s to the mid-1970s that simultaneously saw great technological advance and some radical cultural changes, but also an increased focus on traditional aspects of life. This was especially the case in Wales, where there was a renewed focus on local concerns. It was also a period where the Conservative Party, partly due to time in opposition, refocused its attention on Wales, driven to some extent by the rise in political nationalism from the mid-1960s. The final substantive chapter begins in 1975, when Margaret Thatcher became Conservative leader. More importantly for our purposes, however, was the elevation of a 'new species' of Welsh Conservative to the Wales brief, which had far-reaching implications for the governance of the nation after the party re-entered office in 1979. This final chapter covers the Thatcher period and the calamity the party faced from the mid-1990s. Each chapter is foregrounded by a discussion of how the party communicated British-wide electoral issues in Wales, the challenges many of its candidates often faced in doing so, how they and the party were perceived, and how this appeared to impact on the party's electoral fortunes in Wales. Attention is paid to communication strategies, including the messages that appeared to land well amongst the party's core supporters. A discussion of who these supporters were and where they were found is included. Welsh-specific policies and wider questions about devolution are then the focus. Each chapter ends with a reflection on ordinary members, what they did for the party, how thy used it as a social vehicle, what they thought about key issues, and what this tells us about parts of post-1945 Welsh society.

Taken as a whole, the work argues that political traditions in Wales after 1945 were primarily shaped by Labour. A theme running throughout this book is the difficulties the Tories faced in many parts of Wales because of the skill and success of their main opponents. However, it also argues that it would be wrong to suggest that there is 'no cultural or intellectual tradition of Welsh

Conservatism at all'.[115] Those who were prominent in the party, including prospective parliamentary candidates, represented and communicated a kind of centre-right conservatism that many Welsh people warmed to and voted for. Via its devolutionary concessions in the 1950s, through to the actions of a reforming Welsh Office in the 1980s, the party was also a major player in shaping modern Wales and, whilst it did not believe in the creation of a National Assembly, it laid much of the groundwork that allowed one to be formed. The party rarely changed the nature of Wales's political culture, but its attempts to adapt to it are equally interesting. The party had substantial grassroots in the form of keen rank-and-file activists in the parts of Wales where it was stronger. These people helped ground the party into various communities and normalised it in parts of Wales that do not get enough attention in history books or contemporary commentary. The Welsh dimension of the Conservative Party has always been uncertain, but the party has roots in Wales, and a detailed study of what grew from those roots is long overdue.

---

[115] Steven, ap Gareth and Baston, 'The Conservative Party', 77.

1
DEFEAT AND THE RESPONSE TO LABOUR, 1945–1951

Writing at the end of the 1950s and reflecting on the years since the Second World War, the enigmatic H. W. J. Edwards noted that a self-professed Conservative in the south Wales Valleys was either 'an eccentric, a loon, or a publicity seeker'.[1] He was right in that the politics of coalfield areas had long been so anti-Conservative that to be an outspoken Tory there was highly unusual.[2] Working-class Conservatives in Wales did exist, however, and a small number even fought general elections for the party in this period. The most prominent of these was Harry West, an ex-miner that the Tory hierarchy were keen to have in parliament. He fought the semi-industrial Cardiff South East in 1951, making much of his humble background and gaining over 23,000 votes in the process – although this was not enough to beat the seat's incumbent Labour MP, James Callaghan. West's career, however, whilst interesting, should not obscure the nature of the Conservative Party in these key years after the war. Candidates from manual labouring backgrounds were rare and the Conservatives found much more success in areas that were less industrial, and more 'British' in their outlook. In these places, it pitched itself as a party that would resist the encroaching, controlling forces of socialism. People voted for it and thousands of keen people were drawn to its flag, wanting to be members.

---

[1] H. W. J. Edwards, 'A tory in Wales', *Wales*, 32 (1958), 24.
[2] H. W. J. Edwards, *The Good Patch* (London, 1938), p.12; also see F. J. Harries, *A History of Conservatism in the Rhondda* (Pontypridd: Glamorgan County Times, 1912).

This chapter scrutinises these elements of the party in the key period from the end of the war until 1951: years that encompassed a resounding Conservative defeat at the first post-war general election and a consequent shift in the party's rhetoric and presentation in response. It discusses how the Tories communicated with swathes of Wales that had become deeply loyal to Labour, and where being a Conservative equated for some to being 'a loon'. Their difficulty in making any progress in such areas highlights some of the key problems the party faced in Wales, despite the fact that after the war, and for all its weaknesses, it had policy ideas for the nation, some interesting prospective parliamentary candidates like Harry West, and a huge number of people at the grassroots who worked for, and advertised, the party.

ANTI-SOCIALISM

The Conservative Party in Wales, as in most parts of Britain, fought the 1945 general election by emphasising the importance of Winston Churchill and his role in winning the Second World War. It was certainly the case that Churchill had achieved icon status in the eyes of many members of the electorate. In Wales, this admiration demonstrated the firmly British identity felt by many voters and their belief that the country had been on the right side in the war.[3] One Swansea woman was far from alone in writing to the Tory leader to ask for a signed photograph, adding 'we pray for you in your great efforts to make these islands of ours great once more'.[4] Not everyone, of course, thought that Churchill would make a good peacetime leader. For some, the Tory Party itself was discredited, not least because of the legacy

[3] Denbighshire Record Office [DRO], DD/DM/80/7, Colwyn Bay Conservative Association minute book, annual report 1955; Anthony Seldon, 'Conservative Century', in Anthony Seldon and Stuart Ball (eds), *Conservative Century: The Conservative Party Since 1900* (Oxford: Oxford University Press, 1994), p. 53; Martin Johnes, *Wales Since 1939* (Manchester: Manchester University Press, 2012), pp. 199–200.

[4] Conservative Party Archive, Bodleian Library, Oxford [CPA], Conservative Central Office [CCO], 1/9/526, Letter Mrs D. A. Jeremiah to Winston Churchill, undated *c.*1951.

of the 1930s and the 'preventable poverty' associated with the Depression that had hit parts of Wales especially hard.[5] Labour built on their inter-war success in Wales and made 1945 a true breakthrough moment. Led by Clement Attlee, it won a landslide victory across Britain and showed how deep its roots had penetrated in many parts of Wales, securing massive majorities in seats like Ebbw Vale, Aberdare and Llanelli. In the latter, James Griffiths's majority of 34,000 was the largest in the UK.[6] The scale of Labour's victory was a huge shock for the Conservatives.

However, the war and electoral defeat offered the party a chance to rethink various things, including its policy positions. They also retuned their tactics when it came to attacking Labour. Whilst there was some degree of consensus and similarity between the two main parties after the war, there were also fundamental differences.[7] A period of continued rationing and austerity, and a greater role for the state, including a planned economy, allowed the Conservative party to accuse Labour of being both ineffective at governing and overly controlling of people's personal lives.[8] The two issues often entwined, with the Conservatives linking 'control' over things like rationing to the

[5] This is an old argument. See Robert Blake, *The Conservative Party from Peel to Major* (London: Heinemann, 1997), pp. 254–5. Also see Geraint Thomas, *Popular Conservatism and the Culture of National Government in Inter-war Britain* (Cambridge: Cambridge University Press, 2020), pp. 265–6.

[6] Kenneth O. Morgan, 'Power and Glory: War and Reconstruction, 1939–1951', in Duncan Tanner, Chris Williams and Deian Hopkin (eds), *The Labour Party in Wales* (Cardiff: University of Wales Press, 2000), p. 173.

[7] The debate surrounding 'post-war consensus' is a long running and fascinating one. See: Tim Bale, *The Conservatives Since 1945: The Drivers of Party Change* (Oxford: Oxford University Press, 2016), p. 27; Simon Heffer, 'Traditional Toryism', in Kevin Hickson (ed.), *The Political Thought of the Conservative Party Since 1945* (Basingstoke: Palgrave Macmillan, 2005), p. 197; John Ramsden, *The Age of Churchill and Eden, 1940–1957* (London: Longman, 1995), p. 175. For a crucial debate on the subject, see Paul Addison, 'Consensus Revisited', *Twentieth Century British History*, 4/1 (1993), 91–4, and Dennis Kavanagh, 'The Postwar Consensus', *Twentieth Century British History*, 3/2 (1992), 175–90.

[8] Ina Zweiniger-Bargielowska, 'Rationing, Austerity and the Conservative Party Recovery after 1945', *The Historical Journal*, 37/1 (1994), 173–97; Stephen Brooke, 'Labour and the "Nation" after 1945', in Jon Lawrence and Miles Taylor (eds), *Party, State and Society: Electoral Behaviour in Britain Since 1820* (Aldershot: Scolar Press, 1997), p. 161.

concept of a socialist state constraining individual freedom and even opening the door to the kind of Communism evident in the Soviet Union.[9] As in Scotland, where, in the words of one historian, this issue was the 'principal divide' between the two parties, so was it a clear feature of the difference between the main parties in Wales.[10] Many Welsh Tories attempted to draw clear parallels between Labour's ideas and Communism.[11] They were continuing an old theme that had been a part of inter-war political debate (campaigners had been making this argument in north-east Wales as early as 1906, for example, and David Lloyd George had said that 'Socialism has no interest in liberty' in 1925).[12] It was these ideas that underpinned Churchill's notorious 'Gestapo' speech during the 1945 general election campaign, when he implied that Labour would need heavy-handed reinforcement to implement its policies. The theme proliferated after the Second World War.[13] As the *Western Mail*, showing its Conservative sympathies, put it in 1945, 'Socialism is inseparably interwoven with totalitarianism', adding that this should not be 'overstated or overblown'.[14] The Tories encouraged the use of 'Socialism' instead of 'Labour' when attacking their opponents, as the latter could be linked with 'honest British toil', whereas 'Socialism' sounded like a dangerous, foreign ideology.[15]

---

[9] Matthew Cragoe, 'Defending the Constitution: the Conservative Party and the Idea of Devolution, 1945–74', in Chris Williams and Andrew Edwards (eds), *The Art of the Possible: Politics and Governance in Modern British History, 1885–1997: Essays in Memory of Duncan Tanner* (Manchester: Manchester University Press, 2015), p. 162. Also see Matthew Cragoe, '"We Like Local Patriotism": The Conservative Party and the Discourse of Decentralisation, 1947–51', *English Historical Review*, 122/498 (2007).

[10] Malcolm Petrie, 'Anti-Socialism, Liberalism and Individualism: Rethinking the Realignment of Scottish Politics, 1945–1971', *Transactions of the Royal Historical Society*, 28 (2018), p. 199.

[11] CPA, PUB 229/9/17, J. J. Hayward election address, Cardiff South East, 1950; J. F. Lynam election address, Swansea East, 1950.

[12] Thomas Wyn Williams, 'The Conservative Party in North-East Wales, 1906–1924' (unpublished PhD thesis, University of Liverpool, 2008), p. 144; WPA, C/1/60, campaigning material aimed at Liberals.

[13] Blake, *The Conservative Party*, p. 251.

[14] 'I stand for the freedom of the individual', *Western Mail*, 5 June 1945.

[15] Blake, *The Conservative Party*, p. 262.

Statements like 'enterprise is essential to prosperity' encapsulated a common Conservative theme for the entire period Labour was in government from 1945 to 1951. Candidates the length and breadth of Wales also fused it with their belief in a 'Christian way of life' or 'Christian civilisation'.[16] Donald Walters, who ended up as the most senior Welsh Tory activist in the 1980s in his role as Party Chairman in Wales, was twenty at the time of the 1945 election. He remembered the stark contrast and the 'clear cut distinction' between 'Socialism' and its proposals for state ownership versus the Conservative insistence on free enterprise.[17] The theme developed as Labour spent more time in office, a period that was marked by continued austerity and state control of industry (some of which the Tories agreed with).[18] At the 1950 general election, candidates from both of the two main parties chose to mention, in different ways of course, issues like farming and agriculture, social services and housing in the leaflets they distributed to voters in each constituency. On housing – perhaps the issue of the period that mattered most to voters[19] – twenty-nine Tory candidates focused on some variation of 'homes', whilst twenty-three Labour candidates did. However, whereas only four Labour candidates directly spoke about the role of the state, or on the theme of 'individual freedom', nineteen prospective Tories mentioned the subject, most quite prominently and sometimes quite colourfully.[20] A drab uniformity associated with left-wing politics was contrasted with liberty, portrayed as 'all that is noble in this life'.[21] In some cases, messages like the 1951 manifesto slogan 'set the people free' were written on election addresses in larger font than the name of the party, candidate or

---

[16] See CPA, PUB 229/9/17, Nigel Birch election address, West Flint, 1950; Auberon Herbert, election address, Aberavon, 1950.

[17] Interview, Sir Donald Walters, 19 January 2015.

[18] D. E. Butler (ed.), *The British General Election of 1951* (London: Macmillan and Co. Ltd, 1952), p. 56.

[19] Matthew Francis, 'Searching for Constructive Conservatism: A Short History of the Property-owning Democracy', *Conservative History Journal*, 2/3 (2014), 12.

[20] Figures compiled by the author from CPA material.

[21] CPA, PUB 229/8/16, Charles Stuart Hallinan election address, Cardiff Central, 1945; E. H. H. Green, 'The Conservative Party, the State and the Electorate, 1945–64', in Lawrence and Taylor, *Party, State and Society*, p. 181.

constituency.[22] One Tory candidate argued that 'Socialism, while planning everything for the people, cannot plan for individual tastes'.[23] The message certainly filtered down to the electorate, with one costermonger in Cardiff arguing that, as a businessman, he was 'definitely voting Conservative' because 'I believe in free enterprise. I don't want to be pushed around'.[24]

Large parts of the country, however, especially in the industrial southern parts of so-called 'Welsh Wales', were far from friendly territory for the Conservatives and this critique of Labour would have fallen on many deaf ears. The urban geography of many of these places, where people were clustered together in back-to-back houses, fostered a further sense of solidarity.[25] Even as the process of de-industrialisation gathered pace through the post-war decades, and younger people became more mobile, the 'trinity of work, family and community socialising' was reflected 'in the value of Labourism' and this was especially potent in this immediate post-1945 period.[26] As the Labour candidate for the Valleys seat of Aberdare told voters, they should: 'Think Labour, Talk Labour, Vote Labour'. To add to the Conservatives' woes, evidence suggests that a dominant political culture in certain places impacted on voting patterns, where voting for Labour in an already strong Labour seat became contagious, reinforcing existing electoral behaviour.[27] Such unfavourable circumstances for the Conservatives did not stop the party critiquing Labour in these areas. Such rhetoric about the dangers of Socialism was intended to apply to

---

[22] See CPA, PUB 229/9/17, Charles Hallinan election address, Cardiff West, 1950.

[23] 'Conservative Challenge After 20 Years', *Merthyr Express*, 4 June 1949.

[24] 'Mr. and Mrs. Cardiff say their election piece', *Western Mail*, 24 October 1951. See Petrie, 'Anti-Socialism', for very similar statements made by Unionists in Scotland.

[25] For excellent evocations of this, see the work of Dai Smith, especially the opening to his *Wales! Wales?* (London: Allen & Unwin, 1984); David Butler and Richard Rose, *The British General Election of 1959* (London: Macmillan, 1960), p. 11.

[26] David Adamson, 'The New Working Class and Political Change in Wales', *Contemporary Wales*, 2 (1988), 16.

[27] Robert Waller, 'Conservative Electoral Support and Social Class', in Seldon and Ball, *Conservative Century*, p. 583; David Jeffery, *Whatever Happened to Tory Liverpool? Success, Decline and Irrelevance Since 1945* (Liverpool: Liverpool University Press, 2023), chapter two.

the national, and even global, situation. But it also filtered down to much more local concerns, particularly frustration with remote central government.[28] Some candidates used the theme to take a swipe at an overly restrictive culture at local government level as well. Echoing Churchill, the National (Conservative) candidate for Caerphilly wrote to the *Western Mail* to complain about what he considered to be an already existent 'Socialist Gestapo' in south Wales. He argued that no one, if they were 'an employee of the local authority, would dare openly declare himself a Conservative or work for the Conservative Party'.[29] A nepotistic 'jobs for the boys' culture was identified by Tories as a real problem.

Conservative messages about state control or nationalisation of key industries would, however, have had some purchase in industrial Wales. A cartoon in the *Western Mail* in 1950 showed a woman in traditional Welsh dress reading a newspaper that detailed the profits of the steel industry. The caption read: 'voting for Nationalisation, Ma?'[30] As that cartoon suggested, these themes of 'control' and 'individual freedom' was aimed at women in particular. The party's messaging was designed to tie in with general disquiet about continued rationing at the turn of the decade and the impact this had on feeding a family. In the words of one Tory-supporting woman, 'what right-minded woman is going to submit to state control in the shape and furnishing of her home, in her shopping, in her housekeeping, in her clothes'.[31] The Conservatives had long addressed women about domestic and financial matters and their freedom to organise their own affairs.[32] In the post-1945 years, women in particular were frustrated by shortages and the impact this had on the home, resulting in the formation of a number of protest organisations, like the British

[28] Cragoe, 'We Like', 983.
[29] 'Socialist "Gestapo" in South Wales', *Western Mail*, 2 July 1945.
[30] 'Voting for Nationalisation, Ma?', *Western Mail*, 14 January 1950.
[31] 'Why I am Going to Vote for Churchill – by Maurine Steen', *Western Mail*, 5 July 1945.
[32] David Thackeray, *Conservatism for the Democratic Age: Conservative Cultures and the Challenge of Mass Politics in Early Twentieth-century England* (Manchester: Manchester University Press, 2013), p. 134.

Housewives' League.[33] As one Welsh Conservative MP wrote in 1949, women, 'who bear the children and cook the food do not lose touch with the fundamental realities', and they voted Tory because (unlike men) they were 'less easily persuaded by pure nonsense'.[34]

The party focused its attention on women for more self-interested reasons, too: their vote was vital for its electoral success. Women voted Conservative in this period in much greater numbers than their male counterparts. Indeed, without the women's vote in Britain, there would have been an unbroken rule of Labour government from 1945 to 1979.[35] Historians and commentators have offered a range of explanations as to why right-leaning politics resonated with female voters, including women's natural conservatism; their involvement with like-minded organisations, such as the Church; the effective way in which the Tories targeted women with conservative ideas about household budgets and the cost of living; the party's positive policies like equal pay in the public sector; the masculine and more macho nature of cloth-cap trade unionism; and the confrontational nature of the workplace versus the domestic sphere.[36] A mix of these factors is likely to provide some answer,

---

[33] Zweiniger-Bargielowska, 'Rationing', 181.

[34] Nigel Birch, *The Conservative Party* (London: Collins, 1949), p. 44.

[35] Pippa Norris and Joni Lovenduski, 'Gender and Party Politics in Britain', in Pippa Norris and Joni Lovenduski (eds), *Gender and Party Politics* (London: Sage Publications, 1993), p. 38.

[36] Stuart Ball, *Portrait of a Party: The Conservative Party in Britain, 1918–1945* (Oxford: Oxford University Press, 2013), p. 84; Beatrix Campbell, *The Iron Ladies: Why Do Women Vote Tory?* (London: Virago, 1987); Adrian Bingham, 'Conservatism, Gender and the Politics of Everyday Life, 1950s–1980s', in Clarisse Berthezène and Julie V. Gottlieb (eds), *Rethinking Right-wing Women: Gender and the Conservative Party, 1880s to the Present* (Manchester: Manchester University Press, 2018), pp. 156–74; Joni Lovenduski, Pippa Norris and Catriona Burness, 'The Party and Women', in Seldon and Ball, *Conservative Century*, p. 611; G. E. Maguire, *Conservative Women: A History of Women and the Conservative Party, 1874–1997* (Basingstoke: Macmillan, 1998), p. 119; Ross McKibbin, 'Class and Conventional Wisdom: the Conservative Party and the "Public" in Inter-war Britain', in R. McKibbin, *The Ideologies of Class* (Oxford: Clarendon, 1990), p. 285; Morgan, 'Power and Glory', pp. 183–4; Martin Pugh, 'Popular Conservatism in Britain: Continuity and Change, 1880–1987', *Journal of British Studies*, 27/3 (1988), p. 268; Ina Zweiniger-Bargielowska, 'Explaining the Gender Gap: the Conservative Party and the Women's Vote, 1945–1964', in Martin Francis and Ina Zweiniger-Bargielowska (eds), *The Conservatives and British Society, 1880–1990* (Cardiff: University of Wales Press, 1996), pp. 196, 202.

and it also explains why the party regularly spoke directly to women. Across Britain, many more Conservative candidates than Labour ones included a message from their wife in their election addresses during this period, and always targeted female voters in their capacity as housewives and mothers.[37] In Wales, twelve Tory candidates did so in 1950, whereas six Labour ones did. Wives usually spoke about household management and prices and of 'the hard lot the housewives have had to bear [. . .] Socialism means levelling down not levelling up'.[38] In the early 1950s, most voters would not have frowned upon a wife's message on the grounds of its conservatism, and Labour was yet to become the more culturally radical party that it was in the 1960s. The Tories deployed their wives more regularly, not because it was a purely Conservative thing to do so, but because they had a tailor-made critique of household budgets and prices that they knew women voters were receptive to.[39]

In parts of 'British Wales', the salience of issues like household management, food prices and the domestic sphere lay behind Conservatives doing things like co-opting, for example, prominent meat traders to send letters out to other similar businessmen calling for the Tories to be supported.[40] Evidence suggests that such messages were landing on willing ears and the targeting of women, in particular, was reaping benefits. By 1951, prospective parliamentary candidates reported back to Conservative Central Office (CCO) that whilst many men seemed satisfied with Attlee's government, 'their womenfolk are getting worried over the cost of living'.[41] One man in

---

[37] R. B. McCallum and Alison Readman, *The British General Election of 1945* (Oxford: Oxford University Press, 1947), p. 93.

[38] Figures compiled by the author. However, as election addresses have often been archived by being stuck into scrapbooks, this figure might be a little inaccurate: a wife's address often appeared on the back of these documents, where the glue was added. CPA, PUB 229/9/17, Ivor Thomas election address, Newport, 1950; Arthur Russell election address, Pontypool, 1950.

[39] Maguire, *Conservative Women*, pp. 120–1.

[40] CPA, CCO 1/7/520, Midgley to Spencer, 12 August 1949.

[41] CPA, CCO 1/8/536/2, Body to Woolton, 5 December 1950.

Cardiff, interviewed as part of a survey, said that he was voting Conservative 'for the simple reason that if I vote otherwise my wife – who has very strong Conservative views – will cut off my rations!'[42] The party also addressed women voters in a variety of other ways. Mobile cinema vans, a key feature of inter-war campaigning tactics, remained a useful tool after the war. Again, these were deployed in the more receptive parts of Wales, with one spending fourteen days in the Monmouth constituency in April 1948, playing mild party propaganda to willing audiences.[43]

In early examples of television broadcasts, Patricia Hornsby-Smith, the Conservative MP, addressed housewives directly about the cost of living.[44] However, the television was far from a permanent fixture in every living room in the early 1950s. Whilst the wireless was crucial during elections, Tories in Wales still engaged with a long-term feature of political campaigns dating from the late nineteenth century: the public meeting, especially stump and town hall speeches.[45] In big urban centres like Cardiff, prominent Tories and soon-to-be MPs, like David Llewellyn, would regularly meet queues of women voters when speaking at places like the Cory Hall. According to the *Western Mail*, they wished to 'felicitate' Llewellyn after a speech on prices and household management.[46] Twenty thousand people could be relied on to turn up in Cardiff for the star attraction that was Churchill during the 1950 general election campaign.[47] But, as Jon Lawrence has shown, it was also in areas away from the major metropolitan hubs that large meetings continued to be especially

---

[42] 'Mr. and Mrs. Cardiff say their election piece', *Western Mail*, 24 October 1951.

[43] Stuart Ball, Andrew Thorpe and Matthew Worley, 'Elections, Leaflets and Whist Drives: Constituency Party Membership in Britain Between the Wars', in Matthew Worley (ed.), *Labour's Grass Roots: Essays on the Activities of Local Labour Parties and Members, 1918–1945* (Aldershot: Ashgate, 2005), p. 17; WPA, GB0210 MONION, file 1, Monmouth Unionist Association minute book, 9 November 1948.

[44] Butler, *The British General Election of 1951*, p. 67.

[45] Jon Lawrence, *Electing Our Masters: The Hustings in British Politics from Hogarth to Blair* (Oxford: Oxford University Press, 2009), pp. 185–6.

[46] CPA, CCO 1/7/519, Llewellyn to Thomas, 28 September 1948; 'Socialists sent up cost of living', *Western Mail*, 17 September 1952.

[47] H. G. Nicholas, *The British General Election of 1950* (London: Macmillan, 1951), p. 94.

popular.[48] The former cabinet minister Oliver Stanley brought in a crowd of 12,000 people when he addressed a meeting in south-east Wales in 1948.[49] One and a half thousand turned up, in apparently terrible weather, to listen to David Maxwell Fyfe, the Home Secretary (and, as we shall see, the first Minister for Welsh Affairs) speak in Brecon in 1953.[50]

Such methods and messaging appear to have had an impact.[51] From a historic defeat in 1945, the Conservative Party recovered significant ground at the 1950 general election, reducing Labour's majority to a tiny number of seats in parliament. In Wales, the Tories captured suburban Cardiff North, with David Llewellyn becoming the seat's MP. When Attlee went to the country again in 1951, the Conservative party also won the seats of Conway and Barry – a reoccupation of 'old fortresses', as the *Western Mail* chose to report it – and witnessed a swing of 7.1 per cent to it compared with the 1945 result.[52]

There was a further dynamic at play in Wales, closely related to the anti-socialist theme, that had an impact on elections in some key constituencies: the relationship between the Tories and the National Liberal Party.[53] The National Liberals were a splinter faction of the Liberals that had broken away from its old party in 1931 over debates surrounding tariffs and free trade, and consequently tended to lean, politically, towards the Conservatives.[54] After the war, although the National Liberals continued to have their own separate organisations with candidates standing under their own banner, many did so with the express endorsement of the Tory hierarchy, pledging that

[48] Lawrence, *Electing Our Masters*, p. 153.
[49] Ramsden, *The Age of Churchill*, p. 122.
[50] CPA, CCO 1/10/508, Oliver to Hare, 28 November 1953.
[51] 'All parties appealing to Liberals and Women', *Western Mail*, 22 October 1951.
[52] 'Welsh figures', *Western Mail*, 27 October 1951.
[53] 'Anti-Socialists', *Western Mail*, 14 January 1950.
[54] Sir Henry Morris-Jones, *Doctor in the Whip's Room* (London: Robert Hale, 1955), p. 97.

'both parties' would 'resolve to banish Socialism'.[55] 'Tacit anti-Socialist arrangements' had existed between Tories and Liberals in the inter-war years and this kind of arrangement developed into something very close to a formal alliance in our period, with National Liberal MPs like Emlyn Garner Evans, who sat for Denbigh from 1950 to 1959, displaying messages from the Tory leadership in his election literature.[56] All of this was in the spirit of the Woolton-Teviot pact, named after a cordial agreement struck between the two chairmen of the Conservative and the National Liberal parties. As can be imagined, however, the situation on the ground was not always cordial. 'Considerable confusion' was caused within local Conservative parties about who exactly they were supporting, and some became frustrated that they did not have their own 'true blue' Tory candidate to rally behind.[57] The constituencies listed in table 3 did not field a Conservative candidate in the stated general elections.

Unlike Conservatism in England, which was generally stronger, the number of pacts in Wales reflected the relative weakness of the Tories there – something mirrored in areas of Scotland.[58] The highest-profile National Liberal in Wales during this period was Gwilym Lloyd George, the MP for Pembrokeshire from 1929 until 1950. At the end of the War, Lloyd George was the only Liberal member to remain within the government.[59] He regularly spoke at joint meetings of the Liberal and Conservative associations in Pembrokeshire, consistently warning about the dangers of socialism.[60] Whilst Gwilym's sister, Megan Lloyd George, would

---

[55] CPA, CCO, 1/7/507, Jones to Woolton, undated letter c.1949; Ramsden, *The Age of Churchill*, p. 200.

[56] Geraint Thomas, 'The Conservative Party and Welsh Politics in the Inter-war Years', *English Historical Review*, 128/533 (2013), 893; Williams, 'The Conservative Party in North-East Wales', chapter six. CPA, PUB, 229/11/13. For more on the local dynamics in Denbigh, see CPA, CCO 1/10/515, Denbigh Basic Report, 31 December 1953.

[57] 'The National Liberals', *Western Mail*, 2 February 1950.

[58] Petrie, 'Anti-Socialism', p. 204.

[59] J. Graham Jones, 'Major Gwilym Lloyd-George and the Pembrokeshire Election of 1950', *Journal of the Pembrokeshire Historical Society*, 11 (2002), 101.

[60] Alun Wyburn-Powell, *Defectors and the Liberal Party 1910–2010: A Study of Inter-party Relationships* (Manchester: Manchester University Press, 2012), p. 135.

end up as a Labour MP (for the neighbouring constituency of Carmarthen), his politics leant rightwards. When Lloyd George was re-adopted in the Pembrokeshire constituency for the 1950 contest, as a National Liberal, the head of the Conservative

Constituency	General elections	Details
Cardigan	1945, 1951, 1955, 1959	Supported the Liberal MP for the seat, Roderic Bowen. Fielded a candidate in 1950.
Carmarthen	1945, 1950, 1951, 1955, 1957 by-election	Supported the Liberal MP for the seat, Rhys Hopkin Morris.
Denbigh	1945, 1950, 1951, 1955	Supported the National Liberal candidate Sir Henry Morris-Jones in 1945 and his successor Emlyn Garner Evans in the following three general elections.
Gower	1945, 1950, 1951, 1955 (1959 as a 'National Liberal and Conservative')	Supported the National Liberal candidates. Michael Heseltine stood in 1959 under the joint label.
Merioneth	1955, 1959	Supported the National Liberal candidate in 1955; fielded no candidate against a Liberal in 1959.
Montgomery	1951, 1955	Did not oppose the Liberal MP and party leader, Clement Davies.
Pembrokeshire	1950, 1955	Supported National Liberal candidate Gwilym Lloyd George in 1950; supported an Independent candidate in direct fight against the sitting Labour MP in 1955.
Swansea East	1945	Supported National Liberal candidate, Rowe Harding, who stood in Gower in 1950 and 1951.
Swansea West	1945, 1950	Supported National Liberal candidate Sir Lewis Jones.
Wrexham	1945, 1950, 1951, 1955	Joint Conservative and National Liberal Association supported a National Liberal candidate.

Table 3: Liberal and National Liberal candidates supported by the Conservative Party in Wales, 1945–1959.

Association took the chair.[61] As one account remarked after Lloyd George's defeat to Labour's Desmond Donnelly in that election, there was a 'large reservoir of support for the [Conservative] Party in Pembrokeshire', with members of the Liberal and the Conservative organisations seeing similarities in one another's politics.[62]

The situation in Pembrokeshire had been relatively harmonious, but it was not like that everywhere. Some local Tories considered it simply a 'sign of weakness' not to stand a Conservative candidate in a seat. Activists in Flint East were personally contacted by senior party figures like Lord Woolton, who displayed obvious anger at their desire to field a 'full-blooded Conservative' in the 1950 contest, causing the Deputy Chairman of the party, J. P. L. (Jim) Thomas, to write in despair that it was 'ridiculous' that 'a Welsh seat, of all places should penalise a candidate for being prepared to stand under the joint title'.[63] No doubt he had in mind both the precarious nature of the Conservative vote in much of Wales, as well as the long-term ties to the 'Liberal' label. However, the fact that the local party went ahead and simply stood a Conservative candidate anyway did demonstrate how constituencies had some autonomy from 'the centre'.

The greatest row over the National Liberal matter, however, happened in Swansea West where the Conservatives were 'outraged' about the decision to field Sir Lewis Jones, the seat's National Liberal MP between 1931 and 1945, as the anti-socialist candidate again in 1950.[64] An ideological tug of war between the party hierarchy and the local Conservative Association in

---

[61] Jones, 'Major Gwilym', 113.

[62] CPA, CCO 1/8/542, Miss Risdale's Report from Pembrokeshire, October–December 1950.

[63] The local Tories won the day in this instance and fielded a Conservative candidate. CPA, CCO 1/9/534, Garmonsway to the GD, 7 November 1951; CPA, CCO, 1/7/516, Woolton to Summers, *c.*12 January 1949; CPA, CCO 1/7/516, Summers to Thomas, 10 December 1948; CPA, CCO 1/7/516, Thomas to Woolton, 17 December 1948.

[64] 'Candidate Adopted at Swansea', *Western Mail*, 9 March 1948; CPA, CCO 1/7/525, James to the GD, 11 November 1948.

Swansea ensued. When Lewis Jones was defeated in 1950, the Tories hurriedly selected their own candidate to fight the seat for the next election, which they correctly predicted would come quickly.[65] This, at least, was a sign of some sort of energy amongst the grassroots. In the neighbouring seat of Gower, little resistance was put up to the National Liberal candidate, the former Welsh rugby player, W. Rowe Harding, standing for the seat. Ultimately, this was because the Tory association there was so weak and the party had no hope of winning the constituency.[66]

CLASS AND LANGUAGE

No such pacts existed in the Valleys of industrial Wales, where the Conservatives were often the only receptacle for the anti-socialist vote. It was a mark of how effective at politics Labour had become in these areas that the Tories often communicated poorly there. Even though Anthony Eden could pack out a public meeting in the Labour stronghold of Merthyr Tydfil in 1951, with crowds being marshalled outside, and even though the Tories were able to muster 6,000 votes in this seat, Labour dominated.[67] Sitting MPs drew on their long historical connections with their own communities. Caerphilly's Ness Edwards deliberately emphasised not Churchill's role in the Second World War, but the part he played in the notorious Tonypandy Riots of 1910. At the 1950 election, sixteen different Labour candidates referred to the 'terrible years' of the Depression – often simply referring to it as 'the 1930s' – which were 'lean, hungry and hard years . . . under Tory rule'.[68] Seven Tories brought up the subject too, doing so as a means of arguing that the Conservatives were now different, that

---

[65] CPA, CCO 1/8/526, Garmonsway to Watson, 6 February 1951.
[66] CPA, CCO 1/9/530, Garmonsway to Hare, 7 November 1952; CPA, CCO 1/7/530, Gower Basic Report, July 1949.
[67] 'Surprise at Eden's Merthyr Meeting', *Western Mail*, 12 October 1951; Johnes, *Wales Since 1939*, p. 56.
[68] CPA, PUB 229/9/17, Iori Thomas election address, Rhondda West, 1950.

mistakes were made and that suffering was endured in Wales as a result.[69] A handful of Tories, however, were much more robust, and perhaps tin-eared, in addressing the 'lie' that Conservatives had created unemployment in those years.[70]

In private, senior party officials despaired of Labour's Welsh voters, especially in the Valleys, thinking them 'a very sentimental race and swayed by oratory of which plenty is to be found amongst the Socialists'.[71] Frustration that people did not think closely enough about political issues was never far away. Local constituency parties were often left scratching their heads, wondering how they could appeal to voters who were Labour 'more by tradition than inclination'.[72] Elements of this attitude sometimes seeped out into public rhetoric. On the whole, Conservatives communicated in these seats in a way that was befitting a party that knew it had no hope of winning. In the process, many stereotypes were reinforced and the party's weaknesses were laid bare. Contemporary commentators and historians alike have picked up on how a candidate fighting a winnable or marginal seat tended to produce sober, constrained or even dull material.[73] In contrast, and particularly so in this era where election addresses were less standardised, someone fighting a hopeless seat communicated in more unorthodox ways. This was certainly true in Wales, where some of the election addresses in the Valleys sounded dismissive, aloof or flippant. Instead of writing the date and location in the corner of his address (as was common at the time), one candidate simply wrote 'somewhere in Wales', almost as if to emphasise his lack of connection to the seat, whilst another lectured the voters on the debt they owed Churchill before almost instructing them to vote Conservative by writing: 'go to it

---

[69] Figures compiled by the author from CPA material. See CPA, PUB 229/9/17, George Nicholls election address, Rhondda East, or Lionel Haddrill election address, Merthyr Tydfil, 1950.

[70] See CPA, PUB 229/9/17, Owen Lewis address election address, Abertillery, and Lewis Jones election address, Swansea West, 1950.

[71] CPA, CCO 500/24/56, 'Review of the Welsh political situation', 1 March 1950.

[72] CPA, Howe MS 326, Welsh forum number 6, March 1962.

[73] Butler and Rose, *The British General Election of 1959*, p. 133.

Aberdare!'[74] Others pleaded to at least be given consideration – 'bear with me for a short while in order that I may put my point of view to you' – whilst others adopted the tactic of not even putting the Conservative Party's name on the front of their leaflet, despite this being an era where CCO were insisting on it.[75] This sometimes went hand in hand with colouring the leaflet in red so that it might appear on first glance to be a Labour publication.[76]

The party did spend some time wondering how it could look and sound less aloof and less 'posh'. Local Tory activists on the ground would cry out for someone who was 'used to talking to the working man!'[77] The Conservative party knew that support tended to drift away from it further down the occupational scale. But it was aware that some working-class people, like manual labourers, voted Conservative. As a result, the Tories fielded a disproportionately large number of 'ordinary' people as parliamentary candidates in Wales compared to other areas of Britain.[78] In 1950, the party as a whole had seven 'workers' fighting seats for it. Of this tiny number, three stood in Wales.[79] In 1951, that figure was fifteen and four respectively, with Wales therefore having a hugely disproportionate number of these working-class men standing under the Conservatives' banner.[80] This was perhaps a reflection of the high number of working-class people in Wales, and it was no doubt some kind of response to the successes of Labour. In 1950, nearly 60 per cent of Tory candidates across the UK had been privately educated, but this was less than 50 per cent in Wales, again confirming that the party was making a small but noticeable effort to

---

[74] CPA, PUB 229/8/16, Major Davies election address, Ogmore, 1945; Captain George Clover election address, Aberdare, 1945.
[75] CPA, PUB 229/9/17, Lionel Haddrill election address, Merthyr Tydfil, 1950; Thackeray and Toye, 'An Age', 7.
[76] See CPA, PUB 229/9/17, Jim Driscoll election address, Rhondda West, 1950.
[77] David Butler and Donald Stokes, *Political Change in Britain: the Evolution of Electoral Choice* ([1969] Suffolk: Macmillan Press, 1974), pp. 76–7; CPA, CCO 1/7/516, Summers to Thomas, 19 October 1948.
[78] Eric A. Nordlinger, *The Working-Class Tories: Authority, Deference and Stable Democracy* (London: Macgibbon and Kee, 1967), p. 163.
[79] Nicholas, *The British*, p. 52.
[80] Butler (ed.), *The British General Election of 1951*, p. 41.

address its upper-middle-class profile.[81] Such action also contrasted with the inter-war years when, across Britain, there were very few examples of working-class Tories standing in any seats.[82] In Wales, very few attempts to field such people had been evident at all. The ex-miner Gwilym Rowlands served as the MP for Flintshire from 1935 to 1945 and was 'the most visible representative of working class Conservatism' in the House of Commons at the time.[83] Sam Thompson, who stood in the January election of 1910, came from an ordinary working-class background. However, almost all would-be Tory MPs were landowners, or worked as barristers, diplomats or doctors.[84]

All of which made those small number of candidates in the early 1950s, who mainly stood in 'Welsh Wales' and were from humble backgrounds, more significant. In 1950, the self-declared 'working class chap' George Nicholls stood in Rhondda East, whilst Caerphilly's candidate, Ken Lloyd, grew up in a 'two up and one down . . . and [I] am proud of it'. He was also a trade unionist who articulated the case for Conservative reform of those organisations.[85] Others, like Arthur Russell, standing in Pontypool, might have been an accountant at the time he stood for election, but he made an effort to stress the fact that he had left school at fourteen, educated himself and was 'A REAL workingman' candidate, which presumably was a dig at the seat's MP, Granville West, a well-known solicitor.[86] In 1951, Jim Bowen,[87] another trade unionist, who played rugby locally, stood in Ebbw Vale; in Llanelli the party fielded a factory worker; in Swansea East, the

---

[81] Bale, *The Conservatives*, p. 15. Figures compiled by the author using Ivor Thomas Rees, *Welsh Hustings: 1885–2004* (Llandybie: Dinefwr Press, 2005).

[82] John Ramsden, *The Age of Balfour and Baldwin, 1902–1940* (London: Longman, 1978), pp. 55–6.

[83] Edwards, *The Good Patch*, pp. 92–3.

[84] Williams, 'The Conservative Party in North-East Wales', p. 72; Felix Aubel, 'Welsh Conservatism, 1885–1935: Five Studies in Adaptation' (unpublished PhD thesis, Lampeter University, 1996), pp. 27–8; Ball, *Portrait*, p. 269.

[85] CPA, PUB 229/9/17, Kenneth Lloyd election address, Caerphilly, 1950.

[86] CPA, PUB 229/9/17, Arthur Russell election address, Pontypool, 1950.

[87] Not to be confused with the entertainer who later hosted the television show *Bullseye*.

candidate Jack Hope had worked in the town's docks since he was thirteen and was on the waiting list for a council house.[88] He described his former and present employment as: 'labourer, farm labourer, forestry worker, assistant surveyor, taxi driver, garage assistant and game-dealer's assistant'.[89]

Historians have touched upon the ways in which CCO, and its various regional Area Offices, wanted more working-class candidates. The argument goes that local activists, who made the final decision on who to pick as their candidate, were reluctant to accept them, wanting people of distinction or prestige as well as someone with money who could cover day-to-day expenses.[90] However, the evidence from Wales, whilst not contradicting that, offers a different perspective. Here, the party hierarchy was almost universally hostile or dismissive about these men. Part of this certainly boiled down to money. Requests for help with higher than normal election expenses from these less financially secure individuals were almost always met with blunt memos that the candidate was 'a difficult man'.[91] Another (admittedly large) expense bill left the party's General Director – who was normally so reserved – 'horrified'.[92] The speeches of people like Lloyd in Caerphilly were noted by party officials as being 'pathetic' and he was dismissed as 'inexperienced', without any evidence of the party helping him improve.[93] In the run-up to the 1950 election, Jim Thomas wrote specifically about the Welsh situation, saying: 'how very awkward these working men candidates are'.[94] There is plenty of evidence to suggest that the grassroots wanted

---

[88] Rees, *Welsh Hustings*, p. 30; CPA, CCO 1/8/538, Ebbw Vale Basic Report, 21 February 1951; 'Election candidates in Wales: Llanelly', *Western Mail*, 18 October 1951; CPA, CCO 1/8/525, Swansea East Basic Report, 16 February 1951; CPA, PUB 229/9/17, Jack Hope election address, Swansea East, 1950.

[89] 'Aberdare', *Western Mail*, 20 May 1955.

[90] Bale, *The Conservatives*, p. 59.

[91] CPA, CCO 1/8/523, James to the GD, 1 June 1950.

[92] CPA, CCO 1/7/507, James to the GD, undated; CPA, CCO 1/7/507, the GD to Thomas, undated.

[93] CPA, CCO 1/7/529, Caerphilly Basic Report, c. July 1949; James to Thomas, 14 July 1949.

[94] CPA, CCO 1/7/529, Thomas to the GD, 13 July 1949.

suave, middle-class men, but the Wales Area Office and CCO seemed to do little to encourage them to change their stance, acting exasperated by the quality of working-class Tories who understandably had little political experience. They also thought that a candidate had to 'impress business', a core Tory vote.[95]

There was only one exception to this, and that was the case of Harry West. He was an ex-miner who pitched himself as being in a position to know 'the needs of the people', with his electioneering material stating that he was 'A man of the people' very prominently.[96] CCO 'badly want[ed] him in parliament', not least because West led the efforts in Wales to connect with grassroots trade unionists.[97] Although he fought James Callaghan in Cardiff South East in 1951, having contested the Liberal stronghold of Montgomery the year before, it is telling that the party did not try to crowbar him into a more winnable seat. We should not be drawn into concluding that this smattering of working-class candidates in 1950 and 1951 somehow gave the party in Wales any sort of proletarian image. Harry West was an important Conservative figure, but he was part of the one or two per cent of Conservative candidates across Britain who came from manual labour backgrounds in those two elections in the early 1950s.[98] Whilst that proportion was higher in Wales, they were still a small minority who would never have made the party feel anything other than resolutely middle class. In 1950, 107 candidates across Britain had attended Eton College alone, including Conservatives in Wales, like Nigel Birch.[99] Grassroots Tories, with their power to choose candidates, became increasingly restless about the role of trade unions in society as the post-war period wore on, and this

---

[95] WPA, GB0210 CARCON, file 15, Cardiff South East Executive Committee minute book, 1 November 1954.

[96] Kenneth O. Morgan, *Callaghan: A Life* (Oxford: Oxford University Press, 1997), p. 101; CPA, PUB 229/10/13. Not to be confused with the Harry West who led the Ulster Unionist Party in the 1970s.

[97] CPA, CCO 1/8/520, Thomas to James, 20 May 1950; CPA, CCO 1/8/520, Basic Report Cardiff South East, 28 September 1950.

[98] Bale, *The Conservatives*, p. 15

[99] Bale, *The Conservatives*, p. 15

may underpin why anyone connected to the world of unionised heavy industry was shunned.[100] Consequently, distinctions between the Conservatives and Labour were easy to identify, and Labour simply had a much stronger record in Wales of selecting candidates who looked far more like the electorate.[101]

Figure 2: Harry West's election address to the voters of Montgomery, 1950.

---

[100] Green, 'The Conservative Party', pp. 194–5.
[101] Morgan, 'Power and Glory', pp. 174–5.

If class was one of the key factors that the Conservatives needed to consider in industrial Wales, rural constituencies presented different challenges. Here, concerns about things like agriculture dominated, but the Welsh language was also of real importance. Admittedly, in huge non-urban seats on the border with England, like Brecon and Radnor, where the language did not play a major role in the majority of day-to-day life, the party could find suitable candidates with relative ease by drawing them from the farming community, for example.[102] However, a candidate's Welsh-speaking ability was the key priority in *y fro Gymraeg*, or Welsh-speaking Wales. Those seats were (in this period) Anglesey, Caernarfon, Merioneth, Cardigan, and Carmarthen. These were places where Welsh was often the language of everyday life, as well as being central to the identity of the people who lived there.[103] In places like Ceredigion or on the isle of Anglesey, eighty per cent of people spoke the language in the early 1950s.[104] The fact that the Tories often found it difficult, or simply did not seem to try, to recruit people who could speak Welsh to stand for it demonstrated another of its key failures. In contrast, the Labour Party was almost always able to regularly field Welsh-speaking Welshman in *y fro Gymraeg*, like Cledwyn Hughes, Thomas William Jones or Goronwy Roberts. In 1951, for example, all five of Labour's candidates in *y fro Gymraeg*, as well as in thirteen other seats, spoke Welsh – although senior Labour figures admitted that finding these people was not always easy.[105] At some elections the Tories could only manage to put up one Welsh speaker in any of these five key seats. Table 4 breaks up parliamentary constituencies along Balsom's Three

[102] Janet Davies, *The Welsh Language* (Cardiff: University of Wales Press, 1999), p. 70.
[103] Denis Balsom, 'The Three-Wales Model', in John Osmond (ed.), *The National Question Again: Welsh Political Identity in the 1980s* (Llandysul: Gomer Press, 1985), p. 6.
[104] Johnes, *Wales Since 1939*, p. 181.
[105] Figures compiled by the author using Rees, *Welsh Hustings*; Morgan, 'Power and Glory', p. 181.

Wales model (discussed in the introduction).[106] It shows that, for Wales as a whole, most Welsh-speaking candidates were put forward by the Tories in *y fro Gymraeg* in the whole period that this book covers, but the party never managed to field a clean sweep of Welsh speakers in these seats at any election.

General election	Welsh speakers in *y fro Gymraeg* (five seats)	Welsh speakers in 'Welsh Wales'	Welsh speakers in 'British Wales'
1945	2	1	0
1950	3	1	1
1951	3	1	1
1955	2	1	0
1959	2	0	1
1964	1	0	1
1966	1	0	1
1970	4	0	2
1974 Feb.	4	1	3
1974 Oct.	3	1	2
1979	3	1	1
1983	4	0	1
1987	4	0	2
1992	4	4	3
1997	5	2	4

Table 4: Number of Welsh-speaking candidates fielded by the Conservative Party at each general election, 1945–1997.

As we can see, the party could occasionally find people who could speak Welsh to stand for it, but this was not a common occurrence. At the heart of Welsh-speaking Wales was the

[106] For a useful critique of the model, see Roger Scully and Richard Wyn Jones, 'Still Three Wales? Social Location and Electoral Behaviour in Contemporary Wales', *Electoral Studies*, 31 (2012), pp. 656–67.

isle of Anglesey, whose coastline was also the boundary of the parliamentary constituency. It had once been said that if a roof could be put over the island, it would become one large Methodist chapel, such was the commitment to the idea of Welsh-speaking Nonconformity which, at the beginning of this period at least, reflected a reasonably homogeneous society.[107] Conservative candidates J. O. Jones in 1950 and O. M. Roberts in 1951 were, respectively, a 'Welsh speaking working man candidate', and 'a good mixer [who] is Welsh speaking', according to the Wales Area Office's profiles of them.[108] Tellingly, Jones's ability to speak Welsh was considered his greatest attribute, not the fact that he was working class.[109] When the party produced electioneering material in seats like Anglesey, they appeared bilingually. Indeed, the Tories were becoming sensitive to this issue. In 1950, for example, eight of its candidates issued bilingual election addresses, all from the more Welsh-speaking areas of the country. One further candidate included a token section of a few lines. Labour issued slightly more bilingual addresses (eleven), with a further three including a tokenistic section.[110] Looking at these documents, it is clear that the Tories were not oblivious to the importance of Welsh in certain constituencies.

However, the Conservatives' inability to field a full team of Welsh-speaking candidates in *y fro Gymraeg* had long been considered its Achilles heel.[111] On one hand, the party's primary weakness was surely its inability to make any breakthroughs in a swathe of industrial seats in the south and north-east of Wales. However, on the other hand, those seats in Welsh-speaking Wales would have been, in England, typical Tory targets. A blend of factors relating to history and identity, including the anglicised image of the party in the areas, made voters wary of Toryism. Grassroots party members, many of whom spoke

---

[107] 'Keith looks like having best chance of success', *Western Mail*, 31 May 1983.
[108] CPA, CCO 1/8/507, Anglesey Basic Report, 31 August 1951.
[109] CPA, CCO 1/7/507, Anglesey Basic Report c.1948.
[110] Figures compiled by the author using Rees, *Welsh Hustings*.
[111] Aubel, 'Welsh Conservatism', p. 106.

Welsh themselves, understood the importance. The chairman of the Caernarfon Tories begged CCO in 1949 to tell him immediately if 'any suitable' Welsh-speaking person was placed on the candidate's list.[112] It was significant that the descendants of old Tory families, like the Williams-Wynns, who had dominated landed politics in the nineteenth and early twentieth centuries, felt the need to at least say they were learning the language when they stood in seats like Merioneth in 1950.[113] (It was a step up from one Tory candidate in 1929 telling an audience that his lack of skills in the language was due to his parents having failed to provide him with 'a Welsh-speaking nanny'.[114])

Candidates promising to learn, however, was often the best the party could manage. When Dr George Little stood in Cardigan in 1950, he committed to learning more of the language, justifying himself in public and private by saying that he had been born in Cardiff, had 'so many Welsh friends' and had been taught by 'a Welsh-speaking Welshman' at school.[115] The fact he needed to say such things spoke volumes, as did the local association's deep frustration that they had not recruited someone with the 'essential' characteristic of being able to speak the language.[116] A social study of rural Wales found voters thinking that 'the voice of Welshness' in the Ceredigion Conservative Association was 'almost silent', hence why Little's monoglot status weighed so heavily against him in an area where Welsh was widely used for things like hustings or public meetings.[117] This trend, with the party doing reasonably well in in so-called 'British Wales', versus terrible performances in much of 'Welsh Wales' and the Welsh-speaking heartlands, would set the tone for the rest of the century.

---

[112] CPA, CCO 1/7/59, Roberts to Thomas, 23 June 1949.
[113] CPA, CCO 1/7/534, Merioneth Basic Report, 13 June 1949.
[114] Aubel, 'Welsh Conservatism', p. 99.
[115] CPA, CCO 1/7/511, Little to Thomas, 2 April 1949.
[116] CPA, CCO 1/8/511, Cardigan Basic Report, 31 August 1950; CPA, PUB 229/9/17, George Little election address, Cardigan, 1950.
[117] P. J. Madgwick, Non Griffiths and Valerie Walker, *The Politics of Rural Wales: A Study of Cardiganshire* (London: Hutchinson and Co, 1973), p. 215; CPA, CCO 1/9/511, Garmonsway to Watson, 30 September 1951.

A MINISTER FOR WELSH AFFAIRS

Despite the party's presentational issues in the Welsh-speaking heartlands of Wales, this period did at least witness the Conservatives engaging proactively with specific policy for the nation. The party knew that its un- or even anti-Welsh image was grounded in a long period of history, outlined briefly in this book's introduction. Regardless of differing opinions on this issue, it is fair to say that the landed gentry of the nineteenth century were by no means promoters of any distinctive sense of Welsh nationhood.[118] As prime minister in the inter-war years, Stanley Baldwin attempted to make the party's appeal more Welsh. As Geraint Thomas has shown, Baldwin – who had an important Welsh-speaking special adviser – claimed a knowledge of Welsh culture, incorporating old Nonconformist loyalties in Wales into his wider 'Christian politics' (a bold move in an era when David Lloyd George, the unrivalled master of capturing the old Nonconformist vote, was still active).[119] In a speech made to the Conservative Party's Central Council in 1951, the Chairman of the Merioneth Conservative Association outlined how opposition propaganda portrayed the Conservatives as 'never likely to take the slightest interest in Wales and the special interests of the Welsh nation'. He continued that 'it is the more damaging because so far as the past is concerned there is a great element of truth in it'.[120] And that was coming from a Conservative.

By the early 1950s, however, the party could claim that this sort of attitude was in the past, not least because it created, in 1951, the first central government position relating to Wales: the

---

[118] See Tomos Dafydd Davies, 'A Tale of Two Tories?: The British and Canadian Conservative Parties and the National Question' (unpublished PhD thesis, Aberystwyth University, 2011), p. 11; Andrew Edwards, *Labour's Crisis: Plaid Cymru, the Conservatives, and the Decline of the Labour Party in North-West Wales, 1960–74* (Cardiff: University of Wales Press, 2011), p. 25; Kenneth O. Morgan, 'Swansea West', in his *Modern Wales: Politics, Places and People* (Cardiff: University of Wales Press, 1995), pp. 300–1.

[119] Thomas, 'The Conservative Party', 891, 895.

[120] CPA, CCO 2/2/17, Central Council 1951, motion 13, text of speech made by the Chairman of the Merioneth Conservative Association.

Minister for Welsh Affairs. The party's critical re-assessment of itself after the war also included the subject of Wales, and how much autonomy was available to it.[121] Both the severity of the inter-war depression, and the hardship of the war itself, had led some to call for a stronger voice representing Welsh interests at cabinet level. There had been long discussions over the issue, culminating in 1937–8 when the Liberal Party put forward proposals for a Secretary of State for Wales.[122] Some Labour MPs made similar calls, with the South Wales Regional Council of Labour supporting these proposals during the war.[123] Alongside this, the movement known as *Undeb Cymru Fydd* (The New Wales Union), run by middle-class Welsh intellectuals, was established in 1941. Its aim was to safeguard what its leadership perceived as a threat to the social, linguistic and educational interests of Wales.[124] Members of the relatively new Plaid Cymru, like a young Gwynfor Evans, argued more forcefully for the importance of recognising Wales's distinctiveness, saying in 1945 that 'unless Wales is recognised as a nation for the purposes of Government, she cannot hope to live'.[125]

More important than all these forces, however, was the attitude of the new Labour government. Its MPs from Wales were divided on the subject of governmental representation for Wales. That split was broadly along two lines: those who were Welsh speaking and represented rural constituencies, like Goronwy Roberts, MP for Caernarfon, were more in favour of offices for Wales, such as a Secretary of State. Meanwhile, those from the industrial south, like Aneurin Bevan, were less so.[126] The party's

[121] J. Graham Jones, 'The Parliament for Wales Campaign, 1950–1956', *Welsh History Review*, 16/2 (1992), 207.
[122] James McConnel, '"Sympathy Without Relief is Rather like Mustard Without Beef": Devolution, Plaid Cymru, and the Campaign for a Secretary of State for Wales, 1937–1938', *Welsh History Review*, 22/3 (2005), 535–57.
[123] R. Merfyn Jones and Ioan Rhys Jones, 'Labour and the Nation', in Tanner, Williams and Hopkin, *The Labour Party*, p. 248.
[124] Jones, 'The Parliament', 211.
[125] CPA, PUB 229/8/16, Gwynfor Evans election address, Merioneth, 1945.
[126] Jones, 'The Parliament', 207. Roberts co-founded *Llais Llafur*, a broadsheet that argued for a Secretary of State for Wales.

leadership, which believed in centralisation, were also lukewarm on the matter, with Prime Minister Clement Attlee and his deputy Herbert Morrison rejecting calls for a Secretary of State for Wales outright. For them, such a minister would 'isolate' the nation, not promote its needs.[127] Labour did, however, set up the Council for Wales and Monmouthshire, an appointed body that advised the government on Welsh matters.[128] In response, Conservatives standing for election in Wales did not ignore this issue. Especially in those more Welsh-speaking or rural areas, prospective Tory candidates, like Caernarvon Boroughs's David Price-White, made frequent speeches advocating the formulation of distinct policy for Wales. He even did so at the party's annual conference.[129] In some seats like Cardiff South East, where a young James Callaghan was fighting his first election campaign in the city, the Conservative candidate emphasised the need for a Secretary of State.[130]

Although a Secretary of State was not official Conservative policy, some candidates' rhetoric was undoubtedly a response to wider political discussions and a desire not to be seen to be ignoring Wales. These discussions were also bound up with the wider critique of socialism. As Matthew Cragoe has demonstrated, the Tories believed in powers trickling down from central government to local areas – from Whitehall to town halls – in contrast to the more centralising instincts of Labour. In resisting 'the aggressive imperialism of the Soviet Union abroad' during a period when Cold War tensions were ratcheting up, and tying this in with a critique of Labour's wish to build up a supposedly over-mighty state at home, devolution of powers was presented as a way of decentralising government and spreading power out into the

---

[127] Jones, 'The Parliament', 208; Martin Johnes, *Wales: England's Colony? The Conquest, Assimilation and Re-creation of Wales* (Cardigan: Parthian, 2019), p. 147.

[128] Wyn Thomas, *Hands off Wales: Nationhood and Militancy* (Llandysul: Gomer Press, 2013), p. xiv.

[129] Cragoe, 'Defending', p. 165; Jones and Jones, 'Labour and the Nation', p. 249; CPA, PUB 229/8/16, Price White election address, Caernarvon Boroughs, 1945.

[130] CPA, PUB 229/8/16, Colonel Sir Arthur Evans election address, Cardiff South, 1945.

country.[131] For Churchill, speaking at a huge rally in Cardiff, devolving some powers to Wales would act as an alternative to Labour's 'handcuffs of centralisation'. It is in this context that senior Tories began talking of 'local patriotism', linking it with 'a restoration of individual freedom'. Something like a Minister for Welsh Affairs would also typify, in Churchill's words, the nation's 'distinctive needs'.[132] Conservatives had some experience in the field. The party had created a Scottish Office as far back as 1885 and had long believed that an effective way of demonstrating their 'pro-Scottish' credentials was to grant more administrative devolution to Scotland.[133] There had been a National Conservative Council for Wales and Monmouthshire since 1921, established with the purpose of allowing the Conservatives to 'speak with a more unified voice on political issues specifically affecting the Principality'.[134]

It is in these contexts that the party's announcement of a Minister for Welsh Affairs must therefore be understood. Such a thing was not quite the 'startling departure' from previous ways of thinking that one historian presented it as being.[135] Nevertheless, it was highly significant, and it is worth scrutinising the circumstances that led to the pledge in the first place.[136] A key moment happened in 1947, when the party's Research Department sent their Wales policy specialist, a highly intelligent young brigadier, on a journey around the nation to report back on what was happening there. He was Enoch Powell, who had risen to be one of the youngest-ever professors of Greek (at the

[131] Matthew Cragoe, 'We Like', 967.
[132] Cragoe, 'We Like', 973; Cragoe, 'Defending', p. 165.
[133] James Mitchell, *Conservatives and the Union: A Study of Conservative Party Attitudes to Scotland* (Edinburgh: Edinburgh University Press, 1990), p. vii.
[134] Aubel, 'Welsh Conservatism', p. 22; Matthew Cragoe, 'Conservatives, "Englishness" and "Civic Nationalism" Between the Wars', in Duncan Tanner, Chris Williams, W. P. Griffith and Andrew Edwards (eds), *Debating Nationhood and Governance in Britain, 1885–1939: Perspectives From the Four Nations* (Manchester: Manchester University Press, 2006), p. 200.
[135] Jones, 'The Parliament', 209.
[136] For some details, see Cragoe, 'We like', 971–2; Cragoe, 'Defending', p. 165; Simon Heffer, *Like the Roman: The Life of Enoch Powell* (London: Phoenix Giant, 1998), p. 164.

age of twenty-five, at the University of Sydney). He would go on to become a long-serving MP, infamous for his 1968 speech on immigration and as one of the most prominent voices against the Common Market after Britain joined it in 1973. Although not Welsh, Powell had ties 'of study and affection' to the nation, and could speak Welsh fluently, alongside many other languages.[137] His Wales tour took in almost every part of the country and he wrote up two reports on the 'industrial' and the 'rural' scenes there.

Powell's work demonstrated his trademark sharpness of mind. He noted that many Welsh seats, especially the rural ones, would be 'solidly Conservative' were they in England. He argued that there existed in Wales a distinct political dynamic. Opponents of the Conservatives played upon the fact that social, religious and cultural factors meant the Tories were often perceived as strangers there.[138] He also noted that patterns of living, and a sense of community, were especially strong in Wales, with people in industrial areas 'cling[ing] to their pithead settlements, or house rows, however unsatisfactory, with a more than aboriginal attachment'. He continued that 'a policy which disregards these prejudices, inconvenient and hampering though they may be, will evoke little response in South Wales'.[139] He understood, however, how and why parts of Wales were different. Powell concluded that Wales had both special 'needs' and a special 'outlook', which had to be addressed more specifically by the Conservatives.[140] Although he warned against over-promising anything for fear of looking like the party was 'vote-catching', he stressed that many people in rural Wales 'use habitually and for preference a language [that is] not English'. Therefore, agriculture and rural roads needed support, and better facilities for the use of Welsh were called for.[141] In the 'terra incognita' of 'industrial Wales' Powell called for a new kind

[137] Quoted in Heffer, *Like the Roman*, p. 164.
[138] CPA, CCO 4/2/183, Report on Rural Wales, 20 February 1948, p. 2.
[139] CPA, CCO 4/2/183, Report on Industrial Wales, 26 May 1948, p. 9.
[140] CPA, CCO 4/2/183, Report on Rural Wales, 20 February 1948, p. 3.
[141] CPA, CCO 4/2/183, Report on Rural Wales, 20 February 1948, pp. 3, 4–6, 8–10.

of economic policy that was both 'radical and fresh', which should pivot on better housing, education (because 'industrial problems [cannot] be solved or even understood except in the context of social conditions') and industrial diversification.[142]

Perhaps the most important thrust of Powell's argument, however, rested on the idea of representation. Whilst many of the significant things that his report mentioned about industry and the economy sounded quite a lot like what the Labour government was proposing, this element was different. Powell thought that a dedicated government Minister for Welsh Affairs was necessary. It became official policy in the late 1940s, announced by R. A. Butler in the House of Commons and at the party's 1948 conference in Llandudno. Powell's report was formally written up in the fully bilingual pamphlet called *The Charter for Wales*, which was released on 1 March, 1949 – St David's Day.[143] It was part of a series of other documents, the most prominent being the *Industrial Charter*, which formed the basis of the Conservative's policy positions in the late 1940s. It is significant that one was devoted specifically to Wales, sitting alongside other documents on big topics like agriculture and imperial policy.[144] The pledge of a minister, alongside warm words for Welsh industry, hill farmers, culture and the language, featured in the party's 1950 and 1951 general election manifestos.[145]

When the Tories won in 1951, they duly introduced the Minister for Welsh Affairs, with senior party figures presenting the post as the 'watchdog for Wales'.[146] Whilst the minister role was not in itself likely to have been responsible for improved fortunes for the party in Wales, the fact that it was part of a wider popular

---

[142] CPA, CCO 4/2/183, Report on Industrial Wales, 26 May 1948, pp. 2–3.
[143] Heffer, *Like the Roman*, p. 124; Powell did not write the Welsh version himself, despite his skills.
[144] John Barnes and Richard Cockett, 'The Making of Party Policy', in Seldon and Ball, *Conservative Century*, pp. 367–8.
[145] Kenneth O. Morgan, *Rebirth of a Nation: Wales 1880–1980* (Oxford: Oxford University Press, 1982), p. 379.
[146] CPA, CCO 500/24/101, Anglesey speech by Lord Woolton, 2 August 1951.

programme of 'freedom' and decentralisation is important.[147] The position was initially filled by the Home Secretary, David Maxwell Fyfe, or 'Dai Bananas' as he supposedly became known in Wales (Dai being a shortened version of David, and Fyffes a banana importing company).[148] Privately, party officials cheered that they had managed to wrongfoot their Labour and Liberal opponents by coming up with their own coherent message on this subject. The party's position was announced while Labour was reviewing a decision about setting up a flimsier-sounding Advisory Council for Wales.[149] Many more Tories mentioned Welsh-specific policies in their election addresses at the beginning of the 1950s. In 1950, eighteen did so, compared with only five Labour candidates.[150] Conservatives would no doubt have been pleased with coverage from (admittedly loyal) newspapers like the *Herald of Wales* and the *Western Mail*. The former noted that 'the party has suddenly walked very firmly onto the Welsh political stage – so firmly, indeed, that it may cause much anguish in the other parties and movements'.[151] The latter argued in an editorial that 'the Socialists have nothing comparable to offer'.[152] No doubt buoyed by such coverage, party officials thought that Powell had 'more than justified the expense of [his] journey'.[153] Powell was certainly the key intellectual driving force behind convincing the party that Wales needed specific governmental representation. In arguing that a minister was an essential, or a sine qua non, as he put it, he is no doubt a significant architect of administrative devolution in Wales, if only because he helped create the

---

[147] Cragoe, 'Defending', p. 167.

[148] It is hard to find any original evidence of this name being used, but it is quoted in many works of secondary literature, and memoirs. See, for example, Morgan, *Rebirth*, p. 379; Ramsden, *The Age of Churchill*, p. 246; David Rosser, *A Dragon in the House* (Llandysul: Gomer, 1987), p. 66.

[149] John Gilbert Evans, *Devolution in Wales: Claims and Responses, 1937–1979* (Cardiff: University of Wales Press, 2006), p. 39.

[150] Figures compiled by the author using CPA material.

[151] 'Just What is the New Tory Offer to Wales?' and 'A Plan Labour Cannot Oppose', *Herald of Wales*, 2 June 1951.

[152] 'Tory Offer to Wales', *Western Mail*, 26 January 1950.

[153] CPA, CCO 4/2/183, Hopkinson to Pierssene re Enoch Powell, 28 January 1948.

conditions that spurred on further processes over the next several decades.[154] A post like a Minister for Welsh Affairs would probably have been created eventually, but Powell was able to articulate the case for it, deploying his ability to understand both Wales and the Welsh language (although as an Ulster Unionist MP much later in his career, he would become increasingly hostile to the idea of devolution).[155]

Alongside ministerial representation, the party's broader self-presentation in Wales shifted in the early 1950s, too. Whilst the party's Wales Area Office officials were the first to grumble about the 'emotional Celtic temperament' of the Welsh people, which was responsible for hampering Conservative fortunes, they also recognised that the party had made mistakes by not grappling with 'Welsh problems and . . . history' closely enough in the past.[156] Therefore, the party began producing things like the film 'Land of my Fathers', which portrayed Conservatives as capable of protecting 'the interests of all Wales'.[157] After the film was shown to the Cardiff North Conservative Association, the *Western Mail* commented that it 'features a wide range of activities in Wales. Industrial and rural scenes are admirably balanced'. The narrator even had 'a convincing Welsh accent'.[158] In the inter-war years, the party had been notoriously bad at supplying Welsh-speaking seats with bilingual literature.[159] It got better in this respect at the 1945 and 1950 elections, but there was a real upsurge in the number of bilingual posters and campaigning material in 1951, recognising in the process aspects of Welsh difference.[160] In subtle

---

[154] CPA, CCO 4/2/183, Report on Rural Wales, 20 February 1948, p. 9.

[155] Paul Corthorn, 'Enoch Powell, Ulster Unionism, and the British Nation', *Journal of British Studies*, 51/4 (2012), pp. 967–97.

[156] CPA, CCO 500/24/101, Wales and Monmouthshire Area 1951 General Election Report, undated, *c*.November 1951; CPA, CCO 500/24/56, CPC Wales and Monmouth Area General Election 1950 Report.

[157] CPA, CRD 2/45/4, Draft introduction to 'Land of my Fathers', undated.

[158] 'Wales is Theme of Tory Film', *Western Mail*, 4 January 1950.

[159] Thomas, *Popular*, p. 213.

[160] CPA, CCO 500/24/101, General Director's memorandum, 31 October 1951.

but very noticeable ways, the Conservatives were helping to make specifically Welsh issues more prominent.

However, we must be careful not to over-egg this. Powell himself wrote that Wales 'should be treated as a separate entity *when the occasion demanded*' (my emphasis).[161] It is almost certain that he and all senior Conservative figures in this period thought that there were only relatively few such occasions. Linguistically and culturally, parts of Wales were different, although Powell also noted that some of Wales's border constituencies (all in so-called 'British Wales') felt hardly 'Welsh' in this sense at all. In wider economic and social terms, Wales was part of Britain and we must be cautious of making direct links between Powell, the Minister for Welsh Affairs post and the politics of twenty-first-century Wales, with its own devolved parliament. Similarly, although Anthony Eden told a large crowd at Merthyr Tydfil in 1951 that 'Wales has her own way of life', he also stressed the importance of the United Kingdom, whilst noting that 'unity is not uniformity'.[162] Conservative politicians in Wales constantly did things that symbolised the Britishness of their outlook, like hoisting Union Jacks above their constituency Conservative clubs.[163] As the historian Paul Ward has written, Welshness was distinctive, but in this period is was encompassed by Britishness.[164] Although it was never expressed intellectually so at the time, the party could convincingly have claimed it was acting within good unionist principles, recognising the distinctiveness of Wales whilst ensuring it remained closely tied to the United Kingdom.[165]

---

[161] Evans, *Devolution*, p. 49.
[162] '"New and Just Status" if offered to Wales', *Western Mail*, 12 October 1951.
[163] 'We Can Return 12 Tories', *Western Mail*, 16 January 1950.
[164] Paul Ward, *Unionism in the United Kingdom, 1918–1974* (Basingstoke: Palgrave Macmillan, 2005), p. 90.
[165] Richard Finlay, 'Thatcherism, Unionism and Nationalism: A Comparative Study of Scotland and Wales', in Ben Jackson and Robert Saunders (eds), *Making Thatcher's Britain* (Cambridge: Cambridge University Press, 2012), p 170.

GRASSROOTS LEADERSHIP

Post-war rethinking by the Conservatives also had an important impact on the rank-and-file membership, a body that tells us a great deal about both the party, more broadly defined, and wider Welsh society in this period. These people became a strategic focal point for the central party in the immediate post-war years, with a huge upsurge in numbers of people joining the Tories. Historians have differed in the emphasis they place on who or what was responsible for this, including their interpretations of the role of Lord Woolton, who was made Conservative Party Chairman by Churchill in July 1946. Woolton certainly set about making significant changes to the organisation of the party, although much of what he is credited for had been put into motion before he took up his post, including in the pre-war years.[166] A key plank of the 'new' strategy concerned growing the party's grassroots membership, which in turn would help raise significant funds for the Conservatives. Very successful recruitment drives, in the form of 'Operation Doorstep' in 1946 and 'Operation Doorknocker' in 1948, temporarily boosted the number of paid-up members of the party in Britain to approximately 2.25 million.[167] At its peak in the early 1950s, the party had three million members throughout Britain, compared to Labour's one million, although trade union membership compensated for that disparity.[168] This represented the Conservative's best-ever membership numbers, and it made the party able to boast the largest membership figures for any political party in post-war Western Europe.[169] In

---

[166] Bale, *The Conservatives*, pp. 43–4; Anthony Seldon, 'Conservative Century', in Seldon and Ball, *Conservative Century*, p. 42; Ramsden, *The Age of Churchill*, p. 103.

[167] Bale, *The Conservatives*, p. 18.

[168] Paul Whiteley, Patrick Seyd and Jeremy Richardson, *True Blues: The Politics of Conservative Party Membership* (Oxford: Clarendon Press, 1994), p. 2; Gidon Cohen and Lewis Mates, 'Grassroots Conservatism in Post-War Britain: A View From the Bottom Up', *History*, 98/330 (2013), 202.

[169] Patrick Seyd and Paul Whiteley, 'Conservative Grassroots: An Overview', in Steve Ludlam and Martin J. Smith (eds), *Contemporary British Conservatism* (London: Macmillan, 1996), p. 63.

Wales, these numbers were sometimes impressive. The Barry constituency association, for example, has drawn the attention of British historians because of its 'astonishing' membership figure of 11,000 in the early 1950s, which was nearly half the Conservative vote at the 1951 general election.[170] This kind of number was akin to numbers in English Home Counties seats, like solidly Conservative Maidstone.[171]

Those people who led these associations are worth scrutinising in some detail because, in volunteering to organise, coordinate and advertise the party, they give some sense of what Conservatism 'on the ground' in Wales would have looked and sounded like. Sitting at the head of these associations was usually a symbolic figure in the form of a President, a role which was particular to Conservative associations, as there was no equivalent figure in the other main parties.[172] Even for the Tories, however, the President was 'normally a titular position held uncontroversially by a person of prominence'.[173] In the immediate post-1945 years, Conservative association presidents were a hangover from the inter-war years and even the late nineteenth century. Many of them were aristocratic.[174] Even though the landed elite's retreat from Tory politics had been happening since the beginning of the twentieth century, and especially as a result of the First World War, they still continued to 'contribute handsomely' to Conservative associations, offering 'patronage and guidance'.[175] The tail end of this process could be witnessed in the late 1940s. The presidents of each Welsh constituency's Conservative association in 1948 are outlined in table 5.

---

[170] Ramsden, *The Age of Churchill*, p. 112.
[171] Ball, *Portrait*, p. 168.
[172] Ball, Thorpe and Worley, 'Elections', pp. 8–9.
[173] Cohen and Mates, 'Grassroots', 212.
[174] Ball, Thorpe and Worley, 'Elections', p. 12. For an excellent overview of the links between the landed elite and local Tory politics in Wales in the inter-war period, see Williams, 'The Conservative Party in North-East Wales', particularly chapter one.
[175] Gerard Charmley, 'The House of Dynevor and Conservative Politics, 1910–1939', *The Conservative Party History Journal*, 1/9 (2009), 29, 32.

Constituency	President
Aberavon	The Earl of Jersey
Aberdare	Gwilym Jones
Anglesey	The Marquess of Anglesey
Barry	Sir Ivor B. Thomas
Bedwellty	Viscount Tredegar
Brecon and Radnor	Alderman G. R. Davies
Caernarfon	Lord Penrhyn
Caerphilly	The Earl of Plymouth
Cardiff North	Arthur Meggitt
Cardiff South East	The Countess of Plymouth
Cardiff West	Mr A. McTaggart Short
Cardigan	Sir G. Fossett Roberts
Carmarthen	Lord Dynevor
Conway	Lord Penrhyn
Denbigh	Sir Robert Williams-Wynn
Ebbw Vale	A. S. Huxley
Flint East	Hugh Pritchard
Flint West	Lt Col. W Franklin Bevan
Llanelli	Major H. E. Trubshaw
Merioneth	Sir Charles Phibbs
Monmouth	Mrs Lionel Whitehead
Newport	A. M. C. Jenour
Ogmore	The Earl of Dunraven
Pembrokeshire	Rt Hon. the Earl of Cawdor
Pontypool	Albert Truman
Rhondda East	Sir Gwilym Rowlands
Wrexham	Sir Watkin Williams-Wynn/The Dowager Lady Williams-Wynn

Table 5: Conservative association presidents in constituencies that information was available for, *c.*1948.

Such upper-class patrons were often a feature of Conservative politics in the Home Counties of England. As one historian of the party wrote, it was not unusual for a new Tory candidate to turn up in a seat and find that 'their President was a Duke and their chairman a Lord Lieutenant of the County'. This was also a feature in Wales too, where more presidents were titled than the average in England at around the same time.[176] As we have seen, Labour were already making the political weather in Wales, partly by casting the Conservatives as out of touch and their representatives incompatible with industrial areas and working-class people. At least part of the Conservatives' problem in Wales was indeed their unrelatability to ordinary voters, and these presidents were, to some extent, a reflection of that. However, amongst Conservative-minded people, at least, such figures give a sense of the admiration for status, title and hierarchy that grassroots Conservatives clearly valued. In an era before things like the rise of satirical comedy, consumerism, youth culture and the end of Empire had fundamentally undermined the concept of deference, a certain appreciation of hierarchy was clearly on display.[177] To demonstrate this, when Carmarthen's president, Lord Dynevor, died in 1956, his obituary in *The Times* was headed 'Welsh Feudal Chieftain'.[178] He was not an outlier. The young Eton-educated seventh Marquess of Anglesey, for example, stressed that an ancestor of his had fought bravely at the battle of Waterloo. His family home was a neo-Gothic mansion, Plas Newydd, that overlooked the Menai Strait and contained a small military museum within it.[179] He was one of seven Conservative association presidents in this period who had attended Britain's most prestigious public school, Eton College, and several more had gone to other highly exclusive institutions.[180] Caerphilly's association's

---

[176] Ramsden, *The Age of Churchill*, p. 124; Ball, *Portrait*, p. 148.
[177] Florence Sutcliffe-Braithwaite, *Class, Politics, and the Decline of Deference in England, 1968–2000* (Oxford: Oxford University Press, 2018), p. 9.
[178] 'Lord Dynevor: Welsh Feudal Chieftain', *The Times*, 9 June 1956.
[179] 'The 7th Marquis of Anglesey', *Daily Telegraph*, 15 July 2013.
[180] The other Old Etonians were: the Marquess of Anglesey, the Earl of Jersey, Viscount Tredegar, Lord Penrhyn, the Earl of Plymouth, the Earl of Dunraven.

DEFEAT AND THE RESPONSE TO LABOUR, 1945–1951   75

president was the young Earl of Plymouth, who was responsible for giving St Fagan's Castle to the National Museum of Wales.[181]

Many of those still heading constituency parties were members of established, old, political families. From the very beginning of associational politics in the aftermath of the 1832 'Great' Reform Act, politics was based on patronage and money supplied by wealthy aristocrats.[182] The Cawdors in Pembrokeshire, the Williams-Wynns in Denbighshire, the Penrhyns in north-west Wales or the Tredegars in Monmouthshire were all names associated with this practice.[183] Hence, it is significant that the Earl of Cawdor was Pembrokeshire's president after 1945 (although he also spent most of his time in Scotland),[184] whilst Denbighshire's president was the eighty-six-year-old Sir Robert Williams-Wynn, 9th Baronet. He had been Lord Lieutenant of Denbighshire and, for over fifty years, the Master of the Flint and Denbigh Foxhounds.[185] The wonderfully named Windham Wyndham-Quin, also known as the Earl of Dunraven, was the ninety-one-year-old president of the Ogmore constituency, which he had geographical ties with: his home – Dunraven Castle – was close by. He was from an old political family that had contested elections in Wales in the early nineteenth century and he took a 'life-time interest in Welsh culture and customs'.[186] Clear links with industry and capital were evident across the board, again emphasising the typically Tory profiles of these presidents. Wyndham-Quin had been a coal pit owner and Lord Penrhyn came from a long line of slate-quarry owners.[187] Major H. E. Trubshaw owned the Western Tinplate works in Llanelli and was that constituency's president.[188] A. M. C.

[181] 'Welsh Castle to be Outdoor Museum', *Daily Telegraph*, 23 February 1946.
[182] Matthew Cragoe, *Politics, Culture and National Identity in Wales, 1832–1886* (Oxford: Oxford University Press, 2004), pp. 84, 101.
[183] Cragoe, *Politics*, p. 88, 99; Aubel, 'Welsh Conservatism', p. 24.
[184] 'Earl Cawdor', *The Times*, 12 January 1970.
[185] 'Sir Watkin Williams Wynn', *The Times*, 14 May 1949; 'Sir Watkin Williams Wynn', *The Times*, 27 November 1951.
[186] Cragoe, *Politics*, p. 218; 'Obituary: Earl of Dunraven', *Daily Telegraph*, 24 October 1952.
[187] Johnes, *Wales: England's*, pp. 81–2.
[188] See *https://www.llanellich.org.uk/files/192-brian-trubshaw*. Accessed 8 December 2016.

Jenour, in Newport, was also a prominent businessman.[189] Cardiff West's president, Arthur McTaggart Short, was a successful (and very wealthy) businessman, shop owner and future president of Cardiff's Chamber of Trade, who was also involved in other groups like the Boy Scouts.[190]

Connections with groups like the Scouts, but also with parts of wider community and civic life, including Justices of the Peace (JPs), or ceremonial roles like Sheriff, were common.[191] Much of this echoes the arguments made by Mathew Cragoe regarding political figures promoting a sense of 'civic nationalism' in this period, where common state institutions, like parliament and the monarchy, could be used to promote a sense of Britishness and, in some parts of Wales, resulted in Welsh people becoming invested in wider British networks.[192] This was especially relevant in the wake of the Second World War, where a sense of national unity was often on display.[193] It is worth widening out Cragoe's thesis to suggest that these common institutions could also involve things like the Church (and to an extent chapels), as well as organisations like the Boy Scouts, the Red Cross, the Women's Institute, the British Legion or the Rotary – many of which, although non-partisan and part of a much wider world of civic sociability, were nonetheless bastions of conservative ideals.[194] Even though president figures would often have been accused of being the voice of the old Anglican landlords, their presence can also be seen as evidence of this wider interest in common groups or institutions, many of them respectable, or charitable, which formed part of

---

[189] 'Dividends for 400 Workers', *Daily Telegraph*, 29 October 1949.
[190] 'Mr A. McTaggart Short', newspaper and date unknown.
[191] Ball, *Portrait*, pp. 148–9.
[192] Cragoe, 'Conservatives', pp. 198–9; Cragoe, 'Defending', p.180; Philip Lynch, *The Politics of Nationhood: Sovereignty, Britishness and Conservative Politics* (Basingstoke: Macmillan, 1999), p. 2; Janet Johnson, 'Did Organisation Really Matter? Party Organisation and Conservative Electoral Recovery, 1945–1959', *Twentieth Century British History*, 14/4 (2003), 411.
[193] Johnes, *Wales: England's*, p. 148.
[194] Helen McCarthy, 'Parties, Voluntary Associations and Democratic Politics in Interwar Britain', *The Historical Journal*, 50/4 (2007), 892, 901.

the architecture of broader British life.[195] Whilst this would have had less impact in industrial 'Welsh Wales', or in the Welsh-speaking heartlands, so-called 'British Wales' would have been more receptive.[196]

The majority of people outlined in table 5 were plugged into wider community life via such networks. Sir Charles Phibbs was typical in being a local JP and the Sheriff of Merioneth, for example.[197] Cardigan's Sir George Fossett Roberts would later become President of the National Library of Wales.[198] Some had served with distinction in one of the two world wars and had 'a good war record'. Several Presidents, such as Rhondda East's Sir Gwilym Rowlands, were ex-MPs – although Rowlands, who we met earlier, was a local man 'from old Rhondda stock' who had served as MP for Flintshire during the inter-war years.[199] Interestingly, Hugh Pritchard, from East Flint, and Pontypool's Albert Truman were described as a trade union official and a 'local tradesman' respectively.[200] However, we should not let this pair obscure the fact that there were more knights of the realm and more old Etonians filling such positions than people with ordinary working-class jobs.

The patronage that this elite continued to offer local Conservatives was quite blatant, with the party utilising their names, fortunes, wealth, rank and title.[201] This is obvious from the fact that they continued to stay in post into old age and that things like constituency correspondence often had the president's name prominently displayed on letter headings. Displays of generosity from some of these people were significant, sometimes replicating the role of a pre-war parliamentary candidate in an era when

---

[195] Cragoe, 'Defending', p. 180; Lynch, *The Politics*, p. 2; Johnson, 'Did Organisation', 411.
[196] McKibbin, 'Class', pp. 262, 284–5.
[197] 'Obituary', *Daily Telegraph*, 4 July 1964; Ball, *Portrait*, p. 269.
[198] 'Sir George Fossett Roberts', *The Times*, 10 April 1954.
[199] Edwards, *The Good Patch*, pp. 92–3.
[200] CPA, CCO, 1/8/516, East Flint Basic Report, 31 August 1950.
[201] Johnson, 'Did Organisation', 412; David Cannadine, *Aspects of Aristocracy: Grandeur and Decline in Modern Britain* (London: Yale University Press, 1994), p. 1.

a prospective MP was allowed to spend their own money more liberally in a seat.[202] The Marquess of Anglesey, for example, gave the agent in the constituency that bore his name a 'new Morris 8 car, free of all charge' in 1948.[203] Car ownership in the late 1940s was uncommon, with fewer than two million owned nationwide, but it would have proved invaluable for that role.[204] Even if the assets of this elite were dwindling or under threat, it was commonplace in the 1940s and early 1950s for many presidents to show off the symbols of their prestige as a means of drawing people's attention to the Conservatives. This was visible in all corners of Wales, be it the 'grand parade of the Flint and Denbigh Hounds' by the Williams-Wynn family for the Flintshire and Denbighshire annual fete; the opening up of Margam Castle by its owner (Mr David Evans-Bevan, described by the central party as 'rather a valuable person *financially* to us') in the Aberavon seat, which 2,000 people attended; or events in the grounds of country houses in north Wales, such as the Faenol Estate near Caernarfon, or at Brogyntyn Hall, owned by the prestigious Tory family the Ormsby-Gores (Lord Harlech) (see figure 3).[205]

However, in a sign that the presidency did not matter very much in the grand scheme of things, it was sometimes a role filled by people who did not have a strong connection with the area but who were willing for their names to be used in a ceremonial capacity. There is little evidence to suggest, for instance, that the ninth Earl of Jersey, a member of the famous Villiers family with an estate in Middlesex, ever went to the resolutely anti-Conservative Aberavon constituency even though

[202] This could also be the case for some Labour candidates. See Duncan Tanner, 'Labour and its membership', in Duncan Tanner, Pat Thane and Nick Tiratsoo (eds), *Labour's First Century* (Cambridge: Cambridge University Press, 2000), pp. 253–4.

[203] CPA, CCO 1/7/507, Anglesey Basic Report, c. 1949.

[204] Michael Pinto-Duschinsky, 'Bread and Circuses? The Conservatives in Office 1951–1964', in Vernon Bogdanor and Robert Skidelsky (eds), *The Age of Affluence 1951–1964* (London: Macmillan, 1970), p. 56; *Aberdare Leader*, 30 June 1945.

[205] CPA, CCO 1/8/527, Garmonsway to Watson, 20 June 1950; DRO, DD/PN/203, poster; CPA, CCO 1/8/527, Thomas to Lady Maxwell Fyfe, undated; 'In Memoriam: Sir David Evans-Bevan', *Daily Telegraph*, 1 October 1973.

Figure 3: A scene from a Conservative Party rally and fete at the country mansion, Brogyntyn Hall, owned by the Ormsby-Gore family, 1949.

he was nominally its president (although he was vaguely related, by marriage, to Lord Dynevor).[206] Sometimes, simply having 'a name', like the Earl of Jersey, associated with the constituency was most important. Other presidents were shunted into the position because of their old age which, far from giving them a sense of gravitas, meant they were 'of little use', as CCO often put it.[207] Mrs G. Williams, the President in Pontypridd in the early 1950s, had been 'a tremendous worker for the party for many years', but she was by this point 'over 90 years of age and very deaf'.[208] This implication that presidents had simply passed their prime is revealed by the fact that several of the people listed in table 5 were dead a couple of years after that information was compiled. Also spurring on change in this area were the policies of the Labour government after the war. High death-duties or leasehold reform forced many aristocrats to transfer their assets to tenants or

---

[206] Anthea Palmer, 'Obituary: the Earl of Jersey', *Independent*, 23 October 2011.
[207] CPA, CCO 1/8/513, Llanelli Basic Report, 20 September 1950.
[208] CPA, CCO 1/8/533, Pontypridd Basic Report, 28 September 1950.

property companies.[209] Penrhyn Castle, home of Lord Penrhyn, and its grounds, for example, were taken over by the Treasury in settlement of death duties in 1951.[210]

Unlike the president, an association's chairman was a much more significant role.[211] The chairman, who tended to be a local worthy, businessman or stalwart of the party, would conduct meetings and often set the standards of the association.[212] It was usually their job to ensure that the association functioned on a day-to-day basis and to set the expectations for its wider fundraising campaigns.[213] In the eyes of the party, and especially the Wales Area Office, 'first class' chairmen were a key ingredient for a strong, functioning association.[214] Similarly, those perceived to be bad at the job were the subject of concern. When Sir Charles Price, the Chairman of the Pembrokeshire Association and 'one of the biggest old muddlers I have ever come across' finally resigned the chairmanship of the association there in 1950, there was nothing short of delight in Central Office.[215] Many of these weaker chairmen, unsurprisingly, were found in those areas of 'Welsh Wales' where the party already struggled, compounding its problems there. In the late 1940s, such people were described as 'lack[ing] sufficient power of leadership' or 'not at all popular'.[216] There were apparently several 'dictators'.[217] This was hardly the way to foster an atmosphere where people would volunteer their

---

[209] David Cannadine, *The Decline and Fall of the British Aristocracy* (London: Papermac, 1996), pp. 638–9; David Cannadine, *Lords and Landlords: the Aristocracy and the Towns, 1774–1967* (Leicester: Leicester University Press, 1980), pp. 428–9.

[210] 'Penrhyn Castle for the Nation', *Western Mail*, 13 October 1951.

[211] Stuart Ball, *The Conservative Party and British Politics 1902–1951* (London: Longman, 1995), p. 22.

[212] Ball, Thorpe and Worely, 'Elections', p. 9.

[213] Stuart Ball, 'Local Conservatism and the Evolution of the Party Organisation', in Seldon and Ball, *Conservative Century*, p. 268; British Library Sound and Moving Image archive, C1688/18, Richard Bourne interview.

[214] CPA, CCO 1/8/512, Carmarthen Basic Report, 26 October 1950.

[215] CPA, CCO 1/8/542, Thomas to the GD, 17 July 1951; CPA, CCO 1/8/542, Maxse to Greville, 9 October 1950.

[216] CPA, CCO 1/7/518, Aberdare Basic Report, undated, c.1948.

[217] CPA, CCO 1/11/534, Caerphilly Basic Report, 13 November 1956; CPA, CCO 1/7/523, Rhondda East Basic Report, 11 July 1949; CPA, CCO 1/7/531, Neath Basic Report, July 1949.

time to work for the party. In the safe Labour seat of Bedwellty, in the Monmouthshire valleys, it was perhaps a fitting metaphor for the moribund state of the local association there that the 'unpopular' chairman was an undertaker.[218]

Seats like Bedwellty not only had Labour majorities of around 25,000 in the post-Second World War years, they also exhibited a labour culture, with both a big and a small 'l', that was not just expressed at election times but was embedded into everyday life. This was reflected in grassroots politics. These were areas where, as we have seen, Labour politics was woven into wider society and where a 'blue [Conservative] poster' in a window could invite 'a half brick into the sitting room'. In such places, people who did feel instinctively Conservative sometimes kept that feeling to themselves.[219] Sir Norman Lloyd-Edwards remembered growing up in Merthyr Tydfil in the 1940s, in a household that was almost certainly Conservative, but where his parents felt as if they could not admit their political allegiance.[220] Whilst the vast majority of political campaigning was peaceful, courteous and even good natured, violent incidents did demonstrate anti-Conservative feeling. In the 1945 general election the driver of one Conservative candidate's car was 'grabbed by the neck and nearly throttled . . . My face was cut and bruised; my tie was wrenched away and my collar was pulled off' when a group of demonstrators attacked him.[221] The Wales Area Agent noted in the late 1940s that people in coalmining constituencies were 'afraid to come out into the open and admit they are Conservative', or felt 'intimidated'.[222] (Ten years later, Francis Pym, the future Foreign Secretary, recalled being told in hushed tones by a woman in Rhondda West that she would vote Tory – before shooing him away because she did not

---

[218] CPA, CCO 1/8/537, Bedwellty Basic Report, c.October 1950.
[219] 'A busload of hope for Tryer Tuck', *Western Mail*, 1 May 1979 – this article referred to earlier days when such a fate seemed a possibility.
[220] Interview, Sir Norman Lloyd-Edwards, 7 July 2015.
[221] 'Cardiff Election Hooliganism', *Western Mail*, 20 June 1945.
[222] 'The Steelworkers who will vote for a Conservative', *Western Mail*, 6 October 1959; CPA, CCO 1/7/537, Bedwellty Basic Report, July 1949.

want the neighbours to see them talking to one another.)[223] Other party officials complained of the perennial problem of party supporters being 'reluctant to display party colours', even in seats held by Tories.[224] A sense of social stigma, interwoven with a long political tradition, almost certainly stopped some Tory supporters in Wales becoming members of, let alone campaigners for, the party.

Memories of the 1930s, and admiration for the way Labour had conducted itself in local government, solidified that loyalty. As a result, going against the grain, politically, by leading a local Conservative association in such places understandably resulted in people being labelled 'an eccentric' or 'a loon', in the words of the writer H. W. J. Edwards.[225] Hence, when an official from the Tredegar Electricity Board popped his head above the parapet and became chairman for the Conservatives in Ebbw Vale – Aneurin Bevan's seat – in the early 1950s, the Wales Area Office felt it necessary to report back to CCO that such an ordinary thing to do in this case meant he 'should be admired for his bravery'.[226] Here we see, through the prism of the grassroots, how a political culture shaped by Labour could become so dominant all the way down to associational level.

Nevertheless, in the years immediately after the war, the Conservative Party invested resources into Welsh seats, including these weak ones, as part of its wider strategy to improve the party's fortunes post-defeat. The focus was on facilitating leadership figures, hence almost all seats had professional help in the form of an agent. In fact, despite the tranche of weak seats in 'Welsh Wales', all of these, bar three, had a dedicated agent at the turn of the 1950s, which struck a contrast with the twenty-one seats that

---

[223] 'The Steelworkers who will vote for a Conservative', *Western Mail*, 6 October 1959.
[224] WPA, GB0210 CONLES, file 43, D. Elwyn Jones to All Clerks-in-charge, undated, 1974.
[225] Edwards, 'A tory in Wales', 24.
[226] CPA, CCO 1/8/538, Ebbw Vale Basic Report, 21 February 1951.

had no such person before the war.[227] Conventional wisdom had it that an agent was the glue that held a local organisation together, often acting as administrator, clerk, adviser, public relations officer and caretaker rolled into one.[228] Despite other political parties employing agents, historians consider the Conservatives' version as an especially strong organisational asset, and contemporaries considered this to be 'probably the most important development in party electoral organisation' during the period.[229] Agents were trained by the central party and then employed by constituencies, with some extra funds often coming from CCO if the association could not afford to pay the full salary. Many of the recruits were ex-servicemen who found themselves at a loose end after the war and who appreciated the kind of structure and discipline that came with the role.[230]

Again, scrutiny of the agent role reveals a range of things about the party in Wales, and about wider Welsh society. In 'Welsh Wales', where poor or unpopular leaders sometimes struggled to maintain even a skeleton association, agents often kept some sort of show on the road.[231] This sometimes meant doing so via force of personality, where the agent in question was described as being, for example, 'of the rough and ready type'.[232] On the other hand, however, it was easy to identify cracks in the party's Welsh machine by just how regularly agents across the country were criticised by the Area Office, prospective parliamentary candidates or grassroots leaders for being 'incompetent', 'inclined

---

[227] Ball, *Portrait*, p. 196; CPA, CCO 2/4/14, list of Agents. In 1950, 527 of 542 constituencies in England and Wales employed full-time agents: Bale, *The Conservatives*, p. 20.

[228] For comments on Labour agents, see Steven Fielding, 'The "Penny Farthing" Machine Revisited: Labour Party Members and Participation in the 1950s and 1960s', in Chris Pierson and Simon Tormey (eds), *Politics at the Edge: The PSA Yearbook 1999* (Basingstoke: Macmillan, 2000), p. 177; Sir John Major, 'Foreword', in Jean M. Lucas (ed.), *Between the Thin Blues Lines: The Agent's View of Politics* (Canada: Trafford, 2008), p. v; Anthony Kilminster, 'A Baptism of Fire', in Lucas, *Between*, p. 69.

[229] Nicholas, *The British*, p. 22; Bale, *The Conservatives*, p. 20; Ball, 'Local Conservatism', p. 284.

[230] Ramsden, *The Age of Churchill*, pp. 103–4.

[231] CPA, CCO 18/532, Garmonsway to Perrin, 16 January 1951.

[232] CPA, CCO 1/8/529, Caerphilly Basic Report, 20 February 1951.

to get excited and when in this mood is likely to upset volunteer workers', 'fat, idle, and incompetent' and 'too lazy to get out of bed'.[233] In one winnable seat, Denbigh, the agent supposedly refused to cooperate in any way with CCO, withholding basic information about the local association.[234] In the Barry seat, Jim Thomas described how, during a meeting he had with the association's chairman there, 'at high tea . . . I asked cheerfully how the Agent was doing and [he] became scarlet in the face and said he could not answer that question in front of his wife . . . [the agent is] much too bumptious and extremely rude'.[235]

Lack of finances were at the core of many of these problems. Whilst CCO could help fund an agent's salary, some of the money had to come from local associations. Neither could the central party tell agents where to go. The result was an old problem: CCO could not intervene to evenly distribute talent, meaning that marginal constituencies, which might have benefited from a strong agent, did not always receive one because such people stayed in safe seats where their job was more pleasant.[236] Hence, Wales with its lack of safe seats, simply did not attract, or could not afford, some of the best people. A typical kind of agent's salary in 1950 was £400 to £450 per annum in a 'sole constituency', potentially doubling to a maximum of £800 if the agent had more than two years' service under their belt, or experience of a general election.[237] Some in Wales were paid over £800 per year, like the agent in Conway, which was a considerable drain on that association's finances. The Cardigan constituency in the 1950s found that the agent's salary was fifteen times the cost of renting their offices and fourteen times what they spent on producing all

---

[233] CPA, CCO 1/7/529, Caerphilly Basic Report, c.July 1949; CPA, CCO 1/8/513, Llanelli Basic Report, 20 September 1950; CPA, CCO 1/9/542, Hare to Garmonsway, 25 March 1953; CPA, CCO 1/12/513, Notes on interview with J. H. Davies, 26 November 1957.
[234] CPA, CCO 1/8/514, Denbigh Basic Report, 31 August 1950.
[235] CPA, CCO 1/8/528, Thomas to Garmonsway, 2 October 1950.
[236] Bale, *The Conservatives*, p. 20; Ramsden, *The Age of Churchill*, p. 106. For the longer view, see Ball, *Portrait*, p. 175.
[237] Nicholas, *The British*, p. 25.

their political material. The association later dispensed with their agent altogether as a cost-cutting exercise.[238]

Despite their variation in quality, an agent's management, organisational and administrative skills were seen as particularly important. This is one of the reasons why – on top of the fact that they were able to get their agent's certificate after 1945 – so many in Wales in the immediate post-war years were women. Women, as we will see, played a huge role at the grassroots in the form of chief fundraisers and, sometimes, campaigners. They were conspicuous by their absence from the president and chairman roles, though, with notable but very rare exceptions. However, in the very early 1950s, there were seven women in the agent role in Wales. It is significant that the less public-facing and more administrative elements of the role were seen as suitable for a woman. Party figures were quite explicit about this, with Conway's Susan Risdale praised by the Wales Area Office for being 'excellent' because of her feminine 'gift . . . of administration'.[239] However, it is important to note that almost all the associations that had women agents during the early 1950s were (apart from Conway) hopeless seats for the Tories, located in so-called 'Welsh Wales'. The party was to some extent able to boast about the fact that, unlike Labour, which had one female agent in the Brecon and Radnor seat in 1950, it had seven performing the equivalent role.[240] But this was slightly disingenuous because almost all were working in seats the Conservatives would never win and were not being paid a great deal to do so. All seven were, unsurprisingly, a 'Miss' and probably young, although very scant records survive about any of them. We do know that the grassroots were often resistant to positions being taken up by a female in the first place.

---

[238] CPA, CCO 1/8/510, Finance sheet, 31 May 1950. For an overview of agents' salaries in the early 1950s, see Nicholas, *The British*, p. 25. CPA, CCO 1/12/539, Newport Basic Report, 14 April 1958; CPA, CCO 1/12/539, Oliver to the CCO, undated, c.1958.

[239] CPA, CCO 1/11/515, Conway Basic Report, 1 August 1956.

[240] 'Women as Party Agents', *Western Mail*, 22 February 1950. The seats were Cardiff South East (Miss Midgley), Pontypool (Miss Lewis), Aberavon (Miss Wilson), Abertillery (Miss Lewis), Pontypridd (Miss Hiley), Gower (Miss Maitland), and Anglesey (Miss Browning). All were unmarried and working in unwinnable constituencies.

Cardiff West drew up an advert for an agent in 1950, stipulating that only men should apply (although when a second version appeared later, the line about sex had been removed).[241] In discussions about an agent in the semi-industrial seat of Newport, it was noted that '*he* should be a *man* of strong personality' (my emphasis).[242]

Grassroots Conservative politics, therefore, remained strictly gendered in this immediate post-war period, with men filling the overwhelming bulk of public-facing roles and women doing much more administrative tasks, often in thankless circumstances. Many of these young women performing the agent role in the early 1950s also bore the brunt of the Wales Area Office's disapproval. Some of this criticism focused on their sex, patronisingly noting their bossiness, gossipy ways, or their irrationality. An official memo referred to one, for example, as 'an over earnest and wild young woman'.[243] In the Abertillery seat, a new agent, Miss Rhodes, was described as 'a tremendous dictator' who refused to let the Conservative candidate post his addresses via a free postal grant. She instead insisted that he walked everywhere for his own good. As part of information told 'very privately', it was also rumoured that this candidate and agent had fallen out over her 'flighty performance' with a 'prominent Conservative'. Jim Thomas, the party's Deputy Chairman, who had been born in Carmarthenshire, conveyed this gossip in his typically sardonic way, finding that it added to the fun of the story to write, 'so we flounder again on the rock of Celtic Romance!'[244] The 'dictator' theme cropped up quite regularly, with women agents almost always the recipient of such criticism.[245] In yet another example of female agents not living up to CCO's high standards, the agent in Anglesey, Miss Browning, was reprimanded for supposedly 'telling

---

[241] CPA, CCO 1/8/521, Draft advertisement for Agent, *c.*16 June 1950; CPA, CCO 1/8/521, Advertisement for Agent, 2 February 1951.

[242] CPA, CCO 500/8/4, 'Summary recommendations', *c.*January 1958.

[243] CPA, CCO 1/14, 521, Davies to the COO, 16 April 1962.

[244] CPA, CCO 1/8/536/1, Thomas to the GD, *c.*April 1950.

[245] See, for a slightly later example, CPA, CCO 1/14, 521, Davies to the COO, 16 April 1962.

tales' about the uncooperative nature of the Wales Area Office. CCO replied by saying that it was time 'we tore a strip off her [for] this sort of disloyalty'.[246] As with working-class parliamentary candidates, the records again suggest that the central party had no real sense of how to encourage or nurture those who would have been real assets for it.

WOMEN, YOUTH AND CLUBS

The tone that CCO took towards female agents does, however, paint only a very partial picture of the relationship between women and the Conservatives in this period. Historically, women across Britain were drawn to the party in huge numbers as voters, as we have seen, but also as members. From 1883, the Primrose League acted as a society for Tory women to campaign, canvas, undertake voter registration, even though they themselves were not enfranchised.[247] It also offered a wide range of social activities.[248] From 1918, the party began to take women particularly seriously, and women's branches at the grassroots level were encouraged to raise money through 'social fundraising'.[249] This continued after 1945, where women both voted Conservative and joined the party in greater numbers than men, responding particularly enthusiastically to the party's post-war recruitment drive.[250]

Records of exactly how many people did so are always tricky to pin down because local parties jealously guarded their data and the numbers they supplied are often suspiciously rounded. But there is good evidence of some quite staggering figures that also reveal the extent to which women members outnumbered men.

[246] CPA, CCO 1/7/507, Dodd to James, 27 June 1949.
[247] It was not exclusively a women's organisation. See Ball, *Portrait*, p. 153, for more details.
[248] Pugh, 'Popular Conservatism', 257, 259.
[249] Ramsden, *The Age of Balfour*, p. 251.
[250] Andrew Thorpe, *Parties at War: Political Organisation in Second World War Britain* (Oxford: Oxford University Press, 2009), p. 149.

In Swansea West in 1948, for example, the association had 350 male members, in contrast to 2,450 who were women.[251] Of the 11,000 members that the Barry Association boasted in the early 1950s, 6,000 of these were from women-only branches, 2,500 were from its joint branches (which were often made up of a majority of women), whilst 2,500 people were in the men-only branches.[252] Many of these members were actively interested in politics, too. The meeting to choose a candidate to fight the Cardiff South East seat in advance of the 1950 general election was attended by 1,100 people, many of them women.[253] When a young Peter Thorneycroft won the Monmouth seat in the 1945 by-election, his victory speech was delivered to a group 'largely composed of women', who he thanked for 'neglect[ing] their homes, their husbands and their children'.[254] Despite these huge numbers, Welsh women who were Conservatives are often sidelined from the narrative of political women in the twentieth century. When the celebrated historian Deirdre Beddoe gave the annual Welsh Political Archive lecture in 2004 on the subject of 'women and politics in twentieth century Wales', no mention was made of Tories.[255]

It is important to not get too carried away here. The Barry seat had nothing approaching 6,000-plus women on hand to organise local events, knock on doors, attend branch meetings or contribute to general political discussions. Nevertheless, the sources reveal a vibrant political culture amongst women in certain seats in 'British Wales', which sits in contrast to the general lack of enthusiasm identified amongst their respective Labour groups.[256] They had their own separate branches and leadership

---

[251] CPA, CCO, 1/7/521, Cardiff West Basic Report, 1949.

[252] CPA, CCO 1/8/528, Barry Basic Report, 21 February 1951; Ramsden, *The Age of Churchill*, p. 112.

[253] WPA, GB0210 CARCON, file 15, Cardiff South East Executive Committee minute book, 13 July 1948.

[254] 'Capt. Thorneycroft increases majority', *Abergavenny Chronicle*, 2 November 1945.

[255] Deidre Beddoe, 'Women and Politics in Twentieth Century Wales', *National Library of Wales Journal*, 33/3 (2004), 333–47.

[256] Tanner, 'Labour', pp. 256–7; Andrew Walling, 'The Structure of Power in Labour Wales, 1951–1964', in Tanner, Williams and Hopkin, *The Labour Party*, p. 209.

figures, with each umbrella association's chairman almost always being assisted by a vice chairman who was a woman. In particular, women's groups were always considered crucial for the work they did as fundraisers. The conventional view is that Conservative women sat in backrooms 'busily addressing envelopes at long trestle tables', as well as laying on food and drink at fundraising events.[257] There is much truth in that: when local associations compiled lists relating to who had raised the most money over a given time period, women's groups were always at the top.[258] The post-1945 period is especially important in this regard because the 1949 Maxwell Fyfe Report ruled that, contrary to previous practices, prospective or serving MPs could not offer large sums of money to their respective associations (often 'buying' the seat in the process).[259] Instead, money had to be raised locally in order to maintain things like agents, an office and a car, and to cover election expenses.[260] Further reforms, namely a scheme where each constituency forwarded an annual sum of money known as a 'quota' to CCO, accentuated the importance of local people power.[261] Of course, money was donated to the Tories by businesses and wealthy individuals, but the funds raised by local associations topped this up and certainly seemed 'more defensible in a democratic age'.[262]

Fundraising events organised by women tell us a range of things about post-war Welsh society, including the ability of middle-class

---

[257] McCallum and Readman, *The British*, p. 180.
[258] Maguire, *Conservative Women*, p. 141. For an anecdotal and partisan account of women's work in local Conservative politics, see Rupert Morris, *Tories: From Village Hall to Westminster: A Political Sketch* (Edinburgh: Mainstream, 1991). For an example, see WPA, GB0210 CARCON, file 18, Cardiff West Executive Council minute book, 30 January 1956.
[259] Ball, *The Conservative Party and British Politics*, p. 112.
[260] Ramsden, *The Age of Churchill*, p. 136.
[261] Ball, *The Conservative Party and British Politics*, pp. 112–13; David Butler and Michael Pinto-Duschinsky, 'The Conservative Elite, 1918–1978: Does Unrepresentativeness Matter?', in Zig Layton-Henry (ed.), *Conservative Party Politics* (London: Macmillan, 1980), p. 189. The quota was calculated by a sliding-scale formula based on the share of the vote the Conservatives received in that area at the last general election
[262] John Ramsden, *The Winds of Change: Macmillan to Heath, 1957–1975* (Essex: Longman, 1996), p. 75; Bale, *The Conservatives*, p. 20.

people to wring significant amounts of cash out of other members of the middle class, even in a period of real austerity. They did so by effectively interweaving the social and the money-making elements of politics (association committees were often called things like 'The Social (Money Raising) Sub-Committee').[263] In 1949 alone, the women of the Conway Association raised £525 from their Ball, £609 from the Conwy Castle Fair and £691 from the Christmas Fair – £600 being roughly equivalent to £19,000 in 2023's prices.[264] The Annual Monmouth Fete was such a large event that it had a variety of separate organisational committees organising it.[265] Other associations experimented with less conventional events that aligned with the profile of the constituency, like a comic dog-show on the rural, agricultural isle of Anglesey, or a fly-casting competition in coastal Cardigan. Such events, which were apparently 'popular', raised small sums like £100, which were still important amounts of money.[266]

Just as significant was the fundraising and social work done by bands of women in the 'Welsh Wales' seats that were resolutely anti-Conservative.[267] In the Valleys seat of Rhondda East, which the Wales Area Office described acidly as 'extremely Socialist and Communist', it was a 'small band' of women who kept the 'party flag flying'.[268] At the same time, in Caerphilly, ten or so miles south-east of the Rhondda, there was reportedly 'little enthusiasm' for the party, 'apart from [amongst] the women'.[269] In Aneurin Bevan's steadfastly Labour seat of Ebbw Vale, 'nothing [is] done' except by a 'very good nucleus in the

---

[263] WPA, GB0210 CARCON, file 18, Cardiff West Executive Council minute book, 27 May 1957.
[264] CPA, CCO 1/8/510, Finance Sheet 31 May 1950.
[265] WPA, GB0210 MONION, file 6, Monmouth Conservative Association minute book, 30 January 1956.
[266] CPA, CCO 1/7/507, Fete pamphlet, 24 August 1949; CPA, CCO 1/11/516, Cardigan Basic Report, 21 September 1956.
[267] Ball, *Portrait*, p. 164.
[268] CPA, CCO 1/7/523, Rhondda East Basic Report, 11 July 1949.
[269] CPA, CCO 1/7/529, Caerphilly Basic Report, c.July 1949.

women's branch'.[270] At a similar time in Merthyr Tydfil, another staunchly anti-Conservative constituency, there were 300 women members of the Conservative Association.[271] Such was the significance of the Merthyr Women's first-ever Annual Dinner and Social Evening, in March 1951, that the Party Chairman, the popular Lord Woolton, wrote a personal message wishing them well.[272] In another safe Labour seat, Pontypool, women organised the conventional monthly tea meetings, whist drives, bridge drives, garden parties and bring-and-buy sales that successfully advertised a local Tory presence in the seat, keeping the association alive.[273] By showing that being a Conservative was not totally alien, these women were doing something significant for the party. After all, even in the 'extremely Communist' Rhondda East, over 3,000 people voted Conservative in 1951, whilst 7,500 people did so in Merthyr Tydfil.[274] This small band of activists were representing a minority position in the constituency, but it was a significant one, nonetheless.

Associational life therefore provided opportunities for groups of women in Wales, including for those who wanted to argue their cases on both local and national topics. It is worth focusing on a couple of these more dramatic arguments. Disputes in constituency associations over things like who should be the party's prospective parliamentary candidate show, as Cohen and Mates have argued, that local political associations could be the turf on which ideological ideas were thrashed out by women.[275] One such incident from the north Wales seat of Conway demonstrates this. It was driven by a group of women activists, who demonstrated a huge amount of political agency in the process. In advance of the 1951 general election, the constituency ditched its previous

---

[270] CPA, CCO 1/7/538, Ebbw Vale Basic Report, July 1949.
[271] CPA, CCO 1/7/522, Merthyr Tydfil Basic Report, undated.
[272] CPA, CCO 1/8/522, Garmonsway to Greville, 23 February 1951; Woolton to Merthyr Women, c.25 February 1951.
[273] CPA, CCO 1/12/545, AGM Report 1957.
[274] Arnold J. James and John E. Thomas, *Wales at Westminster: A History of the Parliamentary Representation of Wales 1800–1979* (Llandysul: Gomer Press, 1981), p. 158.
[275] Cohen and Mates, 'Grassroots', 213.

candidate, David Price-White, a local solicitor from Bangor who had served as MP for a neighbouring seat from 1945 to 1950. They replaced him with Peter Thomas (who would go on to win the seat and later serve as Secretary of State for Wales between 1970 and 1974).[276] However, the Bangor Women's branch of the association took great umbrage at their local man having been dropped. Mirroring similar disputes from the period, such as one in Newcastle North, the women orchestrated a significant campaign in favour of reinstating Price-White.[277] They wrote open letters to the local newspaper and collected a 600-strong petition in favour of him being reinstated. Although their cause ultimately failed, it fundamentally challenges some of the narratives about passive Tory women.

In a similar incident during the same period, women were at the heart of more disruption, this time in the Swansea West seat. Again, this event mirrored something that happened in another Newcastle constituency, where a particular branch of the women's association refused to be pulled into the central constituency association. The women of Newcastle West saw it 'as a downgrading of their status'.[278] Although what happened in Swansea West did not rumble on for as long as the Newcastle dispute, the parallels are interesting. Under the 1948 redistribution of seats, the Mumbles Women's branch came into the orbit of Swansea West. The women refused to join the Women's Section of the association, arguing that they should exist as an autonomous body, paying quotas and subsidies directly to the association and not to the pot contributed to by all of the other women's branches.[279] The rumour was that the women from Mumbles were angry at the Women's Committee acting like an exclusive social club.[280] In a Wales Area report outlining

[276] 'Socialists Hold 25 out of 36 Welsh Seats', *Western Mail*, 27 July 1945.
[277] CPA, CCO 1/8/510, Macmillan to Woolton, 5 October 1950. The women in question stressed that Price-White being a 'Bangor man' had nothing to do with their anger, but it could well offer some explanation.
[278] Cohen and Mates, 'Grassroots', 216.
[279] CPA, CCO 1/8/526, Swansea West women report, *c.*1950.
[280] CPA, CCO 1/8/526, James to the GD, 16 May 1950.

all of this, the women were referred to as 'rebels' who needed to 'fall into line'.[281] The dispute became so intense that the Swansea West Conservative Association was left in the very rare position of having no women's vice chairman for a period of time.[282] Again, like the women from Bangor, they demonstrated a sense of political self-confidence far removed from the stereotype of the hidden, backroom loyalist. This, unsurprisingly, was not the view taken by the Wales Area Office, who saw Swansea West as a winnable seat, the prospects for which were diminishing because of the women's actions and the consequent lack of coordination of the local campaign.[283]

Like women, young people were formally incorporated into the structure of the Conservative Party after the war, under the umbrella of the Young Conservatives (YCs). Its forerunner was the Junior Imperial League (JIL) which had encouraged political work and participation. The JIL had been set up in 1906 after electoral disaster and, similarly, the YCs was launched in 1946 as part of the party's wider recruitment drive.[284] Woolton and other Conservative leaders thought a youth movement 'could play a major role in recovering the party's electoral strength'.[285] In its heyday, the YCs was an enormous organisation. It had 160,433 members across Britain in 1949.[286] In Wales at the end of the 1940s, a rough guide to YC membership numbers, complied from the records that have survived or those that were available, is outlined in table 6.

---

[281] CPA, CCO 1/8/526, Swansea West women report, c.1950.
[282] CPA, CCO 1/8/526, Swansea West Basic Report, 20 September 1950.
[283] CPA, CCO 1/8/526, Swansea West Basic Report, 20 September 1950. A fiery streak remained amongst the women of Swansea West, however, with a large group going on strike in the mid-1960s and refusing to work for the party until the 'hopeless' Agent for the constituency was sacked. See CPA, CCO 1/14/545, Davies to the COO, 9 March 1964.
[284] Ball, 'Local Conservatism', p. 274; David Willetts, 'The New Conservatism? 1945–1951', in Stuart Ball and Anthony Seldon (eds), *Recovering Power: The Conservatives in Opposition Since 1867* (Basingstoke: Palgrave Macmillan, 2005), p. 176.
[285] Zig Layton-Henry, 'The Young Conservatives, 1945–1970', *Journal of Contemporary History*, 8/2 (1973), 146.
[286] Ball, 'Local Conservatism', p. 275.

Constituency	Young Conservative members
Aberavon	210
Aberdare	No figure
Abertillery	0
Anglesey	24
Barry	400
Bedwellty	0
Brecon and Radnor	500
Caernarfon	25
Caerphilly	120
Cardiff North	400
Cardiff South East	100
Cardiff West	100
Cardigan	60 (including affiliated university branch members)
Carmarthen	100
Conway	100
Denbigh	250
Ebbw Vale	100
Flint East	250
Flint West	336
Gower	No figure
Llanelli	41
Merioneth	0
Merthyr Tydfil	50
Monmouth	No figure – 4,000 total members in the entire constituency
Montgomery	No figure
Neath	30
Newport	300
Ogmore	No figure
Pembrokeshire	251
Pontypool	No figure, but two branches
Pontypridd	No figure
Rhondda East	No figure
Rhondda West	0
Swansea East	50
Swansea West	180
Wrexham	350

Table 6: Number of Young Conservatives in each Welsh constituency, c.1949.

Total Welsh YC membership 1949 was roughly 4,238, based on these figures, although this may well be a minimum estimate, because there is no surviving data for several important constituencies, like Monmouth. Of course, as with women, numbers on paper did not translate to regular attendance at meetings and certainly not to active workers and campaigners for the party. Nonetheless, it should come as no surprise that seats in 'British Wales', where the party was always stronger, like Barry, Denbigh and Flint West, had healthy numbers in their ranks. In the geographically huge Brecon and Radnor constituency in the early 1950s, there were sixty individual branches of the association, four of which were 'strong' YC groups.[287] Parts of 'Welsh Wales' even had some kind of YC presence, with a hundred members in Ebbw Vale and fifty in Merthyr Tydfil in the early 1950s. In Neath, nearly a third of the 321 members of the association there were YCs, a tribute to their leader Idris Pearce, who was thought of as talented and inspirational, demonstrating how effective a single person could be.[288] Neath, however, was an anomaly. The fact that other anti-Tory constituencies had no YCs at all, in this national heyday of the organisation, again drives home the fact that constituencies in south Wales were some of just the 'handful' of seats across the entire UK that did not have 'at least' a single branch in this period.[289] Even strong seats like Conway, which had 4,000 registered members, supposedly had only twelve YC members.[290] Just as someone like Idris Pearce could be inspirational, so could other leading figures be 'pompous and pedantic' and therefore an active turn-off.[291]

YCs could at least bring their energetic and youthful enthusiasm to a campaign trail.[292] In particular – and this was often the case in Wales – they could be relied upon to go to

---

[287] CPA, CCO 1/9/516, Brecon and Radnor Annual Report, May 1953.
[288] CPA, CCO 1/11/536, Neath Basic Report, 24 August 1956.
[289] Ramsden, *The Age of Churchill*, p. 119.
[290] CPA, CCO 1/11/515, Conway Basic Report, 1 August 1956.
[291] CPA, CCO 1/11/540/1, Newport Basic Report, 18 September 1956.
[292] Jean Lucas, 'The 1949 By-Elections', in Lucas, *Between the Thin Blue Lines*, p. 41.

marginal or even hopeless seats to knock on doors.[293] A typical and symbolic example of this in this period was YCs from Cardiff being bussed up to Valleys seats like Rhondda West.[294] YCs also helped at party social events, or organised their own. Their events inevitably had a more youthful feel, with activities like dances or pancake races serving the triple function of affording entertainment and friendship for young people, the raising of funds for the local association, and the advertisement of the party to the public more broadly.[295] At big constituency-wide events, YCs would often provided the vim and brought other people with them to make such events a success. Many association meetings acknowledged the role they played in this regard.[296]

A final feature of grassroots Toryism that is important for our understanding of local political dynamics is Conservative clubs. Often referred to as 'Con' clubs, they were member-exclusive organisations which to some extent looked like public houses, with a bar, and snooker and billiards tables. As well as that, games rooms were common and reading rooms were also to be found in many establishments.[297] Clubs were separate independent bodies from the Conservative Party, but to varying degrees most were indirectly connected to it – hence the name.[298] Indeed, the model rules produced by the Association of Conservative Clubs stated that all members of a club should seek to 'further and promote the Conservative cause' and that they should be 'members of a Conservative association'.[299] This was rarely the case, however, especially in parts of Wales.

---

[293] Layton-Henry, 'The Young Conservatives', 147.
[294] CPA, CCO 1/8/524, 1950 General Election comments, undated.
[295] Ramsden, *The Winds*, p. 92; CPA, CCO 2/5/19, Howard Davies itinerary, undated.
[296] See, for example, WPA, GB0210 CARCON, file 18, Cardiff West Conservative and Unionist Association, 10th Annual Report, c.1956.
[297] Philip Tether, *Clubs: A Neglected Aspect of Conservative Organisation* (University of Hull: Hull Papers in Politics, 1988), p. 57.
[298] Tether, *Clubs*, p. 1. Some were not called 'Conservative Clubs' and were named Salisbury Clubs, for example.
[299] Glamorgan Archives, Cardiff [GA], D1042/2, Rules of the Conservative Club booklet.

The long-term history is again worth considering. In 1881, Wales received its first piece of specific legislation, in the form of the Sunday Closing Act. Gladstone supported it and it stemmed from 'orchestrated pressure' from Welsh Nonconformists.[300] The club movement was beginning to be rolled out around the same time. It was done so in the spirit of Disraelian 'one nation' and 'working class' pitches to the electorate. The hope was that clubs would extend the reach of the party amongst newly enfranchised working people. In this period, Conservatives also became associated with offering the working classes the freedom to have a quiet drink, in contrast to their more puritanical Liberal opponents.[301] This partly accounted for Tory support bases in seaside areas, like Blackpool, Southport, Brighton, or in areas like Wolverhampton, as Jon Lawrence has shown.[302] Whilst the party found few loyal friends in parts of industrial Wales, clubs were popular there. The more liberal attitude to the serving of drink was likely to have been behind this. The original architect's drawings of the Ton & Pentre Club in the Rhondda, for example, show that of all the rooms in the entire building, the bar was by far the largest.[303] The number here is striking: one writer noted in 1912 that clubs were a real feature of the south Wales Valleys, whereas Conservative-minded people were not.[304] In the seat of Aberdare in 1948, a constituency which at best could sustain a skeleton association and only a 'few keen [party] workers', total membership of the network of clubs was 2,000.[305] In Caerphilly, a constituency with 'little enthusiasm' for Conservatism, club membership totalled 1,756 in 1949.[306]

---

[300] Morgan, *Rebirth*, p. 36.
[301] Ball, *The Conservative Party*, p. 8.
[302] Jon Lawrence, *Speaking For the People: Party, Language and Popular Politics in England, 1867–1914* (Cambridge: Cambridge University Press, 1998), p. 107; McCallum and Readman, The British, p. 262.
[303] GA, D276/4/21, Pentre Conservative Club: proposed library plans, elevations, sections, July 1949.
[304] See Harries, *A History of Conservatism*, pp. 61–116.
[305] CPA, CCO 1/7/518, Aberdare Basic Report, undated, c.1948.
[306] CPA, CCO 1/7/529, Caerphilly Basic Report, c.July 1949.

In contrast, it is no coincidence that the rural, temperate, more traditionally Liberal areas of Wales, like Carmarthenshire, had virtually no clubs at all.[307]

The social element of clubs, therefore, was key. 'The stimulation sought was evidently liquid rather than political', especially in south Wales, where clubs offered their patrons not lively political debate, but a 'convivial pint and a chat' about the daily grind, their jobs or women – and where that pint could often be bought more cheaply than in a pub.[308] The extent to which the social again trumped the political is clear from the regular criticisms, by the Wales Area Office, of 'inactive' or 'useless' clubs, even though they had huge membership figures. Reference to 'so-called Con clubs' was common.[309] The Llanelli constituency contained eleven clubs at the beginning of the 1950s, but only one was 'vaguely political'.[310] When Jim Thomas went to Caernarfon in 1949 to attend the Annual General Meeting, held in the Assembly Room above the Conservative club, he reported back that the meeting was

> a disgrace. It was a Saturday night, the attendance [at the meeting] was 50 [and] over 100 people were drinking beer on the floor below, but they had not the energy to climb the stairs. The Agent was almost in tears at the end of the evening.[311]

---

[307] CPA, CCO 1/7/512, Carmarthen Basic Report, 1949.

[308] Kenneth O. Morgan and Peter Stead, 'Rhondda West', in David Butler and Anthony King (eds), *The British General Election of 1966* (London: Macmillan, 1966), p. 247; Ramsden, *The Age of Churchill*, p. 113; Dominic Sandbrook, *White Heat: A History of Britain in the Swinging Sixties* (London: Little, Brown, 2006), p. 198; Lawrence Black 'The Lost World of Young Conservatism', *The Historical Journal*, 51/4 (2008), 994; Edwards, *The Good Patch*, p. 159.

[309] 'Monmouth Club's "Sitting on the Fence" Complex', *Weekly Argus*, 2 February 1946; WPA, GB0210 CARCON, file 32, C. Stuart Hallinan Election Expenses; CPA, CCO 1/11/524, Cardiff North Basic Report, 25 July 1956. See also, for criticism of inactivity, CPA, CCO 1/7/517, Flint West AGM Agent's Report, 11 June 1949; CPA, CCO 1/8/510, Davies to Thomas, 26 June 1951.

[310] CPA, CCO 1/8/529, Llanelli Basic Report, 20 June 1951.

[311] CPA, CCO 1/7/509, Thomas to James, 15 December 1949.

CONCLUSION

So much of what the Tories did and said after 1945 was a response to defeat by the Labour Party and a reaction to what that government was doing in office. Anti-socialism defined its rhetoric, but also its actions. To an extent, it lay behind the idea of decentralising power which, in Wales, took the form of proposing, and then creating, a Minister for Welsh Affairs on the party's return to office. Despite this interesting move, what is perhaps most notable is the extent to which the party did and did not modify the way it communicated its wider ideas to the Welsh people. By 1945, Labour had captured the hearts and minds of much of the Welsh electorate, and the Tory response to this was uncertain. Yes, it fielded a handful of working-class candidates in urban areas and some Welsh speakers in the rural heartlands, but rarely did it feel as if the party was speaking directly to those voters who were inherently suspicious of it. It robustly critiqued 'Socialism' in a manner that gained it some friends in so-called 'British Wales', whilst sounding aloof or incompatible with those places that were clearly enthusiastic about Labour politics. Many ordinary people, however, did respond positively to its messages. Conservative politics at the grassroots in the five or six years after the war was a vibrant mixture of socialising, day-to-day organisational work and engagement in the substance of the politics of the moment. People – especially women – were undoubtedly attracted to the party, as members and voters, by its messaging. To some extent, everything that happened in this short but important period set the tone for the rest of the twentieth century, although circumstances changed somewhat when the party re-entered government in 1951 at the tail-end of a long period of post-war austerity.

2
AFFLUENCE AND A CHANGING WALES, 1951–1964

In 1959, a twenty-six-year-old Michael Heseltine went to a selection meeting in the Gower constituency, where the Conservative and National Liberal Parties were choosing a candidate to contest the forthcoming general election. Very shortly afterwards, he was picked to fight the seat, partly because no one else had put themselves forward for the role.[1] Heseltine was Welsh and a local man, having been born and brought up during his early years in the neighbouring seat of Swansea West. His anglicised household, comfortable upbringing and private-school education in England, however, had given him clipped enough tones for Aneurin Bevan – in the final year of his life – to taunt Heseltine on the campaign trail for having 'the voice of an Englishman'.[2] Heseltine would rarely refer to this campaign in later life and he came nowhere close to winning what at the time was a safe Labour seat, but his experience is nonetheless revealing.[3] As a well-spoken 'local boy' he represented both what people thought a typical Tory was, but what many Conservative voters and activists liked their representatives to be. Although his family wealth stretched back much further in time, Heseltine's well-heeled demeanour did encapsulate something of the spirit

---

[1] Interview, Lord Heseltine, 24 July 2014.
[2] Interview, Lord Heseltine, 24 July 2014; Michael Crick, *Michael Heseltine: A Biography* (London: Penguin, 1997), p. 12.
[3] In a 2016 diary for the *Spectator*, he wrote briefly about 'his earliest political experiences' without mentioning anything to do with the fact that he had, in 1959, fought Gower. See Michael Heseltine, 'Diary', *The Spectator*, 22 October 2016.

of the end of the 1950s, with Prime Minister Harold Macmillan riding the wave of a growing sense of affluence in the country.

This chapter will explore many of these themes and will focus in particular on how this greater feeling of affluence determined how the party communicated and operated in Wales. On one hand, the circumstances of the period worked in the Conservatives' favour. As the face of a more middle-class section of the population, some parts of the electorate appeared more receptive to its messages about self-improvement, especially when that was communicated by 'local boys' who had themselves done well in life. Affluence was an uneven phenomenon, however, and many in Wales remained less receptive to the party. The 1950s also brought with it concerns about traditional Welsh ways of life, as well as alternative distractions for people who might once have joined a political party to give them something to do. Both posed problems for the party in Wales, to which they attempted to respond.

'LIFE'S BETTER WITH THE CONSERVATIVES'

The period from the early 1950s to the mid-1960s witnessed many significant changes in British society, none more so than economic growth and an increased sense of affluence. For many, this meant living standards improved, with labour-saving devices and 'positional' goods beginning to be acquired by many households.[4] A greater sense of security was felt by more people than ever before.[5] The Conservative Party believed that these economic circumstances were naturally creating more Conservative-minded people in Wales and that with the 'surge in

---

[4] Dominic Sandbrook, *Never Had it so Good: A History of Britain from Suez to the Beatles* (London: Abacus, 2015), p. 100.

[5] Peter Hennessy, *Having It So Good: Britain in the Fifties* (London: Penguin, 2006), p. 518; Martin Johnes, *Wales Since 1939* (Manchester: Manchester University Press, 2012), p. 66.

prosperity', the party could 'look forward to better . . . results'.[6] There had always been a small middle class in Wales. Despite the hardship of the 1930s, that period witnessed a rise in material living standards for this minority of people.[7] Not everyone felt such benefits in the 1930s or even into the 1950s, and those who did not had cause to think of the Tories as 'the rich man's party'. Nonetheless, there is no doubt that affluence was steadily becoming more of a feature of Welsh society.[8] Social surveys from the period indicated that people, especially women, saw opportunities and the chance to secure better material wealth for their families if they voted Conservative.[9]

It is this optimism that is so clearly identifiable in the way Conservatives spoke to the Welsh electorate in this period, reflected particularly in the literature the party disseminated across the country and the way its candidates presented themselves. It was able to talk about the 'liberation of the housewife' that was occurring under its watch. All food rationing eventually stopped in 1954. Candidates like a young Geoffrey Howe, fighting the Aberavon constituency in 1955 – the first political campaign in a long career that would see him rise to the offices of Chancellor of the Exchequer and Foreign Secretary in the 1980s – asked voters, especially women, 'which were better for yourselves, your families, and the country? The years of Socialism, or the years of Conservatism that have followed?'[10] This message chimed with some members of the electorate. Questioned about why he was voting for the Conservatives in 1955, one voter close to Howe's Aberavon seat replied that they were 'the only party that offers

[6] Welsh Political Archive, National Library of Wales, Aberystwyth [WPA], GB0210 CARCON, file 18, Cardiff West Executive Council minute book, 10 November 1959.
[7] Stuart Ball, *Portrait of a Party: The Conservative Party in Britain, 1918–1945* (Oxford: Oxford University Press, 2013), p. 108.
[8] Conservative Party Archive, Bodleian Library, Oxford [CPA], CCO 1/7/540, Missioners' special report for week ending 16 April 1949; 'Letter: Tory Benefits', *Western Mail*, undated, c.1959.
[9] Dominic Sandbrook, *White Heat: A History of Britain in the Swinging Sixties* (London: Little Brown, 2006), p. 691; G. E. Maguire, *Conservative Women: A History of Women and the Conservative Party, 1874–1997* (Basingstoke: Macmillan, 1998), p. 134.
10 CPA, PUB 229/11/13, Geoffrey Howe election address, Aberavon, 1955.

hope for the middleman'.[11] Other candidates found particularly personal ways to express these points, especially in the context of the 1959 general election theme of 'Life's Better with the Conservatives'.[12] Posing with his family and their enormous dog, the candidate for Cardiff West, Lincoln Hallinan, told readers: 'We look happy – we are happy – why? – because the Conservatives have made us happy'.[13]

Bound up with this theme of happiness and rising prosperity was a sense that the Tories had managed to guarantee the 'freedom' that had been such a feature of its critique of Labour when that party was in government before 1951. As the historian Stephen Brooke argued, by identifying with voters as 'consumers', rather than 'producers', the Tories captured the mood of the time and in the process were able to portray Labour as statist and collectivist.[14] Indeed, with Cold War tensions having ratcheted up by the end of the 1950s, and with fears of what the Soviet Union was capable of, Conservative rhetoric shifted by encouraging people not to let socialism back into office. Election addresses told voters that only the Conservatives could 'maintain the British way of life', by which they meant allowing people to be free from the kind of state control witnessed in the USSR.[15] During his campaign in Gower, Michael Heseltine wrote: 'In my world, you shall have the right to own, you shall have the power of decision and you will be, above all else, an individual'.[16] Conservative posters that were such a dazzling shade of orange that they remained almost blinding fifty-five years later were produced at the same election, reading 'a fuller life, a better life,

---

[11] 'In Swansea West every head will count', *Western Mail*, 17 May 1955.

[12] Richard Cockett, 'The Party, Publicity and the Media', in Anthony Seldon and Stuart Ball (eds), *Conservative Century: The Conservative Party Since 1900* (Oxford: Oxford University Press, 1994), p. 567.

[13] CPA, PUB 229/12/14, Lincoln Hallinan election address, Cardiff West, 1959.

[14] Stephen Brooke, 'Labour and the "Nation" after 1945', in Jon Lawrence and Miles Taylor (eds), *Party, State and Society: Electoral Behaviour in Britain Since 1820* (Aldershot: Scolar Press, 1997), p. 159.

[15] WPA, Lord Temple-Morris papers, file P1, Hallinan address.

[16] CPA, PUB 229/12/14, Michael Heseltine election address, Gower, 1959.

a freer life. Keep it so. Vote Conservative'.[17] Passing judgement on the party's performance in office in this period, the *Daily Mail* noted that the Tories had entered office trying to prove that 'freedom works' and that they had 'brilliantly succeeded'.[18]

This rhetoric around 'freedom' had direct and real-world implications for local economies and jobs in Wales, which the Conservatives tried to make capital out of in seats like Flint East and Cardiff South East, both of which contained large steelworks.[19] The primary message from the Conservatives was that the steel industry would function better, and therefore continue to employ people, if it operated under private ownership.[20] The press reported that the messaging was popular.[21] In East Flint, the party made a concerted effort to put pressure on the Labour MP, Eirene White, to say whether she agreed with her party's plans on steel nationalisation.[22] In 1959, both seats were nearly won by the Tories, with White clinging on with a majority of just seventy-five.[23]

It is certainly the case that Conservative rhetoric was chiming with sections of the electorate. The party's success in so-called 'British Wales' in the 1950s, where it held on to or gained seats like Cardiff North, Conway, Flint West and Barry, reflects how it had purchase in more suburban, professional and affluent areas. Party members themselves, although unrepresentative of a typical Tory voter, still reveal something about the social groups the party was grounded in. Pictures from various fundraising and social events in these parts of Wales provide clear visual evidence of this solidly middle-class social world. The huge fete and day of activities, for

---

[17] Gwent Archives, D. 1019.1, poster.
[18] *Daily Mail*, 15 October 1964.
[19] David Rosser, *A Dragon in the House* (Llandysul: Gomer, 1987), p. 179.
[20] WPA, GB0210 CARCON, file 35, Cardiff South East Conservative and Unionist Association Executive Committee, 2 February 1959.
[21] 'The Steelworkers who will vote for a Conservative', *Western Mail*, 6 October 1959; Interview, Sir Norman Lloyd-Edwards, 7 July 2015.
[22] Letter, 'Nationalisation', *Flintshire County Herald*, 27 June 1958.
[23] Arnold J. James and John E. Thomas, *Wales at Westminster: A History of Parliamentary Representation of Wales 1800–1979* (Llandysul: Gomer Press, 1981), p. 166.

example, at the Brogyntyn Hall estate outside Oswestry (which was just over the border into England, but would have been attended by many Tories from the Welsh side) attracted hundreds of people, as figure 3 shows. The day included picnics, a dog show, a horse-jumping competition, and a mannequin parade, all set in the spectacular grounds of a country house belonging to the Ormsby-Gore family. Well-dressed men and women, many wearing hats, watch as a woman takes part in one of the event's highlights. Other images from 1960 (figure 4) show groups of women braving the elements to serve refreshments, including tomato soup, to a large group of activists gathered at the grand Faenol Estate in north west Wales, owned by Sir Michael Duff. The Monmouth Association was constantly organising various outings from the constituency that included meals in pleasant restaurants or shows in London's West End.[24] In 1955, they organised a trip to Paris and Holland.[25] For most ordinary people in 1955, such trips would have been unthinkable. Whilst the economy was now recovering, rationing had not long ended and few had the spare cash necessary for such kinds of holidays.[26]

This unrepresentative societal group was certainly attracted to Conservatism, but the party also made significant efforts to speak to those who were aspirational or becoming more socially mobile. Some of its parliamentary candidates reflected this. Emrys Simons, who fought Cardiff West in 1955, for example, was one of nine children of a coalminer from the Rhondda Valley, who worked errands as a boy for pocket money, won a scholarship to study at school and at University College, Aberystwyth, where he read law. This led to him becoming a barrister – a profession long associated

---

[24] WPA, GB0210 MONION, file 4, Monmouth Women's Executive Committee minute book, 25 September 1946; GB0210 MONION, file 4, Monmouth Women's Executive Committee, 12 October 1955.
[25] WPA, GB0210 MONION, file 4, Monmouth Women's Executive Committee, 16 October 1957.
[26] Kenneth O. Morgan, *The People's Peace: British History, 1945–1990* (Oxford: Oxford University Press, 1990), p. 32.

Figure 4: Five women prepare refreshments in the rain at a Conservative fete at the Faenol Estate, 1960.

with the Conservative Party. There were others like him.[27] Into the 1960s, some candidates standing for election had taken advantages of the improved economic and social circumstances of the post-war era of their childhoods and early adulthoods – a stronger economy, affluence, better educational opportunities provided by a raft of grammar schools.[28] When Conservative politicians in Wales argued that 400,000 Conservative voters there could not solely equate to '400,000 bloated capitalists', this was of course true.[29] Its own activists in some constituencies, like Pembrokeshire, were supposedly known locally as 'social climbers'.[30] In the view

---

[27] 'Meet your candidates', *Western Mail*, 13 May 1955; 'Who's your choice?', *Western Mail*, 19 September 1959.

[28] Brian Harrison, *Seeking a Role: The United Kingdom, 1951–1970* (Oxford: Oxford University Press, 2009), p. 51; Johnes, *Wales Since 1939*, p. 123; Selina Todd, *The People: The Rise and Fall of the Working Class, 1910–2010* (London: John Murray, 2015), pp. 389–92.

[29] 'Tories "no class Party"', paper and date unknown, in WPA, GB0210 CONLES, file 5, newspaper scrapbook.

[30] CPA, CCO 1/9/542, Hare to Garmonsway, 25 March 1953.

of one keen observer of the politics of this period, this was important. For him,

> there is something here about the self-made small business families of which there were a large number in urban, and even rural, Wales. The Welsh public schools reinforced this tradition – I was just about the only declared socialist in my own public school's Sixth Form, the other mostly Conservative, as I remember, with just the occasional Liberal and just one or two Welsh nationalists.[31]

A further sign of this socioeconomic change and a greater sense of aspiration could be found in changing residential patterns, not least in the movement of some people within towns from poorer districts to leafier suburbs.[32] A common motif in a number of Conservative election addresses throughout the 1950s was a small drawing of a typical (but, for many, desirable) neat suburban home with a small front garden.[33] Moving westwards in Swansea, for example, had long been associated with going somewhere that 'bore an unmistakable air of affluence and satisfaction' and was a sign of social progress.[34] One woman, who was a member of the local Conservative women's association, viewed her relocation to the pleasant suburbs of Sketty as a symbol of, in her own words, moving 'up a step'.[35] As a commentator noted at the time, the only problem people who lived in areas like Sketty faced was 'staying respectable'.[36] It was partly in this context that a Conservative, Hugh Rees,

---

[31] Professor Sir Deian Hopkin to Sam Blaxland, 21 May 2015.
[32] Florence Sutcliffe-Braithwaite, *Class, Politics, and the Decline of Deference in England, 1968–2000* (Oxford: Oxford University Press, 2018), p. 48.
[33] See for example, Stuart Hallinan election address, Cardiff West, 1950. On the increasing standardisation of these addresses, see David Thackeray and Richard Toye, 'An Age of Promises: British Election Manifestos and Addresses 1900–97', *Twentieth Century British History*, 31/1 (2020), 7.
[34] Kenneth O. Morgan, 'Swansea West', in his *Modern Wales: Politics, Places and People* (Cardiff, University of Wales Press, 1995), p. 292.
[35] Colin Rosser and Christopher Harris, *The Family and Social Change: A Study of Family and Kinship in a South Wales Town* (London: Routledge and Kegan Paul, 1965), p. 83.
[36] 'In Swansea West every head will count', *Western Mail*, 17 May 1955.

won the Swansea West seat in 1959, of which Sketty was a part. This was likely the result both of a political discourse centred on increasing affluence, and of the actual realities of increasing wealth, which was changing the nature of the electorate. But it is also telling that Tory candidates themselves, if they were local, hailed from these particular areas. It was not uncommon in Swansea, for example, for all three of the town's constituencies to be fought by men who lived in the more affluent Mumbles area.[37] Similarly, the party's Wales Area Office regularly asked middle-class types who lived in the pleasant suburbs of Cardiff, like Birchgrove, or the grand seaside town of Penarth, to 'fight the good fight' in neighbouring safe Labour seats.[38] The uneven distribution of party members within certain seats reinforced much of this, especially in industrialised parts of 'Welsh Wales'. In 1950s Aberavon, there were four times as many paid-up members of the Conservative Party in the relatively middle-class seaside town of Porthcawl as there were in all the industrialised parts of the seat (Port Talbot, Baglan and Margam) combined.[39] When a 'successful' fete was held in the (largely industrial) seat of Pontypridd, it took place in the suburban and leafy town of Cowbridge, in the constituency's very southern tip (and right on the border of the much more Conservative Barry seat).[40]

Specific electioneering tactics reflected the extent to which wealth was associated with the party and mattered to its supporters. Antony Eden was met with a fireworks display on one trip to Cardiff, and the prizes from the raffle to mark that event included a 'ladies' and a gents' bicycle'.[41] At East Flint's coronation ball

---

[37] 'This candidate is sure of at least three votes', *Western Mail*, 31 March 1966.
[38] See, for example, 'Tories to fight all Welsh seats', *Western Mail*, 2 March 1966; Kenneth O. Morgan and Peter Stead, 'Rhondda West', in David Butler and Anthony King (eds), *The British General Election of 1966* (London: Macmillan, 1966), p. 247.
[39] CPA, CCO 1/7/527, Aberavon Basic Report, 23 June 1949.
[40] WPA, GB0210 CARCON, file 34, The Glamorgan Group Council of the Wales and Monmouthshire Provincial Area minute book, 2 December 1954.
[41] WPA, GB0210 CARCON, file 15, Cardiff South East Executive Committee minute book, 25 February 1947; 17 June 1947.

in 1953, the raffle's first prize was a television set.[42] Upmarket drinks parties were used by the party as opportunities for senior Tories to engage with a middle-class voter base. Cocktails were a symbol of social status, to such an extent that the Cardiff North MP David Llewellyn – not always the most self-aware of politicians – was left pondering whether the rate at which cocktail parties were organised by the Tories actually 'restricted' the party and hampered its image.[43] Only the Tories could have had a local disagreement over the fact that two separate associations had coincidentally booked Cardiff Castle for a fundraising cocktail party on the same day.[44] Such events were a world away from sandwiches in Nonconformist rural village halls, or from pints of bitter in working men's labour clubs, both of which were the social epicentres of different kinds of politics. In his satirical 1955 novel, *That Uncertain Feeling*, which lambasted the Welsh bourgeoise, Kingsley Amis introduced readers to the frightfully respectable and bourgeois Elizabeth Gruffydd-Williams, the wife of a high-flying local man who lives on the outskirts of town in a house with a gravel drive. Her car, we are told, had 'a leather couch affair which ran across the whole width [and] smelt new'.[45] They also had a cocktail cabinet 'constructed of glass and chromium' that the novel's protagonist marvels at, thinking 'of all the money that must have been spent on the thing'.[46] This middle-class family is clearly resident in one of the nicer, leafier suburbs of Swansea West (although the town in the novel is called Aberdarcy) or from Mumbles. Amis lived for over a decade in Swansea and knew these types of places and people well.

---

[42] John Ramsden, *The Age of Churchill and Eden, 1940–1957* (London: Longman, 1995), p. 237.
[43] CPA, CCO 1/11/524, David Llewellyn to Godfrey Llewellyn, 10 June 1955.
[44] 'Air blue over Tory drinks', *South Wales Echo*, 17 September 1964.
[45] Kingsley Amis, *That Uncertain Feeling* ([1955] St Albans: Panther, 1975), p. 54, 100.
[46] Amis, *That Uncertain*, p. 114.

'LOCAL BOYS' AND ANGLICISED WALES

Despite all this, the party seems to have been most effective at winning the trust of these parts of the electorate when its ideas were mediated 'on the ground' by what were sometimes called 'local boys'. These people were often from the communities they wanted to represent and could therefore most effectively blend big political trends and concerns with local issues.[47] Local activists took the process of selecting a possible member of parliament seriously and knew that the process was one of the few ways in which power was diffused from the party hierarchy to the grassroots.[48] In doing so, they tended to place real emphasis on the need to field someone local. For the *Western Mail* in 1955, having a local candidate for any party was a 'bird in the hand', and contemporary academic commentators also drew the same conclusions.[49] One Nuffield general election study would even go as far as to suggest that there was something specific about Welsh politics that made this theme of localism key.[50] A strong sense of place, family, community and kinship had long been identified as a particularly Welsh trait, akin to the kind of spirit also found in rural or 'parochial' areas like Cornwall, where rank-and-file Conservatives sought similar kind of 'locals' and 'good mixer[s]'.[51] As Taym Saleh has noted about parts of Scotland, regional politics far removed from London was often more local in character, although oral evidence shows such things mattered to grassroots activists in the south east of England

---

[47] For comments on this in the context of a more recent period, see British Library Sound and Moving Image archive, C1688/16, Ken Worthy interview; Andrew Edwards, *Labour's Crisis: Plaid Cymru, the Conservatives, and the Decline of the Labour Party in North-West Wales, 1960–74* (Cardiff: University of Wales Press, 2011), pp. 9, 266.

[48] Stuart Ball, 'The National and Regional Party Structure', and Brian Criddle, 'Members of Parliament', in Seldon and Ball, *Conservative Century*, pp. 170, 158; John Ramsden, *The Winds of Change: Macmillan to Heath, 1957–1975* (Essex: Longman, 1996), p. 124.

[49] 'In Swansea West every head will count', Western Mail, 17 May 1955. F. A. Stacey and E. W. Cooney, 'A South Wales Constituency', in D. E. Butler (ed.), *The British General Election of 1951* (London: Macmillan and Co Ltd, 1952), p. 207.

[50] David Butler and Dennis Kavanagh, *The British General Election of 1979* (London: Macmillan, 1980), p. 311.

[51] Johnes, *Wales Since 1939*, pp. 157–8; Ramsden, *The Winds*, p. 121.

too, whilst the work of Steven Fielding has explored the importance of the theme in the context of local Labour parties.[52] In most cases, however, the focus on localism is something that is brushed over in the broader historiography of post-war politics in Britain.

General election	Number of candidates*	From the area	Educated at some point in Wales [for all primary and secondary][53]	Educated outside Wales
1945	12	6 (50%)	4 (33%) [3]	8 (66%)
1950	25	13 (52%)	13 (52%) [12]	12 (48%)
1951	29	12 (41%)	13 (45%) [12]	16 (55%)
1955	29	13 (45%)	15 (52%) [14]	14 (48%)
1959	31	13 (42%)	14 (45%) [12]	17 (55%)
1964	32	13 (41%)	15 (47%) [12]	17 (53%)
1966	35	15 (42%)	19 (54%) [16]	16 (46%)
1970	32	15 (47%)	20 (63%) [18]	12 (38%)
1974 Feb.	34	17 (50%)	20 (59%) [17]	14 (41%)
1974 Oct.	35	18 (51%)	20 (57%) [18]	15 (43%)
1979	31	12 (39%)	15 (48%) [12]	16 (52%)
1983	35	14 (40%)	16 (46%) [14]	19 (54%)
1987	37	10 (27%)	13 (35%) [10]	24 (65%)
1992	37	12 (32%)	20 (54%) [17]	17 (46%)
1997	37	10 (27%)	19 (51%) [17]	18 (49%)

* The number of candidates that data was available for.

Table 7: Residency and education of Conservative Party parliamentary candidates at each general election in Wales, 1945–1997.

[52] Taym Saleh, 'The Decline of the Scottish Conservatives in North-East Scotland, 1965–79: A Regional Perspective', *Parliamentary History*, 36/2 (2017), 219; British Library Sound and Moving Image archive, C1688/19, Simon Parnell interview; Steven Fielding, 'The "Penny Farthing" Machine Revisited: Labour Party Members and Participation in the 1950s and 1960s', in Chris Pierson and Simon Tormey (eds), *Politics at the Edge: The PSA Yearbook 1999* (Basingstoke: Macmillan, 2000), p. 176.
[53] Ivor Thomas Rees's brilliant collection of biographies, *Welsh Hustings*, provided the raw data for this table – and many of the others in this book. He collected personal details from every candidate who stood for a parliamentary seat in the period 1885–2004. Not every entry for a candidate lists their place of birth, so the author decided to use place of education for this particular exercise instead.

Table 7 demonstrates that the Conservatives often fielded an even mix of parliamentary candidates who were from Wales and those who were not from Wales (a slightly blunt judgement based on whether they had received a majority of their education there; had lived there for a majority of their life; or had grown up there throughout their formative years). In most cases, those who were not Welsh were Englishmen drafted in to fight a seat which was usually unwinnable. What the table also demonstrates, however, is that in most cases when a Welsh candidate was fielded, they hailed not just from Wales but specifically from that local area, judged by the same metrics of schooling, upbringing or residency. Candidates themselves clearly thought this was important to stress. In every election covered by this chapter's period, when Conservatives had a strong connection to the area they were standing for, they mentioned that fact in their election address, whilst very few stressed things like their 'Welsh roots'.[54] Twice as many Tory candidates as their Labour opponents chose to talk about their local connections, although this can be read as a sign that they had to remind voters they were not 'outsiders', whereas many Labour MPs – deeply embedded as they were into their local communities – did not need to make such statements.[55] Nonetheless, the emphasis on the local over the national is highly significant.

The Conservatives were not solely responsible for emphasising this aspect of Wales's political culture, but they consciously embraced it. They must have thought it made a difference and there is certainly evidence that supporters and voters warmed to local candidates. When Geoffrey Howe stood for the party in his home seat of Aberavon in 1955 and again in 1959, the local party there was delighted. 'Not only [is he] a local man' wrote the association's secretary, 'but . . . a name well known and much respected throughout the Aberavon Division'.[56] Howe's father had

---

[54] Although before this chapter's period, at the 1950 general election, every candidate who had this local link mentioned the fact.

[55] Figures compiled by the author using data in Ivor Thomas Rees, *Welsh Hustings: 1885–2004* (Llandybie: Dinefwr Press, 2005).

[56] CPA, CCO 1/11/532, Secretary's Report for 1955.

been the Coroner for West Glamorgan for thirty-three years, as well as Clerk to the Aberavon County Justices. His mother was a Justice of the Peace (JP).[57] Whilst his family were not representative of the population in a seat dominated by a steelworks, they were undoubtedly familiar names and faces. Tellingly, at the 1955 general election, the front of Howe's address to the electorate read: 'Vote for Howe, your local man!'[58] Lord Howe later remembered his campaign as good-natured, with people reacting kindly to him 'because they knew my mother and my family', even if most of them thought he was on 'the wrong side'.[59] At the following election in the neighbouring seat of Neath, the Conservative candidate Idris Pearce, son of local hoteliers, remembered getting 'a very friendly reception . . . it was good being local'.[60]

FARMING
We shall maintain fair prices and orderly marketing for main farm products, and production grants for small farms and farmers on hill and marginal land. We shall continue to extend rural water and electricity supplies - and to oppose any form of land nationalisation.

HOUSES & SCHOOLS
Our target of 300,000 houses a year has been surpassed - with more for sale and more to let. Conservatives will continue helping people to buy their homes and to repair and convert the older houses. Our slum clearance programme, the first since the war, will rehouse 200,000 people a year.

The Conservative Government have improved the rate of school building and the recruitment of teachers. In the next five years we shall provide another million school places, and so bring down the size of classes. Grammar schools must not be swallowed up by mass comprehensive schools; but I believe that each has a place in education to-day.

INDIVIDUAL FREEDOM
Seven out of every ten war-time regulations have gone and we mean to deal with the rest. We shall ensure justice for individuals at the hands of the State. A comprehensive scheme for legal advice and legal aid in the County Courts will be introduced. Local government will be strengthened and reformed.

I do not question the sincerity of our political opponents. All parties pray for peace and desire the prosperity and welfare of the people. These ends are not at issue between the parties. The issue is: Which party has shown, in practice and in prospect, that it knows and can use the means to secure them? If we remember the lessons of yesterday, tomorrow can be bright indeed. A vote for Socialism is a vote for the policy which was tried and has failed. To vote Conservative is to invest in success.

Geoffrey Howe

VOTE FOR HOWE YOUR LOCAL MAN!

Figure 5: Geoffrey Howe's election address stresses to the voters of Aberavon in 1955 that he is a local man.

[57] CPA, MS Howe dep 326, 1955 election address.
[58] CPA, PUB 229/11/13, Geoffrey Howe election address, Aberavon, 1955.
[59] Interview, Lord Howe of Aberavon, 17 July 2014; Geoffrey Howe, *Conflict of Loyalty* (London: Pan Books, 1995), p. 28.
[60] Interview, Sir Idris Pearce, 10 August 2017.

Howe and Pearce were standing in unwinnable Valleys seats, but this theme of localism was especially prominent in Conservative-friendly 'British Wales'. David Llewellyn, for example, the member for Cardiff North from 1950 to 1959, began his election addresses to his constituents with phrases like 'My Dear Neighbour', followed by a description of how long he had lived in the area (although he was originally from Aberdare in the Cynon Valley).[61] When Llewellyn stood down from parliament, a flurry of excitement followed, with seventy-six names initially put forward as his replacement as candidate. This list included William Rees-Mogg (who would later edit *The Times*).[62] From an impressive array of names the association selected local man Donald Box, stressing that he was a 'native of Cardiff and [a] senior partner of a firm of stockbrokers', even if local party members were apparently very concerned about the fact he was divorced.[63] His local credentials, however, trumped any concern about his status as a divorcee.[64] Box had spent previous contests emphasising the fact that 'he had been born and bred' in the local area. In the Newport by-election of 1956 he used this against his Labour opponent, the former minister Sir Frank Soskice, who had been parachuted into the constituency in order to re-enter parliament, having lost his former seat.[65] When Swansea West was narrowly won by the Tories in 1959, the victorious candidate Hugh Rees played heavily on his local connections.[66] He was the 'son of a prominent businessman' and spoke in 'an attractive Swansea accent', noted the *Western Mail*.[67] Even though it was always an easy win for the local press to pass comment on someone being a 'local boy', one paper even described how Rees had set the tone for the campaign in the seat, challenging other candidates

[61] CPA, PUB 229/9/17, David Llewellyn election address, Cardiff North, 1950.
[62] CPA, CCO 1/12/524, Davies to Craine, 1 December 1958.
[63] 'Who's your choice?', *Western Mail*, 6 October 1959.
[64] CPA, CCO 1/10/520, Oliver to Hare, 1 March 1954.
[65] 'Tory candidate appeals to Newport Liberals to support him', *South Wales Argus*, 23 June 1956.
[66] Morgan, 'Swansea West', pp. 295, 296.
[67] 'Tories gamble on their Y-line', *Western Mail*, 2 October 1959.

116   AFFLUENCE AND A CHANGING WALES, 1951–1964

to stress their own connections to the area.[68] Peter Thomas, the MP for Conway from 1951 to 1966, also supposedly had a 'strong following in the constituency as one of its local boys'.[69] On his 1964 election address, his face appeared imposed on a map of his Conway constituency, with key place names highlighted.[70]

Figure 6: Peter Thomas emphasises the importance of place to the voters of Conway in his 1964 election address.

[68] 'Slight swing can sway results', *Western Mail*, 9 October 1964.
[69] 'Eligible', *Western Mail*, 21 September 1959.
[70] CPA, PUB 229/13/16, Peter Thomas election address, Conway, 1964.

Crucially, the places that tended to elect their Conservative 'local boys' were not just the more middle-class parts of Wales, but also the most anglicised areas too, often reflected in the candidates themselves. Even those who were born and bred in Wales had, either through their schooling, their university education, or the nature of their family upbringing, unconsciously or deliberately developed more English accents, or at least less strong Welsh ones. This contributed to a sense – not always fairly – of them as upper middle class, 'respectable' or even 'English'. Hence, Michael Heseltine being accused of having 'the voice of an Englishman' by Aneurin Bevan when he fought the Gower seat in 1959.[71] Peter Thomas, despite being born in the Welsh-speaking Llanrwst area of the Conway constituency, was well-spoken and, in the words of another Anglo-Welsh Tory from the period, 'the type of Welshman the English like'.[72] Geoffrey Howe had a Welsh lilt to his voice, but it was also clear that he was not from a working-class, steelworker's household. When asked, years later, what had happened to his 'fiery' Welsh temperament, Howe responded that 'nothing is more likely to diminish fire than being a Wykehamist' – that is, the product of one of England's most prestigious public schools, Winchester College.[73]

Even Cardiff, which was a surprisingly Conservative city for much of the twentieth century, was described by one schoolbook in 1961 as 'quite English in attitude'.[74] Such areas were also the recipients of more inward migration than most others. After all, the border between England and Wales was remarkably porous. In some of these border areas, or along the north Wales coast, a very large number of people living there were English by birth.[75]

---

[71] Interview, Lord Heseltine, 24 July 2014; Crick, *Michael Heseltine*, p. 12.

[72] Andrew Roth, 'Obituary: Lord Thomas of Gwydir', *Guardian*, 6 February 2008; Interview, Lord Temple-Morris, 17 June 2015.

[73] British Library Sound and Moving Image archive, C1503/12, Lord Howe interview.

[74] Martin Johnes, 'The Making and Development of the Capital City of Wales', *Contemporary British History*, 26/4 (2012), 516.

[75] Graham Day, Angela Drakakis-Smith and Howard H. Davis, 'Being English in North Wales: Immigration and the Immigrant Experience', *Nationalism and Ethnic Politics*, 12/3–4 (2006), 579.

This did not map directly on to Tory support. But, at the same time, there was a stronger link between Englishness and voting Tory, and that bond became even stronger when age and social class were added into the mix.[76] Seats like Monmouth, held by Peter Thorneycroft from 1945 to 1966, are testament to this. Monmouthshire had, since the turn of the century, been the recipient of tens of thousands of largely English incomers.[77] Industrial developments were also bringing in new English immigrants from 'occupationally and socially mobile groups' to work in managerial positions. They were regularly associated with a Conservative vote.[78] The post-war period was an era where industrial patterns were altering, as the closure of heavy industry meant that localised economies were less insular. The new managerial classes, professional and often Anglo-Welsh, or from England, utilised a growing ease of travel. They tended to locate in, or relocate to, the coastal fringes and the suburbs. At the steelworks in Port Talbot in the 1950s, there were occasional grumblings from workers there that the management were all disconnected and English – 'there's not a bloody Welshman among the lot of them'.[79] *The Manchester Guardian* also recognised this, commenting that 'middle as well as top management tends to be English rather than native Welsh . . . locally they live side by side with the local middle class'.[80] Other commentators noted that these 'incomers' tended to share far less of the old radical political spirit that had been a part of many Welsh communities in the past.[81]

---

[76] Richard Wyn Jones, Roger Scully and Dafydd Trystan, 'Why do the Conservatives Always do (Even) Worse in Wales?', in Lynn Bennie, Colin Rawlings, Jonathan Tonge and Paul Webb (eds), *British Elections and Parties Review*, 12/1 (2002), 236, 238–40; Ball, *Portrait*, p. 84.

[77] Chris Williams, 'Monmouthshire – Wales or England?', in H. V. Bowen (ed.), *A New History of Wales: Myths and Realities in Welsh History* (Llandysul: Gomer Press, 2011), p. 93.

[78] Colin Bell, *Middle Class Families: Social and Geographical Mobility* (London: Routledge and Kegan Paul, 1968), p. 11.

[79] James Morris, 'Welshness in Wales', *Wales*, 32 (1958), 17–18.

[80] Quoted in Bell, *Middle Class Families*, p. 12.

[81] Morgan, 'Swansea West', p. 301.

It was not lost on Conservative Central Office (CCO) that electoral support in Wales was grounded in the anglicised communities of certain seats.[82] In Wrexham, a hopeful parliamentary candidate commented that, of the Welsh and English communities in the area, the Conservatives were 'really only representative of the English section'.[83] Even in some places that were very Welsh in character, like Anglesey, the Conservative Association deliberately sought out Welsh people to become members because it perceived itself to be 'far too exclusively English in character'.[84] One local informant told CCO that the Conservatives on Anglesey were known locally as the 'society of snobs'.[85] Again, this very particular group was the subject of ridicule by Kingsley Amis, who called them, through the central character in *That Uncertain Feeling*, 'that upper-class crowd . . . Why couldn't they be Welsh, I wondered, or since they were mostly Welsh by birth why couldn't they stay Welsh? Why had they got to go around pretending to be English all the time?'[86]

Local grassroots leaders who, alongside parliamentary candidates, acted as the face of the party 'on the ground' in this period, were usually drawn from similar backgrounds. The prominence of upper-class and ex-military personnel in Monmouth Association's headquarters in this period led to it being nicknamed 'the War Office'.[87] One key person was Colonel Sir Godfrey Llewellyn, who had a distinguished military career, winning the Military Cross and twice being mentioned in dispatches. His long list of honorifics – CB, CBE, MC, TD, DL and JP – featured atop much local party communication in his role

---

[82] In Enoch Powell's 1948 report on the political situation in, and specific characteristics of, Wales, Flintshire – a Conservative seat – was deliberately omitted from the discussion because it was 'more closely allied to England than to Wales in its characteristics'. See CPA, CCO 4/2/183, 'Report on Rural Wales', 20 January 1948.
[83] CPA, CCO 1/7/515, Lamb to Thomas, undated, *c.*1950.
[84] CPA, CCO 1/7/507, Anglesey Basic Report, undated, *c.*1948.
[85] CPA, CCO 1/7/507, Selwood to the Organising Department, *c.*May 1949.
[86] Amis, *That Uncertain*, p. 208.
[87] Interview, Peter Price, 4 December 2015. Walters's predecessor in this role, the 'terribly posh' Leslie Knipe, did tell the Monmouth Association in 1972 that he 'hoped to learn a little Welsh'. See WPA, GB0210 MONION, file 24, 27 June 1972.

as Chairman of the Party in Wales, a voluntary but key grassroots position. He had chaired the Glamorgan group of constituencies, was a JP and High Sheriff for Glamorgan, Deputy Sheriff and High Lieutenant of Monmouthshire, later becoming Deputy Lieutenant of the new county of Gwent. He had numerous business interests on top of all of this, highlighting how those who got involved in such forms of civic voluntarism around the world often joined multiple organisations.[88] Llewellyn's correspondences – which were sometimes signed off 'Godders' – were full of talk of 'awfully nice fellows' and statements like 'I would not like to leave without saying *au revoir*'.[89] In both demeanour and actions, people like Llewellyn were the epitome of the well-spoken Tory who displayed a sense of 'civic nationalism', tying themselves to core British institutions like the army. They also exhibited as well a sense of 'local patriotism', which we saw in the context of policy for Wales in the previous chapter, but which can also apply here. Such people were closely involved with things like local government positions, choirs or hospital management committees, or flying the flag for local charitable causes or groups. In Carmarthen, the husband-and-wife team, the Protheroe-Beynons, who led the association were active members of the local Anglican church, the farming union and the Girl Guides. Mrs Protheroe-Beynon was proud of founding the first branch of the local Burry Port Girl Guides.[90] Whilst much of this had a distinctly local focus, the way in which party leaders were so clearly bound up with British-wide institutions and organisations, which of course were dominated by English overtones, helped cement the party's anglicised image, albeit in a period where this would have felt quite ordinary for a lot of Welsh people in so-called 'British Wales'.

---

[88] 'Sir Godfrey Llewellyn', *Daily Telegraph*, 6 October 1986. For civic activity in an international context, see Sidney Verba, Kay Lehman Schlozman and Henry E. Brady, *Voice and Equality: Civic Voluntarism in American Politics* (London: Harvard University Press, 1995), pp. 1–2.

[89] See WPA, Huw T. Edwards papers, A2/154, Llewellyn to Edwards, 22 February 1965.

[90] CPA, CCO, 1/14/517/1, Davies to Bryan, 6 September 1962; Rees, *Welsh Hustings*, pp. 239–40.

Other key people, like Cardiff-based Sir Charles Hallinan, were cast from the same mould. Hallinan was variously Chairman, President and parliamentary candidate for Cardiff constituencies and the wider area. He was an upper-middle-class solicitor, with a well-stocked wine cellar, who had commanded a battalion of the Cardiff Home Guard in the war. He was Vice President of the British Legion and through a long career held a range of ceremonial roles, including becoming Lord Mayor of Cardiff.[91] Indeed, a feature of many prominent members of the grassroots in Wales was that they were involved in local government, sometimes representing more Conservative-friendly wards. Hallinan himself was a long-serving councillor in Cardiff. He was talented, but an eccentric, causing irritation to the party as a result. He had 'a crop of grey billowing hair and an eye glass and a bunch of sweet peas or a chrysanthemum in a metal holder in his button hole'.[92] One young activist from the time remembered going into 'Charlie's' office, which he described as 'an Emperor's Palace with busts of Napoleon on the wall', reflecting an admiration for the French leader.[93] On one occasion, after apparently putting his new Rolls Royce into reverse by accident, Hallinan and the car were propelled from the road into the bar of a nearby pub (after which he was supposedly given a Napoleon brandy for the shock).[94] Hallinan's desire for social status, as it was seen by the Wales Area Office, even got him upbraided directly by Lord Woolton. After Hallinan wrote a series of notes to the Chairman of the Party on a range of issues, Woolton scribbled at the bottom of one of the correspondences, 'Please [underlined three times] do not send official letters to my home. How would you like it?'[95] The fact that this prominent Tory in the capital city was considered such a nuisance and an eccentric again speaks volumes about the often shaky position of the party in places like Cardiff.

[91] CPA, PUB 229/9/17, Charles Hallinan election address, Cardiff West, 1950.
[92] CPA, CCO 1/7/519, Thomas to Maxse, 3 February 1948.
[93] Interview, Keith Flynn, 29 September 2015.
[94] Robert Mogbridge, *South Wales Echo*, 2 April 2013.
[95] CPA, CCO 1/12/526, Hallinan to Woolton, 28 November 1957.

POLITICAL CHALLENGES

In the process of appealing to, and reflecting, their more anglicised and middle-class base, the Conservatives did of course reinforce some of the core problems they had in many other parts of Wales, namely that they looked and sounded unsuitable to the electorate there: too 'English', too elitist, and detached from 'ordinary' concerns. This was especially the case when their primary appeal in Wales in this period revolved around symbols of affluence and self-improvement that were more available to some people than others. Working-class people did of course vote for the Tories. Across Britain, they did so in significant numbers, as demonstrated by two groundbreaking studies of working-class Conservatism at the end of the 1960s.[96] Without such voters, the Tories could not win seats and would never have been in government.[97] But there can be no doubt that the party relied on a core of middle-class support in Wales, whilst Labour remained able to capture a solid section of the working-class vote.

Wales therefore presented greater challenges for the Tories. As the *Western Mail* decided to put it in one election year, 'every election has a loser. In some parts of south Wales, these are known as Conservatives'.[98] CCO knew that Welsh miners were, in its own mild phrase, 'a tough audience'.[99] Whilst the party was capable of fielding 'local boys' in seats where it might win, this was rarely the case in places like the Valleys of so-called 'Welsh Wales'. In fact, it was common in this period for lists of local people who might be willing to stand for election being passed to local associations, with every person on the list refusing to do so.[100] One wrote of contesting Wrexham, that the only

---

[96] Eric A. Nordlinger, *The Working-Class Tories: Authority, Deference and Stable Democracy* (London: Macgibbon and Kee, 1967); Robert McKenzie and Allan Silver, *Angles in Marble: Working Class Conservatives in Urban England* (London: Heinemann, 1968).
[97] Todd, *The People*, pp. 1–2.
[98] 'Valleys Tories only stand to lose', *Western Mail*, 11 February 1974.
[99] CPA, CCO 1/8/536/2, Final Report, 8 December 1950.
[100] CPA, CCO 1/8/532, Garmonsway to Thomas, 27 October 1950.

person who should fight that seat was a 'very young energetic man, who has everything to gain and nothing to lose'.[101] Signs of how desperate the party was to field a candidate with some connection to the area were evident when the Wales Area Office seriously considered allowing Alfred Norris to stand for a seat in the early 1950s despite the fact that he was 'quite frank in admitting that he was connected with the British Union of Fascists'.[102]

The results of this were perhaps inevitable. Throughout this period, seats like those in the south Wales Valleys were used as constituencies that offered young aspiring politicians from outside Wales a chance for what was often euphemistically called 'gaining valuable experience'.[103] The process of parachuting keen but unsuitable English public-school boys into the Valleys is a practice associated with more recent times, but it has a long pedigree. Solicitors from the Home Counties were a particularly common sight.[104] Candidates were sometimes as far from 'local' as could be imagined, with those in Llanelli and Rhondda West in 1955 originally hailing from New Zealand and Australia respectively.[105] The contrast a New Zealand solicitor would have struck with the town's sitting MP, the former collier and key member of the Attlee government James Griffiths, would have been stark to anyone following the campaign. When some candidates spoke of presenting their printed election addresses 'with compliments to a proud Valley', this only accentuated that they were not from there; local Labour candidates never did anything similar.[106] CCO conceded that the problem across the board was that 'too many square pegs [were] trying to fit

---

[101] CPA, CCO 1/8/514, Brown letter.
[102] CPA, CCO 1/8/536/3, by-election report, 24 October 1950.
[103] R. B. McCallum and Alison Readman, *The British General Election of 1945* (Oxford: Oxford University Press: 1947), p. 75.
[104] CPA, CCO 1/7/523, James to Thomas, 13 January 1950.
[105] 'More Conservative candidates adopted in south Wales', *Western Mail*, 29 April 1955; 'Meet the candidates: Rhondda West', *Western Mail*, 24 May 1955.
[106] CPA, Various 1950 general election addresses.

into round holes'.[107] Unlike more recent times, when the longlist to fight a hopeless seat consists of dozens of people plotting a future political career, someone like Michael Heseltine, as we have seen, could turn up for the selection meeting in Gower to discover no one else was being interviewed for the position.[108] The hopelessness of fighting a safe Labour seat created a self-perpetuating problem, where fewer suitable people came forward to take on the thankless task.

However, it is also worth examining the other end of the so-called 'political spectrum' and those people in Wales who, far from subscribing to the left-wing values of an area, criticised the Tories for not being robustly conservative enough in this period. The higher echelons of the party were often at odds with both the feeling of their supporters, and parts of the electorate more broadly, especially when it came to issues like immigration or capital and corporal punishment.[109] On the death penalty, women in particular were often satirised as 'blue-rinsed dragons' or as 'a pack of savage matrons in mink baying for blood and flogging and capital punishment', but – stereotypes aside – this reflected broader feelings in the country at large.[110] A party official noted in a confidential report after a trip to a public meeting in Colwyn Bay, in 1956 that there was 'unanimous enthusiastic clap[ping] when I said I was in favour of capital punishment – I don't think there was a single abolitionist present'.[111]

Some Welsh politicians, however, were good at reflecting the mood of this section of the electorate. The MP for Denbigh from 1959, Geraint Morgan, who was considered to be a terrible 'House of Commons man' because he never turned up for debates, was well attuned to politics in other ways. He noted that

[107] CPA, CCO 500/24/56, Wales and Monmouth Area General Election 1950 Report.
[108] Interviews, Lord Heseltine, 24 July 2014, and Peter Price, 4 December 2015.
[109] Stuart Ball, 'Local Conservatism and the Evolution of the Party Organisation', in Seldon and Ball, *Conservative Century*, p. 295.
[110] 'Prisons and Punishment', *Daily Telegraph*, 21 April 1961; Tim Bale, *The Conservatives since 1945: The Drivers of Party Change* (Oxford: Oxford University Press, 2016), p. 84.
[111] CPA, CCO 2/4/14, Katherine Elliot report on Area Tour, 22 February 1956.

'feeling for abolition [of hanging] in the House of Commons was in inverse ratio to the feeling in the country'.[112] In a poll of the electorate in his seat on the separate issue of the use of corporal punishment in schools, there was 'almost 100 per cent backing' for it.[113] When Donald Box, the MP for Cardiff North, made a pledge to vote for the reintroduction of hanging, he was greeted at a public husting 'with cheers and applause'.[114] Speaking in 1961, the future MP Michael Roberts told an audience of party supporters about his worries surrounding 'the decline in the public morality [which] left no room for complacency about our greatest asset – the character of the people'.[115] More broadly, Harold Macmillan's economic policies demonstrated that a gulf existed between the party's hierarchy, some of its activists and certain parts of the electorate. Macmillan was a Keynesian, believing in the theory of the multiplier effect, as well as the need to run short-term budget deficits.[116] He believed in the state and its ability to play a supportive role in areas like industry, influenced by having been the MP for urban and industrial Stockton-on-Tees for much of the 'bad old days' of the inter-war period.[117] Cabinet ministers in the 1950s were sent to Wales, where unemployment rates were significantly higher than in England, to reassure voters there that they would not witness a rerun of the 1930s.[118]

However, Macmillan's approach was far from popular with some voters and key MPs.[119] In January 1958, all three ministers who made up the Treasury team resigned in protest against

[112] 'Denbigh Conservative conference topics', *Weekly News*, 13 May 1965.
[113] 'Return corporal punishment say Denbigh voters', *Liverpool Daily Post*, 29 March 1966.
[114] 'Box pledge on hanging lauded', *Western Mail*, 10 March 1966.
[115] WPA, GB0210 CARCON, file 35, Cardiff South East Executive Committee minute book, AGM, 30 March 1961.
[116] E. H. H. Green, *Ideologies of Conservatism: Conservative Political Ideas in the Twentieth Century* (Oxford: Oxford University Press, 2002), p. 165.
[117] Green, *Ideologies*, p. 160.
[118] CPA, CCO 4/8/370, Notes for Lord Hailsham in Swansea, c.1958.
[119] Robert Blake, *The Conservative Party from Peel to Major* (London: Heinemann, 1997), p. 295.

the Prime Minister's commitment to increase public spending to counter inflation.[120] This was important from the Welsh perspective because the Chancellor of the Exchequer was the Monmouth MP, Peter Thorneycroft. His junior ministers were Nigel Birch, the MP for the north Wales seat of Flint West, and Enoch Powell. Powell, whilst neither Welsh nor a Welsh MP, had ties with the nation, as we saw in the previous chapter. Their actions were supported by many members of the public, who were fearful of inflation, and this was reflected in letters sent to Thorneycroft's Monmouth constituency association.[121] Although he was a senior activist and not just a member of the electorate, its chairman even went as far as to write to the party's chair Lord Hailsham threatening to take him on in the pages of *The Times* if he continued to write 'such nonsense publicly' on subjects like monetary policy.[122] In Birch's Flint West, the response from the wider public was reported to be 'so strong, so spontaneous and so universal[ly positive]' after he had resigned.[123]

This conservatism within the party, and across sections of the electorate, perhaps helps explain why so few women stood as Conservative candidates in this period.[124] Front-line political culture across Wales in the 1950s and early 1960s was a great deal more masculine than it would later become, so this was not a phenomenon exclusive to the Conservatives, but the way the party approached female candidates does reveal something specific about the Tories and their supporters, especially when we consider the fact that the women's vote was so important for the party's electoral fortunes and its strength at the grassroots. The most prominent Conservative women in the public eye remained the wives of candidates, who continued to feature on

---

[120] E. H. H. Green, 'The Conservative Party, the State and the Electorate, 1945–64', in Lawrence and Taylor, *Party, State and Society*, p. 187.

[121] Green, *Ideologies*, p. 193; WPA, GB0210 MONION, file 6, Monmouth Conservative and Unionist Association Executive Committee minute book, 27 July 1956.

[122] CPA, CCO 1/12/544, Jenour to Hailsham, 13 January 1958.

[123] CPA, CCO 1/12/522 West Flintshire Conservative and Unionist Association AGM Report, 28 February 1958.

[124] In fact, no woman was elected as a Conservative MP from Wales until 2019.

many election addresses, styling themselves as 'his staunchest supporter, his most enthusiastic worker, his permanent organiser'.[125]

Table 8 shows how rare it was for women to stand as parliamentary candidates. These figures must be read with the knowledge that Wales had somewhere from 36 to 40 seats between 1945 and 1997. The Tories normally fielded candidates in all constituencies (exceptions being incidents like their pact with the National Liberals, or when they did not oppose George Thomas in Cardiff West during his tenure as Speaker of the House of Commons). Women in Wales had a certain stereotypical image, forged in part by the concept of the 'mam'. But as one newspaper put it in 1955, 'this tendency towards matriarchy has not been reflected in the political history of Wales'.[126] One explanation lies in the decision-making abilities of grassroots Tories, who ultimately chose candidates, and many of these thought that women would be particularly unsuitable in the industrial seats of 'Welsh Wales'. Even though Flint East had a female Labour MP, Eirene White, for twenty years from 1950 to 1970, the Conservative association there thought, on the basis of its semi-industrial character, that it was 'not a division for which a woman would be particularly acceptable, and I think therefore we start off with some little advantage for this reason'.[127] Other seats that had similar sorts of 'industrial characters' took the same attitude, with prominent Conservatives like Pamela Thomas actually being taken off some shortlists because of their sex.[128]

---

[125] 'When they fight, their womenfolk are with them – shoulder to shoulder', *Western Mail*, 29 September 1959.
[126] 'Women candidates in Wales', *Western Mail*, 17 May 1955.
[127] CPA, CCO1/7/516, Summers to Thomas, 19 October 1948.
[128] CPA, CCO 1/14/540, Davies to Bryan, 3 January 1962.

General election	Number of women candidates
1945	0
1950	0
1951	0
1955	1
1959	1
1964	2
1966	0
1970	2
1974 Feb.	1
1974 Oct.	1
1979	1
1983	1
1987	0
1992	2
1997	2

Table 8: Number of women standing as Conservative candidates at each general election in Wales, 1945–1997.

Class and status were again important and in this case they interlinked with sex, determining why Tory women did on rare occasions stand for parliament. The first woman to do so in the post-war era was Revel Guest, the daughter and granddaughter of former MPs, who had grown up with men like Anthony Eden coming to the family home for dinner and who herself later became a successful filmmaker.[129] She was also the direct descendant of 'one of Britain's most gifted and privileged women', Charlotte Guest.[130] When she fought Swansea East at the age of only twenty-three (the age of majority was twenty-one at the time), she had already experienced things that most of the women

[129] Interview, Revel Guest, 19 March 2015. Women had stood for the party before. For example, Gwendolyn Brodrick fought Denbigh in 1922.
[130] Angela V. John, 'Lifers: Modern Welsh History and the Writing of Biography', *Welsh History Review*, 25/2 (2010), 264.

AFFLUENCE AND A CHANGING WALES, 1951–1964   129

in that town, let alone young ones like her, had not. Her election leaflet detailed how she had 'travelled the world'.[131] No evidence survives of why the selection panel chose Guest, but her name and background were probably key factors. The industrial nature of the seat might have dovetailed with the fact that the Guests were prominent industrialists, having owned the Dowlais ironworks, although that would only have accentuated Guest's elite status. Nonetheless, she remembered travelling the constituency with her young female agent, addressing pubs full of coalminers.[132]

Figure 7: Revel Guest's election address to the voters of Swansea East, 1955.

---

[131] CPA, PUB 229/11/13, Revel Guest election address, Swansea East, 1955.
[132] Interview, Revel Guest, 19 March 2015.

Although Guest polled 10,726 votes in Swansea East 'against the odds', the constituency was always safe, and Labour's Dai Mort was never in danger from her challenge.[133] This was evident every time a woman stood for a Welsh seat. When the popular S. O. Davies stood again as the Labour candidate in Merthyr Tydfil in 1959, his challenger was Miranda Greenaway, a barrister from London who was an incongruous figure, 'chatting to men as they left the pit'.[134] This was in a coalmining constituency where, as a future south Wales Labour MP would write: 'Each valley had its superstitions, women and birds being the two most unpopular omens. Just seeing a woman on the way to work was enough to make some miners turn pale and go home for the day'.[135] Despite being one of the Conservative Party's 'major woman figure[s] in local government' in the mid-1960s, coming as she did from a prominent role in the Greater London Council, Shelagh Roberts was selected for the hopeless seat of Caernarfon, where her background as a non-Welsh speaker effectively made her unsuitable, despite her wealth of experience and the fact she had been born in Port Talbot, in south Wales, and educated in Milford Haven, in Pembrokeshire.[136]

Further dynamics specific to Welsh politics posed challenges for the Tories in this period, especially its relations with the Liberal Party in the Welsh-speaking *y fro Gymraeg* constituencies. Whilst the Conservatives maintained their pact with the National Liberals in some constituencies through the 1950s, they also had to consider their attitude to certain Liberal politicians (the National Liberals and the Liberals were separate and should not be confused). Table 3 in the previous chapter provides specific details. Conservatives believed that the presence of a Liberal in a three-cornered parliamentary contest would do more harm to the

[133] CPA, CCO 1/11/530, Swansea East Basic Report, 11 December 1956.
[134] 'Two candidates are "wounded in action"', *Western Mail*, 1 October 1959.
[135] Ann Clwyd, *Rebel With a Cause* (London: Biteback, 2017), p. 5.
[136] Maguire, *Conservative Women*, p. 165; Rees, *Welsh Hustings*, p. 258. Roberts would later go on to serve as a member of the European Parliament, receiving a peerage weeks before she died.

Conservative candidate than the Labour one, again splitting the right-leaning vote.[137] Of course, it had not always been like this. In the late nineteenth century, Liberalism had risen to become the dominant political force in Wales to such an extent that it was considered the political party of the nation, helping to relegate the Tories to a 'marginal irrelevance'.[138] However, what had once been a party wedded to a radical Nonconformism was now much closer to Conservatism, with elected Liberals pushed back into their safest rural heartlands in mid-Wales.[139] As one voter remarked: 'Cardiganshire Liberalism is a damned good Conservative philosophy'.[140] A combination of the growing conservatism of the old Liberalism, anti-Labour feeling, the long political tradition of these areas, and the character of some of the Liberal MPs, all help explain why local Tories in places like Ceredigion 'not only voted' for the Liberal Roderic Bowen in the 1950s, 'but also worked for him'.[141] Whilst some were astonished by this kind of friendliness, senior people within the Conservative Party argued that it would be 'a pity to oppose the right-wing of the Liberal Party', represented by people like Bowen, not least because the Conservatives would have struggled to win anyway in such Welsh-speaking seats, where their anglicised image continually hampered the party's fortunes.[142] Similarly, until a by-election in 1957, the Conservatives in Carmarthen, where there were quite a large number of party members and a vibrant associational life at the grassroots, did not oppose Rhys Hopkin Morris, the seat's right-leaning Liberal MP.

---

[137] CPA, CCO 2/2/17, the GD to Thomas, 31 May 1950.
[138] Kenneth O. Morgan, *Rebirth of a Nation: Wales, 1880–1980* (Oxford: Oxford University Press, 1981), p. 26; Felix Aubel, 'Welsh Conservatism, 1885–1935: Five Studies in Adaptation' (unpublished PhD thesis, Lampeter University, 1960), pp. 19–20.
[139] Johnes, *Wales Since 1939*, p. 37; David Childs, *Britain Since 1945: A Political History* (London: Routledge,1993), p. 66.
[140] P.J. Madgwick, Non Griffiths and Valerie Walker, *The Politics of Rural Wales: A Study of Cardiganshire* (London: Hutchinson and Co, 1973), p. 215.
[141] CPA, CCO 1/8/511, Cardigan Basic Report, 31 August 1950.
[142] CPA, CCO 1/8/511, Thomas to Garmonsway, 18 January 1951.

Most intriguing of all, however, was the situation in Montgomery, the seat of the Liberal leader Clement Davies. In 1951 and 1955, the Tories stood aside for Davies in order to use the seat as a bargaining chip. As the Vice Chairman of the party, John Hare, wrote: 'If we are committed to oppose candidates in the few remaining Liberal seats it will be an open invitation to the Liberals to adopt spoiling tactics in all [our] marginal seats . . . [Therefore], Clement Davies should not be opposed'.[143] No doubt the Conservatives warmed to Davies's messages that Labour had 'no policy' and was 'worn out', but there was much more going on behind the scenes.[144] Secret correspondences between the Deputy Party Chairman and the Wales Area Agent at the time spoke of appeasing Davies 'until Mr Churchill offers Wales to the Liberal Party!'[145] The presence of an exclamation mark at the end of the statement may well suggest that this was a throwaway remark made in jest, but perhaps there is something more to be read into it. Churchill was certainly fond of Clement Davies, offering him a role in his new cabinet on returning to office in 1951 and then requesting that he be left unchallenged by Tories in Montgomery.[146] It is worth speculating whether Churchill, prone to eccentric gestures and wishing in this period to make electoral pacts with his 'Liberal friends', considered going further and offering to stand aside in many more Welsh seats, as an even bigger bargaining chip with the Liberals.[147] After all, there were a number of constituencies in the 1945, 1950 and 1951 general elections where the two groups made significant compromises at the local associational level. A grand pact never happened, and such alliances with other parties fizzled out from the beginning of the 1960s. Making these connections with the party that used

[143] CPA, CCO 1/9/541, Hare to the GD, 27 August 1953.
[144] 'Socialists "worn out – no policy" – Mr Clement Davies', *Western Mail*, 1 September 1957.
[145] CPA, CCO 1/8/542, Thomas to Maxse, 2 May 1950.
[146] Malcolm Petrie, 'Anti-Socialism, Liberalism and Individualism: Rethinking the Realignment of Scottish Politics, 1945–1971', *Transactions of the Royal Historical Society*, 28 (2018), 206; CPA, CCO 1/8/541, Maxse to Garmonsway, 18 August 1950.
[147] Ramsden, *The Age of Churchill*, p. 6.

to dominate Welsh politics, even if the links were tenuous, at least gave the Conservatives some sense of being better plugged into the political culture of Wales, although it of course demonstrated that the party could not win in such places by itself.

'CONSERVATIVES CARE FOR WALES'

When it came to specific matters to do with Wales and its political culture, however, the party did focus on policy-making and ideas surrounding nationhood. They had to tread carefully, because concerns about the threat to a certain kind of 'Welsh way of life' were driven by the very forces of affluence and change that the Tories hoped to capitalise on. Voters had noticed the party's introduction of the Minister for Welsh Affairs role and engaged with it critically. The fact that David Maxwell Fyfe – 'Dai Bananas' – was a Scotsman, as well as the Home Secretary, with a huge amount of other things on his plate, was apparently the subject of more angry letters to some British and Welsh newspapers than anything else after the 1951 general election.[148] In response, an Under-Secretary of State role was set up to avoid the claim that Wales was receiving very 'part-time' attention. It was initially filled by the Cardiff North MP, David Llewellyn, who apparently took up the post with reluctance because he could not speak Welsh. He tried to learn some by listening to Welsh-language gramophone records.[149] After the introduction of these roles, the *Western Mail*, far from the most impartial source on this matter (its editor in the mid-1950 was the godfather of Llewellyn's son[150]), asked whether the Conservatives had 'the right understandings of our problems in Wales'. It added that

---

[148] CPA, CCO 4/4/324, Unsigned memorandum re Wales, 19 October 1951.
[149] 'Home Rule is only Solution to Welsh Problems', *Western Mail*, 16 October 1951; Rosser, *A Dragon*, pp. 66–7.
[150] CPA, CCO 1/12/524, Llewellyn to the Chief Whip, 20 September 1956.

there is far less suspicion of the Tory Party in Wales now than there was 15 to 20 years ago . . . Conservatives are believed to be making determined efforts to interpret the will of the people by forming and adapting their policies on a broad popular front.[151]

It was not simply a case of creating new roles. Under Maxwell Fyfe, the Conservatives were responsible for the gradual transfer of some important administrative functions to Wales. The Cardiff office of the Ministry of Education had responsibility for everyday educational business devolved to it, for example.[152] Conservatives at all levels, from the grassroots to government, tried to make some political capital out of this, stressing the symbolism of this administrative devolution. Prospective parliamentary candidates boasted that 'Wales is being looked after too! Remember that it was a Conservative Government that appointed a Minister for Welsh Affairs who sits in the cabinet. Welsh interests and problems are thus represented at the highest levels'.[153] This was something that the new Prime Minister Anthony Eden chose to stress on a visit to Cardiff in 1955, where he argued that it was an asset that the Home Secretary had oversight of Wales because, as the holder of one of the great offices of state, he was especially influential.[154] The role had passed to Gwilym Lloyd George in 1954, who had been a Tory-backed National Liberal MP in Wales until 1950, and who by 1954 sat for Newcastle North as a Conservative. As a Welsh-speaking member of the dynastic Lloyd George family, he seemed a suitable choice to fill the position.[155]

[151] 'A Poll of the back-benchers in Wales', *Western Mail*, 22 December 1951.
[152] Matthew Cragoe, 'Defending the Constitution: the Conservative Party and the Idea of Devolution, 1945–74', in Chris Williams and Andrew Edwards (eds), *The Art of the Possible: Politics and Governance in Modern British History, 1885–1997: Essays in Memory of Duncan Tanner* (Manchester: Manchester University Press, 2015), p.170.
[153] CPA, PUB, 229/11/13, Roy Rowlands election address, Rhondda East, 1955.
[154] CPA, CRD 2/45/4, Draft speech for Sir Anthony Eden in Cardiff, 5 May 1955.
[155] John Gilbert Evans, *Devolution in Wales: Claims and Responses, 1937–1979* (Cardiff: University of Wales Press, 2006), p. 55.

Figure 8: David Maxwell Fyfe, Home Secretary and Minister for Welsh Affairs, arrives to speak to a large Conservative Party rally in Dolgellau, 1953. Note the many formally dressed women in the audience.

Throughout the 1950s, which was an era of relatively subdued Welsh political consciousness, some in the party were making subtle but genuine attempts to recognise the difference and distinctiveness of Wales. The MP for Barry, Raymond Gower, who was elected in 1951, began lobbying the Board of Trade to permit the description 'Made in Wales' on goods manufactured there, for example.[156] For one grassroots association chairman in Welsh-speaking Wales, the Tories had 'taken immense pains to understand the special needs of Wales'.[157] Indeed, references to things like the 'needs' of the nation as a 'cultural entity' that had to be 'encouraged to develop its fine cultural characteristics' were reasonably common.[158] More bilingual electioneering material

---

[156] 'Welsh MPs Are "Whys" Men of Westminster', *South Wales Echo*, 16 December 1952.
[157] CPA, CCO 2/2/17, Central Council 1951, motion 13, text of speech made by the Chairman of the Merioneth Conservative Association.
[158] CPA, PUB 228/9/17, J. F. Lynan election address, Merthyr Tydfil, 1951.

continued to be produced by the party.[159] The wider context here is important. As the historian Peter Mandler has argued, 'national identity' is a tricky – even 'woolly' – concept to pin down precisely, but being Welsh increasingly meant something to many people in this period.[160] The end of the war did not witness an immediate upsurge in political nationalism, but wider discussions were often framed in terms of the need for better political representation.[161]

However, when MPs like Raymond Gower were calling for more general recognition of Wales, they were not necessarily shaping the debate, but responding to those who were. A key moment in this period was the Parliament for Wales campaign, which played out during the first half of the 1950s. A combination of a pressure group run by middle-class intellectuals, *Undeb Cymru Fydd* (The New Wales Union), Plaid Cymru and some Labour Party members, spent the period calling for self-government. This culminated in the veteran left-wing Labour MP for Merthyr Tydfil, S. O. Davies, presenting a Private Members' bill calling for a Welsh Parliament in 1955.[162] Davies was a particularly significant figure to have done this, because he was from an area – the industrial south – that tended to view devolutionary measures with a sceptical eye. His motive however was protection for Wales against any kind of return to a 1930s-style economy. The Bill was defeated in the House of Commons by 48 votes to 14, the small numbers reflecting, perhaps, how this was not considered to be a major issue of the day. Nevertheless, it marked another significant moment in the fluid debate about the Welsh nation to which the various political parties felt a need to respond.[163] Within some

---

[159] CPA, CCO 500/24/101, Wales and Monmouthshire Area 1951 General Election Report, undated, *c.*November 1951.
[160] Peter Mandler, *The English National Character: The History of an Idea from Edmund Burke to Tony Blair* (Bury St Edmunds: St Edmundsbury Press, 2006), chapter six.
[161] 'Wales Council Chairman Wants Welsh Parliament', *Western Mail*, 17 October 1951.
[162] J. Graham Jones, 'The Parliament for Wales Campaign, 1950–1956', *Welsh History Review*, 16/2 (1992), 207, 226.
[163] Jones, 'The Parliament', 226.

sections of Conservative ranks, S. O. Davies's plan had garnered sympathy. The future Conservative MP Geraint Morgan – at the time a little-known prospective candidate for Merioneth – discussed how he felt great sympathy for the movement.[164]

S. O. Davies's enthusiasm for devolution, however, contrasted sharply with many of his fellow south-Walian Labour MPs, like James Callaghan and George Thomas. The party continued to be conflicted over the issue, although it went into the general election of 1955 promising to maintain the Minister for Welsh Affairs. Similarly for the Tories, there was a fine line to tread. It certainly wanted to be seen as recognising the 'needs' of Wales, whilst remaining solidly committed to the unionist status quo. Evidence of how much this status quo mattered again came from Enoch Powell, who advocated drawing up documents in the early 1950s that would provide a 'handy de-bunking of the Welsh Parliament and Secretary of State theories'.[165] When the Monmouth MP and President of the Board of Trade Peter Thorneycroft gave a speech in Ystradgynlais in 1953, he was provided with notes from the party's Research Department that urged him to 'remember that Wales and England are indissolubly linked as one United Kingdom . . . Any exaggerated attempt at administrative devolution could be . . . disastrous'.[166] Responding to the defeat of the Parliament for Wales Bill in the House of Commons, Gwilym Lloyd George struck a broadly noncommittal tone, noting how the process of devolution had not yet finished.[167] Harold Macmillan used the same kind of conciliatory language on a visit to Cardiff in February 1955, ultimately committing the government to little by saying that 'if Wales is part of the United Kingdom . . . [there] is no reason why the Welsh nation should not have the maximum say in matters affecting Wales'.[168] It was common for Tory politicians to fall back on such imprecise

---

[164] 'Conservatives support the just claims of Wales', *Western Mail*, 4 October 1951.
[165] CPA, CCO 4/4/324, Powell to Thomas, undated, *c.* July 1951.
[166] CPA, CRD 2/45/4, 'Notes for Mr Thorneycroft at Ystradgynlais', undated, *c.* 1953.
[167] Evans, *Devolution*, p. 67.
[168] CPA, CRD 2/45/4, Notes for Harold Macmillan in Cardiff, 25 February 1955.

rhetoric, often simply saying the word 'Wales' several times without adding anything of substance, but they were certainly talking about the subject a great deal more.

The whole debate was given fresh impetus in the mid-1950s, when plans were drawn up to submerge the village of Capel Celyn, in the north Wales valley of Tryweryn, in order to create a reservoir that would provide water for the people of Merseyside. For nationalists at the time, and in the decades since, 'Tryweryn' became a byword for Welsh subjugation to hegemonic and uncaring English rule. The Capel Celyn affair is presented by many historians and in popular television documentaries as a major pivotal moment in modern Welsh history.[169] Even though the material loss at Trweryn was relatively small, Capel Celyn did represent a traditional 'Welsh way' of life that the encroaching forces of affluence and modernisation had not swept away. This had been 'sacrificed' in order to provide water for an English city (where, of course, many Welsh people lived).[170] The village was evacuated and flooded, and the reservoir – which still operates – was built. It was significant that all Welsh MPs (bar one Tory, David Llewellyn) voted against the measure, but to no avail.[171] These 'constitutional structures' allowed some to argue that the wishes of the Welsh people, expressed through their MPs, was going unheard.[172]

Harold Macmillan's government did not ignore the message that came from the Tryweryn affair. Macmillan took opportunities to stress how 'the Welsh point of view is always kept fully before the Cabinet when policy decisions are made', notably via the Minister for Welsh Affairs.[173] Piecemeal but important gestures

---

[169] Wyn Thomas, *Hands off Wales: Nationhood and Militancy* (Llandysul: Gomer Press, 2013), p. xi. Martin Johnes, *Wales: England's Colony? The Conquest, Assimilation and Re-creation of Wales* (Cardigan: Parthian, 2019), pp. 150–3; Huw Edwards, 'The Story of Wales', episode 6, BBC iPlayer.

[170] Michael Cunningham, 'Public Policy and Normative Language: Utility, Community and Nation in the Debate over the Construction of Tryweryn Reservoir', *Parliamentary Affairs*, 60/4 (2007), 631.

[171] Johnes, *Wales Since 1939*, p. 214.

[172] Cunningham, 'Public Policy', 633.

[173] *Western Mail*, 25 September 1959.

like the 1958 Festival of Wales, encouraging the naming of Prince Charles as the Prince of Wales, and the 1959 Eisteddfod Act were all significant. At the end of the 1950s, the striking Red Dragon was declared the official national flag. The Welsh Grand Committee in the House of Commons was set up in 1960 (albeit as a result of pressure from Labour MPs like Ness Edwards) in order to scrutinise measures pertinent to Wales.[174] Whilst many considered it an ineffective talking shop, it was another step in a particular direction.[175] The government also facilitated the 1961 referendum on public houses closing on a Sunday in Wales, which was organised on a county-by-county basis so as to allow areas of rural Wales – such as the kind of place where Capel Celyn had been – to express their own specific views on the matter (which most rural areas did, by voting to stay 'dry' on Sundays). From the end of the 1950s, more and more party literature in Wales began to feature a prominent 'Conservatives Care for Wales' slogan – something that might well have been more gesture politics, or something it felt forced into doing, but which it would certainly not have done even ten years earlier.[176]

None of this should give the impression, however, that the entire population of Wales – let alone those who were drawn to the Conservative Party – actually wanted or cared about gestures or concessions that recognised the unique features of the nation. In fact, many born and bred there were ambivalent about the Welsh language in particular, and some did not like it at all.[177] Economic change, the television and in-migration were all undermining the viability of traditional Welsh-speaking communities, leaving some to think that the language had little

---

[174] R. Merfyn Jones and Ioan Rhys Jones, 'Labour and the Nation', in Tanner, Williams and Hopkin, *The Labour Party*, p. 255.
[175] 'Silent Voice in Westminster', *Abergele Visitor*, 11 May 1963.
[176] *North Wales Weekly News*, c.1962.
[177] Geraint H. Jenkins and Mari A. Williams, 'Introduction', in Geraint H. Jenkins and Mari A. Williams (eds), *'Let's do our best for the ancient tongue': The Welsh Language in the Twentieth Century* (Cardiff: University of Wales Press, 2015), pp. 16–17.

future.[178] Again, the party found itself having to walk a fine line, balancing what it thought Welsh voters as a whole might want it to do, versus what its core supporters tended to think. When the party canvassed a range of its own voters on the topic of how much Welsh should be taught in schools, for example, the results were a mixed bag that tended to reflect where people came from. The Carmarthen Association, for example, located in a part of the Welsh-speaking heartlands, was of the 'firm opinion' that the language should be taught throughout schools, but many other associations gave a less clear-cut view, arguing for voluntary or occasional teaching.[179] Incidentally, a range of mixed reactions was evident in Labour associations as well.[180]

Some people's attitudes on the subject at the time were striking, especially in hindsight. In 1959, a little-known television producer called Wyn Roberts wrote a newspaper column railing against 'small, self-centred groups' in Wales who represented 'nothing but outmoded standards and stuffy idiosyncrasies'. In arguing that the television audience in Wales was small, with only a minority of those people Welsh speakers, Roberts said that to 'see programmes designed for a specific section of such a small audience, cutting out the majority, *really breaks my heart*'.[181] As we shall see, twenty years later Roberts would be the one who, in government and as the MP for Conway, established a Welsh-language television channel and became known to colleagues as 'the minister for S4C'.[182] Roberts almost certainly changed his mind between the late 1950s and the early 1980s (as people are allowed to do), and

---

[178] Janet Davies, *The Welsh Language* (Cardiff: University of Wales Press, 1999), pp. 76–7. This author's grandmother was born in rural north Pembrokeshire in the mid-1930s and spoke virtually no English until her later teenage years, but chose to stop using Welsh when she moved to a more anglicised area and had children in the 1950s and 1960s, believing, in part, that the tide was running against the language and that it was old-fashioned and impractical. Also see Johnes, *Wales: England's*, p. 149.

[179] CPA, MS Howe dep 326, 'Welsh forum number 5, February 1962'.

[180] Daryl Leeworthy, *Labour Country: Political Radicalism and Social Democracy in South Wales, 1831–1985* (Cardigan: Parthian, 2018), p. 466.

[181] 'Producer hits at cultural dictatorship', *Western Mail*, 21 September 1959. Italics in original.

[182] Interview, Nicholas Bennett, 21 December 2015.

the nature of TV had changed considerably in that time too, but his writings in the late 1950s show how there were limits to the kinds of concessions that even some Welsh-speaking Welsh people with Tory inclinations wanted to see.

The debate about Wales and nationhood was, however, increasing in volume. In 1957, the Council for Wales and Monmouthshire published its *Third Memorandum*, which came out strongly in favour of a Secretary of State for Wales.[183] After many months of discussion, Macmillan rejected the proposals. The council's chairman and influential trade unionist, Huw T. Edwards, resigned in fury at what he perceived to be the government's inability to understand Welsh aspirations, accusing the Tories of 'Whitehallism', which is what the party used to claim was one of Labour's great faults.[184] Shortly afterwards, responsibility for Welsh affairs was transferred from the Home Office to the Minister for Housing and Local Government. Thus, Henry Brooke became the new – and rather energetic – Minister, but there was also a vacancy for an Under-Secretary with responsibility for Wales. The choice for this role was limited and the way it was handled yet another piece of evidence demonstrating how the Conservatives often felt awkward in Wales. With no obvious choice to fill this Under-Secretary position, it was decided that David V. P. Lewis, a prominent grassroots Conservative who was also a successful businessman, would be a good option. This marked a rare occasion when a local Tory activist figure in Wales made the successful leap from grassroots politics to ministerial level. Lewis was 'flashed the ermine' and made a life peer in the House of Lords, which entitled him to become a government minister.[185] There followed concern that such a person was inexperienced and unable to take part in House of Commons debates.

---

[183] Johnes, *Wales Since 1939*, p. 47.
[184] Paul Ward, *Huw T. Edwards: British Labour and Welsh Socialism* (Cardiff: University of Wales Press, 2011), p. 117.
[185] David Melding, *Have We Been Anti-Welsh? An Essay on the Conservative Party and the Welsh Nation* (Barry: Cymdeithas y Kymberiaid, 2005), p. 16.

Lord Brecon, as Lewis became, was ultimately a symbol of the government's clumsy but real attempt to connect with Welsh feeling by bringing in someone who had for so long had his ear to the ground in Wales. Lewis used his position in the upper chamber to vigorously defend what were seen as 'Welsh interests'. When, for example, the Lord Lieutenant of Monmouthshire, Lord Raglan, argued in 1958 that the Welsh language was being forced upon some children and parents (which no doubt reflected a significant strand of opinion), Lord Brecon put forward a rebuttal.[186] Despite the peculiar circumstances of his appointment, Tories in Wales, like the Crown Bard of the National Eisteddfod and future Conservative candidate in Anglesey, John Eilian Jones, tried to make political capital out of Brecon. In 1959, Jones wrote: 'What have we done to deserve this? Only 2½ million people live here in Wales. Yet we have received two ministers, one voice in the cabinet and the other living amongst us with a seat in the House of Lords'.[187] The emphasis on 'living amongst us' might well have reflected an anxiety that many senior Tories with responsibility for Wales were not Welsh.

Meanwhile, the Labour Party's position on things like administrative devolution and the representation of Wales became clearer. Three significant resolutions passed by the Welsh Regional Council of Labour led to the party gaining the initiative by pledging to introduce a Secretary of State in 1959.[188] In 1964, the Llanelli MP, James Griffiths, became the first to hold that position when the party won that year's general election. This was a historic moment that ensured Wales was a unit of government for the first time.[189] The Tories did not commit to maintaining the Secretary of State position until they had lost the 1964 election, although by this point they had taken pragmatic steps to ensure

---

[186] WPA, GB0210 CONLES, file 5, 'Papers hit at Lord Raglan' (newspaper unknown), 28 November 1958.

[187] CPA, CRD 2/45/4, Draft column, 'Reviving the Old Country', 31 August 1959.

[188] Jones and Jones, 'Labour and the Nation', p. 254.

[189] Leon Gooberman, '"A Very Modern Kind of English Loneliness": John Redwood, the Welsh Office and Devolution', *Welsh History Review*, 29/4 (2019), 268.

that the policy areas of health, local government, transport and agriculture were overseen by dedicated Welsh teams.[190] Debates about 'the nation' within Conservative ranks also continued. One of the more interesting documents in this field was a pamphlet written for the Bow Group, an organisation founded in 1951 for bright younger Tory members.[191] The pamphlet, titled *Work For Wales: Gwaith i Gymru*, was penned by two up-and-coming prospective Conservative candidates, Tom Hooson and Geoffrey Howe.[192] *Work for Wales* was intended as a 'blue-print' for a specific Welsh Conservative strategy.[193] The pamphlet was addressed to Welsh people, with the authors primarily making specific calls for Welsh economic problems to be tackled, particularly in the context of a new, more diverse, post-war economy. Although it played down the need for a Secretary of State, Hooson and Howe argued that 'the Welsh way of life' – that phrase again – needed special consideration.[194] Although not the main focus of *Work for Wales*, one of the most significant recommendations it made was a move to recognise the 'nationhood and uniqueness of Wales' by differentiating the Conservative Area Council of Wales from its sister area councils and renaming it the 'Conservative Party in Wales'. This would also serve to help the party address itself 'purposefully to a Welsh audience'.[195] The central party acted upon the recommendation.[196]

Alongside this, candidates standing for the party in various constituencies, but particularly in those in *y fro Gymraeg*, tended

[190] Cragoe, 'Defending', pp. 168, 170.
[191] Catherine Ellis, 'No Hammock for the Idle: The Conservative Party, "Youth" and the Welfare State in the 1960s', *Twentieth Century British History*, 16/4 (2015), 446.
[192] When published, Tom Hooson was the Conservative parliamentary candidate for Caernarfon, and Geoffrey Howe the candidate for Aberavon.
[193] Edwards, *Labour's Crisis*, p. 160.
[194] Tom Hooson and Geoffrey Howe, *Work For Wales: Gwaith i Gymru* (London: Conservative Political Centre, 1959), p. 25.
[195] Hooson and Howe, *Work For Wales*, pp. 38, 111.
[196] When Howe took his peerage in 1992 he chose a Welsh title – his birthplace of Aberavon. Historians have pointed towards this as an indication of a Conservative's genuine loyalty and fondness to his Welsh hometown. When interviewed by the author, Lord Howe explained that he chose 'Aberavon' because it 'sounded good'.

to make greater efforts to stress the Welsh dimension of their personal lives and their politics. When Hooson himself stood in Caernarfon in 1959, he described himself as 'a Welshman full of life and ideas' and (giving a significant nod to Welsh political traditions and his family's personal history) 'a Welsh Conservative with Liberal blood' (he was the cousin of Emlyn Hooson, a prominent Liberal politician and Welsh MP).[197] Most candidates tended to discuss Welsh matters in their communications with the electorate, although the focus was usually on generic issues affecting people throughout Britain, but with Welsh case studies.[198] Much has been written about the Conservative Party's historic ability to be 'pragmatic' and shapeshift in accordance with the mood of the time. In reality, when it came to Wales, it was doing little more than making reasonably small gestures in terms of recognising the distinctiveness of the nation, but it knew that gestures mattered in politics. Much of this was driven by a genuine concern that an era of affluence and greater personal mobility would erode a traditional way of life. But such changes without doubt helped shift the dial in favour of more specific discussions about Wales and its distinctiveness.

APATHY AND ACTIVITY AT THE GRASSROOTS

Ironically for the Conservatives, an era of greater affluence helped undermine the strength of grassroots Tory associations. Popular culture, the television and consumer goods were slowly but significantly replacing a desire for people to 'do something', like join their local political party. Through the 1950s and into the 1960s, the political association as an idea or a reality did not die by any means, but it weakened, providing a contrast to the immediate post-war years, when membership numbers soared. Cracks were

---

[197] CPA, PUB 229/12/14, Tom Hooson election address, 1959.
[198] *Western Mail*, 12 September 1959.

visible across Wales, where local records show frazzled association officers fretting about apathy amongst their members.[199] This was particularly prevalent in men's branches, where local chairmen were, to take one example, 'disgusted at the meagre attendance of delegates... 8 attended [out of 28] and no apologies were received for absence'. 'Heated arguments' sometimes took place, not over politics but over the fact that too much was being asked of the men by the party's local leadership.[200] Often, men's branches would merge with women's ones to become 'joint' branches, although this usually meant that women dominated in both numbers and enthusiasm.[201]

Some attempts were made to combat this apathy and to appeal to men. The party believed it could convince more of the working-class members of the population who voted for it to join it.[202] Indeed, people of modest means did sometimes wish to join associations but found that the subscription rate of 2s. 6d was too high.[203] One way of trying to address this was the establishment of a countrywide Conservative trade union movement along the lines of the party's pre-war 'Labour committees'.[204] Across Britain, most attempts flopped, although areas like the West Midlands did meet with some success.[205] By the end of the 1950s there were 166 separate Conservative Trade Union groups in Glamorgan and Monmouthshire (the most heavily industrialised areas). How well

[199] John Ramsden, *The Age of Balfour and Baldwin, 1902–1940* (London: Longman, 1978), p. 48.
[200] WPA, GB0210 CARCON, Cardiff West Conservative and Unionist Association, file 19, Men's Division minute book, 20 October 1949, 6 June 1951, 13 August 1951, 24 January 1952, 23 November 1954.
[201] WPA, GB0210 CARCON, file 7, Penylan Men's Branch minute book, 6 October 1953; 2 February 1956; 'Conservative Branch', *Western Mail*, 23 February 1956.
[202] David Butler and Michael Pinto-Duschinsky, 'The Conservative Elite, 1918–1978: Does Unrepresentativeness Matter?', in Zig Layton-Henry (ed.), *Conservative Party Politics* (London: Macmillan, 1980), p. 186.
[203] Denbighshire Record Office [DRO], DD/DM/80/7, Colwyn Bay Conservative Association minute book, 17 May 1950.
[204] Ramsden, *The Age of Churchill*, p. 117.
[205] Peter Dorey, 'Industrial Relations and "Human Relations": Conservatism and Trade Unionism, 1945–1964', in Stuart Ball and Ian Holliday (eds), *Mass Conservatism: The Conservatives and the Public Since the 1880s* (London: Frank Cass, 2002), p. 139; Ball, 'Local Conservatism', p. 276; Ramsden, *The Winds*, p. 105.

attended they were, or how active, is rarely commented upon in the source material, and a failure to boast about strong numbers was normally a bad sign.[206] The group in industrial Aberavon, where the Port Talbot steelworks were located, was supposedly 'thought much of' countrywide, and its leaders were thanked for their 'perseverance and loyalty' in what must have been a difficult task.[207] They found a support base in the local Conservative Club, where Mr Pandy Rees, a local retired schoolmaster, supported the club, the party and the trade union initiative loyally.[208] However, this appears to have been a one-off. Even in a Conservative seat like Barry, which also had a high number of trade union members from its industries and docks, the trade union group could never take off.[209] Cardiff's most industrialised seat had a place reserved on its executive committee for a Vice Chair who was the trade union representative, but not long after it was introduced it was quietly abolished.[210]

The Young Conservatives (YCs) in Wales met with a more mixed set of results. In the 1950s in particular, the YCs still offered young people entertainment and 'social opportunities' that were not always easy to come by. Educational away-days offered politics and evenings of 'organised gregariousness for the children of the middle classes'.[211] In the words of one YC from the time, post-war Britain 'was a dreary place in which to live'. YC branches, 'with weekly meetings and [. . .] all kinds of affordable social events, prospered and grew'.[212] A common reflection from YC members across the country was that they joined up 'not from conviction

---

[206] Dorey, 'Industrial Relations', p. 139; WPA, GB0210 CARCON, file 34, The Glamorgan Group Council of the Wales and Monmouthshire Provincial Area minute book, 16 February 1960.
[207] CPA, CCO 1/11/532, Secretary's Report, 1955.
[208] CPA, CCO 1/11/532, Aberavon Basic Report, 18 October 1956.
[209] CPA, CCO 1/10/528, Barry AGM Report, 30 April 1954.
[210] WPA, GB0210 CARCON, file 15, Cardiff South East Executive Committee minute book, April 1951.
[211] Lawrence Black, 'The Lost World of Young Conservatism', *The Historical Journal*, 51/4 (2008), 995, 999.
[212] Anthony Garner, 'The Young Conservatives', in Jean M. Lucas (ed.), *Between the Thin Blues Lines: The Agent's View of Politics* (Canada: Trafford, 2008), pp. 4–5.

but for pleasure'.[213] Keith Flynn, who organised a strong band of YCs from the early 1950s in Llandaff, which was in the Cardiff West seat, left the navy and found himself 'bored stiff'.[214] The late 1950s, of course, witnessed the emergence of rock 'n' roll, but not everyone suddenly signed up to this new kind of culture. YCs still provided a source of respectable, less delinquent (if sometimes mocked), fun.[215] This reputation was, for a time, self-perpetuating, aiding further recruitment.[216] In Wales, social outings included holiday weekends in places like Pwllheli, on the Llŷn Peninsula in north west Wales.[217] Middle-class 'luncheon clubs' were frequent in Cardiff North.[218] Picnics were a favourite and barbecues increased in popularity, too, with 800 people attending one in Conwy in 1962.[219] In Keith Flynn's single Llandaff branch, there were roughly 100 people who came to meetings, although Flynn remembered 'perhaps a dozen' who were political; 'the rest were there for fun', although many did turn out at election time for the obligatory political work.[220] The relatively small numbers who were genuinely engaged was an ill omen for what was to come for the YCs, as the following chapter details, but, into the 1960s, the party was able to engage some young people on both a social and a political level.

The political element in particular gave some YCs an opportunity to articulate their opinions on a range of issues. Unsurprisingly, common topics for discussion at branch meetings and weekend schools were on broad, relatively bland themes like 'agriculture' or 'industry'. However, a regular topic in the 1950s and 1960s was a variation on the theme of 'the problems of multi-

[213] Rupert Morris, *Tories: From Village Hall to Westminster: A Political Sketch* (Edinburgh: Mainstream, 1991), p. 18.
[214] Interview, Keith Flynn, 29 September 2015.
[215] Lawrence Black, *Redefining British Politics: Culture, Consumerism and Participation, 1945–1970* (Basingstoke: Palgrave Macmillan, 2010), p. 75.
[216] Zig Layton-Henry, 'The Young Conservatives, 1945–1970', *Journal of Contemporary History*, 8/2 (1973), 147.
[217] Garner, 'The Young Conservatives'.
[218] *Western Mail*, 18 September 1952.
[219] '800 at Tory barbecue', *Weekly News*, 28 June 1962.
[220] Interview, Keith Flynn, 29 September 2015.

racial societies'.[221] When viewed in comparison with other YC groups across Britain, the picture of the many younger activists in Wales is of a more liberal, if ideologically mixed, group of people, conforming broadly to the stereotype of the YCs as being more 'wet' than the party in general.[222] This also reflects the findings of Catherine Ellis's work on the YCs' attitude to social policy.[223] The Conservative Party canvassed all YC Area groups across the UK as part of a short-lived scheme to involve its youth wing in decision making. It feared young people's habits were naturally becoming more inclined to socialism.[224] As part of this process the Wales Area (which took contributions from most constituency YC associations) fed back particularly on the 'society in the Sixties' theme, which asked for ideas about what the coming decade would involve. The Wales YCs concluded that the role of the individual in society was crucial and that good morality was grounded in good home life – common motifs in Conservative philosophy at the time, which stressed the importance of not letting the state become too powerful (much of which we have seen already). They also argued that hereditary peers should be removed from the House of Lords and that young people should be treated less severely by the criminal justice system.[225]

This sat in contrast to other area groups, who took a more robustly conservative line on things like crime and wider societal issues.[226] For the Wessex YCs, there was more need for 'greater parental discipline', a higher rate of criminal convictions and 'less crime' depicted on TV. The South Eastern Area argued that 'Parents should be penalised for the misdeeds of their children' and

---

[221] CPA, CCO 2/5/19, Young Conservative Weekend School programme, 6 March 1960; N. J. Crowson, 'Conservative Party Activists and Immigration Policy from the Late 1940s to the Mid-1970s', in Ball and Holliday, *Mass Conservatism*, p. 171.

[222] David Jarvis, 'The Conservative Party's Recruitment of Youth', in Gaetano Quagliariello (ed.), *La Formazione della classe politica in Europa: 1945–1956* (Manduria: P. Lacaita, 2000), p. 554.

[223] Ellis, 'No Hammock', 451.

[224] Ellis, 'No Hammock', 446.

[225] CPA, CCO 506/14/14, Reports from the Wales and Monmouthshire Area Young Conservative Policy Group.

[226] Jarvis, 'The Conservative', p. 569.

prison officers should be better paid. In various other areas, a mix of views were expressed, but the emphasis tended to be on 'the [sharp] punishment of young offenders' and 'stricter discipline in schools'.[227] Of course, these contributions essentially represent views of the more politicised YCs, filtered through their leadership figures, but they still give a sense of a group of young people in Wales who were slightly more liberal than some of their English counterparts. Their ideas were in keeping with a broadly conservative worldview that stood in contrast to the general atmosphere of the 1960s, but it is also fair to say that they were thoughtful, with the report reflecting ideas having been weighed up.[228]

Conservatism remained, however, most effective at bringing together groups of women. Unlike working-class men, who the party struggled to find much purchase with, middle-class women often did not work in the immediate post-war years. Conservative associations consequently continued to give them something to do. A staggering 500 local members of the Barry association came to London for a weekend trip in 1959. Such people were hardly apathetic members who simply paid their subscriptions and then ignored the party.[229] This was a theme identifiable in many other non-political groups or organisations, like the local chapel or church, charity organisations or sports clubs, as the social survey work of Ronald Frankenberg demonstrated.[230] The party acted as a useful way of bringing like-minded people together under the auspices of politics, resulting in the continued organising of respectable fundraising events.

In the era of the Primrose League, politics had been pitched as a family-friendly pursuit and this remained the case well into the post-1945 period.[231] For women, the Conservative Party's

[227] CPA, CCO 506/14/14, various reports from Wales Area, Wessex Area, South Eastern Area, Home Counties North, West Midlands Area.
[228] Ellis, 'No Hammock', 456.
[229] CPA, CCO, 505/2/10, Hicks to Turner, undated.
[230] Ronald Frankenberg, *Village on the Border: A Social Study of Religion, Politics and Football in a North Wales Community* (London: Cohen and West, 1957), p.104.
[231] Martin Pugh, 'Popular Conservatism in Britain: Continuity and Change, 1880–1987', *Journal of British Studies*, 27/3 (1988), 264.

programme of activities offered the broader excuse for a day out with their children. Of course, it would have been considered an added bonus if some of the young people attending these events became 'socialised' in the process, picking up Conservative ideas at an age when many people are receptive to such things.[232] Party fetes, and especially those large ones in parts of so-called 'British Wales', involved children enjoying things like train rides on miniature railways. Candid photographs from such events show families sitting together on hay bales eating lunch. Throughout the 1950s, the Mathern branch of the Monmouth Association organised an annual children's party, the pictures of which show at least forty children, sitting around long trestle tables, smiling and eating food.[233] Dozens of children, ranging from the very young to those in their teenage years, were pictured attending the Conservative Carnival in Chirk, just south of Wrexham, in 1953 (figure 10).

These events were clearly held, financed and attended by people with money to give. This is one of the ways in which rank-and-file Conservatives struck a contrast with their Labour counterparts. Although Labour's activist base was much more middle class than its voters in general, grassroots socialists often took their politics more seriously – believing there were great fights to be won – and therefore more time was devoted to work than to play.[234] Hence, some contemporary commentary from the period referred to Labour activists as 'tired, careworn [and] grizzled'.[235] In contrast, Tory fundraising emphasised fun, with a more affluent spirt underpinning it, as many of the visuals from that period demonstrate.

---

[232] For a discussion of this, see David Jeffery, 'The Strange Death of Tory Liverpool: Conservative Electoral Decline in Liverpool, 1945–1996', *British Politics*, 12/3 (2017), 390.

[233] *South Wales Argus*, 18 January 1958.

[234] Andrew Walling, 'The Structure of Power in Labour Wales, 1951–1964', in Tanner, Williams and Hopkin, *The Labour Party*, p. 212; Steven Fielding, 'Activists Against "Affluence": Labour Party Culture During the "Golden Age" circa 1950–1970', *Journal of British Studies*, 40/2 (2001), 260.

[235] Quoted in Fielding, 'Activists', 251.

AFFLUENCE AND A CHANGING WALES, 1951–1964 151

Figure 9: Families sit together at a Conservative Party rally at Brogyntyn, 1949.

Figure 10: A large number of children take part in a Conservative carnival in Chirk, 1953.

Such events also gave women a chance to get together with like-minded friends and an opportunity to exercise a form of social leadership. To take an example where these things combined, at one meeting of the Pontypool association in the 1950s, Tory members were taking a ballot for who would be their next chairman. The Wales Area Agent later described how, just before the ballot,

> there was an influx of about 20 women members who were actually attending a whist drive in the room upstairs. They were all members of the association [...] To my amazement they all took a ballot paper and after handing [it] in they trooped back to the whist drive [which was being used as a fundraiser].

The Area Agent added that 'I have not experienced anything like this before [but] it is typical of the unorthodox energies displayed by the women's organisation'.[236] In this case, the women had managed to organise a fundraiser, which doubled as a social event, whilst also taking in the more conventional politics of the association. Outings and trips organised by party members in this period tended to be organised by women. When we therefore talk about local grassroots leaders, women should be considered vital to such discussions.[237]

These elements of class and social leadership have been reasonably well covered in the wider historiography.[238] However, fewer writers critically analyse the political ideas and ideologies of such women, with conventional explanations suggesting that it was precisely the non-political nature of associational life that attracted them to grassroots Conservatism.[239] Contemporaries

[236] CPA, CCO 1/12/545, Oliver to CCO, 28 March 1957.
[237] Sam Blaxland, 'Women in the Organisation of the Conservative Party in Wales, 1945–1979', *Women's History Review*, 28/2 (2019).
[238] Maguire, *Conservative Women*, p. 145; James Hinton, 'Conservative Women and Voluntary Social Service, 1938–1951', in Ball and Holliday, *Mass Conservatism*, p. 114.
[239] Gidon Cohen and Lewis Mates, 'Grassroots Conservatism in Post-War Britain: A View From the Bottom Up', *History*, 98/330 (2013), 207.

had long thought that women's groups had the propensity to get involved in arguments, noting that 'when women get together they are petty and mean and jealous', but there is also no doubt that when they discussed politics, attended events and debated strategy, they were demonstrating a series of firmly held beliefs.[240] As the previous chapter showed, these people were far more politically engaged than is allowed for by the stereotypical image of backroom workers dutifully stuffing envelopes. Large political rallies were held at various times and places across Wales, such as a huge one at Margam Park, near Port Talbot, in July 1953, which 1,000 women attended.[241] This was not just a one-off.[242] Women were interested in political issues and often demonstrated that they knew the details of what they were talking about, whether it be the exact price of a loaf of bread, or the suitability of their prospective parliamentary candidate.[243] In more Conservative-friendly seats, their activities helped local Conservatives ensure the party had some sort of foothold in wider society. It would have been difficult to ignore, for example, a new 'local newspaper' established primarily by the women members in Barry in the mid-1950s. This was used 'regularly with considerable discretion in publicising the activities of the association'.[244] Other strong associations also talked about forming their own constituency 'magazine or broadsheet'.[245] In James Callaghan's Cardiff South East constituency, the provisional name for the Conservative magazine was 'The Tory Punch', but this was eventually rejected in favour of the more neutral 'The South Tory'.[246]

---

[240] Ball, *Portrait*, p. 152.
[241] '1,000 women Conservatives at open-air meeting', *Western Mail*, 3 July 1953.
[242] WPA, GB0210 CARCON, file 15, Cardiff South East Executive Committee minute book, 16 September 1947.
[243] 'Women found "nice" Tory worth wait', Western Mail, 17 June 1970.
[244] CPA, CCO 1/11/533, Barry Basic Report, 31 July 1956.
[245] WPA, GB0210 CARCON, file 1, Cardiff North Joint Executive Committee minute book, 18 July 1952.
[246] WPA, GB0210 CARCON, file 15, Cardiff South East Executive Committee minute book, 16 December 1947.

Many of the party's supposed grassroots supporters, although not female ones, were still to be found in Conservative clubs in this period. Occasionally, especially in 'Welsh Wales', a club was at the heart of a local association, and many supplied meeting rooms or even makeshift offices for the party or prospective candidates.[247] On occasion, well-attended meetings were held there. During one election campaign, the Tonypandy Club in Rhondda mustered up 250 people at one political meeting.[248] However, when it came to politics, most clubs – and club members – were either apathetic or actively unhelpful. Peter Temple-Morris, fighting Newport in 1964 and 1966, would go to each of the ten clubs in Newport (having half a pint in each) in one evening, but remembered 'the worst heckling' he received on the campaign trail coming from some members. It was not that they were anti-Conservative, per se, but they were hosting another skittles team and objected to their game being disrupted by 'something as trivial' as the Conservative candidate's speech.[249] In a rough personal diary kept at the time, Temple-Morris noted that he had received 'no help again!' from the clubs, signing off the diary with the line: 'Good experience but pleased to see the back of it!'[250] Many associations struggled to get any money at all from their local clubs, some of which were considered to be 'in the delinquent class'.[251] Relations varied from club to club, with some friendly establishments found in very Labour seats, whilst stronger Conservative constituencies like Barry had a poor relationship with theirs.[252]

---

[247] The chairman was connected to the Bethcar Club. See: CPA, CCO 1/11/543, Ebbw Vale Basic Report, 18 October 1956; FRO, D/DM/307/15, Agent's Report, 9 August 1947.

[248] CPA, CCO 1/8/524, 1950 general election comments, undated.

[249] Interview, Lord Temple-Morris, 17 June 2015. Also recounted in: Peter Temple-Morris, *Across The Floor: A Life in Dissenting Politics* (London: I. B. Tauris & Co., 2015), pp. 29–30.

[250] Personal diary of Peter Temple-Morris, Friday 16 October 1964.

[251] CPA, CCO 1/11/537, Ogmore Basic Report, 15 November 1956. For other difficulties extracting money, see CPA, CCO 1/9/533, Annual Report, 31 December 1951.

[252] CPA, CCO 1/8/524, 1950 general election comments, undated.

Club members were rarely 'supporters'.[253] Some might have been so on paper to gain access to one, but the situation in Wales could be exactly the opposite, with clubs deliberately conspiring against the Tory Party. Concerns were raised in Flint East that the club had been taken over by people hostile to Conservatism and there were suspicions on Anglesey when the Holyhead Club seemed determined to 'introduce a candidate [to fight a general election] who was completely unacceptable'.[254] Hywel Francis, who was campaigning for the Communist candidate in Rhondda East in 1964, remembered an internal inquiry launched by the Conservative candidate after the number of votes he received was far less than the total membership figures of Conservative clubs in the constituency (which was not a unique occurrence).[255] The Tylorstown Club was reported to have had a number of significant local Communists on the committee, who were not only ensuring that donations did not find their way to the Tory, but were channelling the money to the Communist candidate Annie Powell instead.[256] The Arthur Balfour Conservative Club in Aberbargoed in the constituency of Bedwellty would later host the advice surgeries of Neil Kinnock, the Labour member for the seat.[257]

Perhaps the greatest benefit of these clubs for the party was less tangible or easy to measure. Clubs would certainly have played a role, like fetes and women canvassers did, in attempting to establish the Conservative Party in parts of Welsh society where it would otherwise have had little presence.[258] Those working-class people who certainly voted for the party but were clearly reluctant to get stuck into associational politics might have used 'Con' clubs as their conduit into that very loosely defined sphere of Tory

[253] Ball, 'Local Conservatism', p. 293.
[254] CPA, CCO 1/8/516, East Flint Basic Report, 31 August 1950; CPA, CCO 1/10/512, Anglesey Basic Report, 5 November 1956.
[255] For some raw data, see James and Thomas, *Wales at Westminster*, p. 155.
[256] Interview, Dr Hywel Francis, 28 August 2015.
[257] Interview, Dr Hywel Francis, 28 August 2015.
[258] Thomas Wyn Williams, 'The Conservative Party in North-East Wales, 1906–1924' (unpublished PhD thesis, University of Liverpool, 2008), p. 140.

politics.[259] The most common way in which club members rubbed shoulders with local Conservatives was through organised social events. One historian argued that the 'beer and billiards' nature of Conservative clubs did not automatically create working-class Conservatives, but he suggested that amongst this stratum of people it was likely to have 'extended the party's influence to many who would not otherwise have come within its orbit'.[260] Whilst it is impossible to know if this was the case or not, there is evidence to suggest it might have happened in Wales.

In particular, sport was integral to forging bonds. Skittles matches, played between various Conservative club teams and association's Men's Branches were described as examples of the two groups coming into close contact.[261] Similarly, the only way in which the Grangetown Club in Cardiff seemed to have been involved with the association was when it and the local men's branch organised darts tournaments.[262] The parliamentary candidate for Pontypridd in 1951 was the Sports Editor of the *Sunday Chronicle*. He was a rare example of a candidate who 'spent much time in the clubs, where his sporting background is very acceptable'.[263] The only records of talks held at the Pembroke and Milford Haven Clubs in Pembrokeshire during this time show that they were not about politics, but on horse racing and rugby. Sports-themed entertainment continued to dominate, but it had the power to attract audiences from both the club and associational worlds.[264]

Behind the scenes, some unexpected individuals were determined to diagnose the party's various problems in Wales and revive its fortunes from the grassroots upwards. The most

---

[259] Ramsden, *The Age of Balfour*, p. 257.
[260] Philip Tether, *Clubs: A Neglected Aspect of Conservative Organisation* (University of Hull: Hull Papers in Politics, 1988), p. 53.
[261] CPA, CCO 1/9/535, Newport Men's Branch Annual Report, 31 December 1951; WPA, GB0210 CARCON, file 15, Cardiff South East Executive Committee minute book, 12 January 1951.
[262] WPA, GB0210 CARCON, file 15, Cardiff South East Committee Minute Book, 15 June 1948.
[263] CPA, CCO 1/8/533, Pontypridd Basic Report, 28 September 1950.
[264] CPA, CCO 1/14/547, AGM Report, 28 February 1962.

interesting of these was Basil Lindsay-Fynn. He represented one of the new kinds of businessmen who were willing to donate huge sums of money to the Tory cause in this period. Such people mattered because, despite the often-impressive fundraising efforts of local Conservatives, the party still received in the decades after the war somewhere between 75 and 90 per cent of its donations from wealthy individuals. CCO's Board of Finance, established in 1946, had full-time staff dedicated to raising funds from such people.[265] Lindsay-Fynn was the director of a number of public companies and the owner of a brewery (an old Tory staple), with offices on Savile Row in London. Details about his life are relatively scarce. As well as a great deal of charity work, his obituary in 1988 noted that he was 'an active fundraiser for the Conservative Party and President of a number of London constituency parties'.[266] That he was wealthy is beyond doubt. At the time of his death, he left an estate worth over £4.5 million.[267] From the end of the 1950s and into the mid-1960s, Lindsay-Fynn channelled some of this wealth into the local organisation of the party in Wales in the form of 'practical assistance' to some of the struggling Welsh constituencies, mostly in so-called 'Welsh Wales'.

Lindsay-Fynn's diagnoses of some of the party's problems were at least a focused attempt at offering some possible solutions to the party's woes in Wales. He was willing to plough money into the 'safely held Labour seats of South Wales' to begin a 'long term programme' of Tory revivals in these areas.[268] As one unnamed CCO official reported back after a long conversation with Lindsay-Fynn:

> He thinks we should take a very long view of Wales and to abandon the Valleys is a short-sighted policy. He is very interested in finding a number of young men to go to the Valleys as candidates and live there for a considerable period. He would be prepared to finance

[265] Bale, *The Conservatives*, pp. 20, 97.
[266] Sir Basil Lindsay-Fynn, *The Times*, 26 August 1988.
[267] '£4.5 million will', *Daily Telegraph*, 10 November 1988.
[268] CPA, CCO 500/8/4, Lindsay-Fynn to Poole, 16 October 1958, 15 May 1959.

their sojourn and it would be necessary, apparently, for them to have respectable and enthusiastic wives. [He said that] if we could get our feet into the Welsh Valleys with suitable people and build up a Conservative body of opinion there our children would benefit.[269]

Initially, Lindsay-Fynn proposed donating £50,000 (equivalent to approximately £871,000 today) to the party in Wales.[270] This money came in periodically in the form of small lump sums over the next several years, with Lindsay-Fynn also making one-off gestures like paying the salary of certain agents, or women's organising secretaries.[271] The parliamentary candidates in 1959 for Aberdare (Bernard McGlynn) and Swansea East (Humphry Crum Ewing, who had made headlines several years earlier for trying to play a golf ball from London to Oxford in twenty hours) were his lieutenants.[272] His money led to some associations being breathed back into life, and money donated to Hugh Rees in Swansea West might have helped the Conservatives win that very marginal seat in 1959.[273] Although one CCO staff member was suspicious about what 'he really wants', no record of any favour being asked by Lindsay-Fynn in return survived.[274] Whilst this is not surprising, it could be that he was simply guilty of nothing more than wanting influence and access to senior Conservatives, who effectively fawned over him. It could also have been an example of old-fashioned face-value paternalism. There is some evidence that these slightly eccentric efforts to help rehabilitate the Tory Party in the south Wales Valleys had echoes in other lost causes elsewhere. In 1962, Lindsay-Fynn founded the Friends of Malta group, designed to support the Maltese people and their 'continuing British loyalty', during a period when the presence of

[269] CPA, CCO 500/8/4, CCO to the GD, 9 April 1958.
[270] CPA, CCO 500/8/4, Heath to Poole, 3 February 1958.
[271] CPA, CCO 500/8/4, Memo to Lindsay-Fynn, 4 February 1959; CPA, CCO 500/8/4, Lindsay-Fynn to Bagnall, undated.
[272] CPA, CCO 500/8/4, Lindsay-Fynn to Poole, 15 May 1959.
[273] CPA, CCO 500/8/4, Heath to Poole, 3 February 1958.
[274] CPA, CCO 500/8/4, Bagnall to the GD, 17 December 1959.

British forces was being run down there. This involved paying for schemes like youth clubs and 'comforts for old people'.[275]

There is no way of telling precisely how many schemes, agents, campaigns and general salaries Basil Lindsay-Fynn financed either directly or indirectly, but it was almost certainly a great deal more than the surviving scraps of archival information tell us he did. He continued to drip-feed large sums of money to the party in Wales for eight years, until 1966. His final cheque in July 1966 was accompanied by a note simply saying that the financing would stop.[276] There is no explanation why. Perhaps, as 1966 was a particularly bad general election result in Wales, he thought not only that his cash was being poorly invested, but that Conservatism in large parts of south Wales was a lost cause, after all. This curious case does also demonstrate that, under the auspices of CCO, lone, very wealthy figures could dictate the agenda in constituencies much more than hard-working activists could.

CONCLUSION

This chapter began with a short profile of Michael Heseltine, who typified some elements of Conservatism in Wales in this period. Basil Lindsay-Fynn reflected another. Rich, influential people operating out of sight had always been a feature of Tory politics, but it is significant that, despite the professionalism his associates brought to the campaign trail in the late 1950s and early 1960s, more was needed for a Conservative victory in many parts of Wales than just throwing money at those areas. As someone with no obvious close connections to the Valleys of industrial 'Welsh Wales', it is likely that Lindsay-Fynn underestimated just how embedded the politics and values of Labourism were there.

[275] 'Sir Basil Lindsay-Fynn', *Daily Telegraph*, 26 August 1988.
[276] CPA, CCO 500/8/15, Lindsay-Fynn to Varley, 5 July 1966.

He had understood that resources were needed to try to win people over to the party, and that people wanting to be elected to parliament would be better received if they were grounded in their communities. However, in misunderstanding the strength of the anti-Conservative culture there, he ran up against many of the problems the party had long faced. Being so wealthy and so far removed from the places whose culture he wanted to change cannot have helped, either. These were problems that continued to dog the party as a whole in the 1950s. They did not go away in the decades that followed, as the beginning of the next chapter demonstrates.

3
MODERNITY AND LOCALISM, 1964–1975

In the lead-up to the 1964 general election, the officers of the Cardiff South East Conservative Association shoehorned the England cricket captain, Ted Dexter, into the position of prospective parliamentary candidate. He fought his campaign against the seat's sitting MP, James Callaghan, who became Chancellor of the Exchequer after that election, later rising to become Prime Minister in 1976. At the previous general election, the Tory Party and its local, popular candidate Michael Roberts had reduced Callaghan's majority to a tiny 868 votes, having campaigned hard on pertinent issues, such as Labour's plans to nationalise the steelworks in the constituency.[1] Roberts had intended to fight the 1964 contest but instead took up the headmastership of one of Cardiff's secondary schools. Choosing a headline-grabbing celebrity candidate in his place proved to be a disaster.[2] Dexter's considerable cricketing talents were not matched by political skill. At the very beginning of his adventure he told the association's selection committee that he knew 'more about Italian politics than English' – a comment that was all the more telling considering he was standing for a Welsh seat.[3] On the campaign trail, scenes that could have been written by P. G. Wodehouse saw Dexter being knocked over by his own car after it went rolling down a hill. The

---

[1] Interview, Sir Norman Lloyd-Edwards, 7 July 2015; Conservative Party Archive, Bodleian Library, Oxford [CPA], PUB 229/12/14, Michael Roberts election address, Cardiff South East, 1959.

[2] For a full account of this tale, including the selection process, the campaign and the aftermath, see Sam Blaxland, 'The Curious Case of Ted Dexter and Cardiff South East', *Conservative History Journal*, 2/4 (2015), 8–11; Kenneth O. Morgan, *Callaghan: A Life* (Oxford: Oxford University Press, 1997), p. 195.

[3] Ted Dexter, *Ted Dexter Declares* (London: The Sportsmans Book Club, 1967), p. 113.

same car made more headlines when Dexter was fined for parking illegally outside the party's own offices in Cardiff. He reportedly told steelworkers that Eton would make a good choice of school for their children, whilst apparently observing wryly to journalists that he knew which properties in the area he was canvassing housed Labour voters, because he could see the 'unwashed milk bottles' on the doorsteps.[4]

However, it was not simply Dexter who was to blame for the consequent resounding win for Callaghan and Labour, with the vote swinging away from the Tories more dramatically than it did in most other neighbouring areas, giving Callaghan a 7,841 majority. The constituency party itself should take a significant portion of the blame. Its chairman, the eccentric G. V. Wynne-Jones (often called 'Geevers'), a passionate sportsman and rugby commentator with a 'fruity accent', had overridden objections to Dexter's candidature and used the force of his personality to put his fellow sportsman into the role.[5] The local party fought a muddled campaign, hampered by the fact that its candidate was sometimes in another hemisphere playing cricket. It plastered tone-deaf posters around Cardiff South East with the slogan 'Don't be dim and vote for Jim – Use your head and vote for Ted'.[6]

Despite being an almost comically bad example of a prospective parliamentary candidate, many of the themes evident in Dexter's botched bid to become an MP in Wales – the unsuitability, the snobbishness, the misjudged tone of the campaign, the lack of connection with the people he was meant to engage with, the emphasis on the wrong issues, and, to some extent, his Englishness – speak to some of the key reasons why the Conservatives regularly failed to succeed in Wales.[7] Dexter reflects in microcosm some of

[4] Interview, Lord Morgan of Aberdyfi, 9 September 2015.
[5] Welsh Political Archive, National Library of Wales, Aberystwyth [WPA], GB0210 CARCON, file 35, Cardiff South East Executive Committee minute book, 31 July 1963; Gordon Allan, 'Well Said Sir', *The Times*, 4 January 1983.
[6] Interview, Jonathan Evans, 21 November 2014.
[7] Brian Criddle, 'Members of Parliament', in Anthony Seldon and Stuart Ball (eds), *Conservative Century: The Conservative Party Since 1900* (Oxford: Oxford University Press, 1994), pp. 145–67.

the dilemmas that the party grappled with in the years this chapter covers, a period of undoubted modernisation and social change: he was a dashing 'celebrity' candidate, who would have been recognisable to many voters. However, in being totally unfamiliar with Wales, he reflected a stratum of the party, including those at the grassroots, that continued to struggle with the nature of Welsh political culture. But his story also conceals some of the Tories' attempts to become better attuned to this culture from the mid-1960s. Elements of its Welsh leadership, for example, became markedly more professional. On the whole, the party, spurred on to some extent by the rise of Plaid Cymru, got a great deal better at articulating local concerns, despite this being a period when a range of factors, like modernisation, technological advancement and greater mobility, might have suggested that such a focus would diminish as a priority, not the reverse.

DISCONTENT

When Harold Wilson's Labour Party won the 1964 general election, one of its major themes was modernisation, with Wilson himself emphasising how a new Britain would be forged in the 'white heat' of a technological revolution. What followed was certainly an era of technological advancement and modernity. But the period from the mid-1960s into the 1970s was also characterised by economic woes, inflation and industrial unrest. Trade union power was particularly controversial because of the unions' ability to negotiate wage settlements and deals for their workers whilst other members of the public were coping with static salaries, the rising price of food and inflation. Throughout the period covered by this chapter, the 'cost of living' summarised the chief concern for many who tended to vote Conservative in Wales.[8]

---

[8] 'Price of food up record 20p in £', *Western Mail*, 16 February 1974.

Conservatives in Wales stressed their version of the modernity and 'newness' theme, fully embracing the television as a campaign tool to do so.[9] The party boasted about its record in government, establishing 'new schools, new universities, new roads, new bridges, new hospitals, new factories, new steelworks, new training colleges, new technical colleges, new houses, new flats, new old people's homes, new TV transmitters, new gas works, new oil refineries'.[10] Other candidates asked the electorate if they could 'afford to throw away such progress?'[11] However, on the other hand, the party critiqued much of what it presented as having gone wrong with the country. By the time the 1970 election campaign was in full swing, the Tories were able to deploy six years' worth of criticisms, drawing on their opponents' difficult period in office between 1964 and 1970.[12] Labour certainly faced tough decisions on public spending and the control of wages, whilst overseeing a poorly handled devaluation of sterling.[13] Therefore, it was 'the price of Socialism' or 'the Socialist bill' that inevitably dominated Tory messaging at the turn of the decade. Several candidates compared the prices of staple goods between 1964 and 1970, noting how much more expensive items had become. Strikes, mortgage rates, crime and violence were all presented as being at 'the highest ever'.[14] On one election address whose front pages had a big blue 'X' in a box – like a mark on a ballot paper – voters were told to 'make this your answer to Socialism'.[15] Although the theme of Labour using an over-mighty state to control people's lives was nothing like as prominent as in the immediate post-war

[9] CPA, CCO 1/14/59, Denbigh Conservative and Unionist Association AGM Report, 1962.
[10] CPA, PUB 229/13/16, Donald Box election address, Cardiff North, 1964.
[11] CPA, PUB 229/13/16, Sidney Doxsey election address, Merthyr Tydfil, 1964.
[12] Brian Harrison, *Seeking a Role: The United Kingdom, 1951–1970* (Oxford: Oxford University Press, 2009), p. 499.
[13] Tim Bale, *The Conservatives Since 1945: The Drivers of Party Change* (Oxford: Oxford University Press, 2016), p. 107.
[14] CPA, PUB 229/15/17, John Rendle election address, Abertillery, 1970; Robert Saunders, *Yes to Europe!: The 1975 Referendum and Seventies Britain* (Cambridge: Cambridge University Press, 2018), p. 199.
[15] CPA, PUB 229/15/17, Raymond Gower election address, Barry, 1970.

years, voters in Wales were still being told to vote Conservative for 'Great Britain NOT State Britain'.[16]

It was possible to detect a general sense of anger amongst Conservatives in Wales at what might be loosely characterised as 'decline'. In 1968, the grassroots Chairman of the Party in Wales, Alistair Graesser, wrote a long complaint to the party hierarchy about 'lack of discipline . . . not least in industry [in which] I naturally include trade unions'. He continued that 'discipline in the majority of schools is very lax . . . there is a certain type of youngster who does not understand anything but physical pain and I am sure that the bringing back of the birch would be a very popular move'.[17] To some extent he was sharing the wider views of the electorate, one of whom wrote at the same time: 'I think the people are waiting for some positive statement regarding trade union reform, wild cat strikes, crime . . . what have the Tories suggested in return?????'[18] There were also the inevitable displays of support amongst Conservatives, including some Welsh parliamentary candidates, for Enoch Powell after his 1968 'Rivers of Blood' speech on immigration.[19]

The Tories re-entered office in 1970 promising less government control, trade union reform and no prices and income policies, things that many Conservative voters wanted to hear.[20] However, it and the new prime minister, Edward Heath, failed to live up to most of these expectations.[21] The government pumped money into the economy, nationalised certain industries and, perhaps most damagingly for its reputation amongst its supporters, appeared to fail to curb the power of the trade unions, despite

[16] CPA, PUB 229/17/19, Michael Penston election address, Flint East, October 1974.
[17] CPA, CCO 20/11/39, Graesser to Barber, 14 May 1968.
[18] CPA, CCO 2/7/12, Fletcher to Davies, undated, c.1968.
[19] David Butler and Michael Pinto-Dushinsky, *The British General Election of 1970* (London: Macmillan, 1971), p. 160; Camilla Schofield, 'Enoch Powell and Thatcherism', in Ben Jackson and Robert Saunders (eds), *Making Thatcher's Britain* (New York: Cambridge University Press, 2012), p. 101; CPA, PUB229/15/17, Michael Carter election address, Gower, 1970.
[20] 'We want action, say the Tories', *Western Mail*, 7 March 1966.
[21] Norman Barry, 'New Right', in Kevin Hickson (ed.), *The Political Thought of the Conservative Party Since 1945* (Basingstoke: Palgrave Macmillan, 2005), p. 37.

the Industrial Relations Act 1971.[22] Disquiet amongst many in the electorate was obvious. If normally loyal Conservative associations like Brecon and Radnor were producing news-sheets arguing that Heath was failing to provide 'strength, a purposeful direction [or] an understandable theme', then the general public were even less content.[23] Issues like Heath's determination to enter the European Community, something that the Conservatives were broadly more in favour of in this period than Labour, elicited some hesitant reactions. Voters questioned a number of aspects of the policy, including where it left the old Empire countries, which they wanted Britain to remain aligned with. In 1972, the new Conservative MP for Monmouth, John Stradling Thomas, received a tranche of letters on this subject from his constituents, one of which argued that the party was losing 'quite a number of good voters' because, in turning to Europe, the government was 'alienating . . . our fellow countrymen in the fast-departing Commonwealth countries . . . is our Queen . . . still Queen of Australia or of Austra-alien?'[24]

Unsurprisingly, many of the party's messages and anything that referenced 'the cost of living' was targeted specifically at women, with 'the tribulations of the housewife' a recurring theme.[25] Neither was this something manufactured for political gain. Social surveys from Welsh seats at the time picked up on the cost of running a household as being a real concern amongst female voters.[26] When women listened to their MP, Raymond Gower, give speeches in Barry, they were reportedly 'really on their toes when it came to price rises'. When Gower said that the price of bread (which was fixed by government) had risen to 1s. 9d, 'he was greeted with a chorus of "1s. 10d"'.[27] Even though numbers in the workforce were rising, the Conservatives continued to appeal

[22] Bale, *The Conservatives*, p. 152.
[23] CPA, CCO 1/16/551, News-sheet c. January 1974.
[24] WPA, GB0210 MONION, file 23, Coltman to Stradling Thomas, 1 November 1972.
[25] Butler and Pinto-Dushinsky, *The British General Election of 1970*, p. 157.
[26] Kenneth O. Morgan, 'Swansea West', in his *Modern Wales: Politics, Places and People* (Cardiff, University of Wales Press, 1995), p. 298.
[27] 'Women found 'nice' Tory worth wait', *Western Mail*, 17 June 1970.

to women primarily as the chief organisers of the household.[28] Wives of candidates were utilised again to push the message that prices were too high and households were bearing the brunt. Speaking for her husband, who was contesting Bedwellty in 1970, Penelope Marland argued that 'politicians enjoy elections. Most women think they are a nuisance, but our vote is very important . . . I am a housewife and we all know how much it costs [to feed the family] these days'.[29] Other wives claimed that 'the burden of the Labour government's policy has been felt especially by women at home'.[30] As women's rights became a more commonly discussed topic into the 1970s, the Conservatives spoke to women in much more traditional terms. Whilst Tory and Labour candidates in the October 1974 election featured roughly the same number of messages from their wives on their election addresses – nine versus seven, respectively – thirteen Labour candidates made some reference towards equal pay for women, or even the Women's Liberation Movement. No Tory candidates did so. A difference in approach from the two main parties to women voters was starting, slowly but clearly, to open up.[31]

Heath called a general election in February 1974 in the midst of a series of strikes in various industries and an enormous stoppage in the coal industry.[32] The resultant shortened working week, and lighting restrictions, even had a detrimental effect on those campaigning in that election, with Heath having gone to the country on the theme of 'who governs?'[33] By this point, average household income in Wales was among the lowest in the UK, unemployment was high, and spending on things like sickness

---

[28] G. E. Maguire, *Conservative Women: A History of Women and the Conservative Party, 1874–1997* (Basingstoke: Macmillan, 1998), p. 124.

[29] CPA, PUB229/15/17, Paul Marland election address, Bedwellty, 1970.

[30] CPA, PUB229/15/17, Michael Roberts election address, Cardiff North, 1970.

[31] See, as one example, CPA, PUB 229/17/19, Brynmor John election address: 'A vote for Labour is a vote against sexual discrimination'.

[32] David Butler and Denis Kavanagh, *The British General Election of February 1974* (London: Macmillan, 1974), p. 22.

[33] WPA, GB0210 CARCON, file 35, Cardiff South East Conservative and Unionist Association Executive Committee minute book, Annual Report 1974.

and incapacity was dramatically higher than the UK norm.[34] In both the February and October general elections of 1974 in Wales, support for the party slumped. It received 26 per cent of the vote in February, and then 24 per cent in October, down nearly four percentage points from 1970.[35] However, because of a combination of boundary changes and the electoral system, its number of MPs went up from seven to eight.

CLASS AND THE CONSERVATIVES

Despite being a disappointment for many natural Conservatives, the party in Wales from the mid-1960s to the mid-1970s was speaking to a new, and sometimes receptive, kind of audience. As we have seen in previous chapters, the Tories had always struggled to offer an alternative to the powerful social values, traditions and habits associated with voting Labour in places like the Valleys of 'Welsh Wales'. This period, however, witnessed some of those old class-based structures breaking down.[36] People's voting behaviours became less rigid and in some areas of Wales, which had for decades returned Liberal or Labour members, there was a drift towards the Tories, like in the Pembrokeshire constituency. A brief delve into local election results allows this broader point about the shifting relationship between class and location to be reinforced, because results can be broken down ward by ward to reveal where the Tory vote tended to cluster. In the 1967 local elections in Cardiff, for example, Conservative candidates unsurprisingly polled best in the middle-class villadoms of

---

[34] Saunders, *Yes*, p. 326.

[35] Felix Aubel, 'Welsh Conservatism, 1885–1935: Five Studies in Adaptation' (unpublished PhD thesis, Lampeter University, 1996), p. 443.

[36] See in particular Bo Särlvik and Ivor Crewe, *Decade of Dealignment: The Conservative Victory of 1979 and Electoral Trends in the 1970s* (Cambridge: Cambridge University Press, 1983), which argues that whilst class-based politics and voting behaviour did not disappear in the 1970s, it was seriously weakened. Also see David Denver, *Elections and Voters in Britain* (Basingstoke: Palgrave Macmillan, 2007), for a similar analysis; Patrick Joyce, 'Introduction', in Patrick Joyce (ed.), *Class* (Oxford: Oxford University Press, 1995), p. 3.

Llandaff, Llanishen, Penylan, Plasnewydd, Rhiwbina, Roath and Whitchurch: all grander, more comfortably affluent parts of the city, resplendent with large houses and leafy streets.[37] Despite this, Tories also polled well in, and even won, much more working-class wards, like Cathays, Canton, Grangetown and Riverside, examples of places where an English-speaking working class, or lower middle class, felt less and less tied to the politics of the Welsh-language, rural anti-Conservatism, or to heavily unionised manual labour – all of which had long been factors limiting Tory success in Wales.[38]

In short, the party continued to reflect, and speak directly to, those who were aspirational for a better life and higher social status.[39] In this respect, at least, Edward Heath was an asset for the party, being a living and breathing example of social mobility: a grammar-school boy who made it to the very top, replacing an aristocratic earl as leader of the party.[40] Similar kinds of Conservatives who were far removed from the upper-middle-class stratum of the party became more prominent in Wales. Perhaps the most interesting personification of this was Stefan Terlezki, a councillor in Cardiff, several times a parliamentary candidate in the 1970s, and eventually the MP for Cardiff West from 1983 to 1987. An eccentric Ukrainian whose parents had been prisoners of war, Terlezki presented himself as someone who arrived in Britain 'with £1' in his pocket and had since

> been determined to make the most of the opportunities presented. This meant working hard by day and studying by night for his graduation from the Cardiff College of Food Technology . . . by his self-determination and hard work he has made a comfortable standard

---

[37] Aubel, 'Welsh Conservatism', p. 339.

[38] CPA, CRD 2/22/18, Local election results, 1967. For a wider discussion of this, see Ross McKibbin, 'Class and Conventional Wisdom: the Conservative Party and the "Public" in Inter-war Britain', in R. McKibbin, *The Ideologies of Class* (Oxford: Clarendon, 1990), pp. 284–5.

[39] See for example, CPA, PUB 229/13/16, Graham Partridge election address, Pembrokeshire, 1964.

[40] Bale, *The Conservatives*, p. 132.

of living for his family . . . our way of life offers the opportunities, by working hard, for all to succeed.[41]

Paul Valerio, who stood as a candidate in Wales on two occasions in this period and was active in the Young Conservatives (YCs), was another figure who encapsulated this theme. He was the director of an automatic vending-machine company and a member of a 'well known family of Swansea caterers'.[42] Nigel Evans, also from Swansea, cited aspiration as a driving force behind his Conservative politics. He grew up in a household with a 'small business philosophy' (his father was a shopkeeper) and he came to believe that a desire to better oneself was of great importance.[43]

This should not give the impression, however, that class did not matter and that people did not self-identify as being from a certain class. If anything, in a society not determined by religion or ethnicity, class and self-identification became a default way of framing political choice.[44] The party was still rooted in the world of middle-class 'British Wales', where it continued to do things like convene 'business meetings' in places like Penarth, on the southwestern side of Cardiff, which was accurately described as the apex of 'stately villadom'.[45] It knew it had to court wealth-creators and the upper middle classes. These meetings were attended by shipping directors, estate managers, various captains of industry, engineers, advertisers and solicitors, as well as various managing directors of companies across Wales.[46] The leading lights of the party in Wales during these years, like the MPs Donald Box, Hugh Rees, Peter Thomas and Nicholas Edwards, were all resolutely

[41] CPA, PUB 229/17/19, Stefan Terlezki election address, Cardiff South East, October 1974.
[42] Interview, Paul Valerio 16 October 2014; CPA, PUB 229/14/15, Paul Valerio election address, Neath, 1966.
[43] Interview, Nigel Evans MP, 16 June 2015.
[44] Iain McLean, *Rational Choice and British Politics: An Analysis of Rhetoric and Manipulation form Peel to Blair* (Oxford: Oxford University Press, 2001), p. 204.
[45] Kenneth O. Morgan, *Rebirth of a Nation: Wales, 1880–1980* ([1981] Oxford: Oxford University Press, 1988), p. 128; CPA, CCO 1/11/525, Cardiff South East Basic Report, 20 August 1956.
[46] CPA, CCO 2/4/14, Oliver to the GD, 29 January 1957.

middle class and were drawn from these kinds of professional and managerial backgrounds. Peter Thomas was the son of a respected solicitor, while Donald Box and Nicholas Edwards were bankers.[47] When Box lost his Cardiff North seat in 1966, the longlist of names drawn up for his replacement read like a who's who of Cardiff's middle-class political establishment, with several barristers unsurprisingly making the cut. One, Peter Temple-Morris, described himself as a 'respectable man', his father having once been the MP for a Cardiff seat.[48] Peter Thorneycroft was, in the eyes of his local Monmouth Association, a man of 'stature and courtesy' – both words that carried middle-class connotations (although Thorneycroft would later, as Party Chairman under Thatcher, say that he was 'pained' by the continued desire for middle-class candidates amongst local activists).[49]

Such traits were obviously something the grassroots base admired as well, because they continued to select people primarily from these walks of life.[50] For local Tories, social hierarchy had been fundamental in their choice of candidate well before the Second World War, and that tradition continued for decades afterwards.[51] In the words of the historian Stuart Ball, the party was 'infused by the conventions of British middle class behaviour' and this was no different when it came to candidate selection, where middle-class (often Oxbridge) traits of assurance, authority and articulateness had always been seen as assets.[52] Although place of education is not a straightforward indicator of social class (bright children from

---

[47] Andrew Roth, 'Obituary: Lord Thomas of Gwydir', *The Guardian*, 6 February 2008.

[48] Interview, Lord Temple-Morris, 17 June 2015.

[49] Letters, 'Appreciation', *South Wales Argus*, undated, 1966; Bale, *The Conservatives*, p. 234.

[50] Criddle, 'Members of Parliament', p. 165.

[51] Stuart Ball, Andrew Thorpe and Matthew Worley, 'Elections, Leaflets and Whist Drives: Constituency Party Membership in Britain Between the Wars', in Matthew Worley (ed.), *Labour's Grass Roots: Essays on the Activities of Local Labour Parties and Members, 1918–1945* (Aldershot: Ashgate, 2005), p. 16.

[52] Stuart Ball, 'The National and Regional Party Structure', and Brian Criddle, 'Members of Parliament' in Seldon and Ball, *Conservative Century*, p. 170; Stuart Ball, *Portrait of a Party: The Conservative Party in Britain, 1918–1945* (Oxford: Oxford University Press, 2013), p. 199.

poor backgrounds could win scholarships to elite schools), it is useful to outline the number of Conservative candidates at each election who were educated, either partially or totally in the private sector, in contrast to those who went to a state school. Table 9 presents this data, demonstrating that the numbers were reasonably split at most elections. However, for a period that encompassed the years covered by this chapter, a majority of candidates had gone to fee-paying schools – a significant figure, considering that only around six per cent of the population at the time attended one. In contrast to Labour Party candidates, such numbers are stark. In October 1974, for example, thirty-four of thirty-six Labour candidates had been educated by the state – most of them in grammar schools. Whilst there were far fewer labourers and former miners in their ranks by this point (figures like Ness Edwards and S. O. Davies having died), and far more teachers, academics and solicitors, there were still very few businessmen and landowners. Such people remained features of the Conservative ranks.[53]

Because party members notoriously picked people who looked and sounded like them, this reflected the social superiority and middle-class traits that the membership in Wales continued to exhibit in this period.[54] Monmouth's association organised exotic holidays to places like Paris, Majorca and Rome within the space of a single year (1972). The following year there were more social trips to Majorca and Rome.[55] Conservative fetes, such as the annual, very large one held at the stately home Bodrhyddan Hall in Flintshire, often included the reliably bourgeois delicatessen stall, country stall and the garden stall.[56] Fundraisers in other parts

[53] Figures compiled by the author using Ivor Thomas Rees, *Welsh Hustings: 1885–2004* (Llandybie: Dinefwr Press, 2005), and from various electioneering material in the WPA and CPA.

[54] Michael Rush, *The Selection of Parliamentary Candidates* (London: Thomas Nelson and Sons, 1969), p. 22; Bale, *The Conservatives*, p. 16; Gidon Cohen and Lewis Mates, 'Grassroots Conservatism in Post-War Britain: A View From the Bottom Up', *History*, 98/330 (2013), 205.

[55] WPA, GB0210 MONION, file 24, Monmouth Conservative Association Records, minute book, 1 December 1970, 29 June 1971, 28 March 1972, 1 March 1973.

[56] Flintshire Record Office [FRO], D/DM/307/26, Rhyl, Prestatyn and District Area minute book, 29 April 1961.

General election	Educated privately [entire education]	Educated by the state
1945	9 (75%) [9]	3 (25%)
1950	12 (41%) [12]	17 (59%)
1951	14 (45%) [13]	17 (55%)
1955	13 (46%) [12]	15 (54%)
1959	15 (48%) [12]	16 (52%)
1964	19 (61%) [16]	12 (39%)
1966	18 (53%) [14]	16 (47%)
1970	18 (56%) [15]	15 (44%)
1974 Feb.	18 (51%) [15]	17 (49%)
1974 Oct.	19 (54%) [15]	16 (46%)
1979	20 (63%) [18]	12 (37%)
1983	19 (56%) [17]	15 (44%)
1987	18 (49%) [16]	19 (51%)
1992	8 (22%) [7]	28 (77%)
1997	10 (26%) [9]	28 (74%)

Table 9: Number of Conservative candidates in Wales educated privately or by the state, 1945–97.

of north Wales included a 'champagne and strawberry' event; flute, harpsichord and pianoforte concerts; and paté and wine evenings.[57] The fancy-sounding (and very 1970s) menu from the party's Welsh conference in Llandudno in 1978 included crème portugaise; fillet of sole Dieppoise; sauté chicken chasseur with pont neuf and croquette potatoes; centre fillet of beef Bordelaise; and sherry trifle.[58]

In many respects, then, the party was reflecting the new form that the middle and upper-middle classes were taking in this

[57] WPA, GB0210 WREXCON, file 8, 20 June 1969; GB0210 CONLES, file 8, Conway Conservative and Unionist Association minute book, 24 April 1981; file 25, Llanynys and Rhew Branch, invitation cards.
[58] WPA, GB0210 CONLES, file 18, Llandudno conference menus.

period. The aspirational and self-made were prominent, as were the typical members of the established middle class. The face of the grassroots leadership was also altering significantly. This period witnessed the death knell for the connection between Tory politics in Wales and families like the Cawdors, Penrhyns and the Tredegars. An energy crisis and soaring domestic costs meant the upkeep of such status symbols as grand country houses became impossible, despite increasing land and art values resulting in some fresh, but very temporary, sources of income.[59] Even for a political party rooted in traditionalism and hierarchy, the country was becoming in the late 1960s and early 1970s less devoted to ideas of deference and hierarchy, both of which were undermined by the rise of social and political satirical comedy, consumerism, the Suez Crisis and the end of Empire, the decline of the Church and a greater emphasis on individual choice.[60] Even the upper-class military men who had occupied senior positions in the party were fading away. In their place came a more meritocratic, self-made, managerial and suburban group of people who offered a 'less tweedy' style of leadership.[61] By the end of the 1960s, it was estimated that throughout Britain well over half of constituency chairmen were from business backgrounds.[62] Good examples of such figures in Wales were Donald Walters, who headed up the association in Cardiff North, and Neville Sims, who was the chairman in Barry. One writer noted how the party's landed element had given way to these 'younger, more urban-orientated' leadership figures, citing Walters in particular.[63] Walters was a lawyer and finance company executive and had acted as a long-term director of the merchant banking company Julian S. Hodge.

---

[59] David Cannadine, *The Decline and Fall of the British Aristocracy* (London: Papermac, 1996), p. 652; CPA, CCO 1/16/552, Webster to Wolstenholme, 15 March 1974.

[60] Florence Sutcliffe-Braithwaite, *Class, Politics, and the Decline of Deference in England, 1968–2000* (Oxford: Oxford University Press, 2018), p. 9.

[61] Trevor Fishlock, 'Buoyant Welsh Tories take to the valleys', *The Times*, 11 June 1977.

[62] Bale, *The Conservatives*, p. 148.

[63] CPA, Conservative Research Department [CRD] 4/15/4/2, John Osmond, 'Creative Conflict', in 'The Welsh Dimension' report, 1979.

He also took an active intellectual interest in policy-making.[64] When the new suburban seat of Cardiff North West was created in 1974, Walters was a clear choice to head that association. The seat was solidly Conservative for the nine years that it existed. Walters would become chairman of the party's Wales Area in 1977, the role previously held by Sir Godfrey 'Godders' Llewellyn, who we met in the previous chapter and who was undoubtedly from the older school of local Conservative leaders.[65]

Such changes were symptomatic of many other things associated with voting Tory in Wales that were gaining extra momentum in this period. Although Donald Walters had been born and bred in Wales, this period witnessed a rapid increase in the numbers of retired (and often English) people moving to Wales, especially to its coastal areas, utilising increased ease of movement and better transport links.[66] In the early 1960s, 13 per cent of the Welsh population had not been raised in Wales.[67] By the close of the following decade, this figure had risen sharply to 30 per cent, amounting to 468,000 people.[68] Many parts of rural Wales experienced this inward English migration to such an extent that previous anxieties about depopulation gave way to concerns about repopulation from outside the area.[69] The over-representation of elderly and middle-class people remained centred on coastal areas like the north Wales 'Costa Geriatrica', typified by places like Llandudno, Colwyn Bay, Abergele and Prestatyn – where by the 1970s half the people who lived there had not been born in Wales,

---

[64] Richard Roberts, 'Sir Donald Walters, 1925–2017', *https://www.cardiff.ac.uk/obituaries/obituary/sir-donald-walters*. Accessed 25 September 2019.

[65] David Butler and Michael Pinto-Duschinsky, 'The Conservative Elite, 1918–1978: Does Unrepresentativeness Matter?', in Zig Layton-Henry (ed.), *Conservative Party Politics* (London: Macmillan, 1980), p. 190; Aubel, 'Welsh Conservatism', p. 20.

[66] John K. Walton, *The British Seaside: Holidays and Resorts in the Twentieth Century* (Manchester: Manchester University Press, 2000), p. 158.

[67] Martin Johnes, *Wales Since 1939* (Manchester: Manchester University Press, 2012), p. 125.

[68] Dylan Griffiths, 'The Political Consequences of Migration into Wales', *Contemporary Wales*, 5 (1992), 78; Johnes, *Wales Since 1939*, p. 303.

[69] Day, Graham, Angela Drakakis-Smith and Howard H. Davis, 'Migrating to North Wales: the "English" Experience', *Contemporary Wales*, 21/1 (2008).

and where many Conservative supporters could also be found.[70] As studies of English people moving to north Wales have shown, incomers are very capable of adapting to new environments, but they can also retain an existing sense of themselves, which might include language, cultural habits and political preferences.[71] The Conservative party's own private estimations from this period, and social survey evidence, suggested that 80 per cent of its supporters were 'English speaking monoglots' or, if not born or raised English, then certainly 'English-minded'.[72]

When Conservative Central Office (CCO) profiled seats like Conway, the boundaries of which covered a section of the north Wales coast, it noted that 'a very high proportion of the working population is involved in the tourist trade . . . there are also a large number of retired people, mostly English'.[73] When asked their opinions, voters in Conway, who classed themselves as 'retired business people [from] a high percentage of a fixed income group' were of the opinion that elections should not be a 'hectic affair' and they would tend, on the whole, to stick with voting Conservative.[74] Similarly, Pembrokeshire became a Conservative seat in 1970. It had a significant anglicised profile and was full of small businesses that revolved around tourism, offering seasonal employment opportunities.[75] When one candidate fought the Cardigan seat, which encompassed a swathe of coastline, the best reaction he got was in the 'superior flat territory' of coastal Aberystwyth's boulevards, 'where pensioners peer[ed] from behind curtains'.[76]

---

[70] Janet Davies, *The Welsh Language* (Cardiff: University of Wales Press, 1999), p. 78.

[71] Day, Drakakis-Smith and Davis, 'Migrating', 102–3.

[72] CPA, CRD 4/15/4/2, 'Secret Report: The Welsh Dimension'; P. J. Madgwick, Non Griffiths and Valerie Walker, *The Politics of Rural Wales: A Study of Cardiganshire* (London: Hutchinson and Co, 1973), pp. 34–5.

[73] CPA, CCO 500/26/29, Conway constituency reports *c.* 1969.

[74] 'Hectic', *Western Mail*, 24 September 1959.

[75] Walton, *The British Seaside*, p. 169; 'The toughest battle is over', *Western Mail*, 25 May 1983.

[76] 'Odds are on the canny Cardis when the chips are down', *Western Mail*, 18 February 1974.

LOCALISM

A more mobile population and 'modernisation' was therefore changing the nature of Welsh society and its political culture. But what is so striking about this period is the way in which Conservatives devoted more time and energy, not less, to local and constituency-specific issues, especially in the marginal Tory seats of 'British Wales'.[77] Stressing local people's concerns, or refracting national politics through pertinent local case-studies, was an old feature of British politics, stretching back well before all adults were enfranchised, as Jon Lawrence has shown.[78] Whilst the Conservatives had historically been quite successful at this, Labour had also capitalised on its connections with certain communities, focusing on everyday concerns.[79] Although the heyday of local political campaigns had been in the era of the inter-war National Government,[80] this period witnessed a re-emergence. This can be explained by a number of factors. For some Conservatives in Wales, an era increasingly defined by modernity left them feeling that 'finding adjustments to the rapid changes taking place in this modern world' was 'a painful and difficult process'.[81] The success of Liberal 'pavement politics' and the rise of the nationalist party Plaid Cymru, which tended to focus on relevant, constituency-specific issues, was also important.[82] Indeed, Plaid Cymru's

[77] Jon Lawrence, *Electing Our Masters: The Hustings in British Politics from Hogarth to Blair* (Oxford: Oxford University Press, 2009), pp. 171, 180.

[78] Jon Lawrence, *Speaking For the People: Party, Language and Popular Politics in England, 1867–1914* (Cambridge: Cambridge University Press, 1998), pp. 80–1, 228, 235.

[79] Chris Williams, *Democratic Rhondda: Politics and Society, 1885–1951* (Cardiff: University of Wales Press, 1996), p. 163; Andrew Walling, 'The Structure of Power in Labour Wales, 1951–1964' and Duncan Tanner, 'Facing the New Challenge: Labour and Politics, 1970–2000' in Duncan Tanner, Chris Williams and Deian Hopkin (eds), *The Labour Party in Wales* (Cardiff: University of Wales Press, 2000), pp. 192, 278; Paul O'Leary, 'Order! Order? The Lives of George Thomas, Viscount Tonypandy', in H. V. Bowen (ed.), *A New History of Wales: Heroes and Villains in Welsh History* (Llandysul: Gomer Press, 2012), p. 177.

[80] Geraint Thomas, *Popular Conservatism and the Culture of National Government in Inter-war Britain* (Cambridge: Cambridge University Press, 2020), pp. 20–1.

[81] CPA, CCO 1/14/524, Cardiff North Conservative and Unionist Association AGM Report, 26 March 1963.

[82] David Thackeray and Richard Toye, 'An Age of Promises: British Election Manifestos and Addresses 1900–97', *Twentieth Century British History*, 31/1 (2020), 18.

Gwynfor Evans won his Carmarthen seat having stressed his 'deep roots' in the area.[83] In short, if a candidate was from an area, they were often better placed to focus on potholes or local businesses, presenting themselves as caring for that place because they were from it.

The Conservative Party clearly deemed it important to stress that its candidates, where applicable, were 'local'. In the election of 1966, all fifteen candidates who were able to lay claim to a connection with their seat mentioned the fact in their election addresses. Memories of the Ted Dexter fiasco two years earlier loomed large in Cardiff South East. Despite not giving the best speech, local Tories there chose Norman Lloyd-Edwards on the basis of his 'intimate knowledge of the constituency' as a 'local boy'.[84] The former candidate for the seat, Michael Roberts, had made himself popular with some Tories by making a show of brandishing a form from CCO at meetings. This form was for people who wanted to be considered for English seats if there was a by-election. Roberts would apparently 'exclaim' that 'I did not fill it in! . . . I hoped for the honour of fighting in Cardiff again'.[85] It seemed to have worked for him, because he became the MP for Cardiff North in 1970. Conservative election communications began to feature more examples of putting local people and their concerns quite literally at the centre of documents. In Cardiff, 'the Llanishen businessman, the Gabalfa housewife, the Llandaff pensioner and the Birchgrove first time voter' all had good things to say about the Tories, according to the party's election addresses.[86] In rural seats, like Brecon and Radnor, or Merioneth, the party emphasised 'better rural transport', or the closure of branch railway lines. In Denbigh, 'better retired officers' pensions' was important enough to be flagged up as a key issue.[87]

---

[83] Rhys Evans, *Gwynfor Evans: A Portrait of a Patriot* (Talybont: Y Lolfa Cyf, 2008), p. 260.

[84] CPA, CCO 1/14/525, Davies to Prior, 22 April 1965.

[85] WPA, GB0210 CARCON, file 35, Cardiff South East Executive Committee minute book, AGM, 30 March 1961.

[86] CPA, PUB 229/18/22, Michael Roberts election address, Cardiff North West, 1979.

[87] CPA, MS Howe 326, resolutions to party conference, *c.* 1962.

The conditions of local roads (as more voters became drivers) was a topic mentioned with increased frequency.[88] 'Beating the big drum on national policies', in the view of the *Western Mail*'s chief political reporter, caused 'very [few] reverberations' in many Welsh seats, where small-scale and area-specific issues like depopulation and rural development were of greatest importance 'on the doorstep'.[89] A former Conservative candidate said of his time canvassing in one rural seat: 'you'd never talk national politics to [voters]'.[90]

As the previous chapter demonstrated, commentators had long argued that there was something especially important about the local dimension in Welsh politics, and whilst the Tories did not create that environment, they helped reinforce it. Typifying this for the Conservatives was the MP for Denbigh from 1959 to 1983, Geraint Morgan. Despite not asking a single question in the House of Commons chamber between 1965 and 1973, he was assiduous at dealing with local issues like the lack of television signal in his rural constituency. He sent handwritten letters to constituents, and any local people wishing to visit Westminster would be given guided tours of the palace.[91] Observers at the time put Morgan's popularity down to the fact that he had 'built up a powerful constituency following which, in many places, has successfully cut across traditional party ties'. He was a 'political nonconformist . . . (and greatly liked for it)'.[92] The long-serving MP for Barry and then the Vale of Glamorgan, Sir Raymond Gower, was renowned for maintaining his popularity locally because of the 'remarkable relationship' he 'built up with his

---

[88] Figures compiled by the author using CPA material.
[89] 'County will choose to stay Liberal – but on a minority vote', *Western Mail*, 6 October 1964.
[90] Interview with anonymous.
[91] Sam Blaxland, 'Denbigh Constituency's First and Final Conservative MP: a study of Geraint Morgan', *Denbighshire Historical Society Transactions*, 65 (2017), 87–9.
[92] 'Tory may surprise in four corner fight', *Western Mail*, 19 March 1966; 'Denbigh Division Re-elects Mr Geraint Morgan', *Denbigh Free Press*, 24 October 1964.

[constituents]'.[93] The press noticed that he 'snapped up' any local issue as soon as it was raised.[94] He was one of the first to begin the practice of sending greetings cards to constituents on significant birthdays. In the words of one politician, 'he peddled the popular line, irrespective of party policy'.[95] His long-term campaign slogan was 'At the people's service'.[96] In the difficult election of 1966, Morgan and Gower held on to their seats, whereas some of the party's bigger national names, like Peter Thomas and Peter Thorneycroft, did not. Although there were other factors at play, it is worth noting that Thorneycroft's version of stepping up his campaigning activity in Monmouth in 1966, was to make 'fortnightly visits to the constituency', unlike Gower, who famously attempted to visit every house in his constituency on a regular basis.[97] Morgan's majority in Denbigh, in a fight with the same three parties as the previous election, even went up.[98]

Morgan, however, was not dealing with the issue of leasehold reform. This topic loomed especially large in Cardiff and Swansea, and it had a tangible impact on Conservative fortunes in Wales.[99] In Cardiff, leases were due to run out on significant amounts of land and property, originally from the Bute Estate. Many residents were concerned that they did not have the security necessary to stop them being evicted from their homes.[100] Even in the early 1950s, the Labour Party was bringing up 'security of tenure' a lot in their communication with the electorate, but this reached fever pitch in the mid-1960s. The whole debate played badly for the

[93] 'No positive sign of weakness in an established Tory fort', *Western Mail*, 26 March 1966.
[94] Ibid.
[95] Lord Roberts of Conway, *Right From the Start: The Memoirs of Sir Wyn Roberts* (Cardiff: University of Wales Press, 2006), p. 82.
[96] 'Tory in the hot seat pins his hopes on personal vote', *Western Mail*, 12 June 1970.
[97] 'Defeated M.P.s will prepare to fight another day', *Western Mail*, 2 April 1966.
[98] Arnold J. James and John E. Thomas, *Wales at Westminster: A History of the Parliamentary Representation of Wales 1800–1979* (Llandysul: Gomer Press, 1981), pp. 170, 173.
[99] 'Leases and industry big issues in Wales', *Western Mail*, 18 March 1966; David Butler and Anthony King (eds), *The British General Election of 1966* (London: Macmillan, 1966), p. 102.
[100] Interview, Jonathan Evans, 21 November 2014.

Tories, who opposed elements of proposed reforms to leasehold laws, despite pressure from local associations and the electorate to act. As a consequence, some presented the party as being full of the same old uncaring, landed grandees.[101] Looking on from north Wales, Geraint Morgan noted that the public in places like Cardiff were asking: 'who do these grand landlords think they are?'[102] As a result, Labour managed to unseat Donald Box from Cardiff North – a real achievement, since the seat had long been considered as close as one got to a 'safe' Welsh Conservative constituency. It is difficult to judge the way in which the votes swung in places like Cardiff North or Swansea West because the 1964 campaign saw four parties contest those seats, whereas 1966 witnessed a straight fight between Labour and the Tories. Nonetheless, Box was a real scalp for Labour.

The leasehold issue was indicative of the way parties and the electorate interacted. Gone were the days of enormous attendance figures at big public meetings, despite some politicians still giving public talks.[103] By 1966, major television broadcasts were reaching millions of people and the BBC dedicated more time to specific current affairs broadcasting, the moratorium on election news being broadcast having been lifted in 1959.[104] By the 1970s, the vast majority of British people admitted to spending a 'considerable amount of time' as television viewers.[105] It therefore became the best way for political parties to communicate their message.[106] Enthusiasts for the old ways of election campaigning on the ground told a newspaper reporter that the television was having a 'spoiling effect on local campaigns', with 'the national' campaign

---

[101] CPA, CCO 500/50/1, Nationalism in Wales speech appendix; WPA, GB0210 CARCON, file 34, The Glamorgan Group Council of the Wales and Monmouthshire Provincial Area minute book, 18 March 1964.
[102] 'Surprise for the Tories', *Liverpool Daily Post*, 15 April 1966.
[103] Lawrence, *Electing*, p. 188.
[104] Martin Harrison, 'Television and Radio', in Butler and King, *The British General Election of 1966*, p. 125; Lawrence, *Electing*, p. 170.
[105] Alwyn W. Turner, *Crisis? What Crisis? Britain in the 1970s* (Trowbridge: Aurum, 2008), p. x.
[106] Butler and Kavanagh, *The British General Election of February 1974*, p. 201.

dominating like never before.[107] Even when Edward Heath spoke in Cardiff in 1970, only 'the faithful' turned up to listen to him'.[108] This sits in stark contrast to the hundreds who packed out a hall in the Labour stronghold of Merthyr – of all places – twenty years earlier to hear Anthony Eden speak.[109] TV also changed the way politicians communicated. Commenting on how Donald Box presented himself, the trade unionist Huw T. Edwards wrote that 'he is a very attractive person on TV' because 'he is always so wrong and always so controversial'.[110] An awareness of local feelings, however, still influenced the way the party designed its strategy. It continued to draw up detailed documents in the 1960s and 1970s on how it would run tailored campaigns in marginal seats. This included a blitz of more traditional methods, including large poster campaigns, huge numbers of extra leaflets being delivered through doors, speeches by key figures like the former Chancellor of the Exchequer, Reginald Maudling, large teams of canvassers, and 'an extensive meeting programme covering the main towns, villages and cattle markets'.[111]

Defeat in 1966, however, did allow the party to refresh its crop of Welsh MPs. In the following election in 1970, it won seven seats in total, and the new intake of MPs included the likes of Wyn Roberts, Nicholas Edwards, John Stradling Thomas and Michael Roberts, all of whom would later contribute in various ways to shaping the party's approach to Wales. Significantly, too, they fought good local campaigns in their seats. In all cases, these men were plugged into the areas they represented in parliament, even if they were not originally from there, striking a contrast with the types of Tories who used to represent their seats. When Peter Thorneycroft lost Monmouth in 1966, he was frank about how he would 'sever all ties' with the area.[112] The fact that his Conservative

---

[107] '4,000 floating Liberals hold key to Tory come-back', *Western Mail*, 11 June 1970; Lawrence, *Electing*, pp. 189–90.
[108] 'A True Blue Happening', *Western Mail*, 3 June 1970.
[109] 'Surprise at Eden's Merthyr Meeting', *Western Mail*, 12 October 1951.
[110] WPA, Huw T. Edwards papers, A2/154 Edwards to Morgan, 14 January 1965.
[111] CPA, CCO 500/24/248, 'Marginals in Wales'.
[112] 'Defeated M.P.s will prepare to fight another day', *Western Mail*, 2 April 1966.

successor, John Stradling Thomas, was a (well-connected) Welsh farmer and businessman familiar with the local area demonstrated the direction the party was moving in.[113] The most intriguing case was Nicholas Edwards, who would become the long-term Secretary of State for Wales in the 1980s. He surprisingly won the Pembrokeshire seat in 1970 as the result of a peculiar vote split between an official Labour candidate and the maverick former Labour MP for the constituency, Desmond Donnelly. Edwards was a merchant banker from London who, whilst having familial Welsh connections, was not tied in any way to Pembrokeshire, where politics was often especially parochial.[114] In 1970 (and for the many victories that followed) Edwards's campaigns stressed not that he was a local man, as such, but that he had imbibed all the specific qualities necessary to be a good politician in this part of west Wales. This involved donning huge red rosettes, because blue was not the county's Tory colour at the time (the same was true in other parts of the UK).[115] He also spent more time than many MPs in his own constituency, utilising the sleeper train to his constituency from London Paddington, and wrote a huge number of personal notes to people on House of Commons headed paper – a tactic employed by his colleague Geraint Morgan.[116] For the press, which followed Edwards's career with interest, such things 'tend[ed] to override any political hesitation' voters may have had in supporting him.[117]

Scrutinising the backgrounds of these candidates illuminates this point about localism and candidate selection clearly. Table 7 shows that in the 1966, 1970 and the two 1974 general elections, of those candidates who were from Wales, the vast majority had some close tie or connection with the constituency

[113] Rees, *Welsh Hustings*, p. 287.
[114] Interview, Dr Felix Aubel, 1 September 2014.
[115] John Ramsden, *The Age of Balfour and Baldwin, 1902–1940* (London: Longman, 1978), pp. 259–60.
[116] 'Pembroke – where the answer could lie in the Celtic Sea Oil', *Western Mail*, 20 February 1974; Interview, Lord Crickhowell, 1 July 2013.
[117] 'How the West will be won', *Western Mail*, 2 October 1974.

they stood for.[118] In the October election of 1974, 57 per cent of Tory candidates had received some (or in most cases all) of their education in Wales, with over half of the total number of candidates – 51 per cent – being able to claim some lasting connection to the place they wished to represent in parliament.[119] In contrast, in the election after the First World War, 48 per cent of Conservative candidates in Wales had been educated in private schools in England, and only 35 per cent received a Welsh education.[120] It is telling that when the Flint West Association drew up a list of eight questions it thought most important to ask of a prospective candidate in this period, four related to whether 'he' was local, with the other four relating to whether he was 'politically sound', knowledgeable, of good appearance and a good speaker.[121] Conservative priorities were changing, although the party still lagged behind Labour's record on fielding locals. In October 1974, for example, thirty-one of Labour's thirty-six parliamentary candidates or returned MPs had been educated in Wales, and twenty-seven had direct connections to the seat. This accounted for eighty-six per cent of its personnel – a much higher proportion than the Tories – and no doubt cemented the already established notion that Labour best reflected those communities it represented.[122] Whilst Labour candidates continued to let their reputations and 'localness' speak for themselves, mentioning them in their communications with the electorate less than the Tories did, some Labour candidates were not above emphasising them in very specific ways. One opponent standing against Wyn Roberts in Conway pitched himself as 'alone of the candidates . . . [to have] spent most of his life in the area'.[123] Considering that Wyn Roberts had been born in the neighbouring seat – although educated for some of his schooling at Harrow – this was quite

---

[118] Figures compiled by the author using Rees, *Welsh Hustings*.
[119] Figures compiled by the author using Rees, *Welsh Hustings*.
[120] Aubel, 'Welsh Conservatism', p. 29.
[121] FRO, D/DM/307/48, 'list of questions for potential candidates', c.1978.
[122] Figures compiled by the author using Rees, *Welsh Hustings*.
[123] WPA, GB0210 ROGROB Roger Roberts papers, 2/7 (i), 1979 election leaflet.

a bold swipe. It did prove, however, that politicians across the spectrum thought the issue a salient one.

The Conservative Party continued to be far less successful in most parts of industrial 'Welsh Wales', where it could not replicate this sense of connection to an area. It certainly made some attempts to talk about issues pertinent to these kinds of communities, like private home ownership, or 'better machinery for better utilisation of man power'. Occasionally, local people would stand as a Tory, although it is very telling that when some did they removed the name of the party completely from their election leaflets. Others chose to stand in the seat they were from, out of an element of pride. Jonathan Evans, who would later become an MP, MEP and a prominent Welsh Conservative, stood for the seat of Ebbw Vale in 1974 at twenty-three years of age on the grounds that 'firstly, it was because I was from Tredegar', which was in the constituency. He knew there were vacancies in most of the Valleys seats, but he only applied for this one, because of the 'local connections'.[124]

But this sort of honourable behaviour was dwarfed by some quite extraordinary campaigning tactics. Abertillery, for example, was an industrial seat on the south-eastern edge of the south Wales Valleys, and a Labour stronghold in this period. Labour could win over eighty per cent, and sometimes nearly ninety per cent, of the vote in the 1940s, 1950s and 1960s. Standing there for the Conservatives in the 1970 general election, John Rendle (a local man, who was the son of a steelworker) clearly decided to throw caution to the winds when it came to designing his addresses to the electorate.[125] By the early 1970s, these leaflets, which each candidate would send to all households in a constituency, tended to follow a set template, using the same stock graphics and messaging.[126] Not so in Rendle's case. His did not feature the party's name on the cover. Instead, the majority

---

[124] Interview, Jonathan Evans, 21 November 2014.
[125] Rees, *Welsh Hustings*, p. 248.
[126] Thackeray and Toye, 'An Age', 3.

of the front of the address was taken up by an illustration of a line of sheep, winding down the page (see figure 11). The front animal had a wayward, cross-eyed expression and a vacant smile on its face. 'STOP! don't YOU be one of THESE!' the leaflet commanded. Underneath the line of sheep it continued: 'DARE to be different. VOTE FOR . . .'.[127] Voters had to turn to the inside to find out that it was the Conservative candidate who was implying that most of the electorate were unthinking sheep who needed to be jolted out of their age-old habits and to think for themselves a bit more.

David Purnell rather pompously told the electorate in Aberdare in 1970 that 'you are rightly proud of your heritage and traditions . . . the only tradition I regret is that of returning a Socialist member, a bad habit which I hope will this time be broken'.[128] Abertillery's candidate in October 1974 did not go quite as far as her predecessor by producing a line of dazed sheep on the front of an election address, but she still asked people to 'think carefully. Think twice before you vote . . . can I ask you to look to the future and not to the past?'[129] Such people sounded slightly detached or unfamiliar with the area they supposedly wanted to represent, but their material also carried an implication that Labour voters were stuck in a bygone time and were not thinking rationally. This is all the more interesting because in some respects, a small-c conservative message might have found some purchase in communities where the values of 'deference, hierarchy and organisational loyalty' often found a home.[130] Social surveys from this period demonstrated that even one-fifth of Labour voters found something reassuring in someone who was a member of an elite. Presumably the figure amongst Conservatives would have been considerably higher.[131]

---

[127] CPA, PUB 229/15/17, John Rendle election address, Abertillery, 1970.
[128] CPA, PUB 229/15/17, David Purnell election address, Aberdare, 1970.
[129] CPA, PUB 229/17/19, Pamela Larney election address, Abertillery, October 1974.
[130] Dominic Sandbrook, *State of Emergency: The Way We Were: Britain, 1970–1974* (London: Penguin, 2011), p. 333.
[131] Harrison, *Seeking*, p. 186.

Figure 11: John Rendle's election address to the voters of Abertillery in 1970 implies that the Labour-voting electorate are sheep.

As we will see shortly, the party's private discussions about voters in the Valleys of 'Welsh Wales' resulted in some unusual conclusions about its strategy in these areas, but the party's campaigning tactics in public, too, could be eccentric. As in previous years, this did nothing other than reinforce perceptions that the party was out of touch with these areas at best, and fundamentally incompatible with them at worst.

THE RISE OF NATIONALISM

The Conservatives' sharper focus on local issues in those parts of Wales where it could win was in part a response to the tactics of other political parties, including Plaid Cymru. But the rise of nationalism in this period also spurred the Tories into thinking more carefully about Wales. An especially significant moment came in 1966, when Gwynfor Evans became the first Plaid Cymru MP after the historic Carmarthen by-election.[132] His victory took place in a political atmosphere of discontent with the Labour Party and within an atmosphere shaped, for nationalists, by Saunders Lewis's *Tynged Yr Iaith* (The Fate of the Language) lecture in 1962. This had sparked a campaign to extend the use of Welsh in everyday life.[133] The impact of Gwynfor Evans's victory was augmented by two further by-elections, in Rhondda West and Caerphilly, in 1967 and 1968 respectively, where seemingly impregnable Labour majorities were slashed by Plaid Cymru, which came a very close second.[134] Alongside this, violent incidents were also taking place. Groups like the Free Wales Army set off a series of bombs between 1963 and 1969 in protest at further 'Tryweryn'-style plans to use Welsh land and resources for the benefit of people in England.[135]

Understandably, this made the Conservative Party sit up and take notice, not because it had any hope of winning seats like Rhondda West, but because it was often the target of nationalists' anger. Gwynfor Evans himself painted the Tories as the antithesis of his kind of patriotism. In 1967 he gave a speech in which he argued that 'the Tories count for little in Wales. Because they have never identified themselves with Welsh nationhood they

---

[132] R. Merfyn Jones and Ioan Rhys Jones, 'Labour and the Nation', in Tanner, Williams and Hopkin, *The Labour Party*, p. 255.

[133] John Gilbert Evans, *Devolution in Wales: Claims and Responses, 1937–1979* (Cardiff: University of Wales Press, 2006), p. 117.

[134] Johnes, *Wales Since 1939*, p. 225.

[135] Wyn Thomas, *Hands off Wales: Nationhood and Militancy* (Llandysul: Gomer Press, 2013), p. ix.

are commonly regarded as the party of the Englishry'.[136] The Conservative Party never seriously feared losing all of its Welsh support or seats to Plaid Cymru, but the party took a keen interest in the rise of Gwynfor Evans and his party, not least because another party gave people an alternative option to vote for, which was always a concern. Its research department kept an unusually close watch on what he did and said, drawing up detailed notes on the matter.[137] The two parties were not the polar opposites that some might assume. There was undoubtedly a certain kind of small-c conservatism to Plaid Cymru in this period, evident particularly in figures like Ambrose Bebb, one of the party's founding fathers (whose grandson, Guto Bebb, later abandoned Plaid Cymru for the Conservatives, becoming the MP for Aberconwy).[138] Later, in the 1970s, Plaid Cymru voters would tell researchers that what they most liked about the Tories was 'their conservatism – keep the old traditions'.[139] Gwynfor Evans's statements on the nation being 'the ultimate political manifestation of community', his ideas about the importance of localism and his critiques of materialism would have appealed to some conservative types in Wales.[140] It should not be forgotten that much of the admiration for Evans initially came from the right-wing British press.[141]

Significant evidence from the time indicates that there were lots of undecided 'floating' voters across Wales, who chose between voting either for Plaid Cymru or for the Tories. David Rosser, the *Western Mail*'s astute observer of the Welsh political scene, who was praised by politicians and commentators across politics for the quality of his insight, was of the opinion that voters in a variety of seats who might once have voted Liberal could have turned to

---

[136] CPA, CRD 3/37/1,3, untitled paper by Gwynfor Evans, January 1967.
[137] CPA, CRD 3/37/1,3, List of parliamentary questions asked by Gwynfor Evans, undated, c.April 1968.
[138] Interview, Guto Bebb, 23 June 2015.
[139] Madgwick, Griffiths and Walker, *The Politics of Rural Wales*, p. 205.
[140] Laura McAllister, *Plaid Cymru: The Emergence of a Political Party* (Bridgend: Seren 2001), pp. 66–7.
[141] Evans, *Gwynfor Evans*, p. 265.

either the Tories or the Nationalists.[142] When Geraint Morgan was trying to win the Denbigh seat for the Conservatives in 1959, his canvassers were apparently 'astonished' by the pro-Tory sentiment amongst Welsh-speaking voters in the constituency who were also tempted to vote Plaid Cymru.[143] A little later, data crunching by the Tories concluded that the swing from Plaid to the Tories had been much greater (over ten per cent) than the comparable swing from Labour to the Conservatives at the 1979 general election.[144] In short, the Conservatives realised that the rise of Plaid Cymru and the developing debate on 'the nation' had potential political advantages for them.

Kenneth O. Morgan argued that the Welsh nationalist movement in this period resulted in a 'recognition by the Conservative Party that Wales possesses not only a distinct culture, but a certain political ambition that required adjustment'.[145] This is true, and the party devoted some of its considerable research manpower to exploring the issue in more depth. The whole incident spurred on what Chris Patten, then an officer in the party's Research Department, called the inevitable 'soul searching on the relevance of our political appeal in the outer fringes of the UK'.[146] In order to find out more about this, his team commissioned several 'nationalism' surveys in Wales, including in Evans's constituency, Carmarthen. These questionnaires asked about a range of issues, including the importance of preserving the Welsh language, the preferred nationality of Welsh parliamentary candidates, and Home Rule.[147] The Conservatives were willingly grappling with some big issues – although if Plaid Cymru had known that Tories were using the term 'the outer fringes' to

---

[142] 'The Party without a candidate holds the key in a close fight', *Western Mail*, 23 September 1959; 'Mail's Westminster Man has Died', 25 June 2007.
[143] 'Promise', *Western Mail*, 25 September 1959.
[144] CPA, CRD 4/15/4/3, 'Background statistics, 18 May 1979.
[145] Kenneth. O. Morgan, *Wales in British Politics* ([1963] Cardiff: University of Wales Press, 1983), p. 310.
[146] CPA, CCO 500/50/1, 'Nationalism and Regionalism', paper delivered by Chris Patten, 26 July 1966.
[147] CPA, CCO 500/50/1, Survey of Nationalism, undated, *c.* 1967.

describe Wales, then they would certainly have claimed that the party still had much to learn.[148]

Any such 'soul searching' should also be seen in the context of the wider political and policy review the party conducted in the late 1960s, when it was in opposition. This exercise was 'perhaps the most systematic' process of researching and formulating new ideas and policies in an 'unusually intense and extensive' way.[149] In the Welsh context, research like Patten's surveys and investigations resulted in a 1968 report, 'The Scope for Conservative Advance in Wales'. This marked another significant step in the party's attempt to try to 'understand' Wales, as well as demonstrating that it thought it was important to treat the nation differently, whilst still focusing on the importance of the Union. The report included the old gripes about Welsh politics, lamenting the 'sentimental . . . Celtic temperament' of Welsh people, but it also made more sophisticated attempts than ever before to critique the party's performance there.[150] It argued that an understanding of Welsh culture was imperative and that sympathy for such things should be expressed, most notably through education policy. In addressing the question 'have we been anti-Welsh?' the report argued that the Conservative record on supporting bilingualism and introducing a Minister for Welsh Affairs was good, but the party's ability to present this in a positive manner was lacking. The report also confirmed something that we have encountered already: local personnel at the grassroots were frequently ineffective, and prospective parliamentary candidates often unsuitable for certain localities.[151]

---

[148] The phrase 'the Celtic fringe' was used by Tory historians like Lord Blake to describe Wales. See Robert Blake, *The Conservative Party from Peel to Major* (London: Heinemann, 1997), p. 257.

[149] Stuart Ball, *The Conservative Party Since 1945* (Manchester: Manchester University Press, 1998), p. 116; John Barnes and Richard Cockett, 'The Making of Party Policy', in Seldon and Ball, *Conservative Century*, p. 372.

[150] CRD 3/37/1, 3, Survey: the Scope for Conservative Advance in Wales, 13 December 1968.

[151] CRD 3/37/1, 3, Survey: the Scope for Conservative Advance in Wales, 13 December 1968.

The party knew that tight-knit communities in industrial south Wales, where the Labour Party was especially strong, had for a long time seen voting for 'the Socialists' as 'a way of life', with a broader political culture having been forged by a sense of working-class solidarity.[152] Many of the party's private communications in this period joked about the hopelessness of the Tory cause in so-called 'Welsh Wales'. When the sitting member for Abertillery, the Reverend Llewellyn Williams, was struck down with a heart attack in 1963, the prospect of a by-election could summon only a two-word reaction from the Wales Area Agent, Howard Davies, who sent a note to CCO (with the sitting MP's other profession in mind, no doubt) stating: 'God forbid!!!'[153] When the dreaded by-election came, in 1965, the party's General Director wrote about how the Conservatives in Abertillery might have to use a caravan as a meeting room, noting that 'in a Welsh mining town, someone would probably light a fire underneath it'.[154]

In relation to these areas of 'Welsh Wales', however, the most interesting part of the 1968 report addressed the specific issue of the winding down of heavy industry. It did so with more optimism than those who had written memos about caravans being set ablaze. The document introduced the concept of the 'inward' and 'outward looking Welshmen'. The 'old close-knit industrial communities' supposedly nurtured the 'inward looking' variety that voted Labour. A more 'diversified economy', the report argued, and 'the more the Welsh economy is modernised', the more "outward looking" Welshmen (our friends) there will be'. The break-up of old industries and their replacement with new types was therefore presented in this report as not just probable, but desirable. The report's authors thought that such circumstances, combined with the party's image as 'competent and trustworthy', would soon allow it to attract as much as 45 per cent of the vote in

[152] Kenneth O. Morgan and Peter Stead, 'Rhondda West', in D. E. Butler and Anthony King (eds), *The British General Election of 1966* (London: Macmillan, 1966), p. 249; Johnes, *Wales Since 1939*, p. 122.
[153] CPA, CCO 1/14/541, Davies to the COO, 9 December 1963.
[154] CPA, CCO 1/14/541, Urton to the COO, 28 February 1965.

Wales. Donald Walters, a future Chairman of the Party in Wales, remembered how there was both genuine belief and excitement about the prospect of the Conservatives breaking through in such a way, once heavy industry subsided.[155] In hindsight, this was wishful thinking. Between the end of the Second World War and the end of the century, the Conservatives' vote share in Wales never passed 33 per cent, and in many of the seats where heavy industries used to predominate, the party regularly did so badly that it lost its deposit at general elections. As we have seen, industry may have disappeared, but mentalities, traditions, family and community links remained.[156] The misunderstandings about the nature of Welsh politics made by the likes of Basil Lindsay-Fynn, covered in the previous chapter, had not gone away. What was written in this report, however, adds weight to one of the most persistent criticisms that has been levelled at the Tories in Wales, namely that there was a political motive for winding down heavy industries, especially coal.

This report – although misguided in its conclusions – reflected something important in relation to the party in Wales and across Britain in this period, which was its growing professionalisation.[157] The party had historically been able to adapt to the times and to circumstances, but from the 1960s onwards it certainly became slicker in relation to its presentation, including the way in which it targeted local issues more effectively, as we have seen. In Wales, this new professionalism was most noticeable in relation to specific Welsh issues.[158] In private, the party's research team saw the new role of Secretary of State for Wales as unnecessary, and the new department as 'little more than a Committee of Departmental Regional Controllers'. But they kept this private. The Tory leadership knew that the least they could do was to maintain the

---

[155] Interview, Sir Donald Walters, 19 January 2015; CPA, CCO 500/26/29, Cardiff North constituency profile, undated, c.1969.
[156] Duncan Tanner, 'Facing the New Challenge: Labour and Politics, 1970–2000', in Tanner, Williams and Hopkin, *The Labour Party*, p. 264.
[157] Barnes and Cockett, 'The Making', p. 372.
[158] Bale, *The Conservatives*, p. 118.

status quo.[159] The 'softer' side of Conservatism was emphasised in the context of 'the nation', with the party continuing to write in its news-sheets that it would not only pay attention to Welsh affairs, but would 'care' for the nation, too.[160]

In the same year as the 'Scope for Conservative Advance in Wales' report was published, a Welsh Policy Group was established, with a series of clever people from the professional wing of the party making up its membership. These included Ian Grist, who at the time worked as the Information Officer for the Conservatives in Wales and who was part of a generation of backroom consultants, researchers or party officials who ended up being selected as parliamentary candidates.[161] Grist had been a long-time 'cog in the Tory Party apparatus' assiduously 'maintaining a flow of facts and opinions' about Wales and Welsh policy.[162] His finger was closer to the pulse of Welsh political life than most others, as his astute and clever campaigning literature when he stood for the industrial seat of Aberavon demonstrated.[163] (Amusingly, too, his signature – I. Grist – looked similar to the Welsh for Jesus Christ, *Iesu Grist*.[164]) This new group re-evaluated its approach towards the Union, toying with proposing bold ideas, like the notion of supporting fully fledged devolution for Wales. 'If the Conservative Party is going to propose elected bodies for Wales and Scotland, we might as well do it in a large way and get credit for it', it suggested. This obviously did not come to pass, unlike in Scotland, where Ted Heath, as Leader of the Opposition, signalled his support for a Scottish Assembly.[165]

In another mark of its growing professionalism, the party began systematically profiling its candidates in Wales in an attempt

---

[159] CPA, CRD 3/37/3, Internal report re progression of the role of Welsh Minister, 1969.
[160] 'Lord Brecon 'boosts' Tories', *North Wales Weekly News*, date unknown, c.July 1964.
[161] Criddle, 'Members of Parliament', p. 165.
[162] 'Cardiff North', *Western Mail*, 27 February 1974.
[163] CPA, PUB 229/15/17, Ian Grist election address, Aberavon, 1970.
[164] Ian Grist Obituary, *Daily Telegraph*, 12 January 2002.
[165] CPA, CRD 3/37/3, CRD paper on Welsh Local Government for Mr Heath, undated, c.1969.

to work out how it could encourage more Welsh speakers to stand for it.[166] One person who did was John Eilian Jones, a Bard of the National Eisteddfod described by Grist as 'something of a freak Tory!' because he was so thoroughly Welsh, but a staunch Conservative.[167] Jones joined the Welsh Policy Group and stood for the party on Anglesey in 1964, 1966 and 1970. This was seen as a real coup because not only was Jones a fluent Welsh speaker, but he also, as the Managing Editor of the local *Caernarvon Herald*, had a firm grasp on local affairs. He was also a passionate advocate of Welsh culture and a translator of various works into Welsh. He fought his campaigns by stressing local issues, illustrating his materials with photos of the isle of Anglesey, and by putting the Welsh language at the centre of his campaign.[168] Almost uniquely amongst Conservative (and indeed Labour) politicians, nearly the entire front cover of some of John Eilian's pitches to the electorate were in Welsh.[169] After his adoption as a candidate in the 1960s, the party witnessed an uplift in the number of people joining the local association, in a period when membership figures were going down. Whilst John Eilian did not come close to unseating the sitting Labour MP, Cledwyn Hughes, at either general elections in the 1960s, the vote swung away from Labour on Anglesey, against national trends.[170] He performed better than most Conservatives in 1966, although there was no Liberal fighting the seat at that general election.[171] In 1964, the Plaid Cymru vote on Anglesey was more than halved from its 1959 result, suggesting again that John Eilian's appeal on the grounds of his Welsh identity and knowledge of local politics was a draw for swing voters and Tory members alike.[172]

---

[166] WPA, GB0210 MONION, file 24, 29 January 1974.
[167] CPA, CRD 3/37/3, Grist to Douglas, undated, *c.*November 1967.
[168] CPA, PUB 229/13/16, John Eilian Jones election address, Anglesey, 1964.
[169] CPA, PUB 229/14/15, John Eilian Jones election address, Anglesey, 1966. The only English on this front cover told readers that Jones, pictured, was 'the Conservative Candidate'.
[170] CPA, CCO 1/14/512, Davies to Bryan, 21 October 1963.
[171] James and Thomas, *Wales at Westminster*, p. 173.
[172] 'There is 'something nasty about politics here'', *Western Mail*, 9 June 1987.

Despite the presence of people like John Eilian Jones, and the party's increased professionalism, perceptions of the Tory's class status, of its 'Englishness' and its historic incompatibility with Wales tended to die hard – and sometimes with good reason. Studies of Cardiganshire (as it was often called then) in the 1960s and 70s found that the Liberals successfully continued to portray

Figure 12: John Eilian Jones's election address to the voters of Anglesey in 1966 contained almost no English on the front cover.

themselves as 'classless', whereas in the minds of local people the 'Conservative Party could still be associated with the [. . .] gentry'. One resident noted that the 'the voice of Welshness' in the local Conservative association, was 'almost silent'. Others argued that the Tories needed to show a more 'open and empathetic sympathy towards Welsh culture'.[173] When Trefor Llewellyn was chosen to fight Cardigan in 1974, his lack of skills in the language made him unviable from the outset, according to the *Western Mail*.[174] One candidate standing in a Welsh-speaking seat in the same period noted how he was able to 'greet people' in Welsh: 'I was encouraged to do so because it was polite'.[175] He also remembered that, whilst people spoke Welsh in the association, they often did so falteringly. On one occasion, the association's chairman accidentally referred to the recent carnival winner, in Welsh, as 'Queen of the Cowsheds'.[176] Others, like a young Tristan Garel-Jones, a future MP and minister under Margaret Thatcher and John Major, could 'get by' in Welsh when he fought Caernarfon in February 1974, but his lack of fluency – and the fact he was based in London – frustrated the local association.[177] Despite that, they still chose the non-Welsh-speaking, twenty-one-year-old future MP, Robert Harvey, to fight the following election in the October of the same year. Harvey remembered that the 'only hostility' he would receive on the campaign trail was a result of not being able to speak the language.[178] Again, it might have been the result of a combination of factors, including an increased Plaid Cymru presence in the seat, but the Tory vote at each election in Caernarfon, unlike on Anglesey, dropped.[179]

---

[173] Madgwick, Griffiths and Walker, *The Politics*, pp. 64, 215.
[174] 'How the West will be won', *Western Mail*, 2 October 1974.
[175] Interview with anonymous.
[176] Interview with anonymous.
[177] Interview, Lord Garel-Jones, 11 June 2015; CPA, CCO 1/16/532, Wolstenholme to Grant, 17 April 1974.
[178] Interview, Robert Harvey, 27 November 2015.
[179] See James and Thomas, *Wales at Westminster*, pp. 173, 177, 181 and 186.

Even Peter Thomas, who was Secretary of State for Wales from 1970 to 1974, was portrayed as a somewhat remote figure.[180] He had been the member for Conway until 1966, but then moved to the safe north London seat of Hendon South, which apparently resulted in 'much derision'.[181] Although Thomas's 'Welsh credentials were not questioned', his affluent English seat only bolstered his image as a respectable urban sophisticate, not truly plugged into Welsh life.[182] Nevertheless, it was under Thomas that the party continued to make policy and presentational changes. Peter Price, who was a Conservative candidate for the party on a number of occasions in Wales, remembered the late 1960s and early 1970s as the period when the 'Welsh agenda' in the party really took hold. He recalled how the then Area Agent for Wales, Howard Davies, took up the cause with enthusiasm.[183] Further promotion of bilingualism in public life was encouraged, Labour's 1967 Welsh Language Act having disappointed language campaigners for not obliging public bodies to use or promote Welsh enough.[184] The Conservatives' annual Welsh conference was established in 1972. Meetings of the Wales Area Council, which on several occasions in the 1950s and early 1960s had been held in the English towns of Chester, Shrewsbury and Leominster, began to be held in the geographically central location of Llandrindod Wells although, as one regular attendant remembered, this just made it 'difficult for *everyone* to get to'.[185] Places like Shrewsbury might in reality have been easier for people to access, but holding the event in Wales was again about

---

[180] Interview, Lord Temple-Morris, 17 July 2015.
[181] Morgan, *Rebirth*, p. 394.
[182] Russell Deacon, *The Governance of Wales: The Welsh Office and the Policy Process 1964–1999* (Cardiff: Welsh Academic Press, 2002), p. 26.
[183] Interview, Peter Price, 4 December 2015.
[184] Geraint H. Jenkins and Mari A. Williams, 'Introduction', in Geraint H. Jenkins and Mari A. Williams (eds), *'Let's do our best for the ancient tongue': The Welsh Language in the Twentieth Century* (Cardiff: University of Wales Press, 2015), p. 16.
[185] Interview, Nigel Evans, 16 June 2015.

symbolism.[186] The *Western Mail* passed positive judgement on all of this in 1974, under the headline 'The Tories gain a new identity.' It argued that the party had once been maligned as 'thoroughly anti-Welsh', but that had changed: 'it can now be said that there is such a species as a genuine Welsh Conservative . . . [who] have made a marked attempt to acquire a Welsh identity in recent years'.[187]

Not everyone of a Conservative disposition in Wales was happy about this, of course, particularly in parts of British Wales. In relation to Welsh-language broadcasting, for example, the Monmouth Conservative Association was undoubtedly reflecting the views of a wider group of people when its members sent a resolution to the Secretary of State for Wales, arguing that 'This meeting deplores the [. . .] viewing time allocated to the small Welsh-speaking minority in the Monmouth area'. They asked for transmitters in the area that would actually *block* Welsh-language programmes for those who did not want to watch them.[188] Other people believed that few meaningful or significant changes had taken place in terms of the party's new and more Welsh identity. The current MP for Ribble Valley, Nigel Evans, came of age politically as a YC in 1970s Swansea, but never considered 'Welsh Conservatism' to mean anything significant aside from 'the odd Welsh cheese and wine nights', which resembled a 'self-help group of political misfits'.[189] The party's leadership in Wales, however, was intent on furthering and reinforcing a sense of 'Welshness', with many more significant changes taking place after 1975, which the next chapter covers in detail.

---

[186] Andrew Edwards, *Labour's Crisis: Plaid Cymru, the Conservatives, and the Decline of the Labour Party in North-West Wales, 1960–74* (Cardiff: University of Wales Press, 2011), p. 160.

[187] 'The Tories gain a new identity', *Western Mail*, 26 September 1974.

[188] WPA, GB0210 MONION, file 24, Monmouth Conservative Association, 25 January 1972.

[189] Interview, Nigel Evans MP, 16 June 2015. For Evans the youth movement is now an integral and vital voice within the party.

GRASSROOTS DECLINE

Grassroots Conservatives may have been prominent in trying to resist the party's 'Welsh agenda', but they still had a significant, if diminished, wider role to play in this period. Much of the modernisation and technological change so evident by the end of the 1960s certainly did undermine aspects of their activism, with numbers of paid-up members declining significantly year by year. But in stronger seats some members used cultural change as a reason to 'double and redouble' their work 'on the ground', because modern media and the television made it easier to become 'misinformed'. The Brecon and Radnor Association had a long, earnest conversation about their continued role as 'persuaders' in 1966, concluding that their role remained important.[190] The central party also had cause to encourage grassroots participation. By the early 1970s, only around a third of the party's income came from central donations and reserves; the other two-thirds was raised by constituency associations.[191]

The perennial problem of leadership in Wales, however, remained an issue. Constituency affairs were often run by a handful of strong people, including married couples like the Protheroe-Beynons in Carmarthen, who drove initiatives forward and often guaranteed payment for most of them. Mrs Protheroe-Beynon also raised a considerable proportion of the funds, and stood once as the parliamentary candidate, delivering speeches 'off the cuff' because she had to concentre on 'important things' like 'the housework and the meals'.[192] Such people were considered 'pillars of strength' by the Wales Area Office, but there were not many of them. Wales was also in short supply of effective agents, the role so many believed important for making politics 'on the ground'

---

[190] WPA, GB0210 CONLES, file 65, News Sheet, January 1966.
[191] Bale, *The Conservatives*, p. 158
[192] CPA, CCO 1/14/517/1, Davies to Bryan, 6 September 1962; PUB 229/13/16, Hilda Protheroe-Beynon election address, Carmarthen, 1964; 'Mrs P-B supplies the sparkle', *Western Mail*, 8 October 1964; CPA, CCO 1/14/517/1, Annual Report 31 March 1962.

function effectively.[193] Some, like Bill Weale in Pembrokeshire, D. Woolley in Monmouth or Rowland Syer in Cardiff North, were deemed excellent.[194] Otherwise, advertisements for posts went unanswered, incumbents were considered 'incapable of carrying out . . . duties' to such an extent that they harmed the party cause, and salaries were deemed to be a worrying drain on a seat's finances.[195] As in previous periods, safer seats were more attractive for agents to work in and consequently attracted better people.[196] In 1974, one-third of the most competitive constituencies in Britain were without a full-time Conservative agent, whilst those with huge Conservative majorities were more likely to employ one.[197] Wales, with its lack of safe seats, suffered accordingly, although it should be noted that having a strong agent in a seat like Monmouth or Cardiff North was no guarantor of the party holding those constituencies against a strong Labour challenge.

In 1973, the party attempted reform in this area, introducing a scheme where agents were employed centrally, so that they could be deployed to places that needed them most.[198] Despite this, recruitment – particularly in Wales – remained a problem.[199] For some years, 'missioners' – Central Office employees engaging in 'ground work' in marginal seats with the aim of attracting new members to the party – had been deployed to Wales, with some positive results.[200] This scheme had wound up by the 1970s, with the party opting instead to cluster together weaker constituencies which would come under the supervision of an Organising

[193] CPA, CCO 1/14/531, Davies to the COO, 8 January 1962.
[194] Interview Lord Crickhowell, 1 July 2013; Interview Richard Howells, 17 July 2013; WPA, GB0210 CARCON, file 29, City of Cardiff Conservative Committee minute book, 19 September 1966.
[195] CPA, CCO 1/14/531, Davies to the COO, 8 January 1962; CPA, CCO 1/14/545, Entwistle to Davies, 25 March 1963; CPA, CCO 1/14/545, Davies to the COO, 9 March 1964; Bale, *The Conservatives*, p. 114.
[196] Andrew Thorpe, *Parties at War: Political Organisation in Second World War Britain* (Oxford: Oxford University Press, 2009), pp. 99–100; Bale, *The Conservatives*, p. 20.
[197] Bale, *The Conservatives*, p. 156.
[198] Zig Layton-Henry, 'Constituency Autonomy in the Conservative Party', *Parliamentary Affairs*, 29/4 (1976), 396; Bale, *The Conservatives*, p. 156.
[199] Butler and Kavanagh, *The British General Election of February 1974*, p. 221.
[200] CPA, CCO 500/8/8, Missioner plan, 30 March 1961.

Secretary, who was like a less well-paid agent.[201] One of these roles was filled by Charlotte Bennett, who was in charge of the South East Wales group, which included seats like Abertillery, Bedwellty, Ebbw Vale and Pontypool.[202] The 'grouping' of these unwinnable seats was evidence of the party's strategy of rationalising its resources and of its central machine becoming more professional. However, without an association or an agent to call their own, those small bands of Conservatives in places like Pontypool no longer had their own constituency-based identity, which compounded many of the other problems such seats faced.

It is estimated that the party was, on average, losing 64,000 members a year across Britain in the 1960s. Nowhere was this weakening of the party's grassroots' support base more obvious than amongst the YCs.[203] In 1965, the national YC membership figure was one third smaller than it had been at its 1949 peak.[204] Even deliberate recruitment campaigns in Wales had limited success, failing to counter the growing narrative that the YCs belonged to a different and more old-fashioned age.[205] There was still some hope for the organisation, but this was to be found in more reliably Conservative areas of 'British Wales'. AGMs of the YCs in Cardiff still attracted around 200 people,[206] and members could still be effective canvassers at election time, as some social surveys found.[207] When Nigel Evans became Chairman of the YCs in Swansea West, he remembered it as 'vibrant', describing it as 'half political' (with canvassing and electioneering conducted

[201] Ball, 'The National', p. 193.
[202] Interview, Charlotte Bennett, 29 September 2015. There had been a version of this in Wales's weakest areas for some time. The two Rhondda constituencies were so weak that they were grouped together as early as 1951, under the supervision of an experienced Agent. This mimicked a scheme from the 1930s. See Ramsden, *The Age of Balfour*, p. 228.
[203] D. E. Butler and Richard Rose, *The British General Election of 1959* (London: Macmillan, 1960), pp. 9, 119.
[204] Lawrence Black, 'The Lost World of Young Conservatism', *The Historical Journal*, 51/4 (2008), 993.
[205] Lawrence Black, *Redefining British Politics: Culture, Consumerism and Participation, 1945–1970* (Basingstoke: Palgrave Macmillan, 2010), p. 76; CPA, CCO 2/6/19, Wales and Monmouthshire Area Annual Report, 8 April 1961.
[206] Interview, Jonathan Evans, 21 November 2014.
[207] Morgan, 'Swansea West', p. 293.

when necessary) and 'half social' ('all we did for seven years was play table tennis').[208] This 50/50 analogy mirrors Ramsden's interpretation of the YCs, although evidence from Wales does seem to demonstrate that the scales were weighted much more heavily towards socialising.[209]

Indeed, big YC events that drew in people were almost always social and not political in substance. Six hundred attended barbecues in Wrexham, for example, or a Raft Race in Monmouth in 1965.[210] As other historians have noted, even in the midst 'of feverish election speculation', YCs met to discuss things like their prize draws and dances, 'but nothing regarding an election campaign'.[211] When the Conway YCs met in April 1966, in the aftermath of a terrible result for the party in the constituency, which had lost its strong MP, the only items on the agenda were parties, a barn dance, bowling in Chester, a barbecue and several beach parties. An invitation to the YC Area Conference was turned down by all members, because 'the date clashed with a social function'.[212] One new YC member in Cardiff remembered constructing mock policies to debate, but thought the main attraction was 'socialising' and 'meeting girls'.[213] Another remembered the importance of dances and games nights, which would involve flirting.[214] As the writer Quentin Letts would later say about Tory youth movements, they involved 'more bedhopping than doorstepping'.[215] Even in the youth wing of the Labour Party, whose politics was often deemed as more 'serious', activities were said to be 'of a social nature'.[216]

---

[208] Interview, Nigel Evans MP, 16 June 2015.
[209] Ramsden, *The Winds*, p. 92.
[210] CPA, CCO 2/7/12, Wales and Monmouthshire Area Annual Report 1965–1966.
[211] Taym Saleh, 'The Decline of the Scottish Conservatives in North-East Scotland, 1965–79: A Regional Perspective', *Parliamentary History*, 36/2 (2017), 227.
[212] DRO, DD/DM/730/8, Colwyn Bay Young Conservatives minute book, 13 April 1966, 28 May 1966.
[213] Interview, Chris Butler, 11 May 2015.
[214] Interview, Peter Price, 4 December 2015.
[215] Quentin Letts, 'The year of the cad', *Spectator*, 12 December 2015.
[216] Walling, 'The Structure', p. 208.

Those who remained members seemed to do so out of loyalty and were hardly politically active.[217] Attempts to drum up support within places like universities resulted in very limited success. Even the Conservative Society at University College, Swansea had been able to attract sixty members to its meetings in the early 1950s, but that level of enthusiasm was short lived.[218] By the mid-1960s, 'Soc. Soc.' (the Socialist Society) was much more popular, despite young Tories having a reputation for being better organised than Labour's League of Youth, which later morphed into the Young Socialists.[219] Student Conservatives at Aberystwyth's University college were so actively unhelpful to the party that they became 'the thorn in my flesh' for the CCO staff member charged with liaising with students.[220] By the 1960s, most students seemed to have concluded that a political association could not offer the necessary social opportunities that wider university life could.[221]

This applied to wider life outside universities, too. As we saw in the previous chapter, Keith Flynn had overseen a thriving YC branch in Llandaff in the mid-1950s, but by the mid-1960s his organisation was 'useless'. He remembered that 'it was all dying out. At one meeting . . . six people turned up!' It transpired that these meetings were being held on the same day of the week, and at the same time of the evening, as 'Hancock's Half Hour' was broadcast on television.[222] (Tony Hancock himself had once mocked the very organisation whose meetings people in Cardiff West and elsewhere were skipping to watch television, joking that he did not join the YCs because he 'couldn't play table tennis and

---

[217] Bale, *The Conservatives*, p. 60; Paul Addison, 'Sixty Somethings', *The London Review of Books*, 17/19 (1995), 17–18.
[218] Richard Burton Archives, Swansea University, 'The Conservative Society', *Crefft*, 5 November 1952.
[219] CPA, CCO 506/25/57, Annual Report 1965; Steven Fielding, 'The Labour Party and the Recruitment of the Young, 1945–1970', in Gaetano Quagliariello (ed.), *La Formazione della classe politica in Europa* (Manduria: P. Lacaita, 2000), pp. 579–84; Bale, *The Conservatives*, p. 111.
[220] CPA, CCO 506/25/54, Aberystwyth files.
[221] CPA, CCO 506/25/55, Bangor files, Turner to Purnell, 6 July 1961.
[222] Interview, Keith Flynn, 20 September 2015.

he wasn't looking for a wife'.[223]) Grassroots Tory politics had never been fundamentally ideological. Changing leisure patterns and the allure of the television meant organisations like the YCs – for so long a way of giving young people something to do – inevitably suffered.[224] However, it is important to note that it was still middle-class households that could afford TV sets. There may have been thirteen million of them in Britain in 1964 (compared with one million in 1951) but that still meant a lot of people did not have one.[225] Coming from the more well-off backgrounds that they did, YCs were more likely to be distracted by new programmes that deliberately emphasised a culture that was youth-centric, trendy and urban.[226] CCO was willing to admit that one of the greatest barriers to YC recruitment was that young people were 'under psychological pressure; the rebellious youth syndrome'.[227] The party rightly recognised that as young people became more and more mobile, leaving home to go to university or find work, it was harder to pin down the kind of people who might have been loyal to their locality (despite local issues being stressed more frequently by parties 'on the ground').[228]

Those who remained in the YCs, however, offer a small glimpse into a relatively socially conservative world of the mid-1960s to mid-1970s. As some historians have argued, rapid social change and the rise of youth culture in this period was not an even process.[229] The Sixties was a period of continuity as much as of change. Many of the new ideas about things like sex, morals, music or architecture caused emotions ranging from excitement and

---

[223] Ramsden, *The Winds*, p. 94.
[224] Harrison, *Seeking*, p. 330.
[225] Michael Pinto-Duschinsky, 'Bread and Circuses? The Conservatives in Office 1951–1964', in Vernon Bogdanor and Robert Skidelsky (eds), *The Age of Affluence 1951–1964* (London, 1970), p. 56.
[226] Dominic Sandbrook, *White Heat: A History of Britain in the Swinging Sixties* (London: Little Brown, 2006), pp. 101–2.
[227] CPA, CCO 20/11/47, Johnson Smith to Cope, 11 March 1968.
[228] WPA, GB0210 MONION, file 22, AGM Report 1973.
[229] Sandbrook, *White Heat*, p. 198; Sam Blaxland, *Swansea University: Campus and Community in a Post-war World, 1945–2020* (Cardiff: 2020), see chapter three.

anxiety all the way through to disapproval or disgust.[230] Pictures of groups of YCs show reasonably formal young people, none of whom look like hippies or mods. Twenty-seven of them had their photograph taken at a social event in Colwyn Bay in 1967, and whilst some of the men are sporting open collars, most are in suits and ties and most of the women look relatively formal.[231] Pictures of young Labour members in this period show a difference that is not dramatic, but which is nonetheless noticeable. Firstly, there are more men in these photographs. Whilst most are still quite formally dressed, there are certainly fewer three-piece suits and members have their arms around one another in a way rarely seen in pictures of Conservative members.[232] Other images of Labour and Plaid Cymru activists show people dressed and behaving much more casually, in a way that simply is not evident in any YC gathering.[233] A general resistance to the supposed spirit of the Sixties could be identified in these groups.

In other respects, the party membership in Wales looked worn out, drawn from an ever-narrowing group of people, as was the case across other political parties.[234] Those ordinary people who did stick with it, faithfully attending branch meetings and raising funds, worried that party events were only 'attracting the faithful'.[235] Of the seventeen members of the Nantyglyn Branch of the Denbigh Association in the 1970s, for example, there were three married couples and two Miss Rawlins, who were presumably related.[236] These kinds of small

[230] For a good discussion, see Trevor Harris and Monia O'Brien Castro, 'Conclusion', in Trevor Harris and Monia O'Brien Castro (eds), *Preserving the Sixties: Britain and the 'Decade of Protest'* (Basingstoke: Palgrave Macmillan, 2014), pp. 192–4.
[231] DRO, DD/DM/80/24, Photograph of Young Conservatives at Colwyn Bay, October 1967.
[232] WPA, GB0210 ROGROB, Roger Roberts collection, photos and clippings.
[233] See: 'Cardiff North', *Western Mail*, 17 June 1970; 'Kilbrandon will be principal plank in Plaid platform', Western Mail, 11 February 1974.
[234] Duncan Tanner, 'Labour and its membership', in Duncan Tanner, Pat Thane and Nick Tiratsoo (eds), *Labour's First Century* (Cambridge: Cambridge University Press, 2000), p. 256; Fielding, 'Activists', 250.
[235] WPA, GB0210 CARCON, file 34, The Glamorgan Group Council of the Wales and Monmouthshire Provincial Area minute book, 1 June 1972, 4 June 1974.
[236] DRO, DD/DM/730/2, Nantyglyn Branch minute book.

village-level branches, which in their own way helped bed the party into many communities, started to wind up, with more emphasis placed on the central constituency association. Local record offices are full of minute books, such as that from the Llanddulas Branch, also in Denbigh, where the final meeting expresses a forlorn hope that, one day, the organisation would be resurrected.[237] Few were.

Again, the only element of the party's grassroots that remained reasonably strong was some women's associations, with many examples of women acting as 'the spearhead in *all* association work'.[238] When the Cardiff North West seat was formed in 1974, women underpinned every aspect of the association's financial health. Such women in particular continued to advertise the party to the public and to potential Tory voters, with one association concluding that, when it came to campaigning, 'the Socialists fear the power of the Conservative woman'.[239] Much of this activity continued to take the form of middle-class social-cum-fundraising occasions. In Monmouth in the early 1970s, 'a lengthy but not trifling discussion on – trifle' resulted in fifteen different women volunteering to make desserts for a function.[240] Family life continued to be deliberately woven into much of this, with lunches, film showings or a chance to see Father Christmas features of various events.[241] Women's 'luncheon clubs' remained a popular staple. There were 308 names on the book for Swansea West's version at the turn of the 1970s, meetings of which were held at the Dragon Hotel on the first Friday of every month,

[237] DRO, DD/DM/730/1, Denbigh Conservative Association Records, Llanddulas Branch minute book, 24 February 1977.
[238] CPA, CCO 1/14/522, AGM Report 1964.
[239] WPA, GB0219 CONLES, file 65, Brecon and Radnor Conservative and Unionist Newssheet, June 1964.
[240] WPA, GB0210 MONION, file 25, Abergavenny Branch minute book, 2 October 1973.
[241] DRO, DD/DM/80/22, Newspaper scrapbook, 'A good time – and gifts!', paper and date unknown.

'at 1pm prompt' – that is, on a working day, implying that most members did not work, or were retired.[242]

Of course, Conservative societies were not the only conduit through which middle-class women could gather, organise and take part in events relating to their broader interests. Swansea had a thriving branch of the Women's Gas Federation in this period, for example, which staged plays, put on monthly talks from local notables and experts and organised charity events. Swansea's mayoress was its president. The group was so popular that it had a waiting list for those who wanted to join it. Pictures in the local newspapers showed these groups of women, often gathered in the smarter hotels of the region, dressed in their finery and wearing pearls. One event involved a 'full and varied programme', including floral arrangements, a summer supper and a glass of wine 'to toast the new Prince of Wales'. The parallels between these groups and Tory women, including the photos that were taken of them, are noteworthy. It bolstered the idea that there was significant overlap between Conservative associations and philanthropic, artistic and recreational groups.[243]

Key figures from these Conservative women's associations often led from the front, displaying a level of courage and agency that contrasted strongly with the patronising attitude they faced from other senior grassroots figures. (When the Barry Association, for example, needed to canvass ideas via a questionnaire about local organisation in 1967, the agent privately warned that 'as the majority of our Branches are Womens [sic] Branches the questions have to be as elementary as possible'.[244]) It was not unheard of for a woman like Mrs E. A. Jones from Monmouth to single-handedly recruit fifty new members of the association in one go, for which she received 'a special badge'.[245] Women

[242] West Glamorgan Archives [WGA], D/D CMLC 1, Swansea West Luncheon Club minute book, 5 July 1968.
[243] Ball, *Portrait*, p. 169.
[244] CPA, CCO 1/14/533, Sims to du Cann, 13 March 1967.
[245] WPA, GB0210 MONION, file 4, Monmouth Women's Executive Committee, 26 February 1946.

like Hilda Protheroe-Beynon in Carmarthen (known as 'Mrs P-B'), or Irene Everest in Barry (known as one of Wales's 'Top Tories'), were forceful charismatic campaigners in their own right.[246] They gave regular stump speeches and, in the latter's case, went to campaign in Labour-dominated areas, 'preferably alone' and unaccompanied.[247] Although Everest was quoted as saying that she thought nothing of such actions, the reality would have surely been different. She had been warned that in places like Caerphilly, where she went door-knocking, 'I would probably have my car turned over'. However, her decision to do this kind of work because she found 'hostile looks' from other women 'exhilarating' is telling.[248] Although such women were relatively unusual, they help paint a much more interesting picture of female Tory activists in this period, showing that they were not all the 'powerless' and 'subordinate' actors that the feminist writer Beatrix Campbell portrayed them as in her pioneering work on the subject.[249]

Despite the likes of Irene Everest or 'Mrs P-B', women continued to feature very rarely as parliamentary candidates in Wales, leading some to conclude that it was these very grassroots women members who often blocked their selection. Several historians have agreed, suggesting that it was women on constituency selection panels who were responsible for ensuring that a parliamentary candidate was a man.[250] There is much anecdotal and oral history evidence that implies the same, with women especially keen to select a handsome, young parliamentary candidate who could possibly act as a suitor for their daughter. Some cited resentment that a woman would just turn up on the scene when 'I've been raising money in this constituency for

[246] For much more detail, see Sam Blaxland, 'Women in the Organisation of the Conservative Party in Wales, 1945–1979', *Women's History Review*, 28/2 (2019).
[247] 'Mrs P-B supplies the sparkle', *Western Mail*, 8 October 1964.
[248] 'A day in the life of a top Tory', *Western Mail*, 12 June 1970.
[249] Beatrix Campbell, *The Iron Ladies: Why Do Women Vote Tory?* (London: Virago, 1987), pp. 256, 269.
[250] Ball, 'Local Conservatism', pp. 265–6; Maguire, *Conservative Women*, p. 168.

thirty-five years'.[251] A useful case study demonstrating aspects of this is Kathleen Smith, who stood in Caernarfon in 1970. She had theories, set out in interesting newspaper columns, as to why so few women were selected by local Conservative associations. For her, many women were naturally conservative and thought that men made better politicians. She also observed that some were jealous of those women who did stand.[252]

Smith herself was a talented novelist and writer who also campaigned for a range of liberal causes, including a twenty-hour working week to allow people's 'leisure [to] be more enjoyable and creative'.[253] She was learning Welsh at the time of the 1970 campaign, knew 'what it is to be a woman on a budget', and was a former Assistant Governor of Holloway Prison, the experience of which fed into her novels and writing. Indeed, her progressive attitudes to law and order and penal reform may well have alienated many women party members. She used a long column in the *Western Mail* to argue the case for women being elected to parliament in equal, if not greater, ratios to men.[254] She was in favour of 'the self-determinative prison sentence', and one of her poems, 'Belly Laughter', ended with the lines: 'Be moved to shrug / when puppy wets the rug; / And always move to hug / the culprit'.[255] Perhaps the most interesting question here is why Smith, with such liberal and feminist instincts, was attracted to the Tories in the first place! Her personal archive provides few answers to that question, but is a fascinating record of her literary work which gives a sense of the character of one of the few, and of course unsuccessful, women Conservative candidates in the twentieth century.[256]

---

[251] Interviews with the author; also see British Library Sound and Moving Image archive, C1688/16, Ken Worthy interview; C1688/07, Dame Elizabeth Anson interview.
[252] 'Why not put more women in power?', *Western Mail*, 1 April 1966.
[253] 'Campaigning Miss Smith has to leave hotel', paper unknown, 10 November 1978.
[254] 'Why not put more women in power?', *Western Mail*, 1 April 1966.
[255] NLW ex 2462, Kathleen Smith papers.
[256] NLW ex 2462, Kathleen Smith papers.

CONCLUSION

A period of fast-paced change in Welsh political life also, conversely, meant that more emphasis was placed on local concerns and issues. In places where they already had a foothold, the Tories were relatively well placed to engage with this. The rise of Plaid Cymru in Wales also spurred on a new kind of professionalised pavement politics, where Conservatives thought more specifically about the needs of particular communities. This also encompassed a greater focus on Welsh policy, with the party thinking more deeply about wider perceptions that it was 'un-Welsh'. Much of this was part of an attempt to push back against two major long-term accusations: on one hand, the Conservatives were trying to show that they could be compatible with the slightly different tenor of Welsh politics. On the other, they were trying to distance themselves from their upper-class image. The two – national identity and class – were, in some people's minds, linked. By 1970, the party in Wales was talking more of itself as a movement 'of the people' with 'a real concern for everyone', even going as far as to add that the 'old Tories so feared in Wales have gone'.[257] Even if loyal newspapers like the *Western Mail* agreed, there was little change in the party's fortunes as a result of this. The period from 1975, however, witnessed another change in this regard. That, and the wider legacy of Thatcherism, are the focus points of the final chapter.

---

[257] CPA, PUB 229/15/17, David Purnell election address, Aberdare, 1970, and John Rendle election address, Abertillery, 1970.

4
THATCHERISM AND ITS LEGACY, 1975–1997

In the lead-up to the 1997 referendum on establishing a devolved parliament in Wales, many Conservative politicians and activists called for a 'No' vote. Prominent amongst them was the former MP, Rod Richards, a fluent Welsh-speaking Welshman who prioritised his Britishness and belief in the integrity of the United Kingdom. Richards would become the Conservative group's first, although short-term, leader in the new National Assembly when it was established in 1999. In many ways, he reflected grassroots opinion on devolution and the separate (but interconnected) issue of 'national identity'. Shortly after the establishing of what would later be called the Senedd, one rank-and-file member wrote to the party's senior leadership to say

> I perceive no mandate or desire for 'Welshness' beyond the nationalist hard-core and many people actually support the Tories because they are seen as the British Party. I would sooner scrap the Cardiff office, the whole Welsh Tory concept . . . and go back to being the British Tories.[1]

Had it been made public, this communication would have solidified, in many people's minds, the idea that Conservatives in Wales thought little of Welsh institutions or even Wales more broadly. The party's long-term anglicised and upper-class image certainly had a role to play in that. By the end of the 1990s, some Conservatives thought they were stuck in a loop, where

---

[1] Welsh Political Archive, National Library of Wales, Aberystwyth [WPA], GB0210 CONAGRP, 4/1, Walker to Melding, 17 June 2002, 11 June 2002.

the 'marked hostility' to Conservatism from large chunks of the electorate in Wales never allowed them to articulate their Welsh identity or their place in the nation's politics effectively.[2]

And yet the period under discussion in this chapter encompasses the greatest of the party's efforts to try to sympathise with the 'needs' of Wales and design certain policies on matters such as the language and broadcasting accordingly: to articulate a Unionist message that genuinely recognised Welsh distinctiveness. We begin in 1975, at the point that Margaret Thatcher took over the leadership of the Conservative Party, not just because of Thatcher's momentous impact on Conservatism and the country more widely, but because she appointed important people as her spokesmen on Wales and Welsh Affairs. Aside from uniquely Welsh issues, the party in the 1980s was a great deal more popular in Wales than might be imagined. Its best result at a general election in the twentieth century, in terms of seats won, was in 1983, and its share of the vote, and the number of votes it received in the following election, in 1987, remained almost the same. This chapter will scrutinise how, amongst its core base, many of the Thatcher government's policies were popular – especially, although not exclusively, in its old core constituencies of 'British Wales'. However, by 1997, the party was obliterated in terms of the number of Welsh MPs it had, whilst appearing to have failed to shift the dial in how it was perceived as un-Welsh. The chapter will also demonstrate that a period of relative success for the party in the 1980s did not revitalise the grassroots, which went into a period of further, and indeed terminal, decline.

---

[2] Conservative Party Archive, Bodleian Library, Oxford [CPA], Conservative Central Office [CCO] 180/32, 'The Scope for Conservative Advance in Wales' Report.

THATCHERISM AND WALES

Margaret Thatcher left a legacy in Wales unlike that of most other modern politicians. Industrial disputes and trade union activity were hot topics by the end of the 1970s, with Labour Prime Minister James Callaghan facing the so-called Winter of Discontent at the end of 1978. Resentment towards these unions, and their leaders, who were presented as being unelected whilst also wielding significant power, was often cited as the main reason why people voted for Thatcher in the general election of 1979.[3] She was keen to rein in the trade unions, folding a critique of them into the party's renewed emphasis on the freedom of the individual.[4] Tories in Wales ran with these themes. Labour, they argued, had ruined a once prosperous country and was now the 'party of unemployment'.[5] Various versions of the message that Wales could 'not afford' socialism, or a Labour government, were common.[6] Some swing voters seemed to agree, with one saying that because of 'seething industrial unrest' there was 'discontent throughout the country'.[7] The *Western Mail* ran one of the most partisan leader articles in its post-war history in advance of polling day in 1979, arguing – under the straightforward headline, 'Why you should vote Tory' – that 'trade union activities do need to be made more accountable'.[8] Resentment amongst large parts of the Welsh middle classes clearly spurred them into voting Conservative. The party gained three seats (Brecon and Radnor, Montgomery, and Anglesey), taking its total of Welsh constituencies to eleven. Its share of the vote also rose a substantial nine percentage points

---

[3] David Butler and Dennis Kavanagh, *The British General Election of 1979* (London: Macmillan, 1980), pp. 334–5.

[4] Peregrine Worsthorne, 'Too Much Freedom', in Maurice Cowling (ed.), *Conservative Essays* (London: Cassell, 1978), pp. 147–8; Noël O'Sullivan, *Conservatism* (London: Dent, 1976), p. 29.

[5] CPA, PUB 229/18/22, Michael Roberts election address, Cardiff North West, 1979.

[6] See for example, CPA, PUB 229/18/22, Ralph Tuck election address, Abertillery, 1979; 'Tory "Robin Hood" tactics attacked', *Western Mail*, 17 April 1979.

[7] 'Conservatives hope for double figures this time', *Western Mail*, 20 April 1979.

[8] 'Why you should vote Tory', *Western Mail*, 2 May 1979.

to 32.3 per cent.[9] By Welsh standards, this represented a strong showing for the party and compared well next to, for example, the Liberals' 10.6 per cent or Plaid Cymru's 8.1 per cent.

The 1979 result, bar the interesting case of Anglesey (discussed below), showed however how Toryism remained rooted in the areas of so-called 'British Wales' and its middle classes, or amongst those who defined themselves as such. Despite its increasingly slippery nature, and the breakdown of old economic structures, self or group identification by social class remained strong.[10] For many voters, and indeed politicians, class-based community ties defined their outlook, which was often set in opposition to what they were not. In parts of Wales, this continued to mean not being a Conservative. Even within certain constituencies, this was obvious. Robert Harvey, who sat for Clwyd South West from 1983 to 1987, argued that people 'were never going to vote for [me] on the [more working class] Wrexham side' of the seat, but in the 'much more prosperous' areas of Ruthin and Denbigh, they were far more likely to.[11] One of Aberavon's parliamentary candidates in this period remembered that all the Conservative association members – and most of the Tory voters – were to be found, as before, in the pleasant seaside area of Porthcawl.[12] The joke at the time was that the sitting Labour MP for the seat, John Morris, always failed to canvass in Porthcawl in case he 'woke the Conservatives up!'[13] This continued to go hand in hand with the Conservative vote clustering in the more anglicised parts of towns and the countryside. Although it can only be speculative, the women who ran the Nefyn Branch of the Caernarfon Conservative Association in the late 1970s, for example, were called Susan, Julia, Sally, Mary, Leslie, Laura, Betty and Beryl, suggesting that there was generally an anglicised influence on

---

[9] Felix Aubel, 'Welsh Conservatism 1885–1935: Five Studies in Adaptation' (unpublished PhD thesis, Lampeter University, 1994), p. 443.

[10] David Butler and Denis Kavanagh, *The British General Election of February 1974* (London: Macmillan, 1974), p. 270.

[11] Interview, Robert Harvey, 27 November 2015.

[12] Interview, Paul Warrick, 24 September 2015.

[13] Interview, Dr Hywel Francis, 28 August 2015.

Conservative politics in such parts of Wales that were, on the whole, Welsh-speaking in character.[14]

However, what is noteworthy about the Conservatives in this period is the way in which the party was capable of offering attractive ideas to people outside this core, comfortably middle-class base, including in Wales. As we know, a sizeable chunk of working-class people had always voted Conservative, and small hives of activity in Wales showed that interest in the party was not confined solely to the anglicised or coastal 'fringes'. Indeed, in this period there was a small but strong Mid-Rhondda Conservative branch, founded by local man Peter Leyshon. It was located at the heart of an area in the south Wales Valleys that was notoriously hostile to the party.[15] Leyshon was educated at Tonypandy Grammar School and had worked as a labourer on a building site. A member of the Labour Party until June 1971, he later switched to the Conservatives. He founded the branch and stood for the Tories in the very safe Labour seat of Rhondda three times, appealing for votes on the basis of his connection to the area, something no Tory candidate in Rhondda could have done since the war. His election addresses read 'Peter is for our people . . . You know him, Rhondda born and bred'.[16] Until 1986, a small but enthusiastic band of workers maintained the Mid-Rhondda Conservative Association. They held regular meetings, produced a detailed newsletter, held recruitment competitions and placed officers into dedicated organisational roles.[17]

Once in office, from 1979, the party explicitly targeted such non-traditional voters in Wales, emphasising in particular its

---

[14] WPA, GB0210 CONLES, file 4, Nefyn Branch notebook.
[15] CPA, CCO 1/16/540, Confidential profile – Peter Leyshon, January 1973.
[16] CPA, PUB, 229/17/20, Peter Leyshon election address, Rhondda, October 1974.
[17] WPA, GB0210 RHOCON, Mid-Rhondda Conservative and Unionist Association records.

policy of selling council houses to tenants.[18] Whilst the party continued to have no widespread purchase in Labour strongholds like Rhondda, it tried to grab the attention of swing voters in more receptive places. In 1980, local Conservatives deliberately distributed 22,500 leaflets in Cardiff, mainly to council-house tenants, emphasising a range of issues, including the right they had to buy the property they lived in.[19] More council houses were bought in Wales than England, per head of the population. By 1983, 48,072 had been sold.[20] There is evidence to suggest that being a homeowner made a person more likely to vote Conservative.[21] The Tories explicitly linked this with Welsh values, like the importance of individual pride, self-improvement, work ethic, a small-c conservative interest in the home and rootedness.[22] Thatcher herself talked frequently about 'ordinary people', by which she meant hard workers who lived within their means and abided by the law. This was who the party targeted in Wales.[23] What is particularly interesting is that Conservatives in Wales emphasised the sale of council houses in its communication at

---

[18] Robert Waller, 'Conservative Electoral Support and Social Class', in Anthony Seldon and Stuart Ball (eds), *Conservative Century: The Conservative Party Since 1900* (Oxford: Oxford University Press, 1994), p. 594; Jon Lawrence and Florence Sutcliffe-Braithwaite, 'Margaret Thatcher and the Decline of Class Politics', in Ben Jackson and Robert Saunders (eds), *Making Thatcher's Britain* (Cambridge: Cambridge University Press, 2012), p. 143.

[19] WPA, GB0210 CARCON, file 36, Cardiff North Executive Committee minute book, 19 November 1980.

[20] Sam Blaxland, 'Thatcherism and Wales: Impacts and Legacies', in Antony Mullen, Stephen Farrall and David Jeffery (eds), *Thatcherism in the 21st Century: The Social and Cultural Legacy* (Cham: Palgrave Macmillan, 2020), p. 148.

[21] Martin Johnes, 'What did Thatcher ever do for Wales?', in H. V. Bowen (ed.), *A New History of Wales: Heroes and Villains in Welsh History* (Llandysul: Gomer Press, 2012); Charles Pattie and Ron Johnston, 'The Conservative Party and the Electorate', in Steve Ludlam and Martin J. Smith (eds), *Contemporary British Conservatism* (London: Macmillan, 1996), pp. 51–2.

[22] Duncan Tanner, 'Facing the New Challenge: Labour and Politics, 1970–2000', in Duncan Tanner, Chris Williams and Deian Hopkin (eds), *The Labour Party in Wales* (Cardiff: University of Wales Press, 2000), p. 270; Michael Benbough-Jackson, 'Diagnosing the Blue Dragon Blues: The Dilemma of the Welsh Conservatives', *Planet*, 150 (2001–2), 62–9; Chris Butler, 'The Conservative Party in Wales: Remoulding a Radical Tradition', in John Osmond (ed.), *The National Question Again: Welsh Political Identity in the 1980s* (Llandysul: Gomer Press, 1985), p. 158.

[23] Florence Sutcliffe-Braithwaite, *Class, Politics, and the Decline of Deference in England, 1968–2000* (Oxford: Oxford University Press, 2018), p. 159.

the 1983 general election much more than the country's victory in the Falklands conflict, which is often cited as a key event that helped the party win the subsequent general election.[24] Urban seats like Bridgend, Cardiff West or Newport West, where Peter Hubbard-Miles, Stefan Terlezki and Mark Robinson won narrow, rare victories, demonstrate elements of this. In one district in the Bridgend seat, for example, 14,000 council-house tenants had the opportunity to buy the property they lived in, many of whom did.[25]

An analysis of local election results at the turn of the 1980s across Wales reveals that the Conservative vote was holding up remarkably well within the working-class wards of areas encompassed by 'British Wales'. In Cardiff, where the lack of 'Independent' or Ratepayer candidates allows a clearer analysis to be undertaken, Tories won a majority of votes in the traditional bastions of Conservatism like Llandaff, Penylan, Rhiwbina and Roath. But they also won a majority of votes – that is, over fifty per cent, not just the most votes – in working-class areas like Canton and Grangetown. After the boundaries were redrawn and more local elections were held in 1983, the party still performed well, again gaining a majority of votes in Canton and easily winning in most of its old heartlands.[26] Without these kinds of voters, the party could not have won its narrow victory in Cardiff West, for example. Similar sorts of patterns could be identified in places like Monmouth and the Vale of Glamorgan, where Tory voters were not simply located in the leafier parts of those seats.[27]

---

[24] 'Keith looks like having best chance of success', *Western Mail*, 1 June 1983; 'We will give Wales new industries', *Western Mail*, 30 May 1983; Pattie and Johnston, 'The Conservative Party', p. 42.

[25] 'Wooing the farmers', *Western Telegraph*, 16 April 1979.

[26] For a compilation of this data, see the excellent breakdown of data from Colin Rallings and Michael Thrasher, 'Cardiff Welsh District Council Election Results, 1973–1991': https://www.electionscentre.co.uk/wp-content/uploads/2015/10/Cardiff-1973-1991.pdf. Accessed 7 March 2018.

[27] https://www.electionscentre.co.uk/wp-content/uploads/2015/10/Vale-of-Glamorgan-1973-1991.pdf; https://www.electionscentre.co.uk/wp-content/uploads/2015/10/Monmouth-1973-1991.pdf. Accessed 7 March 2018.

Such results are interesting, given that the Conservatives were operating in a multi-party world. The split vote caused by the arrival of the Social Democratic Party (SDP) in 1981 and the subsequent SDP–Liberal Alliance did not always benefit the Conservatives, but it did make the results in seats like Clwyd South West (which was top of the SDP's Welsh 'hit list') much more volatile, with the Tories, SDP and Labour coming close to winning there in 1983. The Conservative Robert Harvey just made it over the line with 33.8 per cent of the vote, compared with the SDP's 30.2 per cent, and Labour's 27.4 per cent.[28] The Conservatives were lucky in their opponents in the early 1980s. Broadly, Wales continued its tradition of voting for the Labour Party, and the party's leader between 1980 and 1983, Michael Foot, sat for Aneurin Bevan's old seat of Ebbw Vale. But many Tories put a lot of effort into emphasising the dangerous nature of the party's 'lurch to the left'. Julian Lewis, who fought Swansea West in 1983, disrupted a left-wing anti-nuclear weapons 'die-in' protest in the city centre, and subsequently wrote that the support he received for doing so demonstrated that voters in the city were 'overwhelmingly against Labour's nuclear disarmament stance', for example.[29]

Although the Thatcher government had clearly harnessed support from outside its core, traditional vote base, the period after the 1983 victory saw one of the most fractious events of modern Welsh history play out in the form of the 1984–5 miners' strike. The events of that strike are receiving more attention from historians, as well as via popular culture films like *Pride* (2014), set in the Dulais Valley, north-east of Swansea. At the time, tensions ran high. The coal industry had been winding down long before the 1980s. However, the attitude of the prime minister and the government caused leading commentators and writers to talk of the 'sacrifice' of communities and the beginning of a terrible

[28] Interview, Robert Harvey, 27 November 2015; 'Clwyd South West', *Western Mail*, 25 May 1983.
[29] 'Die-in "irrelevant"', *South Wales Evening Post*, 24 May 1983. Julian Lewis personal archive, response to Nuffield College questionnaire, June 1983.

period of decline that hit the south Wales Valleys hardest.[30] But the strike received a mixed reaction and did not end up making Thatcher 'as popular in Wales as a plague of locusts'.[31] As her authorised biographer has pointed out, the fact that the strike was called and continued without a ballot was its most controversial as well as its 'central, distinguishing feature'.[32] At the general election following the strike, the party won more, not fewer, votes in Wales than it had at the election preceding it (499,000 in 1983, versus 501,000 in 1987).[33] Pollsters in Wales picked up that Thatcher still recorded a 'high level of support' in some areas.[34] Attempting to control the trade unions may have been an unpopular move in places formerly dominated by heavy industry, but on the other hand it certainly did appeal to Conservative voters, including those in Wales.[35]

If ever there were a starker display of Wales being 'a singular noun but a plural experience', this was perhaps it. The bruising year-long clash between the government and the National Union of Mineworkers cemented an already strong sense of anti-Conservatism in the old industrial areas, where Thatcher certainly did become a true hate figure (Geoffrey Howe, by this point one of Thatcher's most senior ministers, wrote privately all the way back in 1959 that the closure of coalmines in Wales was among policies 'widely regarded as typically Tory things to do').[36] The Conservatives lost some of their (hyper-marginal) seats with more working-class profiles at the 1987 general election, but the party was comfortably re-elected elsewhere. Other instances also revealed the passions that Tory politics could evoke on both sides

---

[30] Raphael Samuel, 'Introduction', in Raphael Samuel, Barbara Bloomfield and Guy Boanas (eds), *The Enemy Within: Pit Villages and the Miners' Strike of 1984–1985* (London: Routledge and Kegan Paul, 1986), p. 37.

[31] Geraint H. Jenkins, *A Concise History of Wales* (Cambridge: Cambridge University Press, 2007), p. 286.

[32] Charles Moore, *Margaret Thatcher, The Authorized Biography, Volume Two: Everything She Wants* (London: Penguin, 2016), p. 181.

[33] 'Labour's share of Welsh vote sinks', *Western Mail*, 13 June 1987.

[34] 'Hot seat is up for grabs', *Western Mail*, 22 May 1987.

[35] Johnes, 'What did Thatcher', p. 189.

[36] CPA, MS Howe dep 326, Howe to Brecon, 18 October 1959.

of the argument. When 'the Celtic Iron Lady', the MEP for North Wales, Beata Brookes, was re-elected in 1984, she fought off stiff competition from serious political opponents such as Labour's Tom Ellis and Plaid Cymru's Dafydd Iwan. On one hand, she won and polled 60,000 votes. And yet, on the other, she failed to make her victory speech because the volume of 'jeering and booing' at the count was so loud.[37]

This was certainly a period, therefore, when national issues determined the political weather. Some of the electorate, however, continued to see issues in a much more parochial way. Despite being a prominent politician on the national stage and a minister in government continuously from 1979 to 1994, Wyn Roberts was criticised by some of his constituents in Conwy for keeping a 'low profile' in the seat, focusing on big Welsh issues as opposed to 'checking on the dog dirt on Llandudno's pavements'.[38] There is some sporadic evidence suggesting that maintaining a focus on very local issues might have helped the Conservatives in marginal seats, especially in the key 1983 general election. When a senior CCO figure went to campaign in the normally Labour seat of Bridgend, he found that 'everyone' seemed to know the candidate, local businessman Peter Hubbard-Miles. 'I do not know why you need me here', Hubbard-Miles was told.[39] He eventually did win the seat, having asked the electorate to 'be a part of history [and] return a *local* Conservative MP for the first time ever'.[40] Similarly, at the same election and in another marginal Labour-held seat, Newport West, the prospective candidate, Mark Robinson, won the nomination. This was after he had stopped for lunch on the way to the selection meeting and by an extraordinary coincidence was within earshot of the association's selection committee, which was discussing whether a prerequisite for a candidate was that they would live in the constituency in order to soak up local feeling. At

---

[37] 'Beata Victory', *Liverpool Daily Post*, 18 June 1984; 'Beata is back – amid jeers', paper unknown.
[38] '"Absent Wyn" in line for return ticket to Euston', *Western Mail*, 27 March 1992.
[39] 'Home-grown Tory is the frontrunner', *Western Mail*, 1 June 1983.
[40] CPA, PUB, 229/19/13, Peter Hubbard-Miles election address, Bridgend, 1983.

the selection meeting, Robinson told the committee, unprompted, how he would rent a flat in Newport straight away if he became the candidate.[41] His victory – with a wafer-thin majority – was another of the surprises of that election.[42] Nicholas Edwards, despite now being the Secretary of State for Wales, continued the practices covered in the previous chapter, spending more time than previous generations of cabinet ministers would have in his constituency. Edwards's (English) successor, Nicholas Bennett, was also diligent. He wrote a weekly column in the local newspaper and remembered how the most common amendment he would make to letters written by civil servants to his constituents was changing comments like 'your area' to 'our area'.[43] He also asked members of the party and constituents for their views on the big topics of the day, prompting several to scrawl at the bottom of the questionnaire he sent out that they were impressed by this level of 'reaching out'.[44] The local dimension to Welsh politics and the Conservatives' ability to adapt to it in some places tended to endure.

Although not in every instance. For some people, nurturing a reputation as a good 'local boy' was less important. After winning the Clwyd South West seat in 1983, Robert Harvey quickly became a member of the influential House of Commons Foreign Affairs Select Committee, devoting less time to his local constituency. The press, reflecting local opinion, branded him 'The Invisible MP'.[45] A record of an extremely hostile meeting between Harvey and his local party found its way into the archives, where the association – who threatened to deselect him as the candidate – questioned his commitment to the area, suggesting he hold more advice surgeries and attend more events. In response, Harvey apparently argued that 'he did not feel it was necessary to attend carnivals,

[41] Interview, Mark Robinson, 15 June 2015.
[42] Gerald Charmley, 'Parliamentary Representation', in Chris Williams and Andy Croll (eds), *The Gwent County History, Volume 5: The Twentieth Century* (Cardiff: University of Wales Press, 2013), p. 315.
[43] Interview Nicholas Bennett, 21 December 2015.
[44] WPA, GB0210 NICETT, Nicholas Bennett Records, Questionnaires.
[45] 'Who is the invisible MP?', *Western Mail*, 26 May 1987.

county shows, sheep dog trials etc. every year'. The officers 'disagreed with [this] general strategy'. They also argued that Harvey's membership of the Foreign Affairs Committee 'was not particularly useful as far as the constituency was concerned, since the ordinary constituent did not take too kindly to their MP being out of the county on foreign trips'. The response from Harvey was that this was 'ludicrous' and that membership of this body should be thought of an 'honour' for the constituency.[46] In 1987, the Labour Party ran its general election campaign in the seat with the slogan: 'Vote for the Man you will see!'[47] On a fraught election night, the Conservatives lost the seat.

By the beginning of the 1990s, it is noteworthy that the Tories were communicating with the public in much the same way as they had since the war. One of the most prominent Welsh Conservatives in this decade was Roger Evans, who became the MP for Monmouth in 1992. An intelligent and quotable politician, Evans made great copy for the local media, who emphasised the fact that he held press conferences in local castles and rushed about the campaign trail 'in new green wellies and a Barbour jacket' and 'three identical tweed suits'. This Anglo-Welsh brand of Toryism earned him the nickname 'Mr Toad', deployed mainly by political opponents.[48] However, he won the Monmouth constituency, having failed in his bid to capture the much more 'Welsh' Ynys Môn in 1987.[49] Evans's style of presentation, which might have been anathema to many on Anglesey, was much less of a concern for the electorate in anglicised Monmouth. Similarly, when Walter Sweeney won the Vale of Glamorgan seat in 1992, a quarter of the seat's population were in managerial roles, less than six per cent spoke Welsh and nearly three-quarters of properties were owner-occupied.[50]

---

[46] WPA, GB0210 CONLES, file 53, 'Meeting with Robert Harvey', 2 August 1985.
[47] WPA, GB0210 CONLES, file 53, Report re 1987 election campaign.
[48] 'Monmouth: A two-horse race?', *Western Mail*, 30 March 1992.
[49] 'Roger at the battlements', *Western Mail*, 3 April 1992.
[50] 'Fact file: Vale of Glamorgan', *Western Mail*, 28 March 1992.

Another constant was the wider outlook of many of those people the Tories were trying to encourage to vote for them. In the early and mid-1990s, MPs across Wales, like Gwilym Jones in Cardiff North or Nicholas Bennett in Pembrokeshire, issued questionnaires to their constituents to garner their opinions on a range of issues. Hundreds were returned. Many who wrote to their MP identified as current or former Tories and their responses give a stark indicator of the robustly right-wing – and sometimes unpleasant – outlook of parts of the Welsh electorate. Comments included: 'we cannot sustain all this immigration'; 'We were great Britain [sic] . . . not any more'; 'hanging for murder (all types!). Corporal punishment in schools'; and, most disturbingly, 'Black/Asian citizens encouraged to emigrate . . . Mixed-race breeding should be penalised'.[51] Nearly ninety per cent backed 'stiffer penalties for violent crime', with many annotations signalling that the return of the death penalty for murder was long overdue. There was much talk of a 'cultural and moral collapse in Britain', which several people offered thoughtful comments on, relating to the leadership of the Church. Lots of respondents were forthright in their condemnation of an 'appalling' state education system, whilst some called for people to belatedly 'follow the teachings of Enoch Powell'.[52] Bennett asked people to rank their worries in order of importance. 'Inflation/the cost of living' was the most pressing issue for local Conservatives, followed closely by 'law and order'. Unemployment, defence and foreign affairs were ranked as those issues that were of the least importance.

More interesting than these slightly arbitrary ranking systems, however, were the annotations and extra comments that some people decided to plaster liberally over their questionnaires. In doing so, and by making subtle alterations to some of the questions they had been given, it is possible to find evidence of a lot more considered or nuanced thinking in these documents; it was not all just unthinkingly reactionary. As would be expected by the mid-

[51] WPA, GB0210 NICETT, Nicholas Bennett Records, Questionnaires.
[52] WPA, GB0210 NICETT, Nicholas Bennett Records, Questionnaires.

1990s, many voters had simply had enough of the Tories after their long period in office. A common critique was that Thatcher's approach to politics had been positive in many ways, but had either gone too far, or had had unintended consequences: 'Too much privatisation' complained one, who had been a 'voter for over 40 years', whilst another Conservative voter 'since 1945' thought 'the straw that broke the camel's back was . . . privatisation'. 'The Tories . . . are putting economics before people', said another, whilst one man chose to frame it as 'the Conservatives have gone from a fair caring party to a grab all you can sod everyone else party'. On the question of whether privatisation should continue, nearly forty per cent thought that a mix of private and nationalised industries was best, with comments along the lines of nationalisation being 'OK', as long as industries were 'run EFFICIENTLY under government'. Such comments reflected wider public opinion.[53] One respondent argued that it was logical for the state to control certain things like gas, water and electricity, but not heavy industry. Many people argued something along the lines of how Thatcher had 'done wonders for this country . . . but the present government has created a less caring society'. The creation of a Single European Market was deemed 'important' for nearly two-thirds of respondents, and seventy-seven per cent of the documents that survived show people favoured removing the Sunday Trading Laws, although often with the caveat that this should be 'according to the wishes' of the business owner. Jones had also asked his constituents to give him their opinions on the age of consent for homosexual sex, with this issue attracting a wide range of views from the severe, to the eccentric, to the tolerant; from 'I now think it was a mistake to make it legal AT ALL', to 'government and the law should not be concerned with private matters'. Of course, a certain kind of person, normally with trenchant views, who might be eccentric or bored, wrote to their MP or returned a questionnaire. Nevertheless, this body of opinion was representative of a strand of opinion in Welsh society

[53] Pattie and Johnston, 'The Conservative Party', p. 54.

in the mid-1990s, much of it right-leaning but seemingly fed up with the Conservative Party.

Indeed, nothing could save the party from collapse at the 1997 general election. After Britain crashed out of the Exchange Rate Mechanism in 1992, and following a long period in the mid-1990s where the party was portrayed as worn out, at best, and corrupt, at worst, the Tories' term in office ended in 1997 with a huge landslide for Tony Blair's Labour.[54] Not only was the campaign in Wales 'miserable' for those who took part in it, they were struck by houses with 'long gravel drives and a Range Rover parked up' where the occupants intended to vote Labour.[55] One stalwart, out on the campaign trail, admitted to knowing: 'we were toast'.[56] Every seat in Wales was lost, including those that might just have remained Conservative, like Clwyd North West, Monmouth or Cardiff North. This represented the strength of New Labour's messaging, but it once again showed that the Conservative tradition was fragile in Wales. As one Welsh Tory would later write about the aftermath of that election, not even a meeting held in 'genteel suburban ambience [with] Churchill memorabilia, could lift the gloom hanging over a Party seemingly bereft of means or mission'.[57]

A 'NEW SPECIES' OF WELSH CONSERVATIVE

More so than during any previous years, however, the period under study here witnessed a shift in the party's approach to Welsh policy, its rhetoric about Wales and its self-image there. Commenting on the crop of Conservative MPs from Wales who had been elected to Westminster in 1970 and 1974, the *Western Mail* spoke of a new 'species' of 'genuine Welsh Conservative'. In

---

[54] David Butler and Dennis Kavanagh, *The British General Election of 1997* (London: Macmillan, 1997), pp. 24–5.
[55] Interview with anonymous.
[56] Interview, John Winterson Richards, 10 November 2015.
[57] WPA, GB0210 CONAGRP, 2/1, article by David Melding, undated.

particular, it must have been thinking of Wyn Roberts, the MP for Conwy from 1970 to 1997. Roberts was a 'quintessentially Welsh' figure, who had been born on Anglesey and whose first language was Welsh. Whilst he won a scholarship to Harrow School, he retained a personal attachment to north-west Wales, where he became an MP.[58] Roberts was promoted to the front bench alongside the MP for Pembrokeshire, Nicholas Edwards, with Thatcher making the latter a member of her shadow cabinet.[59] CCO had long complained that no one in the House of Commons who was 'closely associated with the affairs of the Principality' was of 'cabinet calibre'. This, it argued, 'hamper[ed] the party's . . . efforts in Wales'.[60] However, in Roberts and Edwards, the party had two Welsh MPs who were clever, politically skilful and, in Roberts's case, undeniably a true Welshman. Here were its 'cabinet calibre' people.

One of the Welsh Affairs team's most pressing issues after the election of Margaret Thatcher as party leader in 1975 was devolution. Between the two general elections in 1974, the Kilbrandon Report came into the limelight.[61] It argued that there was an 'urgent need for a domestic parliament' in Wales and Scotland.[62] What had been a non-issue in the February election for both Labour and the Tories suddenly became a real feature of Labour's electioneering in October. It was one of the things that marked a difference between the two parties in Wales, with Labour candidates addressing the issue directly in twenty different addresses to the electorate, compared to only four Tories doing so (most of them to pour cold water on the idea).[63] Formally, despite Edward Heath's warm attitude towards a Scottish parliament and

---

[58] Lord Roberts of Conwy obituary, *Guardian*, 16 December 2013.

[59] Nicholas Crickhowell, *Wales, Westminster and Water* (Cardiff: University of Wales Press, 1999), p. 14.

[60] CPA, CCO 500/50/1, 'Nationalism and Regionalism', speech appendix, 26 July 1966.

[61] R. Merfyn Jones and Ioan Rhys Jones, 'Labour and the Nation', in Tanner, Williams and Hopkin, *The Labour Party*, p. 256.

[62] 'Parliament for Wales vital, insists Liberals', *Western Mail*, 13 February 1974.

[63] Figures compiled by the author using CPA material.

Thatcher's initial support for the idea, the Tories campaigned against devolution, including a Welsh Assembly, in the subsequent referendum on the matter in 1979.[64] People like the Cardiff North MP, Ian Grist, attempted to introduce 'wrecking' amendments to the Bill as it progressed through parliament.

The campaign itself in 1979 was a bitter one. Although the Labour Party was officially in favour of an elected Assembly, notable Welsh MPs, like Leo Abse and the future Labour leader, Neil Kinnock, were not. The Tories made the case that an Assembly would weaken the unity of the United Kingdom and that it represented an unwanted extra tier of government.[65] Senior figures on the ground urged activists, who were broadly anti-Assembly, to argue their case on those terms, noting at the same time: 'Don't be anti-Welsh'.[66] Undoubtedly fuelled by the grim economic situation at the time, with the cost of the new body being emphasised, every Welsh county voted decisively against the devolution proposals, with 11.8 per cent of the electorate voting in favour of an Assembly and 46.5 per cent voting against it.[67] Bodies like the Wales Trades Union Congress had made the vote about politics, issuing a leaflet saying 'Don't let the Tories win a victory in Wales [by voting no]'.[68] This only made it feel to many Conservatives like they had won more than one victory, and the party made much of the fact that they had judged 'the mood of the Welsh electorate correctly'.[69] This was supported by others at the time, with the Plaid Cymru activist Robin Reeves writing in

---

[64] Robert Blake, *The Conservative Party from Peel to Major* (London: Heinemann, 1997), p. 332.

[65] D. Foulkes, J. Barry Jones and R. A. Wilford (eds), *The Welsh Veto: the Wales Act 1978 and the Referendum* (Cardiff: University of Wales Press, 1983), p. 118; WPA, GB0210 CONLES, file 20, Walters to members, undated.

[66] WPA, GB 0210 MONION, file 24, Letter, 24 October 1978.

[67] Kenneth O. Morgan, *Rebirth of a Nation: Wales, 1880–1980* ([1981] Oxford: Oxford University Press, 1988), p. 405.

[68] Quoted in David Melding, 'The Political Parties and the Welsh Nation', Politics Today: No.18, a Conservative Research Department Paper (3 December 1987), 323.

[69] Lord Crickhowell, 'The Conservative Party and Wales', *The National Library of Wales Journal*, 34/1 (2006), 68; Donald Walters, 'The Reality of Conservatism', in Osmond, *The National Question*, p. 219.

the *Financial Times* that being on the right side of the referendum argument 'boosted Conservative confidence immeasurably and enabled the party to throw off a century-old stigma that it was the "English party"'.[70] Hyperbole aside, the Conservatives did emerged relatively unscathed, helped by the scale of the proposal's defeat and by the fact that those being (unfairly but loudly) accused of being 'anti-Welsh', like Neil Kinnock, were from Labour.[71]

Rejecting devolution was central to the Conservative Party's articulation of its Unionist position in this period, despite some Tories actually seeing devolution as playing into old ideas of power trickling down to individuals, with such a body guarding against an overly bureaucratic centralised state. Heath, now on the back benches, was even a figurehead of the 'Conservatives for the Assembly' group.[72] Of course, one of the party's primary concerns was political. It worried that any new Welsh Assembly would have a permanent 'Socialist majority', but this did not make it 'hostile' to the broader idea of Welsh distinctiveness, even if it were rejecting constitutional change.[73] The wording of the party's 1979 Welsh manifesto stressed that 'we have our . . . characteristics, our history and our language . . . there is no need for new tiers of government to prove that we are different'. Ultimately, however, things like manifestos stressed that other issues were of greater importance. The manifesto deployed some characteristically Conservative issues that it wanted voters to focus on: 'We have always believed that people are much more concerned', it said, 'about personal freedom, law and order . . . about jobs and about prices'.[74]

---

[70] Robin Reeves, 'Tories likely to romp home in north Wales', *Financial Times*, 7 June 1979, p. 3.

[71] Andrew Edwards, *Labour's Crisis: Plaid Cymru, the Conservatives, and the Decline of the Labour Party in North-West Wales, 1960–74* (Cardiff: University of Wales Press, 2011), p. 254; Martin Westlake, *Kinnock: The Biography* (London: Little, Brown, 2001), p. 127.

[72] Foulkes, Jones and Wilford, *The Welsh Veto*, p. 35; WPA, GB0210 CONLES, file 20, 'Conservatives for the Assembly' flyer.

[73] Gareth Elwyn Jones, *Modern Wales: A Concise History* ([1984] Cambridge: Cambridge University Press, 1994), p. 271.

[74] CPA, CRD 4/15/4/2, Conservative manifesto for Wales, 1979.

THATCHERISM AND ITS LEGACY, 1975–1997   231

But as the use of 'we' and 'our' in such documents implied, the party remained conscious of how it used its rhetoric. In the latest in its series of important reports, this time called 'The Welsh Dimension', the party's Wales team argued that 'it is a prime lesson of market research or advertising promotion that <u>it is not what is actually said that matters, but what is seen to be said</u>' (emphasis in original text). The report suggested placing the Welsh dragon more prominently on party literature in Wales to strengthen 'the Welsh image' and to mark 'the herald of a new aggressive Conservatism' (the dragon had already been replacing the YC symbol on party documents for some time).[75] For the first time, the party held its Welsh conference in a Valleys constituency – Ebbw Vale – in 1976. This was heralded as a great step forward, because it would '[never] have been contemplated' to hold it somewhere like this several years earlier.[76] Welsh-language-only versions of the programme were produced for these conferences – a far cry from the occasional token gestures that were commonplace only decades before.[77] Engaging in a natural development from Howe and Hooson's proposed name-change in 1959 – when they had argued that the Conservative Area Council should be renamed to make the party sound more sympathetic to Welsh needs – the report also suggested modifying the party title again to 'the Conservative Party of Wales' because 'the Conservative Party *in* Wales sounds like a foreign invasion'.[78]

Tying this in with candidate selection, 'The Welsh Dimension' argued that 'there should continue to be a bias in favour of candidates with Welsh roots' – by which the authors meant connections with a local area more than anything else. The report continued that well spoken, English candidates, 'like John Ranelagh or Tom Sackville – as nice as they are – do not present

[75] For example, WPA, GB0210 CONLES, file 65, News-sheet, October 1968; CPA, CRD 4/15/4/2, 'The Welsh Dimension' Report, 1979.
[76] WPA, GB0210 CARCON, file 9, Cardiff North West Chairman's Annual Report 1976.
[77] See for example the Welsh-only version of the programme for the Llandudno conference in 1978, WPA, GB0210 CONLES, file 18.
[78] CPA, CRD 4/15/4/2, 'The Welsh Dimension' Report, 1979.

the most fruitful image for their constituencies. There are still vestiges of the "young English gentleman" coming to a hopeless Welsh seat to win his spurs'. Selection of appropriate candidates was important, according to the document, not just for 'the seat itself' but because it 'reflects on the nature of the party in Wales'. However, when it came to the crunch, it was often difficult to translate words into action. Both the list of people drawn up as candidates, and the selection process at the grassroots level, continued to favour young Englishmen who had few or no local connections with an area. This cemented the party's reputation for making 'merely rhetorical appeals'.[79] One candidate in Wales in 1983 thought its candidates 'good' in some of its marginal seats, but in the unwinnable ones, the party's candidates resembled an 'English public school reunion' where fighting the seat was seen as 'a kind of work experience'.[80] The number of candidates with local connections at the 1987 general election plummeted to thirteen, with the number educated outside Wales at twenty-four.[81] For some, this was a result of small associations adopting a 'you'll do' attitude, whilst other candidates pitched themselves robustly as 'a young man with fresh ideas', which had some appeal.[82] Nonetheless, those young aspiring English politicians often cited hostility on the campaign trail due to the fact they were not local,[83] with one remembering that things were thrown at him – although 'nothing designed to kill' – on the basis that he was a 'plummy-voiced Englishman'.[84] Whether it was because of his accent is impossible to know, but it is still significant that he pinpointed this as the likely problem.

---

[79] Tim Bale, *The Conservatives Since 1945: The Drivers of Party Change* (Oxford: Oxford University Press, 2016), p. 251.

[80] Interview, Professor Nicholas O'Shaughnessy, 10 November 2014.

[81] Figures compiled by the author using Ivor Thomas Rees, *Welsh Hustings: 1885–2004* (Llandybie: Dinefwr Press, 2005).

[82] Interview, Sir Desmond Swayne, 8 December 2014; CPA, PUB, 229/19/13, David Tredinnick election address, Cardiff South and Penarth, 1983.

[83] Interview, Philip Circus, 9 August 2015.

[84] Interview, Paul Warrick, 24 September 2015.

On the other hand, this period did witness some success in terms of candidate selection. We have already heard about Peter Leyshon in the 'Welsh Wales' seat of Rhondda, but another example is from the Welsh-speaking *y fro Gymraeg*. In 1978, the Conservatives on Anglesey, or Ynys Môn, as the seat was renamed in 1983, selected Keith Best, a barrister from Brighton, to stand as the candidate there. He spent a great deal of time canvassing in the constituency. He also took the bold move of learning Welsh. He recalled how he demonstrated 'more than just lip-service' to the issue. Once the Welsh speakers 'realised I could understand them', the word spread.[85] Best immersed himself in the area and amongst Welsh speakers enough to be able to conduct interviews in the language by the time the election campaign started. In a shock result that few saw coming, the Tories won Anglesey in 1979, formerly the seat of two heavyweight politicians, the Liberal Megan Lloyd George and Labour's Cledwyn Hughes, and where the Tories had once been rightly considered 'a marginal irrelevance'.[86] The seat had been 105th on the party's target list, and it is very possible that Best's character, enthusiasm and ability to communicate in Welsh helped him win.[87] One historian has argued in the context of an earlier period that Welsh-speaking politicians did not need to underline their Welshness to be effective, but someone like Best would no doubt have benefited from engaging with the language in an era where many people in that area still used it in their daily lives.[88]

Best represented something that was changing amongst Conservatives in Wales, which was also evident in the Welsh Office under Nick Edwards, Wyn Roberts and, from 1987, Peter Walker. These men and their teams undoubtedly engaged

---

[85] Interview, Keith Best, 11 May 2015.

[86] Felix Aubel, 'The Conservatives in Wales, 1880–1935', in Martin Francis and Ina Zweiniger-Bargielowska (eds), *The Conservatives and British Society, 1880–1990* (Cardiff: University of Wales Press, 1996), p. 102.

[87] CPA, CRD 4/15/4/3, Britto to Howarth, 2 March 1981.

[88] Geraint Thomas, 'The Conservative Party and Welsh Politics in the Inter-war Years', *English Historical Review*, 128/533 (2013), 912; Janet Davies, *The Welsh Language* (Cardiff: University of Wales Press, 1999), pp. 70–1.

proactively with a specific policy-making agenda. Some elements of what they did had already been put in train before 1979, and in other respects the party was driven by the never-ending worry that it would always be seen as 'the same old Tories' if it did not try to do things differently in Wales. However, there was also an element of principle in play, with men like Edwards and Roberts believing that a subtly different approach to policy in Wales was both possible and desirable. They were responsible for setting a specific agenda for what happened in 1980s Wales, although the results were undoubtedly mixed, depending on who you were and where you lived. It is of course noteworthy that they were able to set their own agenda in the first place. Thatcher's men entered a Welsh Office that had accumulated a great deal of administrative functions by 1979, with a new funding arrangement (the Barnett Formula) giving the Welsh Office further opportunities for policy deviation from England.[89] From its establishment in 1964, it had been responsible for roads, housing, tourism and local government. Health was added to its remit in 1969, school education in 1970 and agriculture and higher education between 1974 and 1979. By the mid-1980s, the Secretary of State oversaw economic and industrial issues in Wales, as well as marshalling relations with 'Europe'.[90] Through active diplomacy and many foreign trips, Thatcher's Welsh team were able to engage in diplomatic missions to secure a strong chunk of UK investment by overseas firms in Wales, particularly from Japan.[91] As Secretary of State, Edwards was an enthusiastic proponent for the regeneration of Cardiff Bay and set in train the scheme that eventually transformed that part of the capital city.[92] Various road-building or road-improvement programmes were initiated throughout the 1980s, including the A55 in North Wales and the Heads of the Valleys Road. In the years that Thatcher

[89] Russell Deacon, *The Governance of Wales: The Welsh Office and the Policy Process 1964–1999* (Cardiff: Welsh Academic Press, 2002), p. 29.
[90] Blaxland, 'Thatcherism', pp. 141–2.
[91] Crickhowell, *Wales*, pp. 36–7.
[92] Crickhowell, *Wales*, Cardiff Bay chapter.

was in power, 140 miles of new motorways and trunk roads were built, alongside twenty-two new bypasses around towns.[93] Much of the work underpinning this was done by Wyn Roberts, who received large amounts of praise as a consequence, including from political opponents.[94]

The rationale behind many of these policy decisions was that a Welsh Office made no sense 'unless it actually had discrete powers'. A series of publicly funded, semi-autonomous bodies, known as quangos, like the Wales Tourist Board and the Development Board for Rural Wales, set up in 1969 and 1977 respectively, helped bolster the idea of specifically Welsh decision-making.[95] Although these were set up under Labour governments, they continued to be utilised by Conservative personnel, who very much believed in their role.[96] Listing the achievements of the Welsh Office in 1981, Nicholas Edwards heavily praised bodies like the Development Corporation for Wales 'for the fact that there are today over 200 overseas companies operating in Wales employing about 55,000 people'; the Development Board for Rural Wales for 'building small factories, providing social facilities and in helping new businesses to start in villages that resent depopulation'; and the Welsh Tourist Board for sustaining that vital sector.[97]

Under the Tories in the 1980s, therefore, the beginnings of what looked like a Welsh state emerged.[98] The Secretary of State role, in terms of its scope, began to be seen as akin to a 'mini-Prime Minister'.[99] This allowed the Welsh Office team to present their approach as different from the standard Thatcherite model, emphasising a more interventionist, 'flexible and pragmatic' style,

[93] Blaxland, 'Thatcherism', p. 149.
[94] *https://www.walesonline.co.uk/news/wales-news/lord-roberts-conwy-died-age-6405283*. Accessed 24 November 2017.
[95] Johnes, *Wales Since 1939*, p. 294.
[96] Duncan Fallowell, 'The Smallest Kingdom', *Spectator*, 21 March 1981.
[97] Letter, 'Real Wales – Nicholas Edwards', *Spectator*, 28 March 1981.
[98] R. Merfyn Jones, 'Beyond Identity? The Reconstruction of the Welsh', *Journal of British Studies*, 31/4 (1992), 354.
[99] Sam Blaxland, 'Thatcherism', p. 141; Leon Gooberman, "A Very Modern Kind of English Loneliness": John Redwood, the Welsh Office and Devolution', *Welsh History Review*, 29/4 (2019), 629.

including higher levels of public spending on policy areas, such as roads.[100] Thatcher (who was famously uninterested in Welsh affairs, once telling Wyn Roberts that 'you', by which she meant Welsh people, 'contribute nothing'![101]) allowed Edwards, and his successor as Secretary of State, Peter Walker, to do things 'my way'.[102] Whilst such statements have the ring of a boast to them, to a great extent it was true.[103] One of the reasons that Walker – 'the great cabinet survivor of the one-nation strand of Toryism' – was given the role in 1987, despite having no clear connections to Wales, was because he had held a variety of other cabinet portfolios, like agriculture, industry and environment, which the Secretary of State's remit covered.[104] In the job, he increased funding for public bodies such as the Welsh Development Agency, whilst investing in projects like land clearance and more road building.[105]

Both Edwards and Walker concluded that to achieve some successes in Wales, accommodating its dominant left-leaning political culture was better than trying to fight it. Edwards, although brusque, was open to working with a wide range of people. A Labour leader of Cardiff City Council would later call him the best Secretary of State Wales had ever had, whilst Peter Walker, ever the 'wet', happily discussed how he met 'all the leaders of local councils, invariably Labour, and trade union officials to tell them I wanted to work with them and form a team'.[106] However, the Conservatives knew that most of the things that happened in the Welsh Office were policies applicable to the whole of the United Kingdom, but with Welsh

---

[100] Crickhowell, *Wales*, p. 40.
[101] Blaxland, 'Thatcherism', p. 142; Lord Roberts of Conway, *Right From the Start: The Memoirs of Sir Wyn Roberts* (Cardiff: University of Wales Press, 2006), p. 221.
[102] Interview, Lord Crickhowell, 1 July 2013; Peter Walker, *Staying Power: An Autobiography* (London: Bloomsbury, 1991), pp. 202–3.
[103] Leon Gooberman, *From Depression to Devolution: Economy and Government in Wales, 1934–2006* (Cardiff: University of Wales Press, 2017), p. 143.
[104] Walker, *Staying Power*, p. 202.
[105] Walker, *Staying Power*, p. 204.
[106] Sam Blaxland, 'Lord Crickhowell', *Oxford Dictionary of National Biography*, 10 March, 2022; Walker, *Staying Power*, p. 205.

examples; a point of view that was later reinforced by subsequent academic studies of the topic and period.[107] There was room for manoeuvre and for doing things differently, but not – on big national policies, at least – for totally breaking the Thatcherite mould.

One policy field that *was* exclusively Welsh was language policy and associated fields, like broadcasting.[108] Edwards and Roberts addressed this area with particular conviction and financial support to such an extent that it is fair to credit them with helping to revive the language. This alone was a significant thing to have done, given the difficult position any minority language in an increasingly globalised world faced. In 1980, Edwards delivered a speech on the topic in Llanrwst, which he considered to be one of the most important he ever gave. Here, he set out his belief that 'survival' of the language was not enough; 'breath[ing] new life into it' was possible. 'This language . . . is a priceless heritage', he said.[109] There were many in the Conservatives' Wales team who believed that 'conserving' an 'ancient, important [and] lovely' language was – as the party had been arguing for some time – compatible with paternalistic, Tory ideas of preservation, tradition and rootedness.[110] In 1980, Chris Butler, then working in the Research Department and who later became a Conservative MP, laid this out in an official party document. Tellingly, it has a bilingual title, with the Welsh coming first: 'Cymraeg: Iaith ein Plant / Welsh: The Language of our Children'.[111]

In the eyes of people like Butler and Roberts, education was key when it came to the language. Nicholas Edwards was

---

[107] Leon Gooberman, 'Recession and Recovery: the Welsh Office and Job Creation in the 1980s', *Llafur*, 11/3 (2014), 115; Dylan Griffiths, *Thatcherism and Territorial Politics: A Welsh Case Study* (Aldershot: Avebury, 1996), p. 160.

[108] CPA, CRD 4/15/14/1, Nicholas Edwards, Welsh Policy Group Report, 1975. For a study that agrees with this argument, see Griffiths, *Thatcherism*, particularly pp. 114, 159–60.

[109] Crickhowell, *Wales*, p. 63.

[110] CRD 2/45/4, Draft column, 'Reviving the Old Country', 31 August 1959. See Walker, *Staying Power*, p. 204.

[111] CRD 4/15/4/3, Chris Butler, 'Cymraeg: Iaith ein Plant' (1980), p. 18; Interview, Chris Butler, 11 May 2015.

keen to decentralise education to local authorities. For him, 'the widest possible opportunity for children to be taught through the medium of their mother tongue, whether English of Welsh' was key. In particular, he was a strong advocate of bilingualism.[112] This policy area gained momentum so that, by 1988, Welsh had a statutory place on the national curriculum, being taught as a core subject in Welsh-speaking areas and as a foundation topic in all other schools.[113] Before that, only half of secondary school pupils had learnt Welsh, even though this new approach gave most non-speakers a relatively shallow grounding in the language. The Conservative Research Department let proposals for the language pass with minimal fuss. To them, it was one of the few matters that raised 'no problem between national policies and Welsh policies'.[114] 'Active government support' and enormous increases in funding for Welsh-language provisions therefore followed.[115] In contrast to the £350,000 in aid and subsidies the Labour government gave the Welsh language between 1974 and 1979, the Conservatives gave £2.6 million between 1984 and 1985 (Edwards's predecessor, Labour's John Morris, faced some criticism during his tenure as Secretary of State in the late 1970s for not setting bilingualism as a 'long-term objective').[116] Senior people in Welsh public life might have been right to say that Mrs Thatcher would not have lost any sleep if the Welsh language had ceased to exist, but that in some respects was not relevant, because it was not true of those who ran her Welsh Office and therefore made the policies.[117]

---

[112] CPA, CRD 4/15/41/1, Memo, Nicholas Edwards to Welsh Conservative Members of Parliament, undated, c. 1975.
[113] Matthew Day, 'Wyn Roberts: The Blue Dragon? Conservatism, Patriotism and North Wales, c. 1970–1990' (unpublished PhD thesis, Bangor University, 2022), p. 128.
[114] CPA, CRD 4/15/4/2, Policy Document for Wales – observations from CRD, undated, c. 1975.
[115] Crickhowell, 'The Conservative Party', p. 70.
[116] *Western Mail*, 15 March 1979; Johnes, *Wales Since 1939*, p. 316; Blaxland, 'Thatcherism', p. 144.
[117] 'Archdruid's Tory blast', *Liverpool Daily Post*, 4 July 1986.

Consequently, several historians have commented on how Thatcher's 'progressive and interventionist' Welsh Office did more 'than any previous administration to buttress the fortunes, status and legitimacy of the Welsh language', just as they had previously helped create a distinct Scottish institutional order via a process of administrative devolution.[118] This is fair, although it is possible to go another step further when looking at Wales. For an entire generation of young people, introduced to more Welsh on a day-to-day basis, via lessons in school and the consequent use of incidental Welsh, or via the production of bilingual documents, it was impossible to escape the fact that Wales was different. It reinforced for a new generation how Wales had distinct cultural features.[119] As a result, the Conservatives were not only maintaining a sense of identity for some people, they were helping to create it, too. Further moves to encourage bilingualism in public life (in the form of more signs, for example, as well as in education) followed. Peter Walker set up a Welsh Language Board, made up entirely of 'enthusiastic Welsh speakers', whose role it was to promote the language.[120] When the writer James (later Jan) Morris said in 1958 that a foreigner could spend time in Cardiff and Penarth and still think himself in England, this was true. By the end of the 1980s, it would have been much more difficult not to realise you were in a different nation.[121] The *Economist* magazine agreed, claiming (inaccurately) that 'practically no one' in south Wales could read the Welsh on signs, but that their significance was considerable: 'They are a constant reminder that Wales is not England'.[122]

---

[118] James Mitchell, *Conservatives and the Union: A Study of Conservative Party Attitudes to Scotland* (Edinburgh: Edinburgh University Press, 1990), p. x; Andrew Edwards, Duncan Tanner and Patrick Carlin, 'The Conservative Governments and the Development of Welsh Language Policy in the 1980s and 1990s', *The Historical Journal*, 54/2 (2011), 535; Tomos Dafydd Davies, 'A Tale of Two Tories?: The British and Canadian Conservative Parties and the National Question' (unpublished PhD thesis, Aberystwyth University, 2011), p. 20; Martin Johnes, 'The Heroes of Recent Welsh Political History', in H. V. Bowen (ed.), *A New History of Wales: Heroes and Villains in Welsh History* (Llandysul: Gomer Press, 2012), p. 186.
[119] Johnes, *Wales Since 1939*, p. 328.
[120] Walker, *Staying Power*, p. 204.
[121] James Morris, 'Welshness in Wales', *Wales*, 32 (1958), 13.
[122] *The Economist*, 18 November 1978.

THE 'SAME OLD TORIES'

Policies on the use of Welsh in schools and in public spaces offset some of the clumsier aspects of what the government was doing in relation to the language, including its handling of the introduction of a Welsh-language television channel – what became, and still is, Sianel Pedwar Cymru (S4C). The party's 1979 manifesto had promised a fourth television channel for Welsh speakers.[123] Key Conservative figures would later take credit for establishing S4C, but the truth is less clear cut.[124] The government initially backed down on their manifesto commitment and instead suggested that Welsh-language broadcasting be part of the schedules for other television channels.[125] In reaction, Gwynfor Evans, recently dislodged as MP for Carmarthen, threatened to starve himself to death unless the government reverted to its original plan. In a letter to Edwards regarding Evans's threats, Tom Hooson (one of the early architects of a shift in Conservative policy towards Wales) noted how 'the Welsh language [is] in truth the only totally distinctive element in Welsh politics. The possibility of Gwynfor Evans fasting to death is very real, and we should take whatever defensive action we can to avoid the charge that we killed the man'.[126] In 1982, the Conservative government raised the status of Welsh-language broadcasting enormously with the establishment of S4C, but its hand had been forced on the matter – and people remembered Evans's hunger strike as much as the founding of the channel. Nicholas Edwards in particular also became the focus of much protest from langage campaigners, partly because of this incident but also because of his status as a plummy-voiced Tory. On several occasions, he was bundled out of meetings, or forced to stay locked in hotel rooms, because of the numbers and forcefulness of the crowds that were protesting against him. A makeshift bomb was even

---

[123] Crickhowell, *Wales*, p. 21.
[124] Crickhowell, *Wales*, p. 63.
[125] See Crickhowell, *Wales*, 'Welsh-Language Broadcasting' chapter.
[126] CPA, CRD 4/15/4/3, Letter Tom Hooson to Nicholas Edwards, 23 June 1980.

placed on his son's bedroom windowsill one night while he slept. Although Edwards's public reaction to all of this was pragmatic, it is clear from his memoir that he found it particularly unfair that he, his wife and his wider family were targeted in such a way, given the level of political and financial support he gave to the Welsh language.[127]

The language issue aside, the legacy of the Thatcher government in Wales, for many, is undoubtedly the winding down of industry and large parts of the manufacturing base. The pit closure programme and the miners' strike of 1984–5, as we have seen, was an especially intense moment. Despite the Welsh Office citing the replacement of heavy industry with lighter manufacturing, these new jobs were often low-paid, part-time and unskilled, striking a contrast with the purpose and status that something like coalmining had provided.[128] The strike was a major British-wide story in the mid-1980s, but coal and Wales were often linked in the popular imagination, no doubt making it feel like it had a special Welsh resonance. As previous chapters have shown, the Tories had long hoped that the party might one day make inroads into these deindustrialising areas. Memories of the 1984–5 strike, however, supplanted talk of 'the 1930s' in these communities – and were just as potent, reinforcing the notion in these areas of the 'same old Tories'. For reasons including her policies, but also her character, perhaps her sex, and probably her very English image, 'Thatcher' became – for some – a hate figure like none other.[129] As Neil Kinnock, who was not just the Labour leader at the time, but a Welsh MP, would later recall: '[she was] a woman who, without exaggeration . . . was profoundly hated amongst many people and in large parts of the country'.[130] It cannot have helped the Conservative brand

---

[127] Crickhowell, *Wales*, see Demonstrations chapter.
[128] Richard Finlay, 'Thatcherism, Unionism and Nationalism: a Comparative Study of Scotland and Wales', in Jackson and Saunders, *Making Thatcher's Britain*, p. 167.
[129] Martin Johnes, *Wales: England's Colony? The Conquest, Assimilation and Re-creation of Wales* (Cardigan: Parthian, 2019), p. 161.
[130] 'Conversations – Lord Kinnock', BBC Parliament, 24 July 2016.

when – despite saying they would not keep doing this – Valleys seats, where the strike was centred, continued to be used as training grounds for future English MPs, like Tim Yeo, David Tredinnick and Desmond Swayne, to 'cut their teeth'. They tended to be the types of candidates who were busy with their day jobs, living far away and with little time to 'nurture' the seat (slightly later, in 1997, the unwinnable Clwyd South was fought for the Conservatives by a certain Alexander Boris Johnson).[131]

Consequently, this 'Englishness' was the focus of much anti-Conservative rhetoric in 1980s Wales, despite the work and presence of people like Wyn Roberts and Nicholas Edwards. A new pressure group, the Welsh Socialist Republican Movement, for example, produced a spoof 'letter' from Mrs Thatcher to 'the Welsh people'.[132] It began: 'Dear Subjects' and continued:

> I must say how delighted I am to visit the Principality (I much prefer the word 'Principality, don't you? – It reminds us all of your country's status as England's first colony) . . . if you irresponsible Welsh were left to your own devices, you would never be blessed with common sense Conservative governments.[133]

Whilst obviously satirical, this group did not know at the time that Thatcher had privately told an aide that 'the only Conservatives in Wales are the English who moved in' (even if that was not true).[134] The Conservatives did continue to invite this kind of criticism when it came to presentational issues. In the run-up to the 1992 election, with Labour being led by Neil Kinnock, who was dubbed 'the Welsh Windbag' by *Private Eye*, the party was accused of 'patronising' the Welsh when Michael Heseltine 'adopted a thick south Wales Valleys voice to take Mr

---

[131] Neil Hamilton also cut his teeth in this fashion, but as he was raised in Carmarthenshire, he was Welsh.

[132] For more information on this group, see John Osmond, *Police Conspiracy?* (Tal-y-bont: Y Lolfa, 1984), chapter two.

[133] Richard Burton Archives, SC446, 'A Personal Message from the Prime Minister: the Rt Hon. Margaret Thatcher MP'.

[134] Lord Roberts of Conway, *Right*, p. 221.

Kinnock's part' on television. This kind of trivialisation meant that Conservatives could still be accused of mocking Wales. What made the situation stranger is that Heseltine, as we have seen, was from Swansea and was adopting an accent that – his critics relished claiming – he 'forgot to use for 40 years'.[135] To compound this problem, when Nicholas Edwards was replaced as Secretary of State for Wales, his four successors between 1987 and 1997 were all Englishmen who sat for English seats. The first was Peter Walker who, as we have seen, seemed to fit with the left-leaning nature of Welsh politics, where he could act in a more economically interventionist way.[136] David Hunt replaced Walker in 1990. He was dubbed by some as 'Dai Polltax' and had to resort to saying that he could at least *see* Wales from his Wirral constituency, but in his approach to policy he was considered to be cast from a similar mould to his two successors.[137]

The arrival of the very English John Redwood in the Welsh Office in 1994, however, solidified some people's attitudes or concerns.[138] As Leon Gooberman has chronicled, previous Secretaries of State had supported the wider policy thrust from central government, but had 'diluted the impact of such policies', whereas Redwood famously sent some of the money allocated for Wales back to the Treasury, on the Thatcherite grounds that this was the fiscally responsible thing to do.[139] Most well-known is that Redwood seemed perplexed by specific aspects of Welsh culture, seemingly unable to sing the Welsh national anthem on one occasion, which was caught on camera.[140] For Gooberman, Redwood's approach was so tone-deaf that he 'almost terminally damaged the Conservatives in Wales'.[141] He was certainly

---

[135] 'Tories accused of patronizing Welsh', *Western Mail*, 9 April 1992.
[136] Obituary, Lord Roberts of Conwy, *Guardian*, 16 December 2013.
[137] Interview, Lord Hunt of Wirral, 16 June 2015.
[138] Deacon, *The Governance*, p. 32.
[139] Gooberman, 'A Very Modern', 637.
[140] Gooberman, 'A Very Modern', 643. Redwood claims he always knew the words, and that the video is propaganda against him. See: *https://www.youtube.com/watch?v=j3HXNgsl8Yo*, 36 minutes, 50 seconds. Accessed 4 February 2018.
[141] Gooberman, 'A Very Modern', 648.

divisive, but for some in Wales, Tories like Redwood were not the problem. In fact, the kind of social conservatism that Redwood attempted to articulate when Secretary of State for Wales, calling for parents to teach their children the differences between right and wrong, was the kind of message that would have gone down well with many voters. His deputy, Rod Richards – sometimes dubbed Redwood's Rottweiler – also noted that people in the Valleys sometimes had 'no expectations and no self-worth'.[142]

On the Welsh language in particular, there were similarly conservative views amongst parts of the population. In private, the party acknowledged that they had to accommodate the 'vociferous anti-Welsh, anti-Welsh language supporters amongst our ranks'.[143] And as Welsh Tories tried to become more Welsh, they flushed out in greater numbers those who resisted these moves and who wanted the party to prioritise other things. The most eccentric manifestation of this was an eighty-four-year-old man from Ceredigion, Brisbane Jones, who renamed himself 'Mr British Jones' and stood against Gwynfor Evans in Carmarthen, highlighting how people had no party standing up for a British identity, a critique that encompassed the Conservatives.[144] Jones, filmed by the BBC on the campaign trail, was not entirely effective at conveying his argument, telling the reporter: 'there are Joneses all the way up to Orkney!'[145]

The *Western Mail* was again speaking for a significant proportion of the conservative population when it published an editorial arguing that 'many' people in late 1980s Wales resented the Welsh language becoming more prominent in day-to-day life.[146] In 1990, the MP for Pembrokeshire, Nicholas Bennett, asked via a questionnaire what members of the Conservative Association thought about the 'Welsh language'. The options

[142] Gooberman, 'A Very Modern', 644.
[143] CPA, CRD 4/15/4/2, 'The Welsh Dimension' Report, 1979.
[144] 'British Jones will fight', *Western Mail*, 25 September 1974.
[145] Featured in *Tudur's TV Flashback*, series 3, episode 7, BBC One Wales, 24 August 2020.
[146] 'Welsh Affairs', *Western Mail*, 22 May 1987.

for people to tick were admittedly strange and included: 'protect with a Welsh Language Act'; 'current support about right'; 'referendum on devolution'; and 'Wales should remain an integral part of the UK' – all options that dealt with language, national identity and devolution, which, while interwoven, were ultimately separate issues. Respondents dealt with this accordingly, sometimes ticking three out of four boxes, but by far the largest proportion (58 per cent) chose the final option about Wales being 'integral' to the UK. The vast majority of these questionnaires were annotated, often liberally, and most comments went along the lines of: 'scrap the Welsh language' and 'too much emphasis is placed on Welsh and Welsh studies'.[147] Even when party supporters felt more sympathetic to the language, their understanding of it was very shallow. Attempting some token Welsh in a card to congratulate the MP Gwilym Jones for his re-election in Cardiff North in 1992, one party member even spelt 'Cymru' – the Welsh name for Wales – incorrectly, writing it as 'Cwmru'.[148]

Some of this sentiment was reflected by the more Thatcherite Welsh Office under Redwood. One historian has argued that Scottish Thatcherites undermined the Union by not accommodating distinctive Scottish patriotism, and a similar critique could be applied to this short period in Wales in the mid-1990s.[149] Rod Richard, who was the MP for Clwyd North West from 1992 to 1997, a minister in the Welsh Office and a fluent Welsh speaker, was of the opinion that 'the union' of the United Kingdom, and not Wales, was 'key'.[150] Although Richard's election as the leader of the Conservatives group in the new National Assembly falls just outside the time period of this study, it is still worth emphasising that he was the leadership candidate who won after calling for the party to be 'wrapped in

---

[147] WPA, GB0210 NICETT, Nicholas Bennett records, Questionnaires.
[148] WPA, GB0210, GWINES, Gwilym Jones papers, cards of congratulation, 1992.
[149] Finlay, 'Thatcherism', p. 169.
[150] Interview, Rod Richards, 29 April 2015.

the Union Jack'.[151] At the close of the twentieth century, this kind of sentiment mattered enormously to Conservatives in Wales and it was even articulated by Welsh-speaking politicians like Richards.

Various pieces of evidence suggest that Conservative activists, and Conservative-inclined voters more generally, also tended to want to articulate their British identity. In parts of the anglicised Monmouth constituency in the mid-1990s there were 'many people' who remained 'vitriolic about the Welsh language', including people who were themselves Welsh.[152] (In the 1991 by-election in the seat, Screaming Lord Sutch of the Monster Raving Loony Party received more votes than the Plaid Cymru candidate.[153]) One member of the association at the time remembered William Hague, Redwood's successor as Secretary of State, visiting the Abergavenny Conservative Club to address a meeting of around 150 members of the association. Hague announced that he was going from the meeting to watch Wales and England play rugby. Once he had gone, one member of the association asked the rest: 'who is supporting England?' and roughly '70 per cent raised their hands' – many of them Welshmen who objected to the kind of banal nationalism exhibited at a rugby match.[154] However, when Monmouth's MP, Roger Evans, fought Anglesey in 1987, he had been so 'acutely conscious' that the Welsh language was a political issue that he made the 'very rash promise' to learn the language if he were elected. Political and cultural differences within Wales could be very stark, and the Conservatives, like all parties, recognised this and made some attempts to accommodate it.[155] By the end of the 1990s the party's attitude towards Wales appeared – and to some extent was – enigmatic. Under the guidance of Wyn Roberts in particular, it had done more than many would have

[151] Interview, Guto Bebb, 23 June 2015.
[152] Interview, Roger Evans, 20 August 2015.
[153] 'Colourful Candidates', *Western Mail*, 26 March 1992.
[154] Interview with anonymous.
[155] Interview, Roger Evans, 20 August 2015.

assumed to highlight the nation's cultural distinctiveness. And yet, the electorate as a whole seemed unmoved by this, many of its supporters disliked such moves immensely, and the party was still perceived to be anchored (and to some extent was anchored) in English or anglicised communities.

'AGED INACTIVISTS'

This period of relative success for the party in Wales did not result in any upsurge in activity or interest at the grassroots. By the end of our period in the late 1990s, many associations were effectively moribund. One prospective Tory candidates standing in a seat with a large Labour majority remembered being interviewed for the role by 'all five members of the Association!'[156] Those that had always been quite strong, like Brecon and Radnor, or Monmouth, still supposedly had around 2,000 members on the books.[157] Whilst this is a substantial number, it compared unfavourably with membership figures from the halcyon days of the 1950s. Two thousand members in Monmouth was much depleted from the 6,579-strong association in 1953.[158] The figure in Brecon and Radnor was one-third of the total of paid-up members there in 1957.[159] Those who did remain were getting noticeably older. More and more meetings ended with the announcement of deaths, 'serious illnesses', hospitalisations, and excuses for absence because the individuals in question were unable to do something like climb a flight of stairs to the meeting room.[160] Members were becoming the 'aged inactivists' identified by historians of

---

[156] Interview, Sir Desmond Swayne MP, 8 December 2014.
[157] Interview, Lyndon Jones, 7 October 2015.
[158] WPA, GB0210 MONION, file 6, Monmouth Conservative Association minute book, AGM Report, 26 February 1953.
[159] CPA, CCO 1/12/512, Annual Report for 1957.
[160] WPA, GB0210 CARCON, file 30, Cardiff North Executive Committee minute book, 11 February 1963; WPA, GB0210 CARCON, file 35, Cardiff South East Executive Committee minute book, 22nd Annual Report; WPA, GB0210 CARCON, file 36, Cardiff North Executive Committee minute book, 6 December 1971.

associational politics.[161] When fighting Swansea West in 1983, Julian Lewis, the future long-serving MP for New Forest East, allowed himself to be photographed in campaign headquarters 'with party workers'. The three very elderly women who made up these workers stuff envelopes, while Lewis looks on.[162] These 'gerontocracies' were not unique to the Conservative Party; older Labour members found they were not being replaced by those from a younger generation, either.[163] Neither was it a purely political phenomena: organisations that combined social elements with wider religious or community purposes, like chapels, pubs or choirs, also found themselves in decline.[164]

Even if the role of leadership figures in helping to rejuvenate local associations was questionable, it cannot have helped the party that the only element of professional support associations had, in the form of agents, was in further decline in this period. At the end of the 1970s there were only nine qualified agents in Wales.[165] Shortly afterwards, Thatcher's party chairman Lord Thorneycroft – the former MP for Monmouth – reversed a set of previous reforms, and employment of agents was transferred back to associations, which did not solve the problem of under-recruitment.[166] The type of person who filled the role of agent was now very different. Philip Circus, who fought the 1987 general election in Llanelli, had an agent in the shape of eighteen-year-old Robert Buckland (who became the MP for Swindon South in 2005, would later rise to the position of Lord Chancellor

[161] Patrick Seyd and Paul Whiteley, 'Conservative Grassroots: An Overview' in Ludlam and Smith, *Contemporary British Conservatism*, p. 72.
[162] 'Special Focus: Swansea West', *Western Mail*, 2 June 1983.
[163] Steven Fielding, 'The Labour Party and the Recruitment of the Young, 1945–1970', in Gaetano Quagliariello (ed.), *La Formazione della classe politica in Europa* (Manduria: P. Lacaita, 2000), p. 589.
[164] Johnes, *Wales Since 1939*, p. 166; Tim Bale, Paul Webb and Monica Poletti, *Footsoldiers: Political Party Membership in the 21st Century* (London: Routledge, 2019), p. 9.
[165] WPA, GB0210 CONLES, file 18, 1978 conference programme. The qualified agents were in the following seats: Conway, Monmouth, Denbigh, Cardiff North, Pembrokeshire, Brecon and Radnor, Swansea West, Anglesey, Flint West.
[166] Bale, *The Conservatives*, p. 192.

in 2019 and was briefly Secretary of State for Wales in 2022). Buckland – dubbed 'the Teenaged Tory' in the press – had to volunteer in this role, not only because Llanelli was an unwinnable seat for the Conservatives, but also because by this point in time the standing of an agent was quite different from what it had been.[167] Circus described how agents in previous decades had been 'minor Kings', who were often retired colonels.[168] It is very telling that an eighteen-year-old, albeit an ambitious and mature one, filled the void.

At the 1992 general election, the Conservative Party only had 300 full-time constituency agents across the UK (although this was a great deal more than any other political party).[169] This amounted to less than one agent for every two constituencies. The ratio was far worse in Wales, however, where only fourteen out of the thirty-eight constituencies had the services of either a full-time or part-time professional agent, or ones who acted in a voluntary capacity.[170] The contrast with the thirty-two out of thirty-six seats that had the service of an agent or organiser in 1950 was sharp.[171] A sense of bitterness about the whole situation was evident. D. Elwyn Jones, who served for thirty-two years as an agent in Wales, wrote to the Party Chairman in 1991 about how 'disgusted' he was by the dismissive treatment of the agent's 'voice' in local associations.[172] When questioned about what became of agents, Lyndon Jones, who had been involved in behind-the-scenes dealings with the Conservative Party for most of his life, explained how eventually the role of 'campaign manager' took over much of the agent's functions in Wales at the end of this period. When asked who did all of the other things besides managing the

---

[167] *Western Mail*, 22 May 1987.
[168] Interview, Philip Circus, 9 August 2015.
[169] David Butler and Dennis Kavanagh, *The British General Election of 1992* (London: Macmillan, 1992), p. 232.
[170] Swansea Conservative Association private archive, Conservative Party of Wales Council Annual Report 1990/91, p. 1.
[171] CPA, CCO 2/2/17, Wales and Monmouthshire Area AGM Report, 10 June 1950.
[172] WPA, Elwyn Jones papers, Jones to Chris Patten, 31 January 1991. Patten had suggested that Jones was not a very good 'team player'.

campaign itself, like fundraising, he noted that it had passed to 'the volunteers'.[173]

A natural consequence of fewer people joining political associations was that those who remained did appear to take political matters quite seriously. The grassroots therefore offer a small but sharply focused picture of rank-and-file Conservatism in Wales in the latter part of the twentieth century, not least because a greater number of MPs across parties in this period tended to ask their membership for their opinions more often than they ever had.[174] Just as it is possible, if not a bit misleading, to identify a 'constituency left' in the Labour Party over much of this period, where Labour activists were sometimes left frustrated at their party's lack of commitment to 'real' socialist values,[175] so too can we identify frustrations in parts of the Conservative rank and file that the Tories were not 'robustly Conservative' enough. As the party tried to edge towards some more socially liberal positions under the leadership of John Major, it faced robust resistance from senior grassroots figures. There was simply no campaigning, even in the 1980s or 1990s, for the kind of progressive politics or 'equal representation agenda' that was obvious at the grassroots of both Labour and Plaid Cymru.[176] The grassroots chairman of the party in Wales, very shortly after the end of our period, wrote to the Conservative politician David Melding to argue that it was 'quite proper' to continue using the term 'spokes<u>men</u>' (emphasis in original): 'I do not believe that this pandering to the wimin [*sic*] industry does anything in real terms to advance the cause of women in politics . . . It should be no part of the Conservative party's agenda'.[177]

---

[173] Interview, Lyndon Jones, 7 October 2015.
[174] Duncan Tanner, 'Labour and its membership', in Duncan Tanner, Pat Thane and Nick Tiratsoo (eds), *Labour's First Century* (Cambridge: Cambridge University Press, 2000), p. 269.
[175] Tanner, 'Labour', pp. 264–6.
[176] Laura McAllister, *Plaid Cymru: The Emergence of a Political Party* (Bridgend: Seren 2001), p. 190.
[177] WPA, GB0210 CONAGRP, 2/4, Lloyd Davies to Melding, 13 June 2002.

The party certainly could not claim to have advanced the cause of political women in this period. As in previous periods, the grassroots selected very few to stand as parliamentary candidates. No women were picked for winnable seats, aside from, perhaps, Kay Wood in Wrexham in 1983. The front cover of her election address, incidentally, was the first of any candidates to positively emphasise her feminine qualities, with the two o's of her surname becoming eyes with long eyelashes.[178] Inside, she spoke positively about being a mother of a young child. However, the only woman to get elected for the party in the pre-devolution age was Beata Brookes, who became a Member of the European Parliament for North Wales in 1979.[179] She was portrayed as stern, being nicknamed 'the Celtic Iron Lady'.[180] An attempt to make Brookes the candidate for the new Clwyd North West seat in 1983 failed, with Antony Meyer, an Old Etonian established candidate, winning the nomination.[181] Even in 1992, only six per cent of the Conservative parliamentary party were female. None of these were drawn from Wales.[182] Labour had a slightly better record of sending women to parliament from Wales, but considering how many more MPs the party had, it too was still a very low proportion.

Whilst most elements of the grassroots struggled to stay afloat, Conservative clubs did not go into such a dramatic a spiral of decline, but that was probably because of their precisely non-political nature. Numbers attending them certainly dipped, but

---

[178] CPA, PUB, 229/19/13, Kay Wood election address, Wrexham, 1983

[179] For an overview of this broader subject, see Sam Blaxland, 'Welsh Women MPs: Exploring Their Absence', in a special edition of *Open Library of the Humanities*: '"An Unconventional MP": Nancy Astor, public women and gendered political culture', *Open Library of the Humanities*, 6/2 (2020), 1–35.

[180] 'Beata Brookes: former North Wales MEP nicknamed the "Celtic Iron Lady" dies aged 84', *Liverpool Daily Post*, 18 August 2015.

[181] Sam Blaxland, 'Denbigh Constituency's First and Final Conservative MP: a study of Geraint Morgan', *Denbighshire Historical Society Transactions*, 65 (2017), 99.

[182] Joni Lovenduski, Pippa Norris and Catriona Burness, 'The Party and Women', in Seldon and Ball, *Conservative Century*, p. 611.

nothing like as severely.[183] More Conservative clubs were open in the late 1980s than Liberal, Labour and British Legion clubs combined.[184] There were still forty of them in 1988 in what was at the time Mid Glamorganshire (which encompassed core areas of so-called 'Welsh Wales', including the Cynon, Rhondda and Rhymney Valleys).[185] Broadly speaking, clubs remained social realms, offering cheap drink. Minute books from these places demonstrate that the kind of topics that were regularly under discussion included entertainment nights, refurbishment, the redecorating of the billiard room and whether or not Worthington 'E' should be kept on tap because only a few people drank it.[186] When asked about one club, which he 'loved' going to, one activist saw club attendance as attributable to the fact that 'the beer there was cheaper than anywhere else!'[187] When asked what the Conservative clubs did for his cause and his campaign in Newport West in 1983, Mark Robinson replied, 'they were nice to me when I went in to put posters up – that was it'. He added that they were 'not political', although they did at least display his posters.[188]

In Aberavon, Paul Warrick remembered that when it came to Conservative clubs 'the name wasn't indicative of the content'. He describes going into a club on the border between Aberavon and Neath in advance of the 1987 election, saying, in relation to the reaction he got, 'there was outright hostility! And [of all the clubs in the area] that was meant to be *the nice one!*'[189] The Conservative club in Llanelli was still being used as the party's campaign headquarters at election time in 1987. The team of

[183] Paul Jennings, *The Local: A History of the English Pub* (Stroud: Tempus, 2007), p. 211.
[184] John Ramsden, *The Winds of Change: Macmillan to Heath, 1957–1975* (Essex: Longman, 1996), p. 106.
[185] Philip Tether, *Clubs: A Neglected Aspect of Conservative Organisation* (University of Hull: Hull Papers in Politics, 1988), p. 4.
[186] GA, D623/1/14, Caerphilly Conservative Club minute book, 2 July 1971.
[187] Interview with anonymous.
[188] Interview, Mark Robinson, 15 June 2015.
[189] Interview, Paul Warrick, 24 September 2015.

enthusiasts would work upstairs away from members, which the candidate summarised as being a valid metaphor for the non-political nature of the club. He remembered it as a 'good social club with cheap beer'.[190] When one parliamentary candidate was campaigning in the Valleys in 1992, he went to give a speech about party policy in a Conservative club. After the chairman of the club introduced him – during the welcoming applause from the audience – he turned and whispered to the candidate: 'no politics, please'.[191]

Investigating the conundrum of why so many people still went to clubs leads to several possible conclusions. Interviews conducted for this book, archived film clips, and pictorial and written records, all point towards an air of (generally non-politicised) respectability infusing Conservative clubs, despite the cheap booze. This might have attracted a broadly aspirational or conservative type of person, who did not mind going into a club bearing the Tory label, but might not have voted Conservative at election times. Such conclusions can be drawn from the physical contents of Swansea's Salisbury Conservative Club, which closed in 2015. Before all the material and items that had once been in there were either destroyed or sent to several different archives, there was an opportunity to sift through the collection of artefacts, signs, notices, books and receipts, all accumulated over at least a hundred years. The records revealed an institution that was primarily about offering drinks and playing billiards. Trips to sporting or social occasions were common. The club had a sizeable library, with a much higher proportion of books on Tory politics and statesmen than in a similar kind of social club. However, in all the paperwork, including the contracts of the managers of the club, there was no reference to the Conservative Party. Various pictures show a male-only membership, dressed formally.[192]

---

[190] Interview, Philip Circus, 9 August 2015.
[191] Interview with anonymous.
[192] Various items from the Salisbury Conservative Club, Swansea, viewed at the South Wales Miners' Library.

Indeed, this male-only nature of most clubs was important. If women were so much more active at the grassroots level, one explanation could be that men's attention was taken up with 'beer and billiards' in clubs. Film footage of the inside of one unspecified club in Powys in the late 1980s demonstrates how the clientele did look a lot like what the 'typical' Conservative voter was deemed to be by the end of this period. Asked what they thought about the prospect of women being allowed into the establishment in the future, the documentary – edited, of course, for maximum effect – nonetheless captured several seconds of telling footage. A young man with his top button undone and tie pulled down, says in a soft mid-Wales accent that he would like to see 'as many young ladies as possible' come to the club. The scene then cuts to a much older gentleman, in thick-rimmed spectacles, sporting a military-style moustache and a three-piece suit – including a mustard-coloured waistcoat – who says of the plan (in a very posh accent): 'I think it's a rather good idea, myself!'[193]

Those clubs that did allow women in witnessed a shift in the nature of the entertainment they sometimes offered. Remarkable television footage captured in 1988 gave viewers a window on to an event held by the Cardiff Women's Association in the Grangetown Conservative Club. The main entertainment that night was a male stripper, complete with period moustache and mullet hairstyle, who, when asked what made him a successful act, replied, 'I make the women laugh [by] taking my clothes off'. One older lady, in a rose-patterned dress, described the night as 'for a good cause. It's also a good excuse for a night out with the girls'. Another told reporters (in very serious tones), 'I have never seen a strip-show before', before adding that she was really looking forward to it.[194]

[193] Featured in *Tudur's TV Flashback*, series 3, episode 7, BBC One Wales, 24 August 2020.
[194] Featured in *Tudur's TV Flashback*, series 3, episode 7, BBC One Wales, 24 August 2020.

CONCLUSION

In contrast to popular myth, the Conservative Party in Wales received a consistent and reasonably high level of support throughout the 1980s. The party was also at its most proactive when it came to specific policy for Wales during this period. Many communities or areas, however, did suffer. Politicians like Nicholas Edwards subsequently made a robust defence of their time at the Welsh Office, arguing that politicians could not solve everyone's problems and that attracting business investment into some areas of Wales was always going to be difficult. It is undoubtable that people like Edwards did at least try to change things in Wales, going well beyond simply a process of managed decline or treating Wales as just a region of Britain. The revitalisation of the Welsh language in the twentieth century is now spoken about as one of the global linguistic success stories of the twentieth century. Not all of that is purely down to policy-making and politics, but those things play a part. Long periods of Conservative rule after the Second World War could have facilitated the language's decline, or done nothing to discourage apathy, but they did not. Peter Thomas in the 1970s deserves some credit, but it is Thatcher's ministers who are also an important component of the story. When summarising the relative weakness of the Conservatism in Wales between 1885 and 1935, Felix Aubel argued that 'the reason for [the] almost invariably unfavourable Tory electoral position in Wales [is] that Conservatism had simply nothing specifically Welsh, either in policy or appeal, to offer the Principality'.[195] By the end of the twentieth century, a fair-minded person would find it more difficult to level that criticism at the party.

The politics of this was always going to be interesting. By the end of the 1980s, people within the party in Wales had started to wonder if attempts to promote 'Welshness' were backfiring on them. In Scotland, where the party had historically done much

[195] Aubel, 'Welsh Conservatism', p. 439.

to bolster distinctly Scottish institutions, it made, in the words of one writer, 'their own position as the Unionists *par excellence* often difficult to sustain'.[196] Something similar could be said of the Tories in Wales, where they helped reinforce a sense of Welsh distinctiveness that only served to magnify the party's perceived 'Englishness'. After the Tories lost the seat of Ynys Môn in 1987, after the imprisonment of the island's MP Keith Best for a scandal involving the sale of British Telecom shares, a group of party agents in north Wales put together a briefing paper on how to win back the seat. They noted that 'Welshness' satisfied a very human need to belong to a group. However, Plaid Cymru was becoming particularly effective at identifying itself with the language and a sense of belonging. Consequently, 'the core of the Conservative vote' was to be found 'in the English speaking community'.[197] In some ways, then, little had changed from the pre-Thatcher period. Support that Tory ministers had given to things like the language did not seem to have reaped that many political benefits for them, even if they had tangible real-world impacts. In supporting the language and buttressing a sense of Welsh nationhood, however, the party undoubtedly helped cement the idea that Wales was distinct and different, to such an extent that they perhaps made the later idea of devolution palatable, despite not being in favour of a National Assembly themselves. How much the party benefited electorally from any of this is questionable. After decades of engaging with ideas surrounding nationhood and its own place within Wales, there is no clear evidence that the party won new friends.[198] Indeed, it is possible that its 'Welsh agenda' alienated a greater number

[196] Mitchell, *Conservatives*, p. xiv.
[197] WPA, GB0210 KEIFAN, Keith Raffan papers, 'Winning back Ynys Môn', undated, 1987.
[198] Richard Wyn Jones, Roger Scully and Dafydd Trystan, 'Why do the Conservatives Always do (Even) Worse in Wales?', in Lynn Bennie, Colin Rawlings, Jonathan Tonge and Paul Webb (eds), *British Elections and Parties Review*, 12/1 (2002), 243.

of old supporters.[199] Nonetheless, although it might seem like a paradox, the story of the creation of modern Wales should have the Conservative Party at the centre of it.

---

[199] Sam Blaxland, 'Welsh Conservatives: Far From a Contradiction in Terms', *Planet* Extra,*https://www.planetmagazine.org.uk/planet-extra/welsh-conservatives-far-contradiction-term* Accessed 15 April 2021.

CONCLUSION

By its own standards, the Conservative Party in Wales during the period 1945 to 1997 was weak. It governed Britain for most of the twentieth century, yet never found true success in this part of, as the party sometimes called it, 'the Celtic fringe'. For a party with clear messages on a range of subjects, a relatively well-oiled machine, a strong election war chest and enthusiastic grassroots members, to hover at around thirty per cent of the vote was always a disappointment. Its political opponents are right to say that, in the era of universal suffrage, 'Wales has never been a Conservative country. And it never will be.'[1] The fact that the twentieth century is bookended by two terrible results for the party makes it easy to conclude, as one eminent historian has, that 'Welsh Conservatism ended the century as it had begun it: floundering badly and unable to meet the needs of the day'.[2] What this characterisation misses is a much more interesting history between those two episodes. Thirty per cent of the vote is not a trifling figure, and it is still representative of hundreds of thousands of people in Wales – many of them Welsh – who voted, sometimes against the grain of the politics of their local area, for the party. Whilst Wales's Conservative tradition has been, and continues to be 'subdued', as one politician put it in 1959, it is not invisible.[3]

Any book trying to paint a historical picture of a political party from top to bottom, including its grassroots, over a long time-period, will inevitably have to do so using relatively broad brushstrokes. Whilst this work has often homed in on case studies

---

[1] Mike (now Lord) German, quoted in 'Capital Eye', *North Wales Daily Post*, 13 March 2007.
[2] Geraint H. Jenkins, *A Concise History of Wales* (Cambridge: Cambridge University Press, 2007), p. 288.
[3] '"Wales has always had a Tory tradition" says Tom Ellis Hooson', newspaper unknown, 27 February 1959.

to help illustrate certain points, the approach has necessarily had to be one that aims to present a big picture. As the first in-depth, book-length history of the Conservative Party in Wales during any era, it has shone a light on to the nation's second political party. It is sincerely hoped that it will encourage more research and work. There is of course more to be done. Space meant that only passing reference has been made here to a number of important themes, including the presence of Conservatives in local government across Wales, or the role played by a series of Secretaries of State in the late 1980s and 1990s. Inevitably, future readers will want more information on the careers of Welsh MPs and the contributions they made to the major debates of their days. The grassroots of the party, which this work has tried to show are important for a study both of the Conservative Party and of conservatism in post-war Wales, could be the subject of further enquiry. In one of his histories of the party, Stuart Ball listed the nine core functions of local organisations. This book has devoted some time to a discussion of eight of these. Ball's fifth point – the role played by activists in influencing, or at least trying to influence, the opinion of MPs and the party's leadership – could be further scrutinised in the Welsh context, despite the fact that the Conservatives were always hierarchical and placed little emphasis on this kind of 'democratic' participation.[4] Similarly, more could be said about the relationship between constituency parties and their MPs once a candidate was selected, as Duncan Tanner has discussed in the context of Labour.[5] Senior Conservative figures frequently lamented how there were few people in the party rank and file in Wales who were of 'the right calibre to produce at the end of the day policy contributions at a presentable standard',

---

[4] See Ball, *Portrait of a Party: The Conservative Party in Britain, 1918–1945* (Oxford: Oxford University Press, 2013), p. 241; Tim Bale, Paul Webb and Monica Poletti, *Footsoldiers: Political Party Membership in the 21st Century* (London: Routledge, 2019), p. 96.

[5] Duncan Tanner, 'The Recruitment of the Parliamentary Labour Party in Britain (1931–1955), in Gaetano Quagliariello (ed.), *La Formazione della classe politica in Europa: 1945–1956* (Manduria: P. Lacaita, 2000).

but that does not mean that more could not be done to study this topic.[6]

Nonetheless, this book has covered many important themes relating to the party's history. It is clear from all periods that the Conservatives had a support base in Wales, which was firmly, if not exclusively, grounded in the more middle-class, anglicised areas of the so-called 'British Wales' parts of the Three Wales Model. This allowed Conservatives to muster enough support in areas like Pembrokeshire, Monmouthshire, Cardiff, Brecon and Radnor, or along parts of the north Wales coast to regularly win seats in these places. They did so by stressing key British-wide policies, ranging from an emphasis on individual liberty in the immediate post-war years, all the way through to clamping down on trade unionism and allowing people to buy their rental properties in the latter parts of the century. Some of the ways Welsh society changed in the decades after the Second World War made it easier for the party to communicate with the electorate. It tapped into ideas about wealth and upward social mobility in a nation that was becoming, in very broad terms, more affluent. It also undoubtedly capitalised on the fact that Wales's extremely porous border with England allowed for large numbers of people from the latter to move in, no doubt resulting in some of them bringing with them their Conservative outlooks and voting habits. Party reports from across the period acknowledged that this was the case, even if Margaret Thatcher was wrong to say that such people represented the entirety of Welsh Tory voters.

A by-product of this, however, was that the party's actual and perceived 'Englishness' was reinforced. This partly explains why the Tories remained untrusted in parts of Wales where the party seemed unsuited to local political dynamics. The lack of high-profile Welsh speakers in their ranks offers some explanation for the underperformance in the large rural constituencies of mid and north Wales – seats that would likely have been Tory had

[6] Conservative Party Archive, Bodleian Library, Oxford [CPA], Conservative Research Department [CRD] 4/15/4/2, 'The Welsh Dimension' Report, 1979.

they been in England. In the industrial, or de-industrialising, parts of so-called 'Welsh Wales', memories of the Great Depression of the 1930s took a long time to fade. The party failed to articulate itself convincingly in these areas, with the 1980s supplanting and reinforcing old stereotypes. Class, rather than national identity or being a Welsh speaker, mattered more here, although class and nation were undoubtedly fused. It did not help the Tory cause that many of those standing for the party in places like the south Wales Valleys were sometimes as unsuitable as could be imagined: very English, unconnected to the constituency and its concerns, and often dismissive or aloof in their communication style.

The picture is, of course, more nuanced than this in reality. Men like Wyn Roberts in Conwy or Keith Best in Ynys Môn proved that it was possible to be either Welsh speaking, a patriotic Welshman, or someone willing to integrate into an area and learn the language, as well as being a Tory. The Conservatives also had some purchase amongst working-class people outside the industrial areas of 'Welsh Wales', without whom they could not have won seats like Swansea West, Bridgend, Cardiff West or Newport West at various times during this period. The party was especially effective in these areas when so-called 'local boys' were able to mediate the party's policies to the electorate by positioning themselves as effective local voices. Welsh politics had long had a distinctly local dynamic to it, and the Conservatives understood this in the post-1945 years, embracing parochial traditions and taking up hyper-local concerns. The fact that parliamentary candidates were ultimately chosen by local associations also showed that activists valued local connections, specifically, over more generic 'Welsh' ties.

No study of the party in Wales, however, can ignore what the party did specifically 'for the nation'. Conservatives engaged with the concept of Welsh nationhood and administrative devolution throughout the period under study here, acting as the kind of Unionists that encouraged and accommodated an element of 'sub-British' nationality within the existing structure of the United

Kingdom. They were, in part, the architects of contemporary Wales, enacting a series of relevant policies from the early 1950s, beginning with the creation of a Minister for Welsh Affairs. As chapter four in particular demonstrated, the party can lay some claim to buttressing a sense of specific Welsh identity, especially through its legislation relating to the language and education. By ensuring that children in even the most anglicised of areas had to learn some Welsh in state schools, the party may not have created a fully bilingual nation, but it did something immensely symbolic. A new generation of young people had a greater sense that they were from a distinct nation within the United Kingdom. In the process, the party also attempted to alter its own image to make it appear 'more Welsh'. The fact that it failed to achieve this, with studies at the beginning of the twenty-first century showing that the party remained closely associated with many features that were precisely *un*-Welsh, spoke to the way in which the party failed to shape the political narrative in Wales.[7]

Indeed, any talk of Conservative successes should not of course distract from the wider truth that much of Wales is 'Labour Country'. Historically, that party has had enormous majorities – occasionally over 30,000 – in many of the industrial seats in the south. Labour has managed to communicate with the Welsh electorate in a way that the Conservatives were simply not capable of, embedding itself into communities in the process. Many Conservatives at the top and the grassroots levels of the party privately thought this was a defect of the Welsh, a people swayed by oratory and fantasy, who voted out of habit for a party that did little to improve their lives.[8] Occasionally, these frustrations seeped out into its public communications. There should be no doubt, however, that much of what the Conservatives did in Wales was in the face of strong Labour opponents who knew their areas well

---

[7] Richard Wyn Jones, Roger Scully and Dafydd Trystan, 'Why do the Conservatives Always do (Even) Worse in Wales?', in Lynn Bennie, Colin Rawlings, Jonathan Tonge and Paul Webb (eds), *British Elections and Parties Review*, 12/1 (2002), 243.

[8] Kenneth O. Morgan and Peter Stead, 'Rhondda West', in David Butler and Anthony King (eds), *The British General Election of 1966* (London: Macmillan, 1966), p. 245.

and who were simply better at politics. The sporadic optimism the party expressed about success in the Valleys of 'Welsh Wales', where they hoped to erode Labour's strength, was misplaced. Conservatives underestimated the power of those areas' left-wing political culture, rooted in a deep sense of community and history.[9] It is not just that the party could not break through in these places, but that it thought it would be able to do so, that demonstrates its naivety. This incompatibility with an important and large section of the nation is also a key part of the party's history in Wales.

Giving key grassroots individuals some limelight has reinforced many of these core themes, whilst also allowing us to examine the parts of Welsh society in which the party was anchored – and which receive relatively little attention in the wider social histories of Wales. Conservative politics was interwoven with a sense of 'civic patriotism' and local pride. Local members of the elite were part of binding the party together with other British institutions. Such people – like Sir Charles Hallinan or, later, Sir Donald Walters – were both untypical of rank-and-file Conservatives (in that they were especially successful and prominent) and a reasonable representation of the party's grassroots base, representing a firm middle-class respectability that was woven into parts of suburban, non-industrial Wales, or its border constituencies. The wider activist base was more middle class than its voters and certainly more conservative than society at large. This small-c conservatism, evident throughout our period, is an understudied force in modern Wales.[10] The social nature of associational life, with its sherry parties, trifle stalls, and cheese and wine evenings, would no doubt have felt exclusive. It brought into the party's orbit people's friends from their own social groups, making the party about much more

---

[9] Kenneth O. Morgan and Peter Stead, 'Rhondda West', in D. E. Butler and Anthony King (eds), *The British General Election of 1966* (London: Macmillan, 1966), p. 249.

[10] Kenneth O. Morgan, 'Power and Glory: War and Reconstruction, 1939–1951', in Duncan Tanner, Chris Williams and Deian Hopkin (eds), *The Labour Party in Wales* (Cardiff: University of Wales Press, 2000), p. 184–6.

than politics.[11] However, much of the hostility to the party's Welsh agenda came from such groups, demonstrating what a bind the party found itself in: it wanted to feel more in tune with the wider tenor of Welsh political life, but in doing so it often alienated those who made up its core voter base.

EPILOGUE: THE PARTY AND DEVOLUTION

The story told in this book deliberately ended at the 1997 general election. The beginning of the devolution era, which was painful for the Conservatives in Wales, requires a book in its own right. It is worth noting, however, that so much of what conditioned how the party behaved after the referendum on establishing a National Assembly in 1997, and after the first elections to that new body in 1999, cannot be fully understood without grappling with its long-term, post-Second World War history. When trying to draw historical threads together, the most obvious change that has taken place concerns the party's rank and file. The era of mass grassroots campaigning is over. Political parties are no longer the kind of organisations they were in the 1950s, when they at least offered an opportunity for large numbers of people to meet other like-minded souls and 'do something' – be that political activity or engaging in the social life of an association. Similarly, for a party that used to be so well represented by women at the grassroots, the current Conservative Party's membership is now made up of more men than women, by a majority of more than three to one.[12] Many in the party in Wales might not realise that this is far from the natural order of things.

A resurgence in interest in rank-and-file politics in the twenty-first century, however, is possible, as the Labour Party showed across Britain during the years of Jeremy Corbyn's leadership. The contemporary Conservative Party in Wales may find

---

[11] See various recordings in British Library Sound and Moving Image archive, C1688.
[12] Bale, Webb and Poletti, *Footsoldiers*, p. 33.

something of interest in the sections at the end of each chapter of this book which outline how the party once acted as a body that tens of thousands of people wanted to join. The streak of 'true blue' conservatism that ran through that membership then was identifiable in those who remained paid-up members after 1997. Most obviously, this manifested itself in the selection of Rod Richards, the 'fiercely intelligent [but] . . . aggressive' kind of Tory who was made the Conservative group's first leader in the National Assembly.[13] Subsequent selection decisions by the membership have also caused headaches for the party's leadership. In the run-up to the 2001 general election in the winnable Clwyd West seat, for example, the local party sidelined a Welsh-speaking member of the National Assembly for Wales in favour of a retired army major from Northamptonshire who did not live in the constituency. This could be one reason why Labour clung on to a seat that was more naturally Conservative than anything else.[14] Writing to Tory Assembly Members (AMs) after the 2007 election to the Assembly, the group's leader Nick Bourne said:

> We certainly need to tighten up our candidate selection . . . there must be no repetition of some of the horrors that we have been through in the last couple of years. We have to be ruthless about turfing people off the list who will embarrass the party on either personal or policy grounds.[15]

Again, finding and selecting the most suitable candidate is something the party has long struggled to grapple with, although it has yielded some fascinating – and surprising – results in the past, as the stories of people ranging from Harry West, to Ted Dexter, to Keith Best demonstrate.

---

[13] David Melding, 'Refashioning Welsh Conservatism – a Lesson for Scotland', in David Torrance (ed.), *Whatever Happened to Tory Scotland?* (Edinburgh: Edinburgh University Press, 2012), p. 128.

[14] Alan Convery, *The Territorial Conservative Party: Devolution and Party Change in Scotland and Wales* (Manchester: Manchester University Press, 2015), p. 85.

[15] Welsh Political Archive, National Library of Wales, Aberystwyth [WPA], GB0210 CONAGRP, 4/1, Bourne to Conservative AMs, 9 May 2007.

When it comes to candidates, the theme of localism that is so prominent in previous chapter continued to be relevant in the years after 1997, with local associations, despite examples like Clwyd West, tending to select 'local boys' (and more women, too) than ever before. This might well have tipped the balance in some cases. Almost exactly one hundred years after the newspaper *Baner ac Amserau Cymru* wrote that Toryism in Wales was 'barren, effete, dying, and already dead . . . in no enlightened country can it ever have a firm foothold', the Conservatives won the seat of Gower for the first time after a century of Labour representation.[16] The victorious candidate, Byron Davies, was a local man.[17] His connection to the area was surely worth the twenty-seven-vote majority he had. At the 2019 general election, it was noteworthy that many of the successful parliamentary candidates had clear connections to the seats they won for the party. That election also witnessed the first women to be elected as Conservative MPs in Wales.

Despite stories like this, the Conservatives continue to grapple with the left-leaning political culture that characterises Welsh politics. Wales is certainly 'Labour country', as we have seen, but adopting a less right-wing approach in response to that is not straightforward. The party might still talk, in private, about the 'sentimental' Celtic temperament of Welsh voters, although it is far more attuned to national sensibilities and is less likely to use such old-fashioned language now. It clearly despairs, sometimes with a wry smile, of what it sees as the tribal and cultural motives that drive many voters to continue picking Labour.[18] Opening the debate on the Queen's Speech in Parliament in 2016, Dr Phillip Lee, the then Conservative MP for Bracknell, gave a light-hearted account of his experience standing as a Tory in Blaenau Gwent in 2005, when he only managed to poll just over 800 votes: 'Sporting a blue rosette outside the Tredegar Kwiksave takes a certain type

---

[16] Arnold J. James and John E. Thomas, *Wales at Westminster: A History of the Parliamentary Representation of Wales 1800–1979* (Llandysul: Gomer Press, 1981), p. 104.
[17] 'Gower', *Western Mail*, 1 June 1983.
[18] WPA, GB0210 CONAGRP, 4/1, Welsh Conservative SWOT analysis, 24 May 2011.

of character: mostly delusional, perhaps even masochistic', he said. When he asked a lady in Abertillery market why she voted Labour, Lee told the House of Commons (to laughs from both sides) that the response was: 'Don't you get complicated with me!'[19] If anything, Conservative support has begun to map more and more clearly on to the 'British Wales' section of the Three Wales concept, to the extent that the 2019 general election result looked eerily similar to the model originally conceived nearly a hundred years earlier. The Tories' strength in places like Brecon and Radnor, at the expense of the declining Liberal Democrats, compensates for the fact that its old urban fortresses like Cardiff North now look lost forever. The seat of David Llewellyn, Donald Box, Michael Roberts, Ian Grist and Gwilym Jones witnessed one of the strongest swings away from the Conservatives in the entire UK in 2019, driven perhaps by growing numbers of students, public sector workers and urban liberals who now tend to occupy such places.

There are explanations for these patterns. A huge amount of recent research, especially from Cardiff University's Wales Governance Centre, reveals that, despite everything we have encountered throughout this book, the party is unable to shrug off its image as the 'un-Welsh' English party.[20] This certainly helps account for why the constituencies it wins in map on to 'British Wales', and why there appears to be a ceiling of support that it is difficult for the party to break through. This is not for lack of trying. The party continued to develop ideas about its own Welsh identity, especially under its leader of the Assembly group from 1999 to 2011, Nick Bourne. It is this aspect of the party's history that has received the most scholarly attention, not least because Bourne was open in admitting that he thought the party was

---

[19] 'Debate on the Address', House of Commons Hansard, 18 May 2016, vol. 611, col. 10.

[20] Jac M. Larner, Richard Wyn Jones, Ed Gareth Poole, Paula Surridge and Daniel Wincott, 'Incumbency and Identity: The 2021 Senedd Election', *Parliamentary Affairs*, 10 May 2022.

struggling to shake off its 'English' image.[21] However, Bourne's project to change the party in this way has long-term historical underpinnings. Even the discussions he had with his key lieutenant, David Melding, about changing the party's name should be seen in historical context. At one point, Melding suggested rebranding the Conservatives in Wales as 'Ymlaen' – meaning 'forward' in Welsh. Melding had read widely about the tradition of tweaking aspects of the party's presentation. He argued that it might help broaden the Conservative Party's appeal in Wales. Whilst his proposals were rejected, he was certainly following historical precedence, drawing on several occasions since the 1950s where the party in Wales made subtle name-changes, on the advice of men like Geoffrey Howe, in an attempt to feel 'less like a foreign invasion'.[22] The legacy of people like Howe, Enoch Powell, Tom Hooson, Ian Grist, John Eilian Jones, and many other backroom staff in the party's Wales Area Office and its Research Department who grappled with similar issues, lives on in the Conservatives' attempts to assess their position in Wales. Wyn Roberts, especially during his long stint as a Welsh Office minister from 1979 to 1994, was especially important in that story.

Interestingly, however, Roberts viewed the devolution era with a rather critical eye. Commissioned to write a report on how the Conservatives could 'make devolution work better', his conclusions were sceptical of the role the National Assembly was playing in Welsh political life.[23] Of course, it was always possible to be a patriotic Welshman and not believe in the kind of devolution that Wales was granted, but the new generation of Conservatives heading up the party in the Assembly were 'disappointed by [the report's] tenor'. Editing a draft of it, David Melding scribbled exclamation marks of shock on it regularly, scratching out phrases that said the institution 'lacks maturity' and had a 'persistently

---

[21] Convery, *The Territorial*, p. 102.

[22] Interviews, Lord Bourne of Aberystwyth, 7 August 2014, and David Melding, 22 July 2014.

[23] 'Devolution in Wales: The Way Ahead: An Interim Report by Lord Roberts of Conwy' (private copy).

poor reputation in Welsh eyes'. At the end, Melding wrote that the report 'implies abolition' of the Assembly.[24] The document is fascinating, not least because it was authored by the man some credit with paving the way for devolution by bolstering a stronger sense of Welsh identity through education and broadcasting reform. Roberts's attitude reflected the conflicting ideas about Welsh politics, broadly defined, that ran throughout the party. But Bourne, who responded passionately to Roberts about the report, was 'certainly very unhappy... given the way that we have shaped the party in Wales over the last decade to embrace devolution'.[25]

If someone like Roberts could be cynical about the party's attitude to devolution, this was nothing, compared with some of the party's wider membership and supporters. When responding to Bourne's criticisms of his draft report, Roberts claimed to be speaking for these people, arguing that the Conservatives were in danger of becoming 'too similar' to parties like Labour and the Liberal Democrats and 'unrepresentative of our own Welsh Conservatives'.[26] Indeed, something that shines through in the evidence from the devolution era is that the party's core support base remained largely uninterested in the party's 'Welsh image', or sense of its own Welsh identity, much in the same way as they had in the decades after the war. Surveys in the 1960s, 1970s and 1980s had shown that the rank and file thought Welsh issues mattered, but that they should not to be prioritised.[27] In the 2000s, one activist wrote to the Conservative group in the National Assembly arguing that voters cared much more 'about declining real wages, entrenched unemployment... [whilst] our ideas are often abstract'.[28]

When it came to the party's compatibility with Wales, the Tories found themselves in a bind. A 2011 Populus Wales Benchmark poll

[24] WPA, GB0210 CONAGRP, 2/4 (Box 10), 3 of 3, Folder 3/3, Annotations to the Roberts Report.
[25] WPA, GB0210 CONAGRP, 2/4, Bourne to Roberts, 24 September 2008.
[26] WPA, GB0210 CONAGRP, 2/4, Roberts to Bourne, 24 September 2008.
[27] Andrew Edwards and Duncan Tanner, 'Defining or Dividing the Nation? Opinion Polls, Welsh Identity and Devolution, 1966–1979', *Contemporary Wales*, 18/1 (2006), 57.
[28] WPA, GB0210 CONAGRP, 2/4 (Box 8), 1 of 3.

found that only thirteen per cent of those sampled thought the Conservatives were 'a strong voice for Wales'. Analysing the poll in private, the party commented ruefully that this accounted for 'barely 2/3 of those who vote for us' and lamented how, despite decades of effort, 'the Party has made little, if any, progress in appearing more Welsh and less English'. An obvious conclusion to draw from this, of course, is that many who *do* continue to vote for the Tories in Wales do not especially care about the party's 'Welshness'. It is not as simple as dismissing many of those voters as 'English' – although some of them, of course, are. Trying to assume a more 'Welsh' identity, however, was never going to be straightforward. As early as 1957, a senior member of the Conservatives' team in the Wales Area Office argued that any attempts to combat nationalism by making devolutionary concessions could have the opposite effect of giving nationalists a better platform to espouse their vision.[29] This is undoubtedly a thought process that haunts some ordinary Conservatives today.

Those wanting a more 'devo-sceptic' or more robust rightwing Conservatism in Wales, however, have few answers to the question of whether they want Tories ever to be in government in Cardiff Bay. The electoral system in Wales means majority government is very difficult to achieve. For David Melding, the contemporary Conservative Party must try to place itself on 'the optimum centre-right' of Welsh politics, which is not the same as the centre-right of English or wider UK politics.[30] The way the party nearly got into power in 2007 was by convincing the parties to its left – the Liberal Democrats and Plaid Cymru – that it was a potentially suitable partner for a 'rainbow coalition'. It nearly achieved this under the leadership of the more 'centrist' Nick Bourne, who set out to 'detoxify' the party. Whilst many natural Conservatives hate the sentiment that their ideas were 'toxic' in

---

[29] Matthew Cragoe, 'Defending the Constitution: the Conservative Party and the Idea of Devolution, 1945–74', in Chris Williams and Andrew Edwards (eds), *The Art of the Possible: Politics and Governance in Modern British History, 1885–1997: Essays in Memory of Duncan Tanner* (Manchester: Manchester University Press, 2015), p. 172.

[30] Quoted in Convery, *The Territorial*, p. 121.

the first place, it is hard to see under what other strategy the party enters government in Wales, even if a significant vote for UKIP in the 2016 National Assembly elections demonstrated that there is a significant right-wing part of the Welsh electorate.[31] Perhaps many Tory-inclined supporters would prefer the party to be a robustly right-wing party that is permanently in opposition. That is not illogical, especially if those supporters care more about Westminster, although it is an odd position for a 'natural party of government' to take.[32] Whilst the party believes in Wales being very much part of the UK, its own chain of command between the leader of the group in Wales, the Secretary of State for Wales and the Prime Minister is still not clear, and the hopes of senior, pro-devolution Conservatives for a 'fully autonomous' Welsh Conservative Party have not come to pass.[33] Although the nature of such a management structure is unlikely to be worth many votes, it is yet another thing that speaks to the uncertainty the party exhibits in Wales.

At the 2019 general election and the 2021 Senedd election, much of this was revealed again. A (very English) prime minister, Boris Johnson, was able to energise the areas that tended to vote Conservative in Wales, deploying a clear (if simplistic) message about a big national policy – Britain's relationship with the European Union – and winning over the many in Wales who had voted 'Leave' in the referendum on that issue in 2016. The result was one of the party's best-ever performances. However, a firm attempt to bring out the Tory base in 2021 did not work in the way the party hoped it would, not least because those who think of themselves as staunch Conservatives remain sceptical of the drift in Welsh politics towards a more nationalistic and less British direction, and many express this scepticism by simply not turning out to vote. To take one example, at the 2010 general

---

[31] *https://www.bbc.co.uk/news/election/2016/wales/results.* Accessed 22 July 2019.

[32] See Melding, 'Refashioning', p. 132, and Sam Blaxland, 'Welsh Conservatives: Far From a Contradiction in Terms', *Planet Extra, https://www.planetmagazine.org.uk/planet-extra/welsh-conservatives-far-contradiction-term.* Accessed 15 April 2021.

[33] Melding, 'Refashioning', p. 34.

election, 382,730 people voted Conservative in Wales, but in the following year's Assembly election only 237,389 did. Similarly, those figures for the 2019 Westminster versus the 2021 Senedd elections were 557,234 and 289,802 respectively. Of course, many things explain the differences between these figures. Some people think differently about politics when it comes to Welsh affairs and might vote Conservative for Westminster and something else for Cardiff Bay. Political circumstances change dramatically in two years, and 'swing voters' change their minds. But it is also certain that a disproportionately high number of the Conservative Party's core vote simply do not turn out for Senedd elections, for reasons of apathy or because they think the Welsh Parliament is unimportant. Similarly, there is evidence that many Conservatives grassroots campaigners seemed more intent on campaigning to leave the European Union in 2016 than they were in campaigning for the Assembly elections of that year.[34]

One of the most prominent Welsh Tories of the devolution era, and the leader of the Conservative group in the Senedd at the time of the 2021 election, was Andrew R. T. Davies. He firmly represented a side of the party that this book has tried to push into the spotlight: anglicised, rural, identifying as both British and Welsh, and whose views on issues like Britain's membership of the European Union reveal that parts of the electorate are shot through with conservatism. However, Davies took over from another Davies – Paul – who was a different kind of Tory that we have also met in previous pages: bilingual, drawn from a background working in a bank, and more socially liberal. Despite people identifying themselves far less with a social class, the make-up not just of the Tory leadership in Wales, but of its candidates and its small group of prominent activists, remains firmly middle class. In many respects, the threads of continuity from the end of

---

[34] Roger Awan-Scully, 'Is Labour's dominance of Welsh politics under threat?', LSE blog, 29 April 2016, *https://blogs.lse.ac.uk/government/2016/04/29/is-labours-dominance-of-welsh-politics-under-threat/*. Accessed 22 May 2018.

the Second World War and the election of 2021 are striking: *plus ça change, plus c'est la même chose.*

And as the Conservative Party looks to its future in Wales, it is hard to see how it squares the difficult circle that is Welsh politics and the electorate there. It surely wants to remain wedded to its base of British-identifying and broadly socially conservative people, even if both groups are likely to decline in numbers. Any attempt to firm up core conservative messages might alienate some voters and certainly will not attract those from other more left-wing parties – although it might re-energise some apathetic Tories who fail to turn out at election times. On the other hand, any move to the left, or to adopting the language of nationalism, will be anathema to many Conservatives and might have a limited appeal to a left-of-centre voter, who will always choose one of the many parties on that end of the spectrum anyway. A firmly right wing party that was socially and culturally conservative but much more nationalistic may be surprisingly popular in Wales, but that space could not be occupied by the Conservative Party. With Labour still able to command the narrative and win votes, and with the Conservatives still labouring under a reputation as being incompatible with parts of the electorate, it is difficult to see how the Tories, long Wales's second party, will ever better the silver medal position. Whenever the story of the post-devolution party is written, its longer-term history in the twentieth century, and especially since 1945, will be key to understanding this. It will help explain why the party has been more successful than many think, but it will also demonstrate why any forward march by the Conservatives in Wales in the future is going to involve a near-impossible uphill struggle.

BIBLIOGRAPHY

ARCHIVES

Conservative Party Archive, Bodleian Library
Denbighshire Record Office
Flintshire Record Office
Glamorgan Archives
Gwent Archives
Julian Lewis personal archive
Pembrokeshire Record Office
Peter Temple-Morris personal archive
Richard Burton Archives, Swansea University
Salisbury Conservative Club, Swansea, private archive
Swansea Conservative Association private archive
Welsh Political Archive, National Library of Wales
West Glamorgan Archives

AUTOBIOGRAPHIES AND MEMOIRS

Clwyd, Ann, *Rebel With a Cause* (London: Biteback, 2017).
Crickhowell, Nicholas, *Wales, Westminster and Water* (Cardiff: University of Wales Press, 1999).
Dexter, Ted, *Ted Dexter Declares* (London: The Sportsmans Book Club, 1967).
Howe, Geoffrey, *Conflict of Loyalty* (London: Pan Books, 1995).
Lord Roberts of Conwy, *Right From the Start: The Memoirs of Sir Wyn Roberts* (Cardiff: University of Wales Press, 2006).
Morris-Jones, Sir Henry, *Doctor in the Whip's Room* (London: Robert Hale, 1955).
Rosser, David, *A Dragon in the House* (Llandysul: Gomer, 1987).
Temple-Morris, Peter, *Across The Floor: A Life in Dissenting Politics* (London: I. B. Tauris & Co., 2015).
Walker, Peter, *Staying Power: An Autobiography* (London: Bloomsbury, 1991).

HANSARD

Volume 611, 18 May 2016.

NEWSPAPERS

Aberdare Leader
Abergavenny Chronicle
Abergele Visitor
Daily Mail
Daily Telegraph
Denbigh Free Press
Financial Times
Flintshire County Herald
Herald of Wales
Independent
Liverpool Daily Post
Merthyr Express
North Wales Weekly News
Prospect Magazine
Rhyl Journal and Prestatyn Weekly
South Wales Argus
South Wales Echo
South Wales Evening News
South Wales Evening Post
Spectator
The Economist
The Guardian
The Times
Weekly Argus
West Wales Guardian
Western Mail
Western Telegraph

NOVELS

Kingsley Amis, *That Uncertain Feeling* ([1955] St Albans: Panther Books, 1975).

ORAL INTERVIEWS

Felix Aubel
Guto Bebb
Keith Best
Lord Bourne of Aberystwyth
Chris Butler
Charlotte Bennett

Nicholas Bennett
Philip Circus
Lord Crickhowell
David T. C. Davies MP
Jonathan Evans
Nigel Evans MP
Keith Flynn
Hywel Francis
Lord Garel-Jones
Revel Guest
Robert Harvey
Lord Heseltine
Lord Howard of Lympne
Lord Howe of Aberavon
Richard Howells
Lord Hunt of Wirral
David Jones MP
Lyndon Jones
Sir Julian Lewis MP
Trefor Llewellyn
Sir Norman Lloyd-Edwards
David Melding
Lord Morgan of Aberdyfi
Nicholas O'Shaughnessy
Sir Idris Pearce
Peter Price
Sir John Redwood MP
Rod Richards
Mark Robinson
Lord Rowlands of Merthyr Tydfil and Rhymney
Sir Desmond Swayne MP
Lord Temple-Morris
Paul Valerio
Sir Donald Walters
Paul Warrick
John Winterson-Richards

British Library Sound and Moving Image archive

TELEVISION

'Conversations Lord Kinnock', BBC Parliament, BBC iPlayer
Tudur's TV Flashback, BBC iPlayer
Huw Edwards, *The Story of Wales*, BBC iPlayer

SECONDARY LITERATURE

Abrams, Lynn, *Oral History Theory* (Abingdon: Routledge, 2010).

Adamson, David, 'The New Working Class and Political Change in Wales', *Contemporary Wales*, 2 (1988), 7–28.

Addison, Paul, 'Consensus Revisited', *Twentieth Century British History*, 4/1 (1993), 91–4.

Addison, Paul, 'Sixtysomethings', *London Review of Books*, 17/9 (1995), 17–18.

Aubel, Felix, 'The Conservatives in Wales, 1880–1935', in Martin Francis and Ina Zweiniger-Bargielowska (eds), *The Conservatives and British Society, 1880–1990* (Cardiff: University of Wales Press, 1996), pp. 96–110

Aughey, Arthur, *The Conservative Party and the Nation: Union, England and Europe* (Manchester: Manchester University Press, 2018).

Awan-Scully, Roger, 'Is Labour's dominance of Welsh politics under threat?', LSE blog, 29 April 2016.

Bale, Tim, *The Conservatives Since 1945: The Drivers of Party Change* (Oxford: Oxford University Press, 2016).

Bale, Tim, Paul Webb and Monica Poletti, *Footsoldiers: Political Party Membership in the 21st Century* (London: Routledge, 2019).

Ball, Stuart, 'Local Conservatism and the Evolution of the Party Organisation', in Anthony Seldon and Stuart Ball (eds), *Conservative Century: The Conservative Party Since 1900* (Oxford: Oxford University Press, 1994), pp. 261–311.

Ball, Stuart, 'The National and Regional Party Structure', in Anthony Seldon and Stuart Ball (eds), *Conservative Century: The Conservative Party Since 1900* (Oxford: Oxford University Press, 1994), pp. 169–220.

Ball, Stuart, *The Conservative Party and British Politics, 1902–1951* (London: Longman, 1995).

Ball, Stuart, 'National Politics and Local History: The Regional and Local Archives of the Conservative Party, 1867–1945', *Archives*, 22/94 (1996), 27–59.

Ball, Stuart, *The Conservative Party Since 1945* (Manchester: Manchester University Press, 1998).

Ball, Stuart, *Portrait of a Party: The Conservative Party in Britain, 1918–1945* (Oxford: Oxford University Press, 2013).

Ball, Stuart, Andrew Thorpe and Matthew Worley, 'Elections, Leaflets and Whist Drives: Constituency Party Membership in Britain Between the Wars', in Matthew Worley (ed.), *Labour's Grass Roots: Essays on the Activities of Local Labour Parties and Members, 1918–1945* (Aldershot: Ashgate, 2005), pp. 7–32.

Balsom, Denis, 'The Three-Wales Model', in John Osmond (ed.), *The National Question Again: Welsh Political Identity in the 1980s* (Llandysul: Gomer Press, 1985), pp. 1–17.

Barnes, John and Richard Cockett, 'The Making of Party Policy', in Anthony Seldon and Stuart Ball (eds), *Conservative Century: The Conservative Party Since 1900* (Oxford: Oxford University Press, 1994), pp. 347–82.

Barry, Norman, 'New Right', in Kevin Hickson (ed.), *The Political Thought of the Conservative Party Since 1945* (Basingstoke: Palgrave Macmillan, 2005), pp. 28–50.

Beddoe, Deidre, 'Women and Politics in Twentieth Century Wales', *National Library of Wales Journal*, 33/3 (2004), 333–47.

Bell, Colin, *Middle Class Families: Social and Geographical Mobility* (London: Routledge and Kegan Paul, 1968).

Benbough-Jackson, Michael, 'Diagnosing the Blue Dragon Blues: The Dilemma of the Welsh Conservatives', *Planet*, 150 (2001–2), 62–9.

Berthezène Clarisse and Julie V. Gottlieb, 'Introduction', in Clarisse Berthezène and Julie V. Gottlieb (eds), *Rethinking Right-wing Women: Gender and the Conservative Party, 1880s to the Present* (Manchester: Manchester University Press, 2018), pp. 1–10.

Berthezène, Clarisse and Jean-Christian Vinel (eds), *Postwar Conservatism, A Transnational Investigation: Britain, France, and the United States, 1930–1990* (London: Palgrave Macmillan, 2017).

Bingham, Adrian, 'Conservatism, Gender and the Politics of Everyday Life, 1950s–1980s', in Clarisse Berthezène and Julie V. Gottlieb (eds), *Rethinking Right-wing Women: Gender and the Conservative Party, 1880s to the Present* (Manchester: Manchester University Press, 2018), pp. 156–74.

Birch, Nigel, *The Conservative Party* (London: Collins, 1949).

Black, Lawrence, 'The Lost World of Young Conservatism', *The Historical Journal*, 51/4 (2008), 991–1024.

Black, Lawrence, *Redefining British Politics: Culture, Consumerism and Participation, 1945–1970* (Basingstoke: Palgrave Macmillan, 2010).

Black, Lawrence, 'Tories and Hunters: Swinton College and the Landscape of Modern Conservatism', *History Workshop Journal*, 77/1 (2014), 187–214.

Blake, Robert, *The Conservative Party from Peel to Major* (London: Heinemann, 1997).

Blaxland, Sam, 'The Curious Case of Ted Dexter and Cardiff South East', *Conservative History Journal*, 2/4 (2015), 8–11.

Blaxland, Sam, 'Denbigh Constituency's First and Final Conservative MP: a study of Geraint Morgan', *Denbighshire Historical Society Transactions*, 65 (2017), 87–100.

Blaxland, Sam, 'Women in the Organisation of the Conservative Party in Wales, 1945–1979', *Women's History Review*, 28/2 (2019), 236–56.

Blaxland, Sam, *Swansea University: Campus and Community in a Post-war World, 1945–2020* (Cardiff: 2020).

Blaxland, Sam, 'Thatcherism and Wales: Impacts and Legacies', in Antony Mullen, Stephen Farrall and David Jeffery (eds), *Thatcherism in the 21st Century: The Social and Cultural Legacy* (Cham: Palgrave Macmillan, 2020), pp. 139–55.

Blaxland, Sam, 'Welsh Women MPs: Exploring Their Absence', in special edition of *Open Library of the Humanities*: '"An Unconventional MP": Nancy Astor, public women and gendered political culture', *Open Library of the Humanities*, 6/2 (2020), pp. 1–35.

Blaxland, Sam, 'Lord Crickhowell', *Oxford Dictionary of National Biography*, 10 March 2022.

Brooke, Stephen, 'Labour and the "Nation" after 1945', in Jon Lawrence and Miles Taylor (eds), *Party, State and Society: Electoral Behaviour in Britain Since 1820* (Aldershot: Scolar Press, 1997), pp. 153–75.

Butler, Chris, 'The Conservative Party in Wales: Remoulding a Radical Tradition', in John Osmond (ed.), *The National Question Again: Welsh Political Identity in the 1980s* (Llandysul: Gomer Press, 1985), pp. 155–66.

Butler, D. E. (ed.), *The British General Election of 1951* (London: Macmillan and Co. Ltd, 1952).

Butler, D. E. and Anthony King (eds), *The British General Election of 1966* (London: Macmillan, 1966).

Butler, D. E. and Richard Rose, *The British General Election of 1959* (London: Macmillan, 1960).

Butler, David and Dennis Kavanagh, *The British General Election of February 1974* (London: Macmillan, 1974).

Butler, David and Dennis Kavanagh, *The British General Election of 1979* (London: Macmillan, 1980).

Butler, David and Dennis Kavanagh, *The British General Election of 1987* (Basingstoke: Macmillan, 1987).

Butler, David and Dennis Kavanagh, *The British General Election of 1992* (London: Macmillan, 1992).

Butler, David and Dennis Kavanagh, *The British General Election of 1997* (London: Macmillan, 1997).

Butler, David and Michael Pinto-Duschinsky, 'The Conservative Elite, 1918–1978: Does Unrepresentativeness Matter?', in Zig Layton-Henry (ed.), *Conservative Party Politics* (London: Macmillan, 1980), pp. 186–209.

Butler, David and Donald Stokes, *Political Change in Britain: The Evolution of Electoral Choice* ([1969] London: Macmillan Press, 1974).

Butler, Lord (ed.), *The Conservatives: A History From Their Origins to 1965* (London: George Allen & Unwin, 1977).

Campbell, Beatrix, *The Iron Ladies: Why Do Women Vote Tory?* (London: Virago, 1987).

Cannadine, David, *Lords and Landlords: The Aristocracy and the Towns, 1774–1967* (Leicester: Leicester University Press, 1980).

Cannadine, David, *Aspects of Aristocracy: Grandeur and Decline in Modern Britain* (London: Yale University Press, 1994).

Cannadine, David, *The Decline and Fall of the British Aristocracy* ([1990] London: Papermac, 1996).

Caunce, Stephen, *Oral History and the Local Historian* (London: Longman, 1994).

Charmley, Gerard, 'The House of Dynevor and Conservative Politics, 1910–1939', *The Conservative Party History Journal*, 1/9 (2009), 29–32.

Charmley, Gerald, 'Parliamentary Representation', in Chris Williams and Andy Croll (eds), *The Gwent County History, Volume 5: The Twentieth Century* (Cardiff: University of Wales Press, 2013), pp. 301–19.

Charmley, John, *A History of Conservative Politics 1990–1996* (London: Macmillan, 1996).

Childs, David, *Britain Since 1945: A Political History* ([1979] London: Routledge,1993).

Cockett, Richard, 'The Party, Publicity and the Media', in Anthony Seldon and Stuart Ball (eds), *Conservative Century: The Conservative Party Since 1900* (Oxford: Oxford University Press, 1994), pp. 547–77.

Cohen, Gidon and Lewis Mates, 'Grassroots Conservatism in Post-War Britain: A View From the Bottom Up', *History*, 98/330 (2013), 202–25.

Convery, Alan, *The Territorial Conservative Party: Devolution and Party Change in Scotland and Wales* (Manchester: Manchester University Press, 2015).

Corthorn, Paul, 'Enoch Powell, Ulster Unionism, and the British Nation', *Journal of British Studies*, 51/4 (2012), pp. 967–97.

Cowling, Maurice (ed.), *Conservative Essays* (London: Cassell, 1978).

Cragoe, Matthew, *An Anglican Aristocracy: The Moral Economy of the Landed Estate in Carmarthenshire, 1832–1895* (Oxford: Clarendon Press, 1996).

Cragoe, Matthew, *Politics, Culture and National Identity in Wales, 1832–1886* (Oxford: Oxford University Press, 2004).

Cragoe, Matthew, 'Conservatives, "Englishness" and "Civic Nationalism" Between the Wars', in Duncan Tanner, Chris Williams, W. P. Griffith and Andrew Edwards (eds), *Debating Nationhood and Governance in Britain, 1885–1939: Perspectives From the Four Nations* (Manchester: Manchester University Press, 2006), pp. 192–210.

Cragoe, Matthew, '"We Like Local Patriotism": The Conservative Party and the Discourse of Decentralisation, 1947–51', *English Historical Review*, 122/498 (2007), 965–85.

Cragoe, Matthew, 'Defending the Constitution: the Conservative Party and the Idea of Devolution, 1945–74', in Chris Williams and Andrew Edwards (eds), *The Art of the Possible: Politics and Governance in Modern British History, 1885–1997: Essays in Memory of Duncan Tanner* (Manchester: Manchester University Press, 2015), pp. 162–87.

Craig, David M., '"High politics" and the "New Political History"', *The Historical Journal*, 53/2 (2010), 453–75.

Crick, Michael, *Michael Heseltine: A Biography* (London: Penguin, 1997).

Crickhowell, Lord, 'The Conservative Party and Wales', *The National Library of Wales Journal*, 34/1 (2006), 49–99.

Criddle, Brian, 'Members of Parliament', in Anthony Seldon and Stuart Ball (eds), *Conservative Century: The Conservative Party Since 1900* (Oxford: Oxford University Press, 1994), pp. 145–67.

Croll, Andy, '"People's Remembrancers" in a Post-Modern Age: Contemplating the Non-crisis of Welsh Labour History', *Llafur*, 8/1 (2000), 5–17.

Crowcroft, Robert, 'Maurice Cowling and the Writing of British Political History', *Contemporary British History*, 22/2 (2008), 279–86.

Crowson, N. J. 'Conservative Party Activists and Immigration Policy from the Late 1940s to the Mid-1970s', in Stuart Ball and Ian Holliday (eds), *Mass Conservatism: The Conservatives and the Public Since the 1880s* (London: Frank Cass, 2002), pp. 163–82.

Cunningham, Michael, 'Public Policy and Normative Language: Utility, Community and Nation in the Debate over the Construction of Tryweryn Reservoir', *Parliamentary Affairs*, 60/4 (2007), 625–36.

Davies, Janet, *The Welsh Language* (Cardiff: University of Wales Press, 1999).

Davies, John, 'Plaid Cymru in Transition', in John Osmond (ed.), *The National Question Again: Welsh Political Identity in the 1980s* (Llandysul: Gomer Press, 1985), pp. 124–54.

Day, Graham, Angela Drakakis-Smith and Howard H. Davis, 'Being English in North Wales: Immigration and the Immigrant Experience', *Nationalism and Ethnic Politics*, 12/3–4 (2006), 577–98.

Day, Graham, Angela Drakakis-Smith and Howard H. Davis, 'Migrating to North Wales: the "English" Experience', *Contemporary Wales*, 21/1 (2008), 101–29.

Deacon, Russell, *The Governance of Wales: The Welsh Office and the Policy Process, 1964–1999* (Cardiff: Welsh Academic Press, 2002).

Deacon, Russell, *The Welsh Liberals: The History of the Liberal and Liberal Democrat Parties in Wales* (Cardiff: Welsh Academic Press, 2014).

Denver, David, *Elections and Voters in Britain* (Basingstoke: Palgrave Macmillan, 2007).

Dorey, Peter, 'Industrial Relations and "Human Relations": Conservatism and Trade Unionism, 1945–1964', in Stuart Ball and Ian Holliday (eds), *Mass Conservatism: The Conservatives and the Public Since the 1880s* (London: Frank Cass, 2002), pp. 139–62.

Edwards, Andrew, *Labour's Crisis: Plaid Cymru, the Conservatives, and the Decline of the Labour Party in North-West Wales, 1960–74* (Cardiff: University of Wales Press, 2011).

Edwards, Andrew, Duncan Tanner and Patrick Carlin, 'The Conservative Governments and the Development of Welsh Language Policy in the 1980s and 1990s', *The Historical Journal*, 54/2 (2011), 529–51.

Edwards, Andrew and Duncan Tanner, 'Defining or Dividing the Nation? Opinion Polls, Welsh Identity and Devolution, 1966–1979', *Contemporary Wales*, 18/1 (2006), 55–71.

Edwards, H. W. J., *The Good Patch* (London, 1938).

Edwards, H. W. J., 'A tory in Wales', *Wales*, 32 (1958), 24–30.

Ellis, Catherine, 'No Hammock for the Idle: The Conservative Party, "Youth" and the Welfare State in the 1960s', *Twentieth Century British History*, 16/4 (2015), 441–70.

Evans, John Gilbert, *Devolution in Wales: Claims and Responses, 1937–1979* (Cardiff: University of Wales Press, 2006).

Evans, Rhys, *Gwynfor Evans: A Portrait of a Patriot* (Tal-y-bont: Y Lolfa, 2008).

Fielding, Steven, 'The Labour Party and the Recruitment of the Young, 1945–1970', in Quagliariello, Gaetano (ed.), *La Formazione della classe politica in Europa: 1945–1956* (Manduria: P. Lacaita, 2000), pp. 579–84.

Fielding, Steven, 'The "Penny Farthing" Machine Revisited: Labour Party Members and Participation in the 1950s and 1960s', in Chris Pierson and Simon Tormey (eds), *Politics at the Edge: The PSA Yearbook 1999* (Basingstoke: Macmillan, 2000), pp. 172–85.

Fielding, Steven, 'Activists Against "Affluence": Labour Party Culture during the "Golden Age" circa 1950–1970', *Journal of British Studies*, 40/2 (2001), 241–67.

Finlay, Richard, 'Thatcherism, Unionism and Nationalism: a Comparative Study of Scotland and Wales', in Ben Jackson and Robert Saunders (eds), *Making Thatcher's Britain* (Cambridge: Cambridge University Press, 2012), pp. 165–79.

Foulkes, D., J. Barry Jones and R. A. Wilford (eds), *The Welsh Veto: The Wales Act 1978 and the Referendum* (Cardiff: University of Wales Press, 1983).

Francis, Hywel, 'Intellectual Property, First Time Round: The Re-Invention of the South Wales Miners' Library', *Llafur*, 9/1 (2004), 27–31.

Francis, Hywel and David Smith, *The Fed: A History of the South Wales Miners in the Twentieth Century* (London: Lawrence and Wishart, 1980).

Francis, Hywel and Siân Williams, *Do Miners Read Dickens?: Origins and Progress of the South Wales Miners' Library, 1973–2013* (Cardigan: Parthian, 2013).

Francis, Matthew, 'Searching for Constructive Conservatism: A Short History of the Property-owning Democracy', *Conservative History Journal*, 2/3 (2014), 10–17.

Frankenberg, Ronald, *Village on the Border: A Social Study of Religion, Politics and Football in a North Wales Community* (London: Cohen and West, 1957).

Gooberman, Leon, 'Recession and Recovery: the Welsh Office and Job Creation in the 1980s', *Llafur*, 11/3 (2014), 115–27.

Gooberman, Leon, *From Depression to Devolution: Economy and Government in Wales, 1934–2006* (Cardiff: University of Wales Press, 2017).

Gooberman, Leon, '"A Very Modern Kind of English Loneliness": John Redwood, the Welsh Office and Devolution', *Welsh History Review*, 29/4 (2019), 624–51.

Green, E. H. H., 'The Conservative Party, the State and the Electorate, 1945–64', in Jon Lawrence and Miles Taylor (eds), *Party, State and Society: Electoral Behaviour in Britain since 1820* (Aldershot: Scolar Press, 1997), pp. 176–200.

Green, E. H. H., *Ideologies of Conservatism: Conservative Political Ideas in the Twentieth Century* (Oxford: Oxford University Press, 2002).

Griffiths, Dylan, 'The Political Consequences of Migration into Wales', *Contemporary Wales*, 5 (1992), 65–80.

Griffiths, Dylan, *Thatcherism and Territorial Politics: A Welsh Case Study* (Aldershot: Avebury, 1996).

Harries, F. J., *A History of Conservatism in the Rhondda* (Pontypridd: Glamorgan County Times, 1912).

Harris, Trevor and Monia O'Brien Castro (ed.), *Preserving the Sixties: Britain and the 'Decade of Protest'* (Basingstoke: Palgrave Macmillan, 2014).

Harrison, Brian, *Seeking a Role: The United Kingdom, 1951–1970* (Oxford: Oxford University Press, 2009).

Heffer, Simon, *Like the Roman: The Life of Enoch Powell* (London: Phoenix Giant, 1998).

Heffer, Simon, 'Traditional Toryism', in Kevin Hickson (ed.), *The Political Thought of the Conservative Party Since 1945* (Basingstoke: Palgrave Macmillan, 2005), pp. 197–201.

Hennessy, Peter, *Having It So Good: Britain in the Fifties* (London: Penguin, 2006).

Hinton, James, 'Conservative Women and Voluntary Social Service, 1938–1951', in Stuart Ball and Ian Holliday (eds), *Mass Conservatism: The Conservatives and the Public Since the 1880s* (London: Frank Cass, 2002), pp. 100–19.

Hopkin, Deian, 'Llafur: Labour History Society and People's Remembrancer, 1970–2009', *Labour History Review*, 75/Supplement 1 (2010), 129–46.

James, Arnold J. and John E. Thomas, *Wales at Westminster: A History of the Parliamentary Representation of Wales 1800–1979* (Llandysul: Gomer Press, 1981).

Jarvis, David, 'The Conservative Party's Recruitment of Youth', in Gaetano Quagliariello (ed.), *La Formazione della classe politica in Europa: 1945–1956* (Manduria: P. Lacaita, 2000).

Jeffery, David, 'The Strange Death of Tory Liverpool: Conservative Electoral Decline in Liverpool, 1945–1996', *British Politics*, 12/3 (2017), 386–407.

Jeffery, David, *Whatever Happened to Tory Liverpool? Success, Decline and Irrelevance Since 1945* (Liverpool: Liverpool University Press, 2023).

Jenkins, Geraint H., *A Concise History of Wales* (Cambridge: Cambridge University Press, 2007).

Jenkins, Geraint H. and Mari A. Williams (eds), *'Let's do our best for the ancient tongue': The Welsh Language in the Twentieth Century* (Cardiff: University of Wales Press, 2015).

Jennings, Paul, *The Local: A History of the English Pub* (Stroud: Tempus, 2007).
John, Angela V., 'Lifers: Modern Welsh History and the Writing of Biography', *Welsh History Review*, 25/2 (2010), 251–70.
Johnes, Martin, 'For Class and Nation: Dominant Trends in the Historiography of Twentieth-Century Wales', *History Compass*, 8/11 (2010), 1257–74.
Johnes, Martin, 'The Heroes of Recent Welsh Political History', in H. V. Bowen (ed.), *A New History of Wales: Heroes and Villains in Welsh History* (Llandysul: Gomer Press, 2012), pp. 183–90.
Johnes, Martin, 'The Making and Development of the Capital City of Wales', *Contemporary British History*, 26/4 (2012), 509–28.
Johnes, Martin, *Wales Since 1939* (Manchester: Manchester University Press, 2012).
Johnes, Martin, 'What did Thatcher ever do for Wales?', in H. V. Bowen (ed.), *A New History of Wales: Myths and Realities in Welsh History* (Llandysul: Gomer Press, 2011).
Johnes, Martin, *Wales: England's Colony? The Conquest, Assimilation and Re-creation of Wales* (Cardigan: Parthian, 2019).
Johnson, Janet, 'Did Organisation Really Matter? Party Organisation and Conservative Electoral Recovery, 1945–1959', *Twentieth Century British History*, 14/4 (2003), 391–412.
Johnson, Janet, 'Conservative Party Mutual Aid: Myth or Reality?', *Contemporary British History*, 22/1 (2008), 23–41.
Jones, Aled, *Press, Politics and Society: A History of Journalism in Wales* (Cardiff: University of Wales Press, 1993).
Jones, Douglas, *The Communist Party of Great Britain and the National Question in Wales, 1920–1991* (Cardiff: University of Wales Press, 2017).
Jones, Gareth Elwyn, *Modern Wales: A Concise History* ([1984] Cambridge: Cambridge University Press, 1994).
Jones, J. Graham, 'The Parliament for Wales Campaign, 1950–1956', *Welsh History Review*, 16/2 (1992), 207–36.
Jones, J. Graham, 'Major Gwilym Lloyd-George and the Pembrokeshire Election of 1950', *Journal of the Pembrokeshire Historical Society*, 11 (2002), 100–20.
Jones, R. Merfyn, 'Beyond Identity? The Reconstruction of the Welsh', *Journal of British Studies*, 31/4 (1992), 330–57.
Jones, R. Merfyn and Ioan Rhys Jones, 'Labour and the Nation', in Duncan Tanner, Chris Williams and Deian Hopkin (eds), *The Labour Party in Wales, 1900–2000* (Cardiff: University of Wales Press, 2000), pp. 241–63.
Joyce, Patrick (ed.), *Class* (Oxford: Oxford University Press, 1995).
Kavanagh, Dennis, 'The Postwar Consensus', *Twentieth Century British History*, 3/2 (1992), 175–90.

Kellas, James, 'The Party in Scotland', in Anthony Seldon and Stuart Ball (eds), *Conservative Century: The Conservative Party Since 1900* (Oxford: Oxford University Press, 1994), pp. 671–93.

Kendrick, Stephen and David McCrone, 'Politics in a Cold Climate: The Conservative Decline in Scotland', *Political Studies*, 37/4 (1989), 589–603.

Kinnock, Neil, 'Preface' to Duncan Tanner, Chris Williams and Deian Hopkin (eds), *The Labour Party in Wales, 1900–2000* (Cardiff: University of Wales Press, 2000), pp. ix–x.

Kowol, Kit, 'Renaissance on the Right? New Directions in the History of the Post-War Conservative Party', *Twentieth Century British History*, 27/2 (2016), 290–304.

Larner, Jac M., Richard Wyn Jones, Ed Gareth Poole, Paula Surridge and Daniel Wincott, 'Incumbency and Identity: The 2021 Senedd Election', *Parliamentary Affairs*, 10 May 2022, 1–22.

Lawrence, Jon, *Speaking For the People: Party, Language and Popular Politics in England, 1867–1914* (Cambridge: Cambridge University Press, 1998).

Lawrence, Jon, *Electing Our Masters: The Hustings in British Politics from Hogarth to Blair* (Oxford: Oxford University Press, 2009).

Lawrence, Jon and Miles Taylor, 'Introduction', in Jon Lawrence and Miles Taylor (eds), *Party, State and Society: Electoral Behaviour in Britain since 1820* (Aldershot: Scolar Press, 1997), pp. 1–26.

Lawrence, Jon and Florence Sutcliffe-Braithwaite, 'Margaret Thatcher and the Decline of Class Politics', in Ben Jackson and Robert Saunders (eds), *Making Thatcher's Britain* (Cambridge: Cambridge University Press, 2012), pp. 132–47.

Layton-Henry, Zig, 'The Young Conservatives, 1945–1970', *Journal of Contemporary History*, 8/2 (1973), 143–56.

Layton-Henry, Zig, 'Constituency Autonomy in the Conservative Party', *Parliamentary Affairs*, 29/4 (1976), 396–403.

Leeworthy, Daryl, *Labour Country: Political Radicalism and Social Democracy in South Wales, 1831–1985* (Cardigan: Parthian, 2018).

Lovenduski, Joni, Pippa Norris and Catriona Burness, 'The Party and Women', in Anthony Seldon and Stuart Ball (eds), *Conservative Century: The Conservative Party Since 1900* (Oxford: Oxford University Press, 1994), pp. 611–35.

Lucas, Jean M., *The Wandsworth Story* (London: WTCA, 1990).

Lucas, Jean M. (ed.), *Between the Thin Blues Lines: The Agent's View of Politics* (Canada: Trafford, 2008).

Lynch, Philip, *The Politics of Nationhood: Sovereignty, Britishness and Conservative Politics* (Basingstoke: Macmillan, 1999).

Macdonald, Catriona, 'Following the Procession: Scottish Labour, 1918–45', in Matthew Worley (ed.), *Labour's Grass Roots: Essays on the Activities of Local Labour Parties and Members, 1918–1945* (Aldershot: Ashgate, 2005), pp. 33–53.

Madgwick, P. J., Non Griffiths and Valerie Walker, *The Politics of Rural Wales: A Study of Cardiganshire* (London: Hutchinson and Co, 1973).
Maguire, G. E., *Conservative Women: A History of Women and the Conservative Party, 1874–1997* (Basingstoke: Macmillan, 1998).
Mandler, Peter, *The English National Character: The History of an Idea from Edmund Burke to Tony Blair* (Bury St Edmunds: St Edmundsbury Press, 2006).
McAllister, Laura, *Plaid Cymru: The Emergence of a Political Party* (Bridgend: Seren 2001).
McCallum, R. B. and Alison Readman, *The British General Election of 1945* (Oxford University Press: London, 1947).
McCarthy, Helen, 'Parties, Voluntary Associations and Democratic Politics in Interwar Britain', *The Historical Journal*, 50/4 (2007), 891–912.
McConnel, James, '"Sympathy Without Relief is Rather like Mustard Without Beef": Devolution, Plaid Cymru, and the Campaign for a Secretary of State for Wales, 1937–1938', *Welsh History Review*, 22/3 (2005), 535–57.
McIlwaine, Jeremy, 'The Party Archivist', *Conservative History Journal*, 2/2 (2013), 48–9.
McKenzie, Robert and Allan Silver, *Angles in Marble: Working Class Conservatives in Urban England* (London: Heinemann, 1968).
McKibbin, Ross, 'Class and Conventional Wisdom: the Conservative Party and the "Public" in Inter-war Britain', in R. McKibbin, *The Ideologies of Class* (Oxford: Clarendon, 1990), pp. 259–93.
McLean, Iain, *Rational Choice and British politics: An Analysis of Rhetoric and Manipulation from Peel to Blair* (Oxford: Oxford University Press, 2001).
Melding, David, 'Refashioning Welsh Conservatism – a Lesson for Scotland', in David Torrance (ed.), *Whatever Happened to Tory Scotland?* (Edinburgh: Edinburgh University Press, 2012), pp. 127–137.
Miskell, Louise (ed.), *New Perspectives on Welsh Industrial History* (Cardiff: University of Wales Press 2019).
Mitchell, James, *Conservatives and the Union: A Study of Conservative Party Attitudes to Scotland* (Edinburgh: Edinburgh University Press, 1990).
Moore, Charles, 'The Authorized Biographer', *Conservative History Journal*, 2/2 (2013), 42–3.
Moore, Charles, *Margaret Thatcher, The Authorized Biography, Volume Two: Everything She Wants* (London: Penguin, 2016).
Morgan, Kenneth O., *Wales in British Politics, 1868–1922* (Cardiff: University of Wales Press, 1963).
Morgan, Kenneth O., *Rebirth of a Nation: Wales 1880–1980* (Oxford: Oxford University Press, 1982).
Morgan, Kenneth O., *The People's Peace: British History, 1945–1990* (Oxford: Oxford University Press, 1990).
Morgan, Kenneth O., *Modern Wales: Politics, Places and People* (Cardiff: University of Wales Press, 1995).

Morgan, Kenneth O., *Callaghan: A Life* (Oxford: Oxford University Press, 1997).
Morgan, Kenneth O., 'Power and Glory: War and Reconstruction, 1939–1951', in Duncan Tanner, Chris Williams and Deian Hopkin (eds), *The Labour Party in Wales* (Cardiff: University of Wales Press, 2000), pp. 166–88.
Morgan, Kenneth O., 'Hughes, Cledwyn, Baron Cledwyn of Penrhos', *Oxford Dictionary of National Biography*, 8 January 2009.
Morgan, Kenneth O., *Revolution to Devolution: Reflections on Welsh Democracy* (Cardiff: University of Wales Press, 2014).
Morgan, Kenneth O. and Peter Stead, 'Rhondda West', in David Butler and Anthony King (eds), *The British General Election of 1966* (London: Macmillan, 1966), pp. 245–9.
Morris, James, 'Welshness in Wales', *Wales*, 32 (1958), 13–23.
Morris, Rupert, *Tories: From Village Hall to Westminster: A Political Sketch* (Edinburgh: Mainstream, 1991).
Nicholas, H. G., *The British General Election of 1950* (London: Macmillan, 1951).
Nordlinger, Eric A., *The Working-Class Tories: Authority, Deference and Stable Democracy* (London: Macgibbon and Kee, 1967).
Norris, Pippa and Joni Lovenduski, 'Gender and Party Politics in Britain', in Pippa Norris and Joni Lovenduski (eds), *Gender and Party Politics* (London: Sage Publications, 1993).
Norton, Philip (ed.), *The Conservative Party* (Hertfordshire: Prentice Hall, 1996).
O'Leary, Paul, 'Order! Order? The Lives of George Thomas, Viscount Tonypandy', in H. V. Bowen (ed.), *A New History of Wales: Heroes and Villains in Welsh History* (Llandysul: Gomer Press, 2012), pp. 176–82.
O'Sullivan, Noël, *Conservatism* (London: Dent, 1976).
Osmond, John, *Police Conspiracy?* (Tal-y-bont: Y Lolfa, 1984).
Pattie, Charles and Ron Johnston, 'The Conservative Party and the Electorate', in Steve Ludlam and Martin J. Smith (eds), *Contemporary British Conservatism* (London: Macmillan, 1996), pp. 37–62.
Pattie, Charles and Ron Johnston, 'The Conservatives' Grassroots "Revival"', *The Political Quarterly*, 80, 2 (2009), 193–203.
Pemberton, Hugh and Mark Wickham-Jones, 'Labour's Lost Grassroots: the Rise and Fall of Party Membership', *British Politics*, 8/2 (2013), 241–67.
Petrie, Malcolm, 'Anti-Socialism, Liberalism and Individualism: Rethinking the Realignment of Scottish Politics, 1945–1971', *Transactions of the Royal Historical Society*, 28 (2018), 197–207.
Phillips, Rob, 'Conservatives in the Welsh Political Archive at the National Library of Wales', *Conservative History Journal*, 2/6 (2018), 56–7.
Pinto-Duschinsky, Michael, 'Bread and Circuses? The Conservatives in Office 1951–1964', in Vernon Bogdanor and Robert Skidelsky (eds), *The Age of Affluence 1951–1964* (London: Macmillan, 1970), pp. 55–77.

Pugh, Martin, *The Tories and the People, 1880–1935* (Oxford: Blackwell, 1985).

Pugh, Martin, 'Popular Conservatism in Britain: Continuity and Change, 1880–1987', *Journal of British Studies*, 27/3 (1988), 254–82.

Ramsden, John, *The Age of Balfour and Baldwin, 1902–1940* (London: Longman, 1978).

Ramsden, John, '"A Party for Owners or a Party For Earners?" How Far Did the British Conservative Party Really Change After 1945?', *Transactions of the Royal Historical Society*, 37 (1987), 49–63.

Ramsden, John, *The Age of Churchill and Eden, 1940–1957* (London: Longman, 1995).

Ramsden, John, *The Winds of Change: Macmillan to Heath, 1957–1975* (Essex: Longman, 1996).

Ramsden, John, *An Appetite for Power: A History of the Conservative Party since 1830* (London: HarperCollins, 1998).

Randall, Nick, 'No Friends in the North? The Conservative Party in Northern England', *The Political Quarterly*, 80/2 (2009), 184–92.

Rees, Ivor Thomas, *Welsh Hustings: 1885–2004* (Llandybie: Dinefwr Press, 2005).

Robinson, Emily, 'The Authority of Feeling in Mid-twentieth-Century English Conservatism', *The Historical Journal*, 63/5 (2020), 1303–24.

Rosser, Colin and Christopher Harris, *The Family and Social Change: A Study of Family and Kinship in a South Wales Town* (London: Routledge and Kegan Paul, 1965).

Rush, Michael, *The Selection of Parliamentary Candidates* (London: Thomas Nelson and Sons, 1969).

Saleh, Taym, 'The Decline of the Scottish Conservatives in North-East Scotland, 1965–79: A Regional Perspective', *Parliamentary History*, 36/2 (2017), 218–42.

Samuel, Raphael, Barbara Bloomfield and Guy Boanas (eds), *The Enemy Within: Pit Villages and the Miners' Strike of 1984–1985* (London: Routledge and Kegan Paul, 1986).

Sandbrook, Dominic, *White Heat: A History of Britain in the Swinging Sixties* (London: Little, Brown, 2006).

Sandbrook, Dominic, *State of Emergency: The Way We Were: Britain, 1970–1974* (London: Penguin, 2011).

Sandbrook, Dominic, *Never Had it so Good: A History of Britain from Suez to the Beatles* (London: Abacus, 2015).

Särlvik, Bo and Ivor Crewe, *Decade of Dealignment: The Conservative Victory of 1979 and Electoral Trends in the 1970s* (Cambridge: Cambridge University Press, 1983).

Saunders, Robert, *Yes to Europe!: The 1975 Referendum and Seventies Britain* (Cambridge: Cambridge University Press, 2018).

Schofield, Camilla, 'Enoch Powell and Thatcherism', in Ben Jackson and

Robert Saunders (eds), *Making Thatcher's Britain* (New York: Cambridge University Press, 2012), pp. 95–110.

Scully, Roger and Richard Wyn Jones, 'Still Three Wales? Social Location and Electoral Behaviour in Contemporary Wales', *Electoral Studies*, 31 (2012), pp. 656–67.

Seldon, Anthony, 'Conservative Century', in Anthony Seldon and Stuart Ball (eds), *Conservative Century: The Conservative Party Since 1900* (Oxford: Oxford University Press, 1994), pp. 17–65.

Seldon, Anthony, and Stuart Ball 'Introduction', in Anthony Seldon and Stuart Ball (eds), *Conservative Century: The Conservative Party Since 1900* (Oxford: Oxford University Press, 1994), pp. 1–16.

Seldon, Anthony and Joanna Pappworth, *By Word of Mouth: 'Élite' Oral History* (London: Methuen, 1983).

Seyd, Patrick and Paul Whiteley, *Labour's Grass Roots: The Politics of Party Membership* (Oxford: Clarendon, 1992).

Seyd, Patrick and Paul Whiteley, 'Conservative Grassroots: An Overview', in Steve Ludlam and Martin J. Smith (eds), *Contemporary British Conservatism* (London: Macmillan, 1996), pp. 63–85.

Smith, Dai, *Wales! Wales?* (London: Allen & Unwin, 1984).

Smith, David (ed.), *A People and a Proletariat: Essays in the History of Wales, 1780–1980* (London: Pluto Press, 1980).

Stacey, F. A. and E. W. Cooney, 'A South Wales Constituency', in D. E. Butler (ed.), *The British General Election of 1951* (London: Macmillan and Co Ltd, 1952), pp. 197–209.

Steedman, Carolyn, *Dust* (Manchester: Manchester University Press, 2001).

Steven, Martin H. M., Owain Llyr ap Gareth and Lewis Baston, 'The Conservative Party and Devolved National Identities: Scotland and Wales Compared', *National Identities*, 14/1 (2012), 71–81.

Sutcliffe-Braithwaite, Florence, *Class, Politics, and the Decline of Deference in England, 1968–2000* (Oxford: Oxford University Press, 2018).

Tanner, Duncan, 'Labour and its membership', in Duncan Tanner, Pat Thane and Nick Tiratsoo (eds), *Labour's First Century* (Cambridge: Cambridge University Press, 2000), pp. 248–80.

Tanner, Duncan, 'The Pattern of Labour Politics, 1918–1939', in Duncan Tanner, Chris Williams and Deian Hopkin (eds), *The Labour Party in Wales, 1900–2000* (Cardiff: University of Wales Press, 2000), pp. 113–39.

Tanner, Duncan, 'Facing the New Challenge: Labour and Politics, 1970–2000', in Duncan Tanner, Chris Williams and Deian Hopkin (eds), *The Labour Party in Wales* (Cardiff: University of Wales Press, 2000), pp. 264–93.

Tanner, Duncan, 'The Recruitment of the Parliamentary Labour Party in Britain (1931–1955), in Gaetano Quagliariello (ed.), *La Formazione della classe politica in Europa: 1945–1956* (Manduria: P. Lacaita, 2000).

Tanner, Duncan, 'Gender,Civic Culture and Politics in South Wales: Explaining Labour Municipal Policy, 1918–1939', in Matthew Worley (ed.), *Labour's Grass Roots: Essays on the Activities of Local Labour Parties and Members, 1918–1945* (Aldershot: Ashgate, 2005), pp. 170–93.

Tether, Philip, *Clubs: A Neglected Aspect of Conservative Organisation* (University of Hull: Hull Papers in Politics, 1988).

Thackeray, David, *Conservatism for the Democratic Age: Conservative Cultures and the Challenge of Mass Politics in Early Twentieth-Century England* (Manchester: Manchester University Press, 2013).

Thackeray, David and Richard Toye, 'An Age of Promises: British Election Manifestos and Addresses 1900–97', *Twentieth Century British History*, 31/1 (2020), 1–26.

Thomas, Geraint, 'The Conservative Party and Welsh Politics in the Inter-war Years', *English Historical Review*, 128/533 (2013), 877–913.

Thomas, Geraint, *Popular Conservatism and the Culture of National Government in Inter-war Britain* (Cambridge: Cambridge University Press, 2020).

Thomas, Wyn, *Hands off Wales: Nationhood and Militancy* (Llandysul: Gomer Press, 2013).

Thorpe, Andrew, *Parties at War: Political Organisation in Second World War Britain* (Oxford: Oxford University Press, 2009).

Thorpe, Andrew, '"One of the Most Backwards Areas of the Country": The Labour Party's Grass Roots in South West England, 1918–45', in Matthew Worley (ed.), *Labour's Grass Roots: Essays on the Activities of Local Labour Parties and Members, 1918–1945* (Aldershot: Ashgate, 2005), pp. 216–39.

Todd, Selina, *The People: The Rise and Fall of the Working Class, 1910–2010* (London: John Murray, 2015).

Torrance, David, *'We in Scotland': Thatcherism in a Cold Climate* (Edinburgh: Birlinn, 2009).

Torrance, David, 'Centenary Blues: 100 Years of Scottish Conservatism', in David Torrance, *Whatever Happened to Tory Scotland?* (Edinburgh: Edinburgh University Press, 2012), pp. 1–13.

Turner, Alwyn W., *Crisis? What Crisis? Britain in the 1970s* (Trowbridge: Aurum, 2008).

Turner, John, 'The British Conservative Party in the Twentieth Century: From Beginning to End?', *Contemporary European History*, 8/2 (1999), 275–87.

Vaughan, Herbert M., *The South Wales Squires: A Welsh Picture of Social Life* (London: Methuen, 1926).

Verba, Sidney, Kay Lehman Schlozman and Henry E. Brady, *Voice and Equality: Civic Voluntarism in American Politics* (London: Harvard University Press, 1995).

Waller, Robert, 'Conservative Electoral Support and Social Class', in Anthony Seldon and Stuart Ball (eds), *Conservative Century: The Conservative Party Since 1900* (Oxford: Oxford University Press, 1994), pp. 579–610.

Walling, Andrew, 'The Structure of Power in Labour Wales, 1951–1964', in Duncan Tanner, Chris Williams and Deian Hopkin (eds), *The Labour Party in Wales, 1900–2000* (Cardiff: University of Wales Press, 2000), pp. 191–214.

Walters, Donald, 'The Reality of Conservatism', in Wales: Remoulding a Radical Tradition', in John Osmond (ed.), *The National Question Again: Welsh Political Identity in the 1980s* (Llandysul: Gomer Press, 1985) pp. 210–21.

Walton, John K., *The British Seaside: Holidays and Resorts in the Twentieth Century* (Manchester: Manchester University Press, 2000).

Ward, Paul, *Unionism in the United Kingdom, 1918–1974* (Basingstoke: Palgrave Macmillan, 2005).

Ward, Paul, *Huw T. Edwards: British Labour and Welsh Socialism* (Cardiff: University of Wales Press, 2011).

Westlake, Martin, *Kinnock: The Biography* (London: Little, Brown, 2001).

Whiteley, Paul, Patrick Seyd, and Jeremy Richardson, *True Blues: The Politics of Conservative Party Membership* (Oxford: Clarendon Press, 1994).

Willetts, David, 'The New Conservatism? 1945–1951', in Stuart Ball and Anthony Seldon (eds), *Recovering Power: The Conservatives in Opposition Since 1867* (Basingstoke: Palgrave Macmillan, 2005).

Williams, Chris, *Democratic Rhondda: Politics and Society, 1885–1951* (Cardiff: University of Wales Press, 1996).

Williams, Chris, 'Monmouthshire – Wales or England?', in H. V. Bowen (ed.), *A New History of Wales: Myths and Realities in Welsh History* (Llandysul: Gomer Press, 2011), pp. 89–96.

Williams, Chris, 'Introduction', in Duncan Tanner, Chris Williams and Deian Hopkin (eds), *The Labour Party in Wales, 1900–2000* (Cardiff: University of Wales Press, 2000), pp. 1–20.

Williams, David, *A History of Modern Wales* (London: J. Murray, 1977).

Williams, Gwyn A., *The Merthyr Rising* (London: Croom Helm, 1978).

Williams, Gwyn A., *When Was Wales?* (London: Black Raven, 1985).

Worley, Matthew, 'Introduction', in Matthew Worley (ed.), *Labour's Grass Roots: Essays on the Activities of Local Labour Parties and Members, 1918–1945* (Aldershot: Ashgate, 2005), pp. 1–6.

Worsthorne, Peregrine, 'Too Much Freedom', in Maurice Cowling (ed.), *Conservative Essays* (London: Cassell, 1978).

Wright, Martin, *Wales and Socialism: Political Culture and National Identity Before the Great War* (Cardiff: University of Wales Press, 2016).

Wyburn-Powell, Alun, *Defectors and the Liberal Party 1910–2010: A Study of Inter-party Relationships* (Manchester: Manchester University Press, 2012).

Wyn Jones, Richard, Roger Scully and Dafydd Trystan, 'Why do the Conservatives Always do (Even) Worse in Wales?', in Lynn Bennie, Colin Rawlings, Jonathan Tonge and and Paul Webb (eds), *British Elections and Parties Review*, 12/1 (2002), 229–45.

Zweiniger-Bargielowska, Ina, 'Rationing, Austerity and the Conservative Party Recovery after 1945', *The Historical Journal*, 37/1 (1994), 173–97.

UNPUBLISHED THESES

Aubel, Felix, 'Welsh Conservatism, 1885–1935: Five Studies in Adaptation' (unpublished PhD thesis, Lampeter University, 1996).

Davies, Tomos Dafydd, 'A Tale of Two Tories?: The British and Canadian Conservative Parties and the National Question' (unpublished PhD thesis, Aberystwyth University, 2011).

Day, Matthew, 'Wyn Roberts: The Blue Dragon? Conservatism, Patriotism and North Wales, *c.*1970–1990' (unpublished PhD thesis, Bangor University, 2022).

Williams, Thomas Wyn, 'The Conservative Party in North-East Wales, 1906–1924' (unpublished PhD thesis, University of Liverpool, 2008).

PAPERS AND PAMPHLETS

Audickas, Lukas, Oliver Hawkins and Richard Cracknell, 'House of Commons Briefing Paper: UK Election statistics, 1918–2016', 7 July 2016.

Evans, Jonathan, *The Future of Welsh Conservatism* (Cardiff, 2002).

Hooson, Tom and Geoffrey Howe, *Work For Wales: Gwaith i Gymru* (London: Conservative Political Centre, 1959).

Melding, David, 'Unionism and Nationalism in Welsh Political Life: An Essay by David Melding AM to Mark the 20th Anniversary of Devolution in Wales' (Cardiff, 2019).

Melding, David, *Have We Been Anti-Welsh? An Essay on the Conservative Party and the Welsh Nation* (Barry: Cymdeithas y Kymberiaid, 2005).

Melding, David, 'The Political Parties and the Welsh Nation', Politics Today: No.18, a Conservative Research Department Paper (3 December 1987).

INDEX

1960s social change 8, 147–9, 204–6

Aberavon (parliamentary constituency) 73, 78, 94, 103, 109, 113–14, 146, 194, 216, 252
Aberconway (parliamentary constituency) 189
Aberdare (parliamentary constituency) 39, 42, 52–3, 73, 94, 97, 115, 158, 186
Abertillery 86, 94, 185, 192, 202
Aberystwyth, University College 106, 204
Abse, Leo 229
Agents 78, 82–7, 89, 98, 129, 158, 200–2, 248–50, 256
Amis, Kingsley 1, 110, 119
That Uncertain Feeling 1, 110, 119
Anglesey (parliamentary constituency) 13, 15, 58, 60, 73, 86, 90, 94, 119, 155, 195, 215, 224, 233, 256, 262
see also Best, Keith
Anglesey, isle of 58, 60, 195, 228
Anglesey, Marquess of 73, 74, 78
Plas Newydd 74
Anglican
Anglican aristocracy 9–10, 74–7, 197
Anglicised influence 3, 10, 21, 60, 101, 117–21, 131, 176, 188–9, 213, 216–17, 224, 247–8, 261, 263, 273
Attlee, Clement 39, 45, 47
Australia 123, 166

Baldwin, Stanley 11, 62
Balsom, Denis *see* Three Wales Model
Banner ac Amserau Cymru 267
Barry (parliamentary constituency) 13, 15, 47, 73, 88, 94, 95, 105, 109, 135, 146, 153, 166, 174, 179,
Conservative Association 72, 84, 149, 154, 209
see also Gower, Raymond
Bebb, Ambrose 189
Bebb, Guto 189
Bedwellty (parliamentary constituency) 73, 81, 94, 155, 167, 202
Bennett, Charlotte 202
Bennett, Nicholas 17, 222, 225, 244–5
Best, Keith 13, 15, 233, 256, 262, 266
Bevan, Aneurin 22, 63, 82, 90, 101, 117, 220
Bevan, W. Franklin 73
Birch, Nigel 16, 56, 126
Blaenau Gwent (parliamentary constituency) 267–8
Blair, Tony 227
Bodrhyddan Hall 172
Bombs 1, 188, 240–1
Bourne, Nick 266, 268–9, 270–1
see also Devolution
Box, Donald 15, 115, 125, 170–1, 181–2, 268
Bowen, Jim 54
Bowen, Roderic 49, 131
Boy Scouts 76
Brecon (place) 47

Brecon and Radnor (parliamentary constituency) 15, 58, 73, 85, 94, 95, 166, 178, 200, 215, 247, 261, 268
Brecon, Lord (David V. P. Lewis) 141–2
Bridgend (parliamentary constituency) 13, 15, 219, 222, 262
British identity 6, 8, 14, 37–8, 70, 76, 120, 213, 244–6, 273
    see also 'British Wales'
British Legion 76, 252
British Union of Fascists 123
'British Wales' 13–14, 37, 70, 77, 88, 95, 99, 105, 115, 120, 150, 170, 177, 199, 202, 216–17, 219, 261, 268
    see also Three Wales Model
Brogyntyn Hall 78–9, 106, 151
Brooke, Henry 141
Brookes, Beata 222, 251
Buckland, Robert 248–9
Bute Estate 180
Butler, Chris 237–8
Butler, R. A. 67

Caernarfon (parliamentary constituency) 28, 51, 58, 61, 73, 94, 98, 130, 144, 197, 210, 216–17
Caerphilly (parliamentary constituency) 43, 54, 73, 90, 94, 97, 188, 209
Caernarvon Boroughs (parliamentary constituency) 64
Caernarvon Herald 195
Callaghan, James 22, 37, 56, 64, 137, 153, 161–2, 215
Capel Celyn *see* Tryweryn
Capital punishment 124
Cardiff 1, 3, 32, 42, 45–6, 61, 65, 96, 109, 115, 117, 121, 134, 137, 156, 161–2, 168–9, 1 80–1, 202, 203, 218, 219, 239, 261
Cardiff Bay 234
Cardiff Castle 110
Cardiff Central (parliamentary constituency) 15
Cardiff City Council 236
Cardiff North (parliamentary constituency) 15, 47, 73, 94, 105, 115, 147, 171, 174, 178, 181, 201, 227, 229, 245, 268
    Conservative Association 69
Cardiff North West (parliamentary constituency) 13, 15, 175, 207
Cardiff South East (parliamentary constituency) 37, 56, 64, 73, 88, 94, 105, 153, 161–2, 178
Cardiff West (parliamentary constituency) 15, 73, 76, 86, 94, 104, 106, 127, 147, 169, 219, 262
Cardigan (parliamentary constituency) 49, 58, 61, 73, 77, 84, 90, 94, 131, 176, 197
Carmarthen (parliamentary constituency) 49, 58, 73, 94, 120, 178, 190, 240
    1957 by election 131
    1966 by election 188
    Conservative Association 140, 209
Carmarthenshire (county) 98
Castle, Barbara 1
Cawdor family 174
    Earl of Cawdor 73, 75
Ceredigion (parliamentary constituency) *see* Cardigan (parliamentary constituency)
Charter for Wales 67
Churchill, Winston 6, 32, 38, 40, 43, 46, 51, 52, 65, 71, 132
Circus, Philip 248
Civic pride/civic nationalism 11, 76–7, 120

INDEX

Clwyd North West (parliamentary constituency) 13, 16, 227, 245, 251
Clwyd South (parliamentary constituency) 242
Clwyd South West (parliamentary constituency) 13, 15, 216, 222
Clwyd West (parliamentary constituency), 16, 266
Cold War 64, 104
Common Market/European Community 66, 166
Communist Party 155
Conservative Party
  Affluence, rhetoric concerning 102–10, 261
  Anti-Conservative sentiment in Wales 1–2, 3, 18, 20, 37–51, 81–2, 122–5
  Anti-Socialist rhetoric 6, 38–51, 99, 103–5, 141, 164–5, 215, 261
  Attitude to Labour voters 12, 52, 185–7, 191, 192, 267–8
  Conservative Central Office (CCO) 28, 29, 53, 55–6, 61, 79, 82–4, 86–7, 89, 119, 122, 124, 157–9, 176, 178, 192, 201, 204–5, 222, 228
  Conservative Research Department 65, 137, 189, 190, 269
  Electoral performance in Wales 3–4, 10, 11, 13–18, 47, 105, 108–9, 167–8, 180, 218–20, 259
  English voters 117–19, 175–6, 256, 261, 271
  Grassroots membership 4, 6–7, 8, 23–7, 29–30, 33, 35, 48, 50–1, 53, 55–7, 60–1, 71–98, 105–7, 111, 119–21, 126, 141, 144–56, 162–3, 171–4, 191, 200–10, 213, 244, 247–54, 260, 264–5, 270
  Housing policy 41, 67, 108–9
  Links with business 7, 13, 42, 45, 56, 76, 80, 89, 141, 157–60, 170–1, 174
  'Local' candidates 101, 111–17, 177–87, 222–4, 231–2, 262
  Missioners 201
  Modernity, rhetoric concerning 164
  Professionalisation 8, 193–5, 202, 211
  Public meetings 46–7
  Welsh Policy Group 194–5
  Conservative clubs 1, 70, 96–8, 146, 154–6, 251–4
  Swansea Salisbury Club 253
Conway/Conwy (parliamentary constituency) 15, 28, 47, 73, 84, 91, 94, 95, 105, 116, 117, 176, 184, 198, 203, 222, 228, 262
  Conservative Association 29, 84, 90–2
Conwy (County) 3, 22
Corbyn, Jeremy 265
Council for Wales and Monmouthshire 64, 141
Crum Ewing, Humphry 158

Daily Mail 105
Davies, Andrew R. T. 273
Davies, Byron 267
Davies, Clement 49, 132
Davies, G. R. 73
Davies, Howard 192, 198
Davies, Paul 273
Davies, S. O. 130, 136–7, 172
Deindustrialisation *see* Heavy industry
Delyn (parliamentary constituency) 16
Denbigh (parliamentary constituency) 16, 28, 48, 49, 73, 84, 94, 95, 124, 178–9, 180, 190, 206–7

Denbighshire (county) 3, 75
Development Board for Rural
    Wales 235
Development Corporation for
    Wales 235
Devolution 6, 27, 33, 265–74
    Administrative devolution 35,
        63–70, 134, 137, 234–5, 239,
        262–3
    Conservative Party attitude
        towards 6, 194, 256
    Referendum (1979) 228–30
    Referendum (1997) 213
    see also Minister for Welsh
        Affairs; Secretary of State for
        Wales; Home Rule (for Wales)
Dexter, Ted 161–2, 178, 266
Disraeli, Benjamin 97
Donnelly, Desmond 17, 50, 183
Duff, Michael 106
Dunraven, Earl of 73
Dynevor, Lord 73, 74, 79

Ebbw Vale (parliamentary
    constituency) 39, 54, 73, 82,
    90–1, 94, 95, 185, 202, 220,
    231
Eden, Anthony 51, 70, 109, 128,
    134, 182
Edwards, H. W. J. 9, 37, 82
Edwards, Huw T. 141, 182
Edwards, Ness 51, 139, 172
Edwards, Nicholas (Lord
    Crickhowell) 17, 23, 170–1,
    182–3, 222, 228, 233–8,
    240–3, 255
Eisteddfod 139, 142, 195
Eisteddfod Act, 1959 139
Ellis, Tom 222
England 18, 32, 60, 66, 71, 74,
    101, 111, 117, 125, 138,
    175–6, 184, 188, 198, 218,
    232, 239, 242, 261
Eton College 56, 74, 162, 251

European Union referendum, 2016
    272–3
Evans, Gwynfor 63, 177–8, 188–9,
    240, 244
Evans, Jonathan 15, 185
Evans, Nigel 170, 199, 202–3
Evans, Roger 16, 224, 246
Evans-Bevan, David 78
Everest, Irene 209
Exchange Rate Mechanism 227

Faenol Estate 78, 106–7
Farming 58, 66, 67, 120, 273
Festival of Wales 139
First World War 72, 77
Flint East (parliamentary
    constituency) 16, 50, 73, 77,
    94, 105, 109–10, 127
Flint West (parliamentary
    constituency) 16, 73, 94, 95,
    105, 126
Flintshire (parliamentary
    constituency) 16, 77
Flynn, Keith 147, 204
Foot, Michael 22, 220
Francis, Hywel 155
Free Wales Army 188
fro Gymraeg, y' 13, 58–61, 130–1,
    143–4, 233
    see also Three Wales Model

Garel-Jones, Tristan 197
Garner Evans, Emlyn 16, 48, 49
General elections
    1945 5, 7–8, 38, 49, 59, 69, 81,
        112, 128, 132, 173
    1950 5, 41, 45, 46–7, 49, 56, 59,
        60, 61, 67, 68, 69, 88, 112,
        128, 132, 173
    1951 5, 41–2, 45, 49, 56, 58, 59
        60, 67, 69, 71, 91, 112, 128,
        132, 133, 135, 173
    1955 5, 49, 59, 103, 112, 113,
        123, 128, 132, 137, 173

INDEX

1959 5 49, 59, 104, 105, 109, 112, 113, 117, 128, 130, 158, 173, 190
1964 5, 59, 112, 116, 128, 142, 154, 155, 161, 173, 181, 195
1966 3, 5, 7, 59, 112, 128, 154, 159, 171, 173, 178, 180–2, 183–4, 195
1970 5, 59, 112, 128, 164, 173, 178, 182–3, 185, 186, 195, 210
1974 (February) 5, 59, 112, 128, 167–8, 173, 183–4, 197
1974 (October) 5, 59, 112, 128, 167–8, 172, 173, 183–4, 186, 197
1979 5, 59, 112, 128, 173, 190, 215–6, 233
1983 5, 59, 112, 128, 173, 220, 221, 222, 248, 251
1987 5, 59, 112, 128, 173, 221, 224, 232, 252, 256
1992 5, 59, 112, 128, 173, 242, 249, 251, 253
1997 5, 7, 17, 59, 112, 128, 173, 242
2010 272–3
2019 2, 267–8, 272–3
Girl Guides 120
Gladstone, William 97
Gower (parliamentary constituency) 49, 51, 94, 101, 104, 117, 124, 266
Gower, Raymond 13, 15, 135–6, 166, 179–80
Graesser, Alistair 165
Great Depression 11, 12, 38–9, 51–2, 63, 82, 103, 125, 136, 241, 262
Greenaway, Miranda 130
Griffiths, James 22, 39, 123, 142
Grist, Ian 15, 194, 229, 268–9
Guest, Charlotte 128
Guest, Revel 128–9

Hague, William 246
Hailsham, Lord 126
Hallinan, Charles 121
Hallinan, Lincoln 104
Hancock, Tony 204–5
Hardie, Keir 22
Harding, W. Rowe 49, 51
Hare, John 132
Harrow School 184, 228
Harvey, Robert 15, 197, 216, 220, 222
Heath, Edward 165–7, 169, 182, 194, 228–9
Heavy industry 10–11, 21, 32, 66, 75, 105, 114, 118, 129–30, 146, 161–2, 167, 192–3, 215, 241
  Deindustrialisation 42, 192, 220–1, 241
Hendon South 198
Herald of Wales 68
Heseltine, Michael 2, 49, 101, 104, 117, 124, 159, 242–3
Holloway Prison 210
Home Rule (for Wales) 9, 190
Hooson, Emlyn 144
Hooson, Tom 15, 143, 144, 231, 240, 269
Hope, Jack 55
Hopkin Morris, Rhys 49, 131
Hornsby-Smith, Patricia 46
House of Commons 33, 67, 125, 136, 141, 179, 228
House of Lords 141, 148
Howard, Michael 2
Howe, Geoffrey 2, 103, 113–15, 117, 143, 221, 231, 269
Hubbard-Miles, Peter 15, 219, 222
Hughes, Cledwyn 58, 195, 233
Hunt, David 243
Huxley, A. S. 73

Industrial Relations Act (1971) 166
Inflation 163

INDEX

Iwan, Dafydd 222

Japan 234
Jenour, A. M. C. 73, 76
Jersey, Earl of 73, 78
Johnson, Boris 2, 242, 272
Jones, D. Elwyn 249
Jones, Gwilym 15, 73, 225, 245, 268
Jones, J. O. 60
Jones, John Eilian 142, 195, 269
Jones, Lewis 49, 50–1
Jones, 'Mr British' 244
Jones, Thomas William 58
Junior Imperial League 93
Justices of the Peace 76, 77, 114, 120

Kinnock, Neil 12, 22, 155, 229, 230, 241, 242–3

Labour Party
 1945 landslide 39
 Attitude to devolution 63–4, 68, 142–3, 228–9, 230
 Connections with communities 12, 42, 51–2, 57, 81, 113, 168, 177, 184, 192–3, 263, 267–8
 Grassroots membership 27, 81, 112, 150, 248, 250
 Popularity in Wales 3, 4, 7, 11, 22, 34, 51, 53, 99, 159–60, 188, 220
 Role in local government 11, 12, 43, 82
 South Wales Regional Council of Labour/Welsh Regional Council of Labour 63, 142
 Welsh-speaking candidates 58, 60
 Women candidates 251
 Youth movements 206
Leasehold reform 180–1
Lee, Phillip 267

Lewis, Julian 220, 248
Lewis, Saunders 188
Leyshon, Peter 217, 223
Liberal Party/SDP/Liberal Democrat Party 5, 9, 11–12, 56, 63, 68, 97, 130–1, 144, 177, 189–90, 195, 196–7, 216, 220, 252, 270
 see also National Liberals

Lindsay-Fynn, Basil 157–160, 193
Little, George 61
Liverpool 32
Llafur 21
Llandudno 67, 173, 175
Llandrindod Wells 198
Llanelli (parliamentary constituency) 39, 54, 73, 75–6, 94, 98, 248–9, 252
Llewellyn, David 15, 46, 47, 110, 115, 133, 138, 268
Llewellyn, Godfrey 119–20, 175
Llewellyn, Trefor 197
Lloyd, Ken 54, 55
Lloyd-Edwards, Norman 81, 178
Lloyd George, David 10, 40, 62
Lloyd George, Gwilym 17, 48–50, 134, 137
Lloyd George, Megan 48–9, 233
Local elections/government 33, 168–9, 219, 260

MacDonald, Ramsey 22
Macmillan, Harold 32, 102, 125–6, 137, 138–9, 141
Major, John 197, 250
Malta 158–9
Manchester 32
Manchester Guardian 118
Margam Castle 78
Margam Park 153
Marland, Penelope 167
Maudling, Reginald 182
Maxwell Fyfe, David 47, 68, 133–5

INDEX

Maxwell Fyfe Report (1949) 89
  see also Minister for Welsh Affairs
McGlynn, Bernard 158
Meggitt, Arthur 73
Melding, David 23, 250, 269–70
Merioneth (parliamentary constituency) 49, 58, 61, 73, 77, 94, 137, 178
Merseyside 17, 138
  see also Liverpool
Merthyr Tydfil (parliamentary constituency) 51, 91, 94, 95, 130
Merthyr Tydfil (place) 70, 81, 182
Meyer, Anthony 16, 251
Monmouth (parliamentary constituency) 16, 28, 46, 73, 94, 95, 118, 180, 182–3, 201, 203, 219, 224, 227, 246
  1945 by-election 88
  1991 by-election 246
  Conservative Association 90, 106, 119, 126, 150, 171–2, 199, 207, 246, 247
Monmouthshire (county) 3, 75, 118, 261
Monster Raving Loony Party 246
Montgomery (parliamentary constituency) 16, 49, 56, 94, 132, 215
Morgan, Geraint 16, 124, 137, 179–81, 183, 190
Morris, Jan 239
Morris, John 216, 238
Morris-Jones, Henry 16, 49
Morrison, Herbert 64
Mort, Dai 130
Middle class 7, 26–7, 53–4, 56, 89–90, 102–10, 118–22, 146–7, 150, 168–76, 205, 207–8, 215, 224, 253, 261, 273–4
Milford Haven 130
Miners' strike (1984–5) 1, 220, 241

National Union of Mineworkers 221
Minister for Welsh Affairs 6, 62–70, 133–4, 138, 191, 263

Napoleon 121
National Assembly for Wales
  see Senedd (Welsh Parliament)
National Conservative Council for Wales and Monmouthshire 65
National Liberals 12, 16–17, 47–51, 101, 127, 130, 132, 134
National Library of Wales 77
Nationalism 21, 34, 136, 189–90, 246, 271, 274
Neath (parliamentary constituency) 94, 95, 114
New Zealand 123
Newcastle North (parliamentary constituency) 92
Newcastle West (parliamentary constituency) 92
Newport (parliamentary constituency) 73, 76, 86, 94, 154
  Newport by-election, 1956 115
Newport West (parliamentary constituency) 16, 219, 222, 262
Nicholls, George 54
Nonconformity 9, 10, 60, 62, 97, 110, 131
  see also Religion
Norris, Alfred 123

Ogmore (parliamentary constituency) 73, 94
Oral history 30–1
Ormsby-Gore family 78–9

Parliament for Wales campaign 136
Patten, Chris 190–1
Pearce, Idris 95, 114–15
Pembrokeshire (county) 3, 75, 130, 156, 261

Pembrokeshire (parliamentary constituency) 17, 28, 48–50, 73, 75, 94, 156, 168, 176, 183, 201, 228, 261
   Conservative Association 80, 107
Penrhyn family 75, 174
Penrhyn Castle 80
Penrhyn, Lord 73, 80
Phibbs, Charles 73, 77
Plaid Cymru 5, 22, 63, 136, 163, 177–8, 188–90, 195, 197, 206, 211, 216, 246, 250, 256, 271
Plymouth, Countess of 73
Plymouth, Earl of 73, 75
   St Fagan's Castle 75
Pontypool (parliamentary constituency) 54, 73, 77, 91, 94, 152, 202
   Conservative Association 152
Pontypridd (parliamentary constituency) 79, 94, 109, 156
Port Talbot 118, 130, 146
   see also Heavy industry
Powell, Annie 155
Powell, Enoch 65–9, 70, 137, 165, 225, 269
Price, Charles, 80
Price, Peter 198
Price-White, David 64, 92
Pride (2014 film) 220
Primrose League 87, 149
Pritchard, Hugh 73, 77
Private Eye 242
Protheroe-Beynon, Hilda 120, 200, 209
Pwllheli 147
Pym, Leslie 16

Radio 8
Raffan, Keith 16
Raglan, Lord 142
Ranelagh, John 231–2
Red Cross 76

Redwood, John 243–5
Rees, Hugh 13, 17, 108–9, 115–16, 158, 170
Rees, Pandy 146
Rees-Mogg, William 155
Reeves, Robin 229–30
Reform Act (1832) 75
Religion 9, 26, 33, 41, 44, 62, 76, 120, 149, 174, 225, 248
   Church disestablishment 9
   see also Nonconformity
Rendle, John 185–7
Rhondda, 22, 28, 97, 106, 154, 217, 233
Rhondda East (parliamentary constituency) 54, 73, 77, 90, 91, 94, 155
Rhondda West (parliamentary constituency) 81, 94, 96, 188
Richards, Rod 16, 213, 244–5
Right to Buy scheme 218–19, 261
Risdale, Susan 85
Roberts, G. Fossett 73, 77
Roberts, Goronwy 58, 63
Roberts, Michael 15, 125, 161, 178, 182, 268
Roberts, O. M. 60
Roberts, Shelagh 130
Roberts, Wyn (Lord Roberts of Conwy) 15, 28, 140, 182, 184–5, 222, 228, 233–8, 242, 246–7, 262, 269–70
Robinson, Mark 16, 219, 222, 252
Rosser, David 30, 189
Rowlands, Gwilym 54, 73, 77
Russell, Arthur 54

Sackville, Tom 231
Scotland 17, 40, 65, 75, 111, 194, 239, 245, 255–6
Second World War 38, 51, 63, 76, 77
Secretary of State for Wales 15, 63–4, 92, 141, 142, 183, 193,

197, 199, 222, 234–6, 243–4, 260
see also Edwards, Nicholas; Devolution; Thomas, Peter; Walker, Peter
Senedd (Welsh Parliament) 16, 18, 35, 70, 213, 245, 265–74
National Assembly elections
2011 273
2016 272
Senedd election, 2021 272–3
Short, A. McTaggart 73, 76
Sianel Pedwar Cymru (S4C) 140, 240–1
Simons, Emrys 106
Sims, Neville 174
Smith, Kathleen 210
Soskice, Frank 155
South Wales Miners' Library 21
Soviet Union 40, 64, 104
Stanley, Oliver 47
Stockton-on-Tees 125
Stradling Thomas, John 16, 166, 182–3
Suez Crisis 174
Sunday Chronicle 156
Sunday Closing Act, 1881 97
Sutch, Screaming Lord 246
Swansea 21, 32, 38, 108–9, 110, 170, 180, 199, 243
Mumbles 109, 110
Sketty 108–9
University College 204
Swansea East (parliamentary constituency) 49, 54–5, 94, 128–9, 158
Swansea West (parliamentary constituency) 13, 17, 49, 50–1, 88, 92, 94, 101, 108–9, 110, 115, 181, 207–8, 220, 248, 262
Conservative Association 92–3
Swayne, Desmond 242
Sweeney, Walter 15, 224
Syer, Rowland 201

Temple-Morris, Peter 154, 171
Terlezki, Stefan 15, 169–70, 219
Thatcher, Margaret 1, 2, 16, 19, 32, 34, 171, 197, 214–15, 218, 221, 228–9, 236, 238, 241–2, 261
Thomas, George 127, 137
Thomas, Ivor B. 73
Thomas, J. P. L. (Jim) 50, 55, 84, 86, 98
Thomas, Pamela 127
Thomas, Peter 15, 92, 116, 117, 170–1, 180, 198, 255
Thompson, Sam 54
Thorneycroft, Peter 16, 118, 126, 137, 171, 180, 182–3, 248
Three Wales Model 13, 31, 58–9, 261
Tonypandy Grammar School 217
Tonypandy Riots 51
Trade unions 44, 54, 56–7, 71, 77, 163, 165–6, 215, 221, 236, 261
Conservative trade unionists 54, 145–6
Wales Trade Union Congress 229
Tredegar family 75, 174
Tredegar, Viscount 73
Tredinnick, David 242
Trubshaw, H. E. 73, 75
Truman, Albert 73, 77
Tryweryn 138, 139, 188

UKIP 272
Undeb Cymru Fydd 63, 136
Unionism 70
University of Sydney 66

Vale of Glamorgan (county) 3
Vale of Glamorgan (parliamentary constituency) 1, 179, 219
see also Barry *(*parliamentary constituency)

Valerio, Paul 170
'Valleys', the 3, 11, 14, 22, 37,
    51–6, 90–1, 96, 97, 115, 122,
    130, 136, 157–8, 159–60, 168,
    185–7, 192–3, 217, 220–1,
    231, 242, 244, 253, 262–4
    Heads of the Valleys Road 234
    see also 'Welsh Wales'

Wales Area Office 27, 56, 60, 69,
    80, 82, 86–7, 90, 93, 98, 109,
    121, 123, 132, 192, 198, 200,
    269, 271
Wales Tourist Board 235
Walker, Peter 233–4, 236, 239, 243
Walters, Donald 41, 174, 193
Warrick, Paul 252
Weale, Bill 201
Welsh Development Agency 236
Welsh Grand Committee 139
Welsh language 9, 11, 27, 32,
    58–61, 63, 66–7, 70, 133,
    139–42, 190–1, 195, 199,
    231, 233, 237–41, 244–5,
    255–6
    Welsh Language Act (1967) 198
    Welsh Language Board 239
Welsh nationhood/identity 8, 20, 21,
    62, 133, 136, 143, 188–99,
    213, 244–5, 256–7, 262–3,
    270
Welsh Office 28, 234–9, 241, 243,
    255, 269
Welsh Socialist Republican
    Movement 242
'Welsh Wales' 13–14, 42, 54, 66–7,
    77, 80–4, 85, 90–1, 95, 109,
    122–3, 127, 154, 157, 159–60,
    185–7, 192, 252, 261, 264
    see also Three Wales Model;
    'Valleys', the
West, Granville 54
West, Harry 37, 56–7, 266
Western Mail 30, 40, 43, 46, 47, 68,
    69, 111, 115, 122, 133–4,
    178, 189, 197, 199, 210, 211,
    215, 227
White, Eirene 105, 127
Whitehead, Mrs Lionel 73
Williams, Delwyn 16
Williams, Gwyn Alf 9, 20
Williams, Llewellyn 192
Williams, Mrs G. 79
Williams-Wynn family 61, 75, 78
    Williams-Wynn, The Dowager
        Lady 73
    Williams-Wynn, Robert 73, 75
    Williams-Wynn, Watkin 73
Winchester College 117
'Winter of Discontent' 215
Wodehouse, P. G. 161
Wooley, D. 201
Women
    As Agents 85–7, 129
    As Conservative activists/members
        7, 9, 27, 87–93, 149–53,
        206–10, 248, 254, 265
    As Conservative voters 6, 38,
        43–7, 87, 102, 108, 166–7
    As parliamentary candidates/MPs
        126–30, 200, 209–10, 251, 267
    As wives of parliamentary
        candidates 126–7, 167
    The British Housewives' League
        43–4
Women's Institute 76
Women's Liberation Movement
    167
Wood, Kay 251
Woolton, Lord 48, 50, 71, 91, 93,
    121,
    Woolton-Teviot pact 48
Work for Wales: Gwaith i Gymru 143
Working-class Conservatives
    As activists 145–6, 217
    As parliamentary candidates
        53–7, 60
    As voters 37, 53, 155–6, 217–19

Wrexham (parliamentary constituency) 49, 73, 94, 119, 122–3
Wrexham (place) 32, 203
Wynne-Jones, G. V. 162

Young Conservatives 7, 9, 27, 93–6, 146–9, 170, 199, 202–6, 231
   Ideologies 27, 147–8

Ynys Môn (parliamentary constituency) *see* Anglesey

Yeo, Tim 242

Zimmern, Alfred E. 13